Godtalk

Godtalk

Travels in Spiritual America

Brad Gooch

Alfred A. Knopf New York 2002

Portions of this work were originally published in *The New Republic, Out,
Travel & Leisure,* and *W.*

Grateful acknowledgment is made to Christopher Wynn for permission to reprint
a lyric excerpt from "Lessons in Breathing" by Christopher Wynn.
Reprinted by permission of the author.

Library of Congress Cataloging-in-Publication Data
Gooch, Brad.
Godtalk : travels in spritual America / Brad Gooch.—1st ed.
p. cm.
Includes bibliographical references and index.
ISBN 0-679-44709-1
1. Spirituality—United States. 2. United States—Religion. 3. Gooch, Brad, [date] I.
Title.
BL 2525 .G66 2002
200'.973—dc21   2001038828

Manufactured in the United States of America

First Edition

TO THE MEMORY OF

Canon Edward N. West

CONTENTS

ACKNOWLEDGMENTS

From the followers of each of the movements I came to spend time with, I often encountered a combination of suspicion mixed with openness. Eventually—at least with those represented in this book—openness won out. And the trust, generosity, and articulateness of the individuals I talked to made all the difference to this book. My reporting was subtly moved along as much by offhand comments, short conversations in hallways, in cars or on planes, as in formal interviews. I wish to thank all those who participated in the making of this book, some of whom probably aren't even aware of their role. A selective list of many of my collaborators follows; to any whom I've overlooked, I offer my apologies and thanks as well.

My entrée into the Urantia Foundation came about through the hospitality of its staff when I first visited their offices in Chicago, especially Tonia Baney, who is president, and Robert Solone, who works in reader services. Matthew Block shared with me his controversial research uncovering many of the sources of *The Urantia Book*. Mo Siegel, a trustee of the foundation, and the founder and CEO of Celestial Seasonings, was forthcoming about his devotion to the book during my visit to his office in Boulder, Colorado. Lucinda Ziesing shared her memories of Siegel and the place of *The Urantia Book* in his life during the 1960s. Other readers who provided insights were Trevor and Kathleen Swaddling, who ran a branch office of the foundation in Sydney, Australia; Carolyn Kendall, part-time secretary to the movement's founder in the early 1950s, Dr. William Sadler; Robin Jorgenson, leader of the Urantia reading group I attended for several months in lower Manhattan; Paul Thompson; Rick Jones; Nola Smith; and Meredith Sprunger. I especially thank Martin Gardner for taking time to share with me his highly informed, debunking view of *The Urantia Book.*

My steadfast guide to the Siddha Yoga ashrams of Gurumayi in both South Fallsburg, New York, and Ganeshpuri, India, was Sukala (Sandra Matrick), who was the press liaison when I began my project, though she continued to stay in touch even after leaving for law school. I also want to thank her successor, Carol Prunhuber. Although Gurumayi does not speak to writers from outside the community, members of her inner circle did. The support of Swami Durgananda (Sally Kempton) was invaluable, as was my interview with Swami Akhandananda (Daniel Bauer). Among those current and former devotees who agreed to speak with me were Kathleen Parrish, formerly director of the philanthropic PRASAD Project; David Kempton, director of the Muktabodha Indological Research Institute; Philip Baloun, S. Ramachandran, Melynda Windsor, Ericka Huggins, Suhasini (Janet Dobrovolny), and Ryan Haddon. Both Joe Lalli and Arnold Weinstein helped give me a sense of Baba Muktananda, Gurumayi's predecessor. Others who agreed to interviews were Patrick Collins, Arnold Herz, and Harriette Cole. Most ex-devotees who agreed to share their memories wanted to remain anonymous. An exception was Dan Shaw, a former director of public programs and intensives for Siddha Yoga, who is currently a psychotherapist in private practice in New York City.

I wish to thank Deepak Chopra, who took time out from an extremely busy schedule to let me interview him on several occasions, not only for this book but for an article on his Center for Well Being, in La Jolla, California, and at his "Seduction of the

Spirit" seminar, which I attended in Goa, India. I was first introduced to Chopra by Wayne Nathan, an interior designer who worked on the opening party for the La Jolla center. Several members of Chopra's inner circle were patient and informative: Gayle Rose, Dr. Stephen Bieckel, and Dr. David Simon. Quite willing to present me with a more critical view of Chopra were Dr. John Renner, president of the National Council for Reliable Health Information; MacArthur Fellow James Randi; and Dr. Steve Barrett.

No visit to a cloistered community of Trappist monks or nuns is possible without the support of the abbot or abbess. I am indebted therefore to Abbot Timothy Kelly, the abbot of the Abbey of Gethsemani, who has since been succeeded by Abbot Damien Thompson. Among the brothers at Gethsemani who agreed to interrupt their silence to speak with me were Father Alan Gilmore, Brother Paul Quenon, Brother Joshua Brands, and Brother Patrick Hart. Indispensable in giving me a sense of the community were Robert Imperato, a former monk, now professor of religion and dean of arts and sciences at St. Leo College, in Florida; Geshe Thubten Tandhar, a Tibetan Buddhist monk who spent time on retreat; and frequent visitor Patrick Collins. For speaking with me and allowing me to visit their monasteries, I want to thank Abbot John Eudes Bamberger, of the Abbey of the Genesee, in New York, as well as Brother Francis and Brother Augustine; Abbot Francis Kline of Mepkin Abbey, in South Carolina, as well as Father Christian (Aidan) Carr and Father Guerric; Dom Brendan Freeman, of New Melleray Abbey, in Iowa. Gustav Niebuhr, of the *New York Times,* also generously shared with me his observations shortly after his visit to the Abbey of the Holy Trinity, in Utah, as did the Benedictine monk Remy Rougeau shortly after the publication of his novel, *All We Know of Heaven.* Hosting my visit to Our Lady of the Mississippi Abbey was the abbess, Mother Gail Fitzpatrick, as well as Sisters Carol Dvorak, Columba Guare, Sherry Pech, Kate Mehlmann, and Rebecca Stramoski. I received further insight into Our Lady of the Mississippi from the chaplain, Father James Kerndt, and from B. J. Weber, founder of the New York Fellowship, who grew up near the abbey and spent much time with the sisters.

Philip Johnson kindly agreed to speak with me about his architectural design for the Cathedral of Hope, in Dallas, Texas. During my visit to the gay cathedral in Dallas the Reverend Michael Piazza; his partner, Bill Eure; Mona West, the director of spiritual development; and Mary Warejka gave generously of their time. The Reverend Troy Perry told me his life story and the story of his founding of the Metropolitan Community Church during several interviews. For commenting more generally on the phenomenon of M.C.C. and the Cathedral of Hope, I'm grateful to the Reverend Malcolm Boyd and to Jim Mitulski, pastor of M.C.C. San Francisco. The Reverend Mel White and his partner, Gary Nixon, allowed me the rare opportunity of joining Soulforce as a delegate for their meetings with the Reverend Jerry Falwell, with the assurance that I wouldn't report on the event, which was off-limits to the press, in any current newspapers or magazines. I owe much to Susan Friend Harding for sharing her more general perceptions of Jerry Falwell and the Thomas Road Baptist Church.

My chapter on Muslims in New York City would have been nearly impossible without the generosity and wisdom of Feisal Abdul Rauf, founder of the American Sufi Muslim Association and Imam of the Masjid Al-Farah, who introduced me to Muslims active in all aspects of the religion, read the chapter carefully in manuscript in several versions, made suggestions and emendations, and, most important, gave me greater insight into traditional Islam. Also helping me generally with this chapter were Gray Henry Gouverneur, director of the Fons Vitae publishing enterprise; Louis Abdellatif Cristillo, field director of the "Muslim Communities in New York City" mapping project at the Columbia University School of International and Public Affairs; Dr. Shaffiq Essaje, coordinator of the New York City chapter of Al Fatiha, a gay Muslim organization; Salar Abdoh, Hisham Moulay Bouudi, Husayn Fruhstorfer, and Sifraz Khan.

Among those who helped me understand the Sunni and Shiite Muslims practicing in New York City were Imam Fadel Al-Sahlani of the Al-Khoei Foundation in Jamaica, Queens; Sayyed Nadeem Kazmi, senior consultant in humanitarian affairs for the international Al-Khoei Foundation; Al-Haaj Ghazi Y. Khankan, director of interfaith affairs and communications for the Islamic Center of Long Island; Dr. Faroque Khan, Dr. Faiz Khan, Daisy Khan, and Michelle Depew. Likewise helping me understand the growing community of African-American Sunni Muslims were Imam Yusuf Hasan, Muslim staff chaplain at Memorial Sloan-Kettering Hospital; Imam Izak-el M. Pasha of the Masjid Malcolm Shabazz, in Harlem; Imam Wahy Deen Shareef, the director of religious affairs of the WARIS Cultural Research and Development Center, in Irvington, New Jersey; Abdul Alim Mubarek, and Linda Salaam. I am most grateful for the interview granted me by Shaykha Fariha al-Jerrahi, born Philippa de Menil, of the Nur Ashki Jerrahi Sufi Order, and to Wheelock Whitney for sharing with me memories of the funeral of his cousin, Sheik Nur, born Lex Hixon. Members of Feisel Rauf's Sufi circle who agreed to talk with me included Robina Niaz, Pedram Samghabadi, Diana Castro, Shazad Rashid, Saadi Alkhouatli, Samina Imam, and Adnan Ashraf.

A great help in this project was release time from teaching, as well as the academic and sabbatical leaves granted to me by William Paterson University of New Jersey. I particularly wish to thank Provost and Executive Vice President Chernoy M. Sesay, and my colleagues in the English Department, especially Edward Burns and Alice Deakins, as well as the staff of the Sarah Byrd Askew Library, who helped me at various times with my research.

My special thanks go to Sonny Mehta, the publisher of Knopf, who was willing to take a chance on commissioning this book while it was still nothing more than a sketch. This encouragement continued to matter as the project exceeded its original scope and time frame. My editor, Shelley Wanger, showed her usual combination of careful intellect and almost clairvoyant good advice. She has definitely lived up to her reputation as one of the few "real" editors in New York who still take time with words and lines. My agent, Joy Harris, has been a true champion of this book, reading it chapter by chapter and following its ups, downs, turnarounds, and reconfigurations with unwavering support.

Sean Weiss worked during one summer doing research work on the project, as did my friend Michael Scalisi. Most involved in the project all the way through has been Barbara Heizer, who first accompanied me out of curiosity to the ashram of Gurumayi for a New Year's Eve celebration, and whom I then convinced to return several times, and even managed to convince to accompany me to a Promise Keepers rally in Washington, D.C., where she appeared to be the only woman visible for miles. Barbara showed an encouraging interest in the project from its inception, and wound up as the confidante with whom I discussed all of the various choices and problems as they arose. Without her provocative questions and sense of humor, the writing of this book would have been far less of a joy.

INTRODUCTION

One Sunday morning in the summer of 1995, I attended an eleven o'clock worship service at St. John's in the Village, an Episcopalian church in Manhattan's Greenwich Village. Our cozy congregation of about fifty, gathered in the angular brick structure—built as "contemporary" in the 1970s, its long thin windows as opaque as wax paper, registering filmy impressions of passers-by on the street—had just filed back from Communion. All was silent and sunny as the organist played a medley from the balcony to a preppy-looking group that could easily have been transported from a small academic town in New England. I'd often experienced a gentle decompression as the service came to its traditional conclusion. On that particular morning, however, I was suddenly filled with a strong mixture of longing and curiosity, wondering what other forms of worship and spirituality were transpiring outside of our familiar downtown parish, what the seekers were doing.

With such thoughts, *Godtalk: Travels in Spiritual America* began. It was a journey that would include a look at the many different kinds of religious experience being talked about in what some have been calling a "postdenominational" age, and others an "awakening" on the scale of America's two "Great Awakenings"— those of the pre–Revolutionary War era and of the 1840s in the Burned-Over District of western New York State. My own questioning was less existential than journalistic. I was simply intrigued at first about what was happening religiously across America. By the mid-1990s, friends were already talking about their gurus, and their mantras, and the latest self-help books by Louise Hay or Marianne Williamson. "New Age" seemed practically its own proliferating sect, and the shelves of bookstores were filled not only with transcripts channeled from beings from the beyond but with wind chimes, crystals, sandalwood prayer beads, and clay angels. Yale literary critic Harold Bloom dubbed these "New Age and Woodstock toys" in his 1996 book, *Omens of Millennium,* in which he rightly predicted, "I expect that all the apocalyptic fears, yearnings and expectations around Millennium will prove to be false."

There were also memoirs published about personal searches for God that involved a surprising about-face, a conversion not only of the writers but of their usual genre of writing. Tony Schwartz, a reporter for the *New York Times,* whose subsequent book would be a more characteristic biography of Donald Trump, published *What Really Matters: Searching for Wisdom in America,* an account of a midlife crisis that propelled him on a zigzagging track from a meditation retreat in the mountains of Utah to a biofeedback laboratory in Kansas, from a peak-performance workshop at a tennis academy in Florida to a right-brain drawing course in Boston. In *Cloister Walk,* Kathleen Norris wrote an account of two extended residencies at St. John's Abbey, in Collegeville, Minnesota. "I didn't feel ready to do it, but I had to act, to take the plunge," this respected, married, and lifelong Protestant poet stated of the profound permutations worked on her by a decision to spend time with a group of celibate Benedictine monks.

I was as anxious to find God, spiritual centering, peace, and joy as the next person. But as a writer my strongest inspiration has always been to write the book that I want to read but couldn't find on the shelf. At the time, with the exception of articles written in the Saturday *New York Times* by Gustav Niebuhr—the grand-nephew of the great theologian Reinhold Niebuhr—I couldn't find much close-up, detailed reporting on the social aspect of the spiritual scene in America. I knew lots was going on. A steady march of *Time, Newsweek,* and *Life* magazine covers told me so: the Virgin Mary in a blue veil for "The Meaning of Mary"; the illumi-nated toy-like towers of the Salt Lake City tabernacle for "Mor-mons, Inc."; a pre-Raphaelite angel with garlands in her hair for a trendy survey, "On the Trail of Angels." But I remained unsatis-fied about what it was like to be among the believers. What were they wearing? How did they talk? I missed the color and close observation of Frances Fitzgerald's 1986 *Cities on the Hill,* in which she thoroughly investigated Jerry Falwell's Liberty Baptist Church, or the Rajneeshram of Bagwan Shree Rajneesh, in Madras, Oregon.

So I decided to set out on my own. My excitement about the scale of religious fervor provoked epic plans to capture its entire topography in a single sweep, and drew me at first to some extrava-ganzas of spirituality. The biggest show at that moment was Promise Keepers, a Christian men's movement, founded by Uni-versity of Colorado football coach Bill McCartney in 1990, and gaining momentum around the time of the election of the Repub-lican congress in 1994. I first attended one of their rallies at R.F.K. Stadium, in Washington, D.C., in May 1996, where I watched as ten thousand teenage boys sprinted around the sta-dium's track holding aloft tiny white crosses while their fathers, full of Iron Man psychology, chanted "We love you, kids!" (My favorite memory of the trip was the Bahai taxi driver who—when I told him of my project—warned, "Be careful! People who get into religion go *craaazy.*")

That September I watched at Shea Stadium as fifty thousand men—in T-shirts that proclaimed "Be Bold, Be Strong" or "His Pain, Your Gain" (with a logo of a bloody hand with a nail through it)—knelt while singing "Holy, Holy, Holy" on the baselines and the pitcher's mound. The following October, I crowded into a parade box to observe hundreds of thousands of men gathered for a Promise Keepers revival meeting on the Washington mall. It was the pumping up of what the early-twentieth-century evangelist Billy Sunday called "muscular Christianity." That week the Promise Keepers, too, made the cover of *Time,* with a dramatic question superimposed on their praying faces: "Should they be cheered—or feared?" The answer turned out to be: neither. The controversial organization wound up more as a whimper than a bang, partly, some said, from the financial problems arising from not having passed the hat more successfully at their ultimate rally, or from a decision since abandoned to stop charging for admission. Their events are now greatly scaled down, the movement's spirit kept alive mostly in small groups of men in local churches for whom the exhortation to live "an extreme faith," evoking extreme sports, has become popular. I learned an important lesson, though. I wasn't going to find out much by attending these big events. My first attempt at exploration proved to have been an instructive misstep.

Changing my course, I decided to continue researching, with the hope that I would discover my subjects more gradually. And I did indeed find them—or, in some cases, they found me. My guides on a New Age tour of the red canyons of Sedona, Arizona, turned out to be readers of *The Urantia Book,* which led me to try to find the book and eventually the story of its origins. At a friend's birthday, a fashionable events planner was so fervent in communicating his devotion to the Indian female guru Gurumayi that he invited me to ride up in his Jeep Cherokee to her ashram in the Catskills; two days later, an interior designer who had worked on an opening party for Deepak Chopra's Center for Well Being, in La Jolla, California, promised an introduction. While mulling over the possibility of traveling to Iowa to visit the contemplative Trappistine sisters at an obscure cloister, Our Lady of the Mississippi, I ran into the playwright John Guare at the Jefferson Market on Sixth Avenue, who informed me that his cousin, Mother Columba Guare, had been living in that community for decades and had served as its mother superior. An assignment for *Out* magazine took me to the gay Cathedral of Hope, in Dallas; and in writing for *Harper's Bazaar* on the sudden popularity of Middle Eastern filmmakers, writers, and artists, I met an Iranian novelist who helped me slip into my first mosque. Deepak Chopra would file such seeming coincidences under the heading "sychrodestiny"—his alluring notion that there are no accidents.

One afternoon at Gurumayi's ashram, a devotee of hers, and a fellow writer, asked me rather testily what I felt my criteria were for choosing what to include in my book. "Deep whim!" I answered. I now see that my flip answer was indeed the truest explanation. The attraction that I felt varied: sometimes it was intellectual; at other times it seemed there was a social or historical significance for followers, or an intimation that something was truly transforming here. There were also other movements I wanted to write about but from which I eventually drew back. In June 1997, I attended teachings by His Holiness the Dalai Lama at the Nairopa Institute in Boulder, Colorado, where—always smiling and adept at thinking on his feet—he gave his talk in a billowing, summery, striped tent. Tibetan Buddhism has certainly been the example of a religion from a very different culture that has helped America expand spiritually. The Dalai Lama's appearance in an ad for Apple computers only confirms the extent of that assimilation. I was also interested in the Kabbalah, a medieval strain of Jewish mysticism. However, at the time, Madonna, Roseanne, Sandra Bernhard, and Isaac Mizrahi were all taking lessons, and its Talmudic wisdom was receiving plenty of press attention. The decision not to delve further into these areas of interest was calculated simply: they seemed overexposed.

A surprise was how similar my own spiritual résumé was to that of many of the frequent-flyer pilgrims I was meeting. I turned out to be the right age. Most of those keeping the retreat houses and guest dormitories in ashrams bustling were of the genus "boomer." Likewise, many of them had uneven denominational pasts. Growing up in a suburban town in northeastern Pennsylvania in the 1950s and 1960s, I was never baptized. At age twelve, I had my own personal awakening—from coming forward after a screening of the Billy Graham production *The Cross and the Switchblade* at my high school—and had myself baptized by a minister at a local Presbyterian church. My fervor was soon lost in the excitement of poetry and political activism. After graduating from Columbia University in 1973, I lived in Paris, where I became fascinated with medieval Christianity. Inspired by a selection from Thomas Aquinas's *Summa Theologica* titled "Treatise on Happiness"—"Happiness is man's proper good," the saint had written—I fancied that I wanted to be a Trappist monk. And I did live for a time in an experimental semimonastic community of men and women, the Trees, affiliated with the Cathedral of St. John the Divine, in New York City under the direction of Canon Edward N. West. This too passed, however, and I found myself back in local neighborhood parishes.

On the mantle of my fireplace, there is a row of seemingly contradictory items: a nineteenth-century Russian icon painted on a curved piece of wood of Christ Pantocrator (the Judge) holding a globe in His outstretched palm; an Islamic lunar calendar for 2001 (a.k.a. 1421–1422); a blue velvet bag stitched in gold thread with a Star of David containing a prayer cap and a tallith; a greeting card printed with a saying of Buddha's. But such mixing and matching of traditions I found to be quite normal. The standard accusation is that this syncretism is self-indulgent plundering of the world's great religious traditions. It's symptomatic of the navel-gazing "me generation." It's spiritual tourism. But with increasing globalization, worlds *are* colliding. When I visit my alma mater I see a student population that looks quite different from 1973. Not only are there now women at Columbia, there are also many more South Asians, African Americans, and Latinos. The second-generation offspring of Hindu, Muslim, and Buddhist parents who've emigrated to the United States in the past thirty-five years are often quite loyal to their own spiritual traditions. On my travels I even came across an underground network of men and women, including many respected academics and writers, who were simultaneously practicing Islam and Christianity. They're "closet Muslims." Or Universalists in deed as well as word.

I also found myself linked with a whole world of America's seekers by the computer. Spiritual America is definitely plugged in. When I imagined I wanted to be a Trappist in the mid-1970s I visited the Abbey of Gethsemani in the blue hills of Kentucky. Arrangements with the brothers under their strict vows of silence could only be made by "snail" mail, or by calling an ancient phone, which would often ring endlessly and never be answered. Twenty-five years later, I simply typed the Web address www.monks.org and found myself at an inviting home page showing a Kodachrome photo of their sun-drenched white stone abbey rising from green fields, with easy links to click on "Retreat Information" and "Map to Retreat House." Angelic messengers couldn't have been swifter. For better or worse, the Web has put formerly invisible spiritual communities on an electronic map. I've yet to visit a convent or ashram without its own bookstore, full of the appropriate CDs and videotapes. In a world shrunk by communications satellites and twenty-four-hour TV news, the notion that only religion and spirituality should remain unplugged is evidently a nonstarter.

The standard and basically unwavering statistic about American piety over the past fifty years has been that as many as 95 percent of the country will say that they believe in God, depending on how the question is put, while in most of Western Europe the figure is closer to 50 percent. Other poll figures have recently become noticeably higher. The Princeton Religious Research Index, which has tracked the strength of organized American religion since the end of World War II, reported a sharp rise in belief and formal practice since the mid-1990s. When the Gallup Poll asked those surveyed in 1999 if they felt a need to experience spiritual growth, 78 percent answered yes—up from 20 percent in

1994. Nearly half said they'd had occasion to talk about faith in the workplace in the past twenty-four hours. Sales of Bibles and prayer manuals, inspirational volumes, and books about philosophy and Eastern religions have grown faster than any other category, with the market expanding from $1.69 billion to $2.24 billion between 1996 and 2001.

During the five years I was working on this book, the mental map I've relied on to keep my bearings has continuously been redrawn. Most simply put: it's shifted from a flat map of the United States to a whirling globe. In just a half decade, "New Age" seems to have become obsolete as a fuzzy label to cover any expression outside the Judeo-Christian tradition. (Which is not to imply that many denominational churches and synagogues aren't thriving. I just chose to write about variations on a theme rather than the theme itself. Feeling in all fairness that being on the cusp is an almost emblematic posture for our times, I spent more time with believers like the woman who recently confessed to me that she was both Episcopalian and Quaker.) "Self-help" has likewise become inadequate as a catchall description for a genre of popular-wisdom literature caught somewhere between memoir, common sense, and sermon, and still very much in development.

Midway through my traveling and writing, I met Frederic and Mary Ann Brussat, who for more than three decades have reviewed books, movies, and videos on spiritual topics for their Values and Visions review service. Filling the walls of their loft in lower Manhattan were rows of review copies arranged and labeled by topic. "I can always tell what's going to take hold next by watching which books come in," Frederic Brussat told me. "What's next?" I asked, obviously interested. "World religions," he answered, confidently pointing to a nearly empty shelf. His hunch was correct. In the past two years I've been hearing more frequently of American Zen Buddhists visiting Japan, American Tibetan Buddhists studying Sanskrit, American Sufis going on a pilgrimage to Mecca. Spirituality in America has become more sophisticated, more global, more interested in tradition and less in simpleminded expropriation. This cycle has been reflected in my own travels, which revolved centripetally from the outer reaches of *The Urantia Book* or Gurumayi—so beautifully ethereal she seems to be a human hologram—inward to expressions, even if exceptional ones, of more traditional Catholicism, Protestantism, and Islam.

As I was finishing this book last winter, I took a subway uptown to visit the Sufi group I describe in my final chapter. (Without even the excuse of having research to do, I chanted with the Sufis on Friday and then was back on Sunday morning taking Communion at St. John's in the Village.) Daisy Khan, the wife of the group's leader, Feisal Rauf, a graduate of Columbia University with a degree in physics, told me of her husband's recent trip to Portugal. Apparently, thousands of Portuguese were being drawn to Sufism, the mystical branch of Islam, and hundreds of them had been chanting with him during the holy month of Ramadan beneath the high dome of the Lisbon central mosque. "Among them were local Portuguese seeking for something they can't find in their own tradition," she reported, sounding amazed. "They're mostly Roman Catholics. You know how *spiritual* Catholics can be." In the time I'd taken to write this book, more borders had opened between cultures and their religious traditions, and a kind of free trade agreement of rituals and practices had taken hold. I felt convinced that in the next five years more Americans would be traveling with spiritual passports—often dual passports—stamped with some very colorful visas.

Godtalk

One

"He's Only a Thought Away": Sleuthing *The Urantia Book*

On a snowy Tuesday evening in January 1997, I waited in a sitting room on the second floor of a 1908 residence on Chicago's North Side for the Urantia study group to begin. This four-story home, now the headquarters of the Urantia Foundation, had been lived in for more than a half century by Dr. William Sadler, a respected surgeon and psychiatrist born in 1875. Taking a critical approach as a young man, the doctor had debunked psychics, spiritualists, and channelers as frauds in his popular early books, *The Truth about Spiritualism* (1923) and *The Mind at Mischief* (1929). Yet he lives on in thousands of minds as the man responsible for the 2,097-page *Urantia Book,* which was said to have been transmitted during the early part of the twentieth century by celestial beings through a "contact personality," a reluctant Chicago businessman who to this day remains anonymous.

I had come across *The Urantia Book* in 1995, in the New Age capital of Sedona, Arizona, which was the perfect setting for scripture delivered in a *Twilight Zone* manner to have found a readership. My two guides on a tour of Sedona's supposed seven "vortices"—places in the earth believed by many to emit special electromagnetic properties—revealed themselves along the way to be readers of *The Urantia Book.* Intrigued by the oddly titled book, I certainly never expected to follow a string of clues that would lead back to the bourgeois home of a respectable-seeming doctor in the middle of that most American of middle-American cities, Chicago. Nor had I expected to discover that cults, or cult-like groups, are a solid part of our American turn-of-the century tradition. Even more surprising was that their adherents were bankers, doctors, and professors, and their wives, who discussed these writings during Sunday picnics at the home of one of their wealthier members in the upper-middle-class suburb of Oak Park, or at Sadler's summer lodge, in Beverly Shores, Indiana.

This wacky-sounding project was pointedly neglected in the April 28, 1969, full-column obituary of the ninety-three-year-old Sadler printed in the *Chicago Tribune.* The obituary's subheadline read, "He Predicted Organ Transplants in 1917," referring to a lecture he'd once given foreseeing a time "not far distant when wealthy people will take mortgages on internal organs of healthy persons and have the organs transplanted into their bodies at the death of the mortgagor." Sadler's other professional credits were duly listed: author of forty-two books on mental hygiene and health; successful medical doctor and public speaker; faculty member at McCormick Theological Seminary; fellow of the American College of Surgeons; attending psychiatrist at Columbus Hospital. Yet there was no mention of *The Urantia Book.* A separate one-paragraph listing of a memorial service at the Bentley and Son Funeral Home, on North Clark Street, did suggest "a donation to Urantia Foundation" in lieu of flowers.

The contradiction at the heart of Sadler's life story remains glaring. He matured as a doctor at a time when science was optimistically valued as having won the debate between faith and reason. His sizable medical practice gave him much respectability, as did his success in public speaking and lecturing around the country on what was known as "the Chautauqua circuit." The circuit was a popular summer education program of concerts and high-profile public lectures begun on Lake Chautauqua in southwest New York State in the late nineteenth century; it grew by the early twentieth century into a national network that had the effect, in pre-TV days, of a cross between public television and *The Oprah Winfrey Show.* Sadler's self-help book, *The Elements of Pep: A Talk on Health and Efficiency* (1925), as well as short books on such easily digestible topics as sex, teenage dating, and hygiene, sold extremely well. They were balanced by the publication of respected medical textbooks, including the 1,200-page *Theory and Practice of Psychology* (1936). He was bespectacled, Republican, and patriarchal in appearance, and surrounded by an extended family and many friends who looked up to him as a leader and a breadwinner. Sadler's interests in spiritualism were properly skeptical for the time, and his reputation as one of the few psychiatrists sympathetic with churchgoing folk made him the only practitioner many ministers felt comfortable recommending to troubled members of their midwestern congregations. He was a futurist and a dabbler. Yet his was a public face that is certainly difficult—then and now—to reconcile with the sorts of interplanetary, crypto-scientific, and post-Thomistic theological claims mulled over at length in the singular *Urantia Book.*

Since Sadler himself concealed much activity—either duplicitous or divine, depending on interpretation—it seemed fitting that his Frommann & Jebsen–designed residence at 533 Diversey Parkway was likewise not as bourgeois as might at first appear. Described in the *AIA Guide to Chicago* as "this grand flat, the star of this graceless southside stretch of Diversey Parkway," the building's official-looking stone exterior is delightfully fronted by a balcony protected with a metal railing and lavish ornaments that recall the more flamboyant Art Nouveau and Jugendstil styles of their time. Its pixilated architectural details are unusual on an urban stretch now filled with tanning parlors, supermarkets, and a Starbucks coffee shop.

"Doctor," as he was affectionately known, moved into this home in 1912 with his wife, Dr. Lena Kellogg Sadler, setting in motion all sorts of nocturnal and weekend activities to match the pace of his daily routine. He slipped an enticing hint as to what these extracurricular activities consisted of into the appendix to his *Mind at Mischief,* a best-seller published by Funk and Wagnalls in which he treated most matters credited to the supernatural as actually influenced by subconscious drives. Sadler confessed there that he'd been introduced to an individual in the summer of 1911 who was an apparent exception to his thesis, and that he had been present at 250 night sessions recorded by a stenographer: "This man is utterly unconscious, wholly oblivious to what takes place, and, unless told about it subsequently, never knows that he has been used as a sort of clearing house for the coming and going of alleged extra-planetary personalities." The doctor reassured his readers that the message being received was "essentially Christian and is, on the whole, entirely harmonious with the known scientific facts and truths of this age."

On my first visit to the house, I felt as if I'd been dropped onto a Parker Brothers *Clue* game board, with its musty library and wistful drawing room, a stack of hidden motives, and, most definitely, an atmosphere of unsolved mystery. In this eccentric building, Sadler allegedly had investigated the transcriptions of his contact personality—reputed by some to be a member of the Chicago Board of Trade, by others to be Sadler's own brother-in-law and office manager, Wilfred Kellogg. After about twenty years of serving as a human radio, the contact's broadcasts evolved into the 196 finished papers that often arrived handwritten by his bedside—with no witnesses present during the procedure.

Starting in 1923, a middlebrow salon of about thirty doctors, professors, and interested friends, known as "the Forum," formed around Sadler to hear these messages. They had convened for decades in the carpeted sitting room where I was waiting on that snowy evening for our meeting to begin. Sitting at a seminar-style table with a half-dozen veteran *Urantia Book* readers, I glanced occasionally through the room's tall windows toward a residential cross street lined with a few remaining gray stone buildings, elegant two-flat houses, and the bare sticks of trees.

The last person with a strong memory of Sadler and the early history of the Forum, Helen Carlson, had just died a week earlier, at the age of ninety-two. The sister-in-law of Sadler's son, William Sadler Jr., Ms. Carlson moved into the third floor of the building in 1935 and stayed on doing clerical work until her death. In a deposition taken in this room in 1994—as part of a defense against a suit claiming that the Urantia Foundation had no right to copyright materials authored by extraterrestrials—Carlson broke down as she told how her sister had invited her to join the Forum in September 1935 to learn about the papers: "Being a sister, she wanted me to know about them. I'm sorry . . . too many memories." These accumulated papers on various topics were eventually collected in what became known as *The Urantia Book.*

Carlson recalled how they would set up fifty folding chairs for an audience to listen to Dr. Sadler or his son read from the papers typed on yellow sheets. The Forum members would then serve as a focus group, submitting questions to the celestials for further clarification (this transfer of information between the earthlings and the extraterrestrials was never entirely explained) by dropping them into either a fishbowl or a basket resting on a chest of drawers in the center of the room. On my way in, I passed the chest of drawers, which had since been moved into the adjoining foyer.

"I remember at that time everybody was puzzled about personality," Helen Carlson recalled in her deposition. "Somebody asked the question, Well, what is personality? In a short time it just came through in a paper, the definition of personality. That had been in *The Urantia Book,* and now that was a direct answer to the question."

The paper chosen to be discussed was Paper 112, "Personality Survival." "It was Helen's favorite," explained Bob Solone, who worked in the reader services department at the foundation. As we talked, Solone lit a white memorial candle and placed it among the bags of chips, cookies, a bottle of ginger ale, and a tray of tea and coffee on the table in front of us. On an opposite wall hung a black-and-white Ansel Adams print of craggy mountains backed against a dramatically distressed bank of clouds.

Before the meeting began, Solone talked with me about how he came to the group. "I found a used copy over ten years ago in a bookstore my aunt owned in Wisconsin," he said. Solone was a soft-spoken forty-six-year-old Italian American with thin-boned features, wide staring brown eyes, and graying hair, and he moonlighted as a piano player in nightclubs. "I was living in Chicago, so I came here to the foundation. When I first came to the study group, I was just asking questions and asking questions. Eventually, though, the book satisfied all that."

Trevor Swaddling, an Australian from the suburbs of Sydney, joined in to tell how he'd first been given the book as an eighteenth-birthday present in 1976 by his sister, who was a member of a New Age commune led by Fred Robinson, a self-styled prophet who spread news of astrology, reincarnation, and UFOs in Australia during the 1970s. "You know, mud brick houses, growing veggies out in the back," Swaddling summed up the commune.

"My wife, Kathleen, found her book through the same chap," he went on. "When she was a teenager she was living in the same community as my sister. I met her when she was twenty-seven. I sparked her interest in *The Urantia Book* again, and she got it down from her bookshelf and reread it. She's been a reader ever since."

"You have to mollycoddle it a bit," interjected his redheaded wife, Kathleen. "You can't compare *The Urantia Book* to the Bible. We're at the early stages of spreading the word here." Together they ran a branch office for the foundation in Sydney.

Hurrying in from the cold at the last minute was Matthew Block, a short, alert, bantam-weight thirty-eight-year-old with the air of an eternal adolescent or graduate student. He had studied religion and philosophy at the University of Chicago in the

1970s, and was somewhat notorious in Urantian circles for having identified scores of books of the 1920s and 1930s from which portions of *The Urantia Book* had been paraphrased, a discovery construed by critics as proof of plagiarism.

"What are we reading tonight?" he asked as he dropped his *Urantia Book,* with its electric blue cover, on the table.

Soon, Rick Jones, who lives in the property's coach house, rounded out the group.

The choice of Paper 112 was doubly meaningful. Not only was it a favorite of Helen Carlson's, but its theme was death and the afterlife. It's the *Urantia Book* equivalent of a Christian burial service, promising life everlasting. Attributed as "Presented by a Solitary Messenger of Orvonton," "Personality Survival" concentrates on the so-called "Thought Adjuster," elsewhere nimbly described as "the Mystery Monitor," an "actual fragment of God" planted within each person. Our procedure that evening was to rotate around the table as each person read a section, pausing when anyone wanted to comment or ask a question.

"I'm sure that Helen has already woken up in the next mansion world with her Thought Adjuster intact," Bob Solone reassured us, deepening my sense that we were at a séance. He then read aloud the introduction to the paper.

"The evolutionary planets are the spheres of human origin, the initial worlds of the ascending mortal career," Solone began reverently.

As the readings continued, my mind filled with a heady mix of interplanetary travel, abstruse theology, and the grand wish that life could exist on other planets and continue to exist after the unraveling of this mortal coil. If the book were being pitched for a Hollywood movie, it might well be as *"The Ten Commandments* meets *Contact."*

"It's your turn to read, Brad," Trevor Swaddling prompted.

My section, called "The Phenomenon of Death," contained a surprising ban on messages sent from deceased loved ones back to earth. It included a stern dismissal of séances. "It is the policy throughout the universes to forbid such communication during the period of a current dispensation," I read aloud. Reincarnation was likewise nixed by the somewhat stuffy-sounding author of my section: "Never does a departed Thought Adjuster return to earth as the being of former indwelling."

Sections followed on such mystifying topics as "Adjusters after Death," "Survival of the Human Self," "The Morontia Self," and "Adjuster Fusion." The idea of the thought adjuster—a concept sounding to me as ancient as conscience itself—was cause for lively debate.

"What do you think they mean when they say the thought adjusters are pre-personal?" asked Trevor Swaddling.

"The thought adjusters are like the hard disk," explained Kathleen.

"Has anyone studied Kant?" Matthew Block offered. "It's like idealism. It's genius that they can just say that."

"I always thought Clarence in *It's a Wonderful Life* could have been a representation of a midwayer or guardian angel," said Bob Solone. "But not a Thought Adjuster, of course."

"On a more material level, I'm willing to share this," said Rick Jones, thankfully adding some levity by holding up a bottle of ginger ale.

Kathleen Swaddling was the last to read. She was given the culminating paragraph, which evokes none too faintly the King James translation of the Bible. "True it is, you mortals are of earthly, animal origin; your frame is indeed dust," she recited in her strong Aussie drawl. "But if you actually will, if you really desire, surely the heritage of the ages is yours, and you shall someday serve throughout the universes in your true characters—children of the Supreme God of experience and divine sons of the Paradise Father of all personalities."

Although the reading of the paper had taken almost two hours, the meeting didn't break up immediately. Everyone seemed fueled to keep talking about these theological concepts and about the possibilities of a gradual personal evolution toward God. No doubt there were many echoes here of those larger meetings occurring fifty years ago when Dr. Sadler was still alive and the papers hot off the celestial presses.

"Why did the Universal Father go to all this trouble?" asked Rick Jones, reasonably enough, of the complex system of spiritual evolution.

"They explain that," Block answered almost impatiently. "It's to have company. That's not original to *The Urantia Book,* though. It's just a tremendous amplification of what's in any basic catechism."

Focusing on the classroom instruction board at the far end of our conference table, I was now floating in a cloud of thoughts too big, too new, or too out of context to be entirely comprehended. Among lots of diagrams and scratching on a large sheet of white paper a phrase—apparently left over from a previous discussion— was written, in brown marker, that verified the heady nature of the group's chosen path to enlightenment: "He's only a thought away!"

B ack in my room at the Surf Hotel—a 1925 building with a terra-cotta facade, located just a block away—I realized that my evening at the reading group had left me feeling more bookish than galvanized. I kept thinking of books about books. I thought of *The Glass Bead Game,* Hermann Hesse's final novel, published in Germany in 1943, about a group of intellectuals in the twenty-third century occupying themselves with an elaborate game that employs all the philosophical and scientific knowledge of the ages. I thought impressionistically, too, of the short stories of the Argentinian writer Jorge Luis Borges, especially "The Library of Babel," in which he imagines the universe organized as a gigantic library. I half expected to pass the night dreaming of kingdoms of books, of toppling books, of climbing a stairway of books.

Yet for a work that invites being looked at in so many dizzy-ing ways, *The Urantia Book* is remarkably simple in its structure. Skimming through its pages again after the meeting, I realized that it's like a textbook, clearly divided into four parts and made up of 196 distinct papers. Part I, "The Central and Superuniverses," includes thirty-one papers. At the heart of these concentric superuniverses is paradise, which is stationary, ellipsoid, and essentially flat, the abiding place of the great I AM, the metaphysical creative trinity of the Universal Father, the Eternal Son, and the Infinite Spirit. Part II is made up of twenty-four papers on "The Local Universe," our universe, called Nebadon, located near the edge of the superuniverse of Orvonton, which is filled with an aggregation of suns, double stars, globular clusters, star clouds, spiral and other nebulae, and the vast Milky Way. Part III expands to 112 papers on "The History of Urantia," Urantia being the name for the planet Earth, conceived in this cosmology as the 606th planet in a planetary group called Satania, which contains 619 inhabited worlds with 200 more evolving toward becoming inhabited. Part IV contains seventy-six papers on "The Life and Teachings of Jesus," in which Jesus is revealed to have been one of 700,000 "Creator Sons," incarnate on earth to fulfill a requirement for passing a lifetime on a mortal world as part of His celestial job description.

The final section, containing the "Jesus Papers"—the most accessible part of the book—gives a day-by-day account of all the incidents left out of the New Testament concerning Jesus Christ. We learn that when Jesus was fourteen his father died from a derrick collapsing on him; that Jesus visited a university in Athens where he "thoroughly discussed the teachings of Plato"; that he toured much of the Roman world with two natives of India, Gonod and Ganid; that his body in the tomb was speeded forward to complete disintegration, while he appeared again in what was actually a reconstituted spiritual body. Along the way, a few key Christian theological doctrines are handily abandoned: the fall of man; the virgin birth; atonement; bodily resurrection.

One problem in understanding the book comes with its dizzying roll call of otherworldly officials, go-betweens, functionaries, angels, near deities, spirits, bodies, planets, galaxies, stars, transport vehicles, and communication devices somehow linking together various worlds separated by time, space, and moral distance in an updated version of the medieval "chain of being." To complicate matters, this cast of characters and locales are often given neologisms for their names and titles, the terms derived from a strange etymology that results in a kind of Indo-European newspeak: "Caligastia," "Urantia," "Nebadon," "Orvonton," "Morontia." Each of the papers has its own presenter, identified by such theatrical names as Brilliant Evening Star, Mighty Messenger, Vorondadek Son, or Malavatia Melchizedek. The effect is of an exotic linguistic tissue laid over a nuts-and-bolts grid.

For all of the surrounding secret-handshake style of mystery, though, *The Urantia Book* has endured and spread, if not quite flourished, during the nearly half century since its publication. More than half a million copies have been sold in hardback and paperback. Sales jumped from 7,000 in 1990 to 24,700 in 1997, and steadily increased to nearly 38,000 in 2000, a dramatic upturn that seems to represent a genuine trend rather than just some spike on a sales chart. (The hefty hardcover, weighing 4.3 pounds, is now in its fourteenth printing.) It's available in a CD-ROM and an audio version. Translations have been completed in French, Russian, Spanish, Dutch, Finnish, and Korean. Work has begun on Bulgarian, Croat, German, Swedish, Estonian, Lithuanian, Italian, Portuguese, Chinese, Hindi, Farsi, Greek, Indonesian, Italian, Japanese, Polish, Portuguese, Romanian, and Arabic translations. A list of secondary works includes a concordance, a glossary and pronunciation guide, and a collection of illustrations of the artist John Byron's conception of the book's universes. The Urantia Foundation runs home-based branch offices in Sydney, Australia; Caversham Berkshire, England; Helsinki, Finland; Paris, France; and Seville, Spain. A Russian office also opened in 2000. That same year, the Urantia Foundation's Web site recorded thirty thousand hits per month. The International Urantia Association has twenty-six reader associations worldwide. The Urantia Book Fellowship, originally the

Urantia Brotherhood—a spin-off of the foundation—claims roughly twelve hundred official members, with the highest concentrations in the West and the Sun Belt, especially California, Colorado, Florida, and Texas.

The number of actual readers remains a question. (I was told of a homeless man in New York City who discovered the book in a trash bin in Central Park.) Many readers come to groups after reading in solitude for twenty years. The book is often passed on, or lent to friends. Reading groups have never been officially counted, as they tend to sprout, ripen, then vanish or splinter. (A rough estimate from a fellowship official puts the number at about five hundred.) I attended a group in Manhattan that has been meeting regularly on Tuesday evenings for more than a dozen years at the SoHo loft of artist Robin Jorgenson and his wife, Helene, who is a teacher at a parochial grade school. When I joined them, they were in the middle of their third reading of the entire text in sequence. In Boulder, Colorado, I attended a meeting of a robust group with nearly one hundred members who gathered on Friday evenings in the First Congregational Church. During a fierce snowstorm, three adult groups were scheduled simultaneously—studying, respectively, Book I, the "Jesus Papers," and an advanced special topic—as well as a garrulous group of children who met Sunday-school-style in the basement.

The line between reading and worshiping in the Urantia movement is blurred. Some readers simply want to crack open the book and discuss its contents with friends. Others feel invited to a more worshipful, even liturgical response. So far the movement is making up its rituals as it goes along. To Dr. Meredith Sprunger—a retired United Church of Christ minister, practicing psychologist, and confidant of Dr. Sadler's—the singing of "Holy, Holy, Holy" at the fellowship's 1993 international conference, in Montreal, was a "milestone." The 1996 Urantian conference, in Flagstaff, Arizona, began with twenty minutes of inclusive morning worship "ranging from an American Indian dance experience to East Indian (Himou) to classical harp and song." But for most, worship remains as individual as the act of reading. "When I vacuum or do housework, I like to think about God the Father and the universe," one reader informed me.

Because of its insistence on having been written by a committee of extraterrestrial beings, *The Urantia Book* falls for most people to the far left of believability. Yet the history of religion, literature, and popular spirituality is full of somewhat similar claims. Fundamentalist Christians believe that the Bible is the literal, inerrant word of God. Muslims believe that in A.D. 610, Muhammad, in a cave two miles north of Mecca, encountered the angel Gabriel, who revealed to him the words of the Quran. In 1823, Joseph Smith claimed that he was visited by the loosely robed angel Moroni, son of Mormon, who led him to a cache of gold plates revealing the history of the lost tribes of Israel, which he then transcribed into the *Book of Mormon.* (Mark Twain wickedly described the final result as "chloroform in print.") Mary Baker Eddy believed that every word in her *Science and Health,* the basic text of the Christian Science movement, was inspired; the Reverend Sun Myung Moon claimed divine inspiration for the bible he wrote for his Unification Church.

Shelves full of books received, channeled, or otherwise idiosyncratically authored have been passed down from the eighteenth through the twentieth century. Swedish visionary Emanuel Swedenborg's *A Spiritual Key,* published in London in 1784, was written from a series of dreams, beginning in 1743, that included a vision of Christ telling Swedenborg to abandon scientific work in favor of biblical studies, which he did, producing more than thirty volumes of theological commentary. In Swedenborg's emphasis on a spiritual path outside the ecclesiastical structure, he touched many of the popular themes of alternative spiritual movements of the next two centuries in Europe and America. Though a number of Swedenborgian churches and societies were founded after his death, his influence has survived mostly through the poetic writings of Blake, Baudelaire, Strindberg, Emerson, and Yeats. (Blake claimed to have superseded Swedenborg in *The Marriage of Heaven and Hell,* when he wrote: "Swedenborg is the Angel sitting at the tomb; his writings are the linen clothes folded up.")

Spiritualism—as a general belief in the possibility of communication with the spirit world—became quite popular in the later nineteenth and early twentieth centuries, an era of mediums, psychics, and channelers unmatched again until the present. The classic book on the subject is still Sir William F. Barrett's *On the Threshold of the Unseen,* written at a peak moment of spiritualism in 1917. Sir Arthur Conan Doyle wrote approvingly at the time, "Spiritualism is a religion for those who find themselves outside all religions; while on the contrary it greatly strengthens the faith of those who already possess religious beliefs." Indeed, Sadler's hobby of exposing mediums, and the warnings against believing in communications with the dead in *The Urantia Book,* are indications of the popularity of the spiritualist movement, and of the Urantians' attempt to separate themselves from episodes of otherworldly contact that seem on the surface often indistinguishable from theirs. (They find themselves in a similarly subtle dispute nowadays when they protest the shelving of *The Urantia Book* under "New Age" in bookstores, or in their earlier fight—won in 1975—for the Library of Congress to reclassify *The Urantia Book* from "Miscellaneous Occult and Esoteric Sciences" to "Other Beliefs and Movements," and for the Dewey decimal classification to be changed from "Parapsychology and the Occult" to "Other Religions.")

One of the more popular books of the early-twentieth-century spiritualist craze was *The Aquarian Gospel of Jesus Christ,* published by Levi Dowling in 1907 just as the first messages from the celestials were allegedly being received by Sadler's contact personality. Dowling claimed that his *Gospel* had been channeled from "the akashic record"—a term derived from the Sanskrit word *akasha,* meaning the ether or all-pervading space, and referring to a complete and psychically available record of all events that have occurred on the earth plane. Like *The Urantia Book,* the *Gospel* discusses Jesus' exposure to Eastern philosophy, telling of his Vedic studies in India, and of an excursion to Tibet to study at a temple in Lhasa. Edgar Cayce claimed to be transmitting material from this same akashic record in his messages delivered, until his death in 1945, in a normal speaking voice while—like Sadler's either real or fictional contact personality—apparently asleep.

The current revival of spiritualism is evident in the market for channeled books such as those of the thirty-five-thousand-year-old warrior and former Atlantean, Ramtha, channeled by Mrs. J. Z. Knight beginning in 1977, or the entity Seth—of *Seth Speaks* and *The Seth Material*—channeled by Jane Roberts from 1963 until her death, in 1984. Perhaps the most influential has been *A Course in Miracles.* Written in three volumes between 1965 and 1973, the *Course* was supposedly dictated psychically by Jesus Christ to Helen Schucman, with the assistance of her colleague, William Thetford, while both were professors of medical psychology at the Columbia University College of Physicians and Surgeons. The project began when, after three months of involuntarily perceiving a series of intense mental images, the atheistic Schucman heard an inner voice announcing, "This is a course in miracles. Please take notes." One of the course's popularizers, and arguably one of the more effective of its teachers in modern America, has been Marianne Williamson, the author of the best-selling *A Return to Love: Reflections on the Principles of "A Course in Miracles."*

A more recent and even more immediate commercial success is *Conversations with God: An Uncommon Dialogue,* which appeared in three consecutive volumes during 1996 and 1997. In the opening chapter of the first volume—dedicated to such easy-listening artists as Barbra Streisand, John Denver, and Richard Bach—the author, Neale Donald Walsch, explains: "In the spring of 1992, it was around Easter as I recall, an extraordinary phenomenon occurred in my life. God began talking with you. Through me." Walsch details how he was writing down questions about his unhappy life when suddenly, "To my surprise, as I scribbled out the last of my bitter, unanswerable questions and prepared to toss my pen aside, my hand remained poised over the paper, as if held there by some invisible force. Abruptly, the pen began *moving on its own.* I had no idea what I was about to write, but an idea seemed to be coming, so I decided to flow with it. Out came . . . *Do you really want an answer to all these questions, or are you just venting?"* What followed were folksy, far-ranging conversations between God and Walsch on love, economics, politics, science, art, and morals.

Peculiar to *The Urantia Book* in this genre of spiritual literature is the amount of scientific material included. Among the scientific topics addressed technically in the book are the birth of the solar system; black holes (poetically dubbed "dark islands of space"); particle physics; neutron stars; continental drift; the origin of life on earth; planetary atmospheres; and the number of stable elements. Even the skeptical Martin Gardner, a columnist for *Scientific American* and the author of the highly critical *Urantia: The Great Cult Mystery,* admits, "As a science journalist I was fascinated by the enormous amount of science in the *UB.* It is absolutely unique in this respect among all literature said to be channeled by higher intelligences through a person either asleep or in a trance. *UB* science is a strange mix of knowledge widely accepted by mainline scientists during the years the *UB* was crafted, and wild speculation about truths either unknown to science or contradicted by recent science."

In its cataloging of scientific discoveries past and future, the book could be seen as a measure of its times. For between 1911, when Sadler claimed to have first been exposed to the material, and 1935, when the first draft of the last paper was completed, discoveries in science, technology, anthropology, and archaeology were occurring at an increasingly rapid rate. Henry Norris Russell, for instance, had introduced his theory of stellar evolution in 1915; Albert Einstein completed his theory of general relativity in 1917; George Ellery Hale oversaw the installation of the Hooker telescope on Mount Wilson in 1919; Robert Hutchings Goddard launched the first liquid-fuel-propelled rocket in 1926; Clyde Tombaugh discovered Pluto in 1930. Some of these discoveries clearly left impressions on *The Urantia Book,* which, in its generally futuristic feeling, describes galaxies full of intelligent life able to communicate through time and across vast distances. Other discoveries showed up in more specific detail. In 1924, for instance, Edwin Powell Hubble determined that the distance to the Andromeda Nebula was a million light-years. This measurement is confirmed, without attribution, in Paper 15 of *The Urantia Book,* "The Seven Superuniverses": "This far-distant nebula is visible to the naked eye, and when you view it, pause to consider that the light you behold left those distant suns almost a million years ago."

Some of *The Urantia Book*'s scientific theories have been verified over the past decades. Others haven't. The book's notion of the growth of planets by slow accretion over billions of years, known in its day as the "Chamberlin-Moulton hypothesis," proposed by two University of Chicago professors in 1900, is at odds with the big bang theory proposed by Jules Lemaître in 1927 and widely held today that puts the age of the universe at ten to twenty billion years rather than the 875 billion years proposed for the birth of our local universe in *The Urantia Book:* "875,000,000,000 years ago the enormous Andronover nebula number 876,926 was duly initiated." The book's clocking of the speed of light at 186,280 miles per second is close to the present figure of 186,232—though other estimates at the time were closer to the current number: "The limit of velocity for most non-enseraphimed beings is 186,280 miles per second of your time." Its theory of a directional magnetic sense in birds, particularly homing pigeons, has been proved by later science, though the application to humans is still debated: "Thus is the sense of orientation forever fixed in the living beings of the universe."

With scientists at the turn of the century credited with knowing the answers to more and more of life's questions, religious thinkers often felt the need to respond or take sides. Such defensiveness was obvious in relation to the paradigm shift caused by Darwin's theory of natural selection. Madame Helena Blavatsky, the renegade Russian aristocrat and spiritualist medium who founded the Theosophical Society in New York City in 1875, expressed her contempt for Darwin by keeping a stuffed baboon in her parlor dressed in wing collar, tail coat, and spectacles, and holding a copy of *The Origin of Species*. She claimed that man wasn't descended from apes but from spirit beings. Christian fundamentalists in America set themselves up as stubbornly opposed to Darwinism, their opposition based on its refutation of the chronology of Genesis, resulting in a hollow victory in the famous Scopes "monkey trial" of 1925. *The Urantia Book* found a middle path by simply adapting Darwin's theory to its own spiritual purposes, recasting evolution as the basis of a process of supernatural selection in which human beings—beginning at stage one on earth—grow souls that allow them to graduate to successively higher planes of existence.

To explain the hits and misses of Urantian scientific theory—as opposed to the pure record of achievement that might be expected from a divine author—the book contains a disclaimer that turns on the notion of "unearned" science. In Paper 101, "The Real Nature of Religion," the presenter, Melchizedek of Nebadon, explains: "The laws of revelation hamper us greatly by their proscription of the impartation of unearned or premature knowledge. . . . We are not at liberty to anticipate the scientific discoveries of a thousand years. . . . We full well know that, while the historic facts and religious truths of this series of revelatory presentations will stand on the records of the ages to come, within a few short years many of our statements regarding the physical sciences will stand in need of revision in consequence of additional scientific developments and new discoveries."

For detractors this caveat is transparently clever, sparing the book from any objective evaluation. If its scientific theories are disproved, they can be ascribed to the limited science of the times; if they pan out, they are pointed to as evidence of superior intelligence. Ironically, no one spelled out the weakness of such a ploy more plainly than the early Sadler of *The Truth about Spiritualism*, which remains one of the strongest attacks ever written on fraudulent mediums and their methods. In it, Sadler complained of the "spirits" of spiritualism: "If the spirits are so wise, why have they never whispered the principles of some new and great invention to the mediums? Why is it that our mechanical inventions all originate in the brains of our natural-born geniuses, or are worked out in the persistent sweat of such men as Thomas A. Edison? What a time and labor saving it would be if the secrets of the wireless-telegraph, or the principles of an internal combustion gas engine, could be secured at a spiritualistic seance."

The combining of science with literature was accomplished at the time of the writing of *The Urantia Book* not by theologians and spiritualists, but by the newly expanding genre of science fiction. This literary development helped make science entertaining, and thus more palatable to the masses. The author most responsible for making science fiction acceptable was H. G. Wells, who ruled the field after the publication, in 1895, of *The Time Machine.* His success was then exploited by pulp science fiction magazines, especially *Argosy* and *All-Story,* which published Edgar Rice Burroughs's "Under the Moons of Mars" (1912), and Arthur Conan Doyle's "The Lost World" (1912), about an overlooked region where dinosaurs and other ancient beasts still roamed—a conceit revived most recently by Michael Crichton. As entertainment, *The Urantia Book* could well be read as early science fiction. And indeed many of its devotees have a background as science fiction fans.

"I used to read tons of science fiction," Robin Jorgenson of the Manhattan reading group told me. "I loved Asimov, Heinlein, all the really good stuff that went beyond Buck Rogers and space cowboys to philosophy and science. But I stopped reading science fiction after I started reading *The Urantia Book.* Everything else pales in comparison. Not only the outrageousness of its presentation of life on other planets—the one-brained, the three-brained, the nonbreathers—but also its philosophical content, and the organization and patterning of the cosmos. I think that science fiction as an art form was probably intended or hoped for by the celestials. I see it as a precursor to *The Urantia Book.*"

Yet *The Urantia Book* doesn't bill itself as science fiction, but rather as "the fifth epochal revelation," the fourth epochal revelation having been the teachings of Jesus Christ. The grandeur of this claim makes *The Urantia Book* especially rankling to the pious and fundamentalist, as well as to many scientists, philosophers, and literary scholars. By stepping over the line from entertainment to divine inspiration, the book invites reactions far more scathing than its somewhat dated, elegant, usually clean, and usually intelligent prose might otherwise merit. "*The Urantia Book* is remarkable among these types of books claiming divine revelation, in that it is occasionally well written," Martin Gardner admitted to me. "There are parts I can even agree with . . . the mild parts reflecting the liberal Protestantism of Harry Emerson Fosdick popular at the time. But I can't agree that each of these papers was channeled from a supernatural being. And unfortunately it's filled with all kinds of science blunders." This response mildly echoed the much harsher appraisal in his book in which he had complained, "The *UB*'s cosmology outrivals in fantasy the cosmology of any science fiction work known to me. . . . No one can read through the *UB*, or even just parts of it, without wondering how such an incredibly detailed mix of science, ethics, politics, and polytheology ever got set down in one monstrous blue-covered volume."

The Urantia Book does indeed come across on many pages as oddball. Extensive space is devoted to a speculative astronomy not much practiced since the ancient astronomers and not much written about since Dante based his poetic universe for the *Commedia*, in the thirteenth century, on a soon-to-be-discarded Ptolemaic system. The authors manage to accomplish what Einstein spent the second half of his lifetime striving to achieve—a unified field theory—with the advantage of not needing final verification by any scientific instruments. At its most extreme moments, the book's explanations of cosmic astronomy are responsible for such inexplicable statements as: "The triodity of actuality continues to function directly in the post-Havona epochs."

Its delving into prehistory, archaeology, and anthropology seems to be written by a first-class fabulist. We learn, for instance, that Adam and Eve, who materialized on Urantia 37,848 years before 1934, were eight feet tall, with blue eyes, and had bodies that shimmered with light. Mankind evolved from three primary-colored races (red, yellow, and blue) and three secondary-colored races (orange, green, and indigo). That the indigo race, the least advanced of the six, was credited with having migrated to Africa to become the black race remains an embarrassment to many present-day Urantians, harking back to strains of racist eugenics popular in the 1930s.

Politically incorrect or not, however, the spiritual scheme laid out in *The Urantia Book* remains its primary claim on its readers' daily life, determining how they perceive existence, death, and the afterlife—the key concerns of any religious statement. For believers, *The Urantia Book* provides a gently supportive, inspiring view of life delivered by its "inditers" in a tone of distant love. As Matthew Block sensitively confessed in 1997, "The heart of *The Urantia Book,* for me, is its compelling and sublime message of the love of God, expressed through Jesus and other spiritual agencies, and the focus on evolution as a divinely ordained cosmic principle."

For nonbelievers, the reading of the book is much more uneven and problematic—fascinating, inspiring, compelling, haunting, entertaining, annoying, incomprehensible, and always wordy. Urantians speak of getting beyond the question of origins as they submerge themselves in the truths they discover. A few have never even looked into the origins; some have never heard the name Sadler. For them, after all, the authors are celestials, not Chicagoans. But for nonbelievers the questions—which, unfortunately, never quite go away—remain the elementary, investigative ones: Who? Where? When? Why?

A ll of these questions lead back to the mysterious figure of William S. Sadler, the unlikely Moses of the Urantia movement, with his tablets of epochal revelation somehow received from the sky. Whether *The Urantia Book* is a hoax or authentic scripture, Sadler is definitely one of America's homegrown religious leaders, an original along the lines of Joseph Smith, Ellen Smith, and Mary Baker Eddy, though on a smaller scale. Yet he has remained largely hidden from public view. Unlike those others who found new truth in trance material—the Mormon followers of Joseph Smith now number 9.7 million—Sadler eschewed all public exposure or proselytizing. His life story must be read between the lines to find clues to those talents that turned the Urantia movement into more than just a passing Sunday-afternoon aberration in early-twentieth-century Chicago.

Sadler's own point of origin was Spencer, Indiana, where he was born on June 24, 1875, to Samuel Cavins Sadler and Sarah Isabelle (Wilson) Sadler. His father was a graduate of the Chicago Conservatory of Music and a successful Bible salesman. Both his parents were converts to Seventh-Day Adventism, the sect founded by Ellen White to cope with the failure of William Miller's 1844 prediction to his Millerites of the end of the world, a nonevent known at the time as the "Great Disappointment." (White and her followers adopted a "shut door" doctrine—the belief that Christ had entered heaven on the prescribed date but that the remnant church must now worship on Saturdays while awaiting His return and final judgment.)

Growing up in Wabash, Illinois, Sadler exhibited an early predilection for learning and a talent for public speaking. He borrowed history books from his neighbor, General Lew Wallace, who was writing *Ben Hur* at the time. All this knowledge came in handy when Sadler's relative, General McNaught, a onetime chief of scouts to General Ulysses S. Grant, asked him at a family reunion to stand on a rain barrel and give a speech on the battles of history. Sadler claimed that at the age of eight he had addressed a high school commencement in Indianapolis on the subject "The Crucial Battles of History," and at age sixteen he was dubbed "the boy preacher" in a local newspaper for a sermon he delivered at a Fort Wayne church.

Leaving home at age fourteen, Sadler moved to Battle Creek, Michigan, where he worked as a bellhop at the Sanitarium and attended Battle Creek College. The Sanitarium was a highly successful hybrid of a European spa and an American medical clinic. Begun as the Health Reform Institute by the Seventh-Day Adventists in 1866, its exercise crazes and homeopathic remedies drew such prominent nineteenth-century celebrities as George Bernard Shaw, Montgomery Ward, S. S. Kresge, Thomas Edison, Henry Ford, John D. Rockefeller III, and President William Taft, among others, who fasted, irrigated their colons, ate yogurt, and slept beneath the original electric blankets. (The hotel's story was retold in T. Coraghessan Boyle's comic 1993 novel *The Road to Wellville.*) Its impresario, Dr. John Harvey Kellogg, inventor of Kellogg's corn flakes, was a common sight on the grounds as he'd ride by on a bicycle in his trademark white suit, his short white beard flipping in the wind.

Sadler's day job turned out to be very rewarding, since Dr. Kellogg took an interest in him and became his prime mentor. When William K. Kellogg, Dr. Kellogg's brother, began manufacturing health foods in 1893, Sadler was hired as a salesman; at nineteen he was demonstrating the products so well to grocers that the factory had trouble filling his orders. In 1895, Dr. Kellogg, who'd founded the Chicago Medical Mission, sent Sadler to Chicago to serve as its secretary. Experiences working with skid row derelicts became an important source of anecdotes for Sadler's later Chautauqua lectures. Dr. Kellogg also arranged for him to be enrolled as a special student at the Moody Bible Institute for evangelistic instruction. Sadler adhered to the Seventh-Day Adventism of Dr. Kellogg and his family by becoming a licensed minister in 1899 and an ordained minister in 1901, yet after Kellogg split from the church in 1907, Sadler gradually fell away. (Dr. Kellogg was excommunicated by his friend Ellen White, who reportedly suspected him of diverting money from "the San" for new buildings in Chicago rather than for the support of her mission in Australia.)

Years later, Sadler did give a nod to Ellen White in the appendix to his *Mind at Mischief.* Putting her in the same special category as the contact personality of *The Urantia Book,* he claimed that he could find no evidence of deliberate deception in her spiritual writings. He found her a fitting model for the later Urantian enterprise, as White claimed that she had written her books in ecstatic trances, directly inspired by God with the help of the

Book of Revelation's "third angel"; these transcripts, making up the canon of Seventh-Day Adventism, included her best-known *Great Controversy* (1888) and the multivolume *Spiritual Gifts* (1858–64) and *Spirit of Prophecy* (1870–84). "But many years ago I did meet one trance medium, a woman now deceased, whose visions, revelations, etc. were not tainted with spiritualism," Sadler wrote in 1929, apparently of Ellen White. "As far as my knowledge extends, at no time did she claim to be under the influence of spirit guides or controls, or to communicate messages from the spirits of departed beings. Her work was largely of a religious nature and consisted of elevated sayings and religious admonitions."

During this period Sadler exhibited a surprising knack for detective work. While in Battle Creek he formed the Young Men's Intelligence Society. This initiative led to his working in association with the Comstock Society for the Suppression of Vice and the United States Post Office Inspectors to arrest printers and peddlers of pornography in Chicago. He continued to earn money part-time by doing detective work, and, as he later told Meredith Sprunger, he was eventually offered a job in an executive position in the governmental intelligence agency that became the Federal Bureau of Investigation. These skills could certainly have come in handy later in life, either to expose any fraudulence involved in the production of *The Urantia Papers* or, according to a more cynical interpretation, to design a foolproof hoax: to get away, that is, with the perfect spiritual crime.

In 1897, Sadler married Dr. Kellogg's niece, Lena Kellogg, who was working as a nurse at the Sanitarium. In 1899 their first child was born, but lived only nine months. In consoling his wife, Sadler recalled saying, "You can have another baby, and perhaps in the meantime, since you have always wanted to do it, we can study medicine." They entered Cooper Medical College (now part of Stanford University) in San Francisco in 1901, earning their room and board by operating a home for Christian medical students and by tutoring in chemistry. Dr. Kellogg, however, urged them to return to Chicago, which they did, matriculating at the

Rush Medical College of the University of Chicago. They both graduated in 1906 and began their medical practice together. Not just husband and wife, they were also close business associates; they had adjoining offices and performed surgical operations as a team. In December 1907, their second son, William Samuel Jr., was born. The Sadlers traveled to Europe in 1910 to study psychiatry at clinics in Leeds, England, and Vienna, Austria, where they attended classes conducted by Sigmund Freud and Alfred Adler. Sadler put this experience into use in 1930 when he expanded his surgical practice to include psychiatric counseling, which he practiced on the staff of Columbus Hospital.

Though intrigued by the teachings of Freud, Sadler kept his distance from the sexual and atheistic implications of classic Freudian psychoanalysis, establishing a position for himself as one of the few psychiatrists of his time sympathetic with religion. "We recognize that there are other human instincts and impulses just as strong as the sex urge," he wrote in his *Americanitis: Blood Pressure and Nerves,* published by Macmillan in 1925. "First of all there comes the instinct to live, to get food, and then, in many individuals, the religious emotion is very powerful, so that we cannot accept the Freudian doctrine that all our nervous troubles are due to suppression of the emotions and further that the particular emotion suppressed that is responsible for the trouble is the sex emotion."

Sadler's relationships with the Kellogg family continued to expand through the years. In 1912, Lena Kellogg's sister, Anna Bell, married her first cousin, Wilfred Custer Kellogg, whose father had been a circuit-riding minister of the Seventh-Day Adventists' New England Conference. (They had to be married in Wisconsin because of laws banning first-cousin marriages in Illinois.) Wilfred Kellogg had worked briefly as a manager of W. K. Kellogg's Toasted Corn Flake Company but sold his holdings in the company in 1912 to join Sadler as his business manager. The Kelloggs then lived at 2572 Hampden Court, a half block from 533 Diversey. Both families continued to keep in contact with their increasingly wealthy Battle Creek contingent, as evidenced by Sadler's gig from 1937 to 1939 as psychiatric consultant and trustee of the W. K. Kellogg Foundation.

This tightly interwoven, incestuous double family unit became the core of the Urantia movement, or what was called the "Contact Commission." Its original members were the Sadlers and their son, Bill Jr., and the Kelloggs and, perhaps, their daughter Ruth, born deaf. Included in this inner circle as well was Emma Christensen, the adopted adult daughter of the Sadlers, who was conveniently an expert stenographer and was reported to have met the couple when treated by Lena Sadler for an automobile injury. "Christy," as she was known, was employed, beginning in 1922, as the office manager of the national bank examiner's office in Chicago. These were the six or seven witnesses credited with being in the room when the contact personality was delivering his messages from the beyond, and who were solemnly sworn to life-long secrecy about his identity.

The date of the first contact with the "revelators" is disputed, and ranges from 1905 to 1912—Sadler puts the date, allowing for a printing error, at 1911 in his appendix to *The Mind at Mischief.* Lena Sadler was perhaps a key figure in making possible the entire event. Urantian legend has it that she believed early on that something significant was happening, while Dr. Sadler remained skeptical until 1936 and wished to abandon the process at several points but continued on at her insistence. The contact personality was said to have been the husband of a patient of Lena Sadler's; the patient had then consulted with William Sadler because of her concern over her husband's "bizarre behavior." Dr. Sadler later told a member of the Forum that "here was a hard-boiled businessman, member of the Board of Trade and Stock Exchange, who didn't believe in any of this nonsense and who had no recollection of what happened during these strange unwakeable sleep states." (The clue that he was a member of the stock exchange would disallow one of the favored candidates for the never-disclosed identity of the contact personality—none other than Wilfred Kellogg himself.)

"Eighteen years of study and careful investigation have failed to reveal the psychic origin of these messages," Sadler wrote of this gentleman in the appendix to *The Mind at Mischief*, in 1929. "I find myself at the present time just where I was when I started. Psychoanalysis, hypnotism, intensive comparison, fail to show that the written or spoken messages of this individual have origin in his own mind. Much of the material secured through this subject is quite contrary to his habits of thought, to the way in which he has been taught, and to his entire philosophy."

During the crucial first phase of the transmission of the Urantia papers, Sadler, then middle-aged, was extraordinarily energetic. Until 1915, he stayed up all night once a week dictating to two secretaries. He was also keen in those days on gathering materials exposing psychics and other popular clairvoyants. As Bill Sadler Jr. recalled in a talk to a Urantian study group in Oklahoma City in 1962: "My father had in his salad days as a hobby spook-hunting. He was an exposer of mediums. His two running mates were the head of the department of psychology at Northwestern University and Howard Thurston, a professional magician. When you take a psychologist, a physician, and a magician and put them together, God help the medium. . . . My dad was humorously mischievous."

During the Roaring Twenties, Chicago was one of the capitals of American magic and spiritualism, as well as of shady criminal activities. A favorite destination for Sadler, according to his son, was a mind-reading act at the MacVickers Theatre, a vaudeville house on State Street. Showing the tight relationship between spiritualism and cheap entertainment, the Loop was cluttered with venues featuring rising tables, ectoplasm, voices from floating trumpets, and luminous ghosts. Sadler's friend Howard Thurston was one of the most famous magicians in the world, and his show, "The Wonder Show of the Universe," with three railroad cars full of equipment and forty assistants, was the most opulent ever mounted. (Like Sadler, Thurston had attended one of Dwight Moody's Bible institutes; his earlier missionary impulses remained evident as he arranged for a service organization to drive the elderly from nursing homes to his shows, arranged for free performances for orphans, and took magic to the bedside of house-bound invalids.) Sadler was rumored to have been friendly as well with Houdini, who was likewise obsessed with exposing fraudulent mediums—Houdini's exposés of the spiritualist movement include *Miracle Mongers and Their Methods* (1920) and *A Magician among the Spirits* (1924)—though there is no evidence other than hearsay for their collaboration.

The transmission of the Urantian papers went into higher gear in the early 1920s with the informal gathering of the Forum. "It came about when Pop was giving a commencement address at Ames," Bill Sadler Jr. recalled. "I was in high school at the time, and he wrote me a letter saying that we were not church people but that Sunday should be productive as well as a day of rest. He asked what I would say if they invited in some friends and they had a discussion group—kind of a forum—and talked about health and history and politics, et cetera. That group came into existence in, I think, 1922." (Sadler claimed elsewhere that he had been on his way to the University of Kansas to deliver a lecture on Gestalt psychology when he wrote this letter to his son.)

Meanwhile, conversations between the Contact Commission and the revelators had been percolating. As Bill Sadler Jr. told the Oklahoma City reading group in 1962: "One evening they were talking to this chap, a kind of argument came up. They were talking with someone who claimed to be a 'Mighty Messenger.' They asked if he could prove he was a 'Mighty Messenger.' 'No,' he said, 'but you can't prove I'm not, either. If you knew what I know, you wouldn't ask these half-baked questions. You would prepare some of the most deep, searching, and far-reaching questions you could possibly imagine.' My father was half English and half Irish. You can get a reserved reaction from him or he can get damn mad. He got damn mad on this occasion. He said, 'This is ridiculous. We're supposed to be checking out phenomena, and we're challenged!' He said, 'Let's take him up on it.' So the next Sunday was a Forum meeting. They came in on the deal." The first of the questions submitted in response to this invitation by a Forum member was, "Is there a God; and if so, what is He like?"

The papers began to be read to the Forum—starting with Paper 1, "The Universal Father," a direct response to the first question—and the organization was formalized by September 1925 as a closed group of thirty members. Each member signed a pledge that read: "We acknowledge our pledge of secrecy, renewing our promise not to discuss the Urantia revelations or their subject matter with anyone save active Forum members, and to take no notes of such matter as it is read or discussed at the Forum meetings, or make copies or notes of what we have personally read." Membership tickets were issued to the group, which consisted of doctors, lawyers, dentists, ministers, teachers, farmers, housewives, secretaries, and laborers. Anyone who wished to read a paper could stop by during office hours to be given the original to read on the premises, library-style, while the steward of the papers, Wilfred Kellogg, kept precise, careful records of the checkouts.

For at least a decade all contacts with the midwayers had been auditory, delivered through the nighttime drone of the unconscious contact personality. When the papers began appearing, however, they were handwritten, supposedly produced overnight by the sleeping subject, without witnesses. These pages were then typed by Emma Christensen, who checked them against the handwritten materials. Both the handwritten and typed pages were eventually destroyed after the printing plates were manufactured, in 1950. "This individual was never seen to write one of these papers—and don't think we weren't wearing gumshoes looking," Bill Sadler Jr. told the Oklahoma City reading group. "If he wrote them he was more clever than us—he was never observed to write them. We tried everything we could think of to see how this was being done, but were baffled. The text was entirely written in pencil—all in the handwriting of this individual who remarked that if they ever wanted to draw on his bank account he'd be a dead duck, because the bank would pay on their signature."

The first 120 papers were completed by 1935. Then there was a delay before the seventy-six "Jesus Papers" were delivered later in 1935. Sadler, having withheld judgment on their authenticity, claimed to finally have been convinced by the detail and psychological accuracy in the depiction of the twelve apostles, in Paper 139. "I'm a psychiatrist, and I think I know my business, but this paper was a real blow to my pride," he later told Meredith Sprunger. "If I had a half-dozen psychiatrists to help me and years to prepare it, I was convinced that I couldn't fabricate a paper with this ring and genuineness and insight. So I said to myself, 'I don't really know what it is but I do know that it's the highest quality of philosophic-religious material that I have ever read.' "

Whatever his motives, Sadler shifted his guise during the late 1930s from professional observer and facilitator to dedicated leader of the Urantia group. Two events occurred simultaneously with this development. The papers had finally stopped arriving, so most of the remaining work involved copyediting, proofreading, organizing, typesetting, and distributing. Touching Dr. Sadler more personally, though, was the death of his wife, in 1939, at the age of sixty-four (her funeral was held at Chicago's conservative Fourth Presbyterian Church). At the time of her death, Lena Sadler had collected about $20,000 for the publication fund eventually used to prepare the nickel-coated plates for the printing of *The Urantia Book*.

During the 1940s, tensions sometimes surfaced in the Forum as everyone adjusted to the absence of Lena Sadler and to questions of how to deal with the papers. One of the most damning accounts of Dr. Sadler, much used by Martin Gardner in his depiction of the Forum as an early American cult, was a chapter in ex–Forum member Harold Sherman's 1976 paperback *How to Know What to Believe*. Sherman was the author of a series of self-help books as well as of *The Green Man* series of science fiction novels, which introduced the concept of the "little green man from Mars" into popular culture. (Norman Vincent Peale is quoted on the book jacket of one of Sherman's self-help books, *The Dead Are Alive*, deeming the work "a masterpiece.") Always annoyed at Sadler's dismissal of psychic phenomena, Sherman, who coincidentally had also worked as a bellhop and elevator boy at the Sanitarium in 1914, entered into a power struggle with the doctor during a Forum meeting on September 13, 1942, by claiming he was tampering with original transcripts from the midwayers.

Sherman then exchanged a series of disgruntled letters with another disillusioned former associate of Sadler's, Harry Jacob Loose, a Chicago police officer and self-proclaimed psychic, who felt that "something snapped" in Dr. Sadler at his wife's death; he characterized Sadler as a power-mad Svengali. "The truth is that Sadler is mentally unsound," Loose wrote to Sherman. "A paranoiac with a religeo-power complex—feverishly grasping for greater jurisdiction over the mentalities of the many. . . . O that Dr. Lena had lived. How different developments would have been today! Sadler has the usual evidence of long latent, and of these later years, aroused, *mental* sadism, which is just as definite, and fully recognized a condition as physical sadism."

The "editing" phase of *The Urantia Book,* from 1942 to 1955, certainly raises some of the more suspicious questions about how this volume came to be. A short history titled *Birth of a Revelation: The Story of the Urantia Papers,* written by Mark Kulieke (whose parents were original Forum members), includes as one of the "forms of contact" the open-ended procedure of "conscious guided writing," in which "Someone other than the human subject who was also a member of the contact group received inner impulses of words and meanings of which he was conscious and which he then wrote down, but which would not be heard or noticed by others."

But the image of Dr. Sadler as a cross between a mad scientist from a 1950s sci-fi film and a strange cult guru doesn't quite hold up. For a master's thesis at Bowling Green State University titled "William S. Sadler: Chautauqua's Medic Orator," G. Vonne Meussing canvassed students from Sadler's tenure as a professorial lecturer on pastoral psychology at McCormick Theological Seminary, in Chicago, from 1930 until 1955. Generally representative was the profile drawn by George F. Bennett, a student of Sadler's in the fall of 1954: "Dr. Sadler appeared quite elderly, rotund, with thick white hair (almost silver), thick gold-rimmed glasses, a heavy-jowled face, almost always wearing a gray suit, starched white shirt, and slightly behind-the-time tie. He walked towards the lectern with short quick strides, spoke in a strong yet soft voice, started lecturing from his manuscript but quickly drifted from it. . . . His speed of delivery and general effect was something like a funny Walter Cronkite might be." Another student compared his looks to Alfred Hitchcock's. A few students commented on the disparity between his engaged speaking presence and a general aloofness with students one on one.

"I thought Dr. Sadler was cute," his part-time secretary Carolyn Kendall recalled to me. "He was calm, definite, quietly directed. He only had one working eye when I knew him. He'd had one eye removed and, as he said, a 'fooler' put in. If he were tickled about something, he'd lift up his shoulder and grin. He was along the lines of Winston Churchill in appearance." Kendall worked for Sadler from 1951 to 1954; the job was procured for her by her father, one of the original trustees of the Urantia Foundation. She conveyed the impression of Sadler as a sort of "Gramps" figure.

On October 12, 1955, *The Urantia Book* was finally printed, at a cost of $100,000, by R. R. Donnelly & Sons Company, in Indiana; the printers were left unnamed in the book in keeping with a code of secrecy. This experience of publication after twenty years of editing was apparently so heady that the Urantia Foundation mailed free copies of the book to a list of cultural leaders they felt might be sympathetic. This mailing included Pearl Buck, Sholem Asche, Ralph Bunche, Arthur Compton, Norman Cousins, Aldous Huxley, Edward R. Murrow, Eleanor Roosevelt, and Edward Teller. The response was not overwhelming. "I think there was one acknowledgment by somebody's secretary," Carolyn Kendall admitted to me.

But Sadler considered the publication a triumph. By the time the papers were all recorded, Sadler estimated that more than three hundred people had taken part in the reading and the submitting of questions. "Doctor wanted to present the books to each of us individually," recalls Forum member Nola Smith, born in 1915 and then living in Phoenix, Arizona. "He wanted to shake hands with everyone. It was quite an evening. He had such a gleam of happiness and joy and pride while handing us the books. We had spent years studying the galley sheets. It was remarkable to be able to finally take the book home with us."

Sadler lived another fourteen years following the book's publication, surviving his grandson, Bill III, who died suddenly in 1955 at age nineteen, perhaps from a brain tumor, and his son, Bill Jr., who died of a heart attack on the day of President Kennedy's assassination, in 1963. Sadler's last book, *Courtship and Love,* was published by Macmillan in 1952. When his next manuscript, *A Doctor Talks with His Patient,* was rejected by his publishers a few years later, he shrugged and said to Carolyn Kendall, "I guess I'm through writing books." Sadler died on April 26, 1969.

In an interview, Emma Christensen related Sadler's "last words," which he delivered on the eve of his death to a small circle of family and friends. "The transition from this world to the next is very easy," she reported as his final, very Urantian message. "There is no pain. It is easy to leave the pains of this world for the pleasures of the next, and I am going to enjoy every moment of it. I am very conscious of everything that is going on here tonight. I could go on visiting with you for hours, but it would be no use. The chapter is closed. The last lines have been written; the book is finished. The world is very real, but the next one is much more real."

"The readers were just very normal folks in the beginning," recalled Caroline Kendall as she sat with me one afternoon in the front parlor of the headquarters of the Fifth Epochal Fellowship, a group of readers descended from the Brotherhood and now simply known as "the Fellowship," in a two-story red brick Victorian a few blocks south of Diversey. "You look at the snapshots of the Forum. Most of the women looked like average housewives. As the book spread to California in the early 1970s, though, there was a whole different group. They were the long-haired people and the hippies. Of course, people back here said, 'Oh goodness, we want young people, but do we want them?' Well, you couldn't stop it. It just sort of filtered out into the world."

The shift described by Mrs. Kendall was generally to the West geographically and to the left sociopolitically—from Chicago bankers to California hippies. This shift has been accompanied by much tension and stress. The Urantia Foundation, established so properly under the laws of Illinois on January 11, 1950, has been hit by a number of crises over the years. Finally, in 1989, the Fellowship seceded, and moved to their own building, accompanied by many of the organization's liveliest and most influential readers. At issue has been control over copyright, distribution, and advertisement. The two "denominations" have only recently begun to reconcile, partly because of the ousting of the unpopular and autocratic president of the foundation at the time of the schism, Martin Myers, and the appointment of Tonia Baney from Maui.

One of the more intriguing and antagonistic of the foundation's legal maneuvers began in 1991, against one of its readers, and a member of the Fellowship, Kristen Maaherra, who designed the first electronic *Urantia Book*. The foundation sued for infringement of copyright, and Maaherra fought back, with the help of the Fellowship, by questioning the foundation's right to copyright materials of nonhuman origin. In the United States, with its tradition of separation of church and state, books of celestial origin are considered beyond legal scope, neither "prohibited nor promoted." As Maaherra's lawyer entertainingly argued, "The work of such spiritual beings would not have qualified for copyright protection under Copyright Office practices and procedures because these beings were not U.S. citizens, or domiciliaries or a citizen or a domiciliary of a country with whom the United States held copyright relations in the 1950s." (*The Course in Miracles* cleverly preserved its own copyright by registering "Anonymous" as the author, with Helen Schucman's name in parentheses.) The foundation's legal team countered that the Contact Commission had directed, financed, and inspired the celestial authors, who could therefore be considered "employees" compiling a "work for hire." In 1995, the United States District Court for the District of Arizona ruled in favor of Maaherra, claiming that the Urantia Foundation's 1983 renewal of copyright was invalid. This judgment was reversed on June 10, 1997, by the United States Court of Appeals for the Ninth Circuit, renewing the foundation's copyright until the year 2030.

Equally troubling to the foundation have been the numbers of channelers piping up around *The Urantia Book,* the very practice of which was anathema for Sadler. In the early 1980s, Vern Grimsley—a Urantian leader and a protégé of Emma Christensen's in an outreach program called Family of God or, inauspiciously, F.O.G., in Berkeley, California—began hearing celestial voices warning him of an impending World War III. Bomb shelters were built by those who believed him, and hundreds of copies of *The Urantia Book* were stockpiled in a cave in Parthenon, Arkansas. By 1991, members of a Urantian group known as the Teaching Mission, or TM—not to be confused with transcendental meditation—came to believe that celestial "Teaching Messengers" had reopened the lines of communication first tested during the writing of *The Urantia Book.* On April 24, 1993, a group who'd been tipped off that Machiventa Melchizedek was returning to earth gathered in a motel in Naperville, Illinois, replaying the Millerite "Great Disappointment" of 1844. The Urantia Foundation has since disowned the Teaching Mission as entirely fraudulent.

Yet most of the Urantia group, which is still growing in the United States and abroad, is made up of readers who are otherwise indistinguishable from churchgoers or spiritual types everywhere. A high profile for the movement is Mo Siegel, the founder of the Celestial Seasonings tea company, in Boulder, Colorado. His early life, as a hippie discovering the book in the late 1960s, fits that of many of those second-wave readers described by Mrs. Kendall. Yet

Siegel's entrepreneurial skills and business success in a country that values such achievements highly make him powerful and visible as that most popular of contradictions, and one quite in keeping with the spirit of the times, a spiritual businessman.

On the day I visited Mo Siegel in February 1997, in his office at the Celestial Seasonings factory in Boulder, signs of this contradiction were evident. Looking like Robert Redford, with strawberry-blond hair and dressed in jeans, a striped polo shirt, and tan cowboy boots, Siegel resembled Central Casting's notion of a successful Western self-made businessman. A treadmill was placed next to a row of windows looking out on the bright flat plains at the foothills of the Rockies. (Siegel was known for having noon meetings while speed-walking around the plant.) Framed behind his desk was a painting of a red rock formation at Lake Palmer, in Colorado, as were pictures of his five children and his second wife, the actress Jennifer Cooke, with whom he lives in a sprawling wooden home across from Boulder's Chautauqua Park, the auditorium built in 1898 for the Chautauqua summer lecture series.

Siegel's more private, mystical side was subtly on display as well. On his desk was a snapshot of Mother Teresa poking him in the chest. Taken in Delhi in the mid-1980s, when Siegel was considering leaving Celestial Seasonings, the photo captures her warning him, as he recalls, "Stay where you are. Grow where you're planted." On one wall hung a painting of his hero Abraham Lincoln, whom he feels was a member of the Destiny Reserve Corps—a class of individuals identified in *The Urantia Book* as being drawn out of obscurity for important missions and numbering no more than a thousand on the planet at one time. As we sat down at a round conference table, Siegel told me, almost reverently, "Carl Sandburg, in one of his classic works on Lincoln, says that it was as though God had taken Lincoln away." (Lincoln was indeed a famous supporter of spiritualism and was reportedly advised by channeled spirits not to delay action on the Emancipation Proclamation.) An artist's swirling, and primarily purple, conception of the universe according to *The Urantia Book* hung above the table.

"I'm a very competitive animal," Siegel admitted before we were settled, referring to the uneasy relation between his business persona and his spiritual life. "That kind of blocks me sometimes. The actual urge to scrap and compete is not so godly. When I get in a supermarket, it's like, 'Knock that shelf! Move that competitor!' It's difficult for all of us in every walk of life to really believe God is within us and to turn our lives over to that spirit within. The Thought Adjuster is a big thing for me. Just realizing God's within you. It's like, '*Hello*—' I'm sometimes pretty amazed by the power of it."

Siegel described himself as having been a lifelong "spiritual scavenger." Born in 1949, he grew up in a small mountain town of five hundred people in Colorado near Lake Palmer. His father was a Jewish businessman; his Christian mother died following an automobile accident when he was two years old. "So I never had my mother's spiritual influence," he said. "My father couldn't raise me Jewish because there wasn't anything Jewish around. But he would take us down to the river sometimes and we'd pray. He was a very spiritual guy." Siegel spent his high school years at a prep school run by Benedictine monks in Kansas City, Colorado. "I met a priest there who took special interest in me," recalled Siegel. "Teilhard de Chardin was what he wanted me to know. I took quickly to Chardin's books. I cared, even as a young man, about the reconciliation of religion and science." (Chardin, a French Jesuit theologian and paleoanthropologist who participated in research in China leading to the discovery of Peking Man in 1923, tried to integrate evolution and theology in an almost Urantian-sounding doctrine of "cosmic evolution." His controversial books, including *The Phenomenon of Man,* were refused publication by the Roman Catholic Church until after his death in 1955.)

During his late teens, Siegel worked briefly at a health-food store in Aspen. He then moved to Boulder. Now a yuppie upper-middle-class university town and winter resort, in those days Boulder was more of an alternative spiritual destination, replete with VW buses painted with rainbows, street folk selling LSD, and swimming holes in the nearby Rockies known for communal skinny-dipping. By 1968, Siegel and his best friend, Wyck Hay, later a founder of the Boulder Urantia study group, were picking wild herbs with the help of Siegel's wife, Peggy, and Hay's girl-friend, Lucinda Ziesing, producing five hundred pounds of their first blend, Mo's 36 Herb Tea. In 1972, they produced Red Zinger Herb Tea, which made a name for the company in health-food stores across the country.

Siegel's business success has been classically entrepreneurial and hands-on. He began his company by setting up shop in an old barn outside of Boulder, driving a beat-up Datsun to sell tea out of its trunk to health-food stores in Chicago, Kansas, and California. He turned this one-man sales operation into a highly successful company, and in 1984 Kraft bought Celestial Seasonings for $40 million. Siegel's stake in the buyout netted him more than $10 million, and he left the business in 1986 to travel and pursue spiritual goals. He cofounded a company that grew algae containing a chemical to help prevent heart disease, and he worked with John Denver on his Wildstar Foundation. But eventually he missed the stimulation of big business. In 1991 he was brought back by the Celestial Seasonings board as CEO, and he invested $3 million of his own money to obtain a 20 percent share. Taking the company public on NASDAQ in 1993, he became chairman of the board of the $60-million-a-year company. In 2000 Celestial Seasonings merged with the Hain Food Group to become the Hain Celestial Group.

Siegel's secret spiritual motor during all these years was *The Urantia Book,* which he discovered in 1968, at about the same time he was picking his first rose hips. "I think the first person who ever told me about it was a friend of mine named Joel Rosenberg, who had a health-food store in Boulder," Siegel recalled. "He ended up being a Jewish rabbi. He told me something about the book, which sounded totally weird—that it was not written by human beings, which I thought sounded like a bunch of garbage. But I picked it up in spite of that claim."

His friend Lucinda Ziesing (who is not a believer of *The Uran-*

tia Book) recalls Siegel's devotion from their first herb-picking expedition together in August 1971: "Mo would read from *The Urantia Book* at nights sitting around the campfire. I loved it when he would read it aloud. It was almost like a fairy tale to me. It was very comforting and full of fantasy about the many kingdoms. I liked hearing what supposedly happened when Jesus went traveling in India. It was like a little folk tale about Jesus that I didn't know." Ziesing also emphasizes that the book was grounded in the 1960s counterculture. "One morning Mo was up early because he had to be in Denver by nine," she said, obviously enjoying the retrospective humor of the situation. "He was accentuating his persona a bit more than usual, even. He was dousing himself with patchouli oil, and hanging herbs off his belt, and he had a God's eye painted on his forehead. Carrying his copy of *The Urantia Book,* which was covered in beautiful leather with these different colored beads hanging off the end of it, he had a big staff and was talking about the 'Brotherhood of Man' and the 'Fatherhood of God.' The way he spoke about *The Urantia Book*—and he believed in it as he believed in the herbal teas—Mo could sell anything to anybody."

Though he has since become a trustee of the Urantia Foundation, Siegel was then guarded about making too public his connection with *The Urantia Book.* During our meeting, he kept the door closed and held all calls. He explained that Celestial Seasonings was a public company, and he didn't want any misperception about the solid line between his personal beliefs and the policies and opinions of the company whose shareholders he represented. He insisted that the name of the company had no connection to his early reading of *The Urantia Book,* with its "Celestial Overseers," "Celestial Recorders," and discussions of "celestial music" and "celestial humor." He explained that "Celestial Seasonings" was Lucinda Ziesing's nickname. "Her best friend was called 'Trish the Dish,' and the guys thought Lucinda was seasoned from heaven," he said. Around the time he named his company, he and his first wife had their first son, and named him Gabriel, after the "Bright and Morning Star" who is chief executive of the universe of Nebadon in *The Urantia Book.* His guardedness appeared to date to the 1980s, when rumors circulated that Celestial Seasonings was involved with an obscure cult.

When discussing *The Urantia Book,* however, Siegel was concentrated and engaged. Gone was the nervous monitoring of the message light on the intercom. "When I did get around to reading Paper 1, I was shocked," he recalled. "When I read the part on God, it connected. I clearly understood what I'd run into. The section on God was just so beautiful I realized I had something here that was completely out of the norm. I walked around stunned for about a month."

As with most of the book's readers, Siegel was particularly compelled by the "Jesus Papers," and had been trying to find a way to publish them separately for several years, though the foundation was opposed to such a violation of the work's integrity. "It is a living, breathing biography of the master's life, the first since the New Testament," Siegel said. "I think that's going to be the most challenging part. Being willing to accept that the Bible isn't the only documentation of the life of Jesus is going to be difficult for a lot of people. Groups like the Mormons believe there are other accounts. But Christian fundamentalists believe there is only the Bible. And they're devoted believers." He's particularly sympathetic to such responses as an acquaintance of his from Boulder is Bill McCartney, the former coach of the University of Colorado at Boulder football team who is currently head of the fundamentalist all-male movement Promise Keepers.

Siegel has an executive's take on the work's complexities—its hierarchy of celestial command, and its spiral of planets, stars, and galaxies. "If you're into administration, it's fantastic," he said. "That's one of the reasons I know it's real. If you want to organize something, it's just too good, it works too well. You could never dream up something like that." In spite of this gut conviction, however, Siegel steers away whenever possible from the very question of origins that tantalizes and attracts new readers. "I believe it in spite of its origin, not because of its origin," he said. "I'm not big on that stuff. It's not a big deal to me if it came from another planet. I don't care much about that. I care about what it does to people's lives."

Most startling of all was Siegel's solid certainty that he had seen the future of religion, and it was *The Urantia Book.* As he shared his enthusiasm for the product, his skills at salesmanship became increasingly obvious, even exaggerated. "I'm convinced it's all going to lead to *The Urantia Book* someday," he said, leaning forward, his blue eyes as sharply focused as pencil points. "Even if it takes five hundred years, that's where it's headed. I think, though, that in this cultural climate it's very possible to make the big shift now. You pick up *Time* magazine. In the last two years I've seen covers on angels, on Jesus, on evolution. Those are three of the biggest subjects in *The Urantia Book* right there. If the book is what it says it is, their timing was impeccable. First of all, before Gutenberg there wasn't even a printing press. Now we're sending space probes and looking at life on other planets. Over half of Americans believe in life on other planets. There's a spiritual hunger."

Siegel siphoned much of this fervor into the Jesusonian Foundation, which he founded in 1984. It is involved in attempting to speed up dissemination and understanding of *The Urantia Book.* In 1987 the foundation sponsored a Christian fellowship prize in religious research of $2,500 for a college student writing a paper evaluating Jesus' concept of the kingdom of heaven as described in *The Urantia Book* and the Bible. They published a catalog, sent representatives to more than two dozen Whole Life Expos around the country, and briefly distributed a paperback version of the book during the period when the copyright was taken away from the foundation. "We've been introducing people all over the country to the book steadily, but we keep a low profile," said Siegel. Siegel's acceptance in February 1999 of an offer to join the main Urantia Foundation as a trustee signaled a strengthening of the truce between the foundation and Fellowship branches.

At the end of our talk, Siegel sent me to meet with Paula Thompson, who was managing the day-to-day operations of the Jesusonian Foundation. Her offices were in a mall of small businesses across the road from the Celestial Seasonings factory. A friendly middle-aged native of the Denver area with a big smile and a dangling cross necklace, Thompson welcomed me into her tidy space, which could easily have been the reception area for an optometrist or a chiropractor, except for the number of maps of the Urantian universe on the walls, and the shelves full of secondary books: *101 Ways to Introduce* The Urantia Book *and Spread Spiritual Truths,* by Vern Grimsley; *A Young Child's Guide to* The Urantia Book, by Mary Ebben; *Through the Eyes of an Angel: Uniting* A Course in Miracles *with* The Urantia Book, by Gerald Rowley; and *David Zebedee and Ruth,* by Helena Sprague, the first historical novel to be based on *The Urantia Book,* concerning the supposed romance and love between David Zebedee and Jesus' "loyal and loving little sister" Ruth. There were also Jesusonian Foundation book bags available and copies of *The Jesusonian Magazine,* with a cover story promising "There Is Life After Death." A soothing New Age Muzak-style tape full of flute, harp, and guitar was playing in the background.

Thompson, who is particularly devoted to Jesus—the slogan of the Jesusonian Foundation is "Reaching Out for the Master"— was given *The Urantia Book* by her first husband while he was confined to a state hospital for drug-related problems in Pueblo, where a Urantian reading group had been put together. She began reading the book in 1975 and finished it two years later, at which time she wrote to the Urantia Foundation to find if there were any other readers in her area. She was given Mo Siegel's name, and he invited her to join the Boulder study group. They now coteach the group's section on the "Jesus Papers" every Friday evening at the main Congregational church, on Pine Street. On the evening I visited the group, Siegel was taking his turn in the basement teaching about Christ Michael to the kids' class, which included his own children.

The Boulder group has been the most active in turning the Urantia movement into a public church, an impulse that has been present for many years. In 1956, a study group in Oklahoma City decided to start the first church based on the teachings of *The*

Urantia Book—the New Christian Church. On August 21, 1994, a group of readers led by Berkeley Elliott celebrated what they believed to be the two thousandth anniversary of Jesus' birth in Jerusalem. Christ Michael's banner of three concentric circles against a blue background was flown from the top of the Mount of Olives. Women in the group held a sunrise service in a hotel garden on the Mount of Olives in remembrance of the women who served with Jesus. Such gestures multiplied during the spring of 1997: the Boulder reading group declared themselves a religious congregation called the Rocky Mountain Spiritual Fellowship, whose symbol is the "banner of Michael"; readers in Oklahoma City purchased a church to establish "the Church of Christ Michael"; Meredith Sprunger announced he was abandoning his forty-year effort to introduce *The Urantia Book* into mainstream Christianity to concentrate instead on establishing religious groups within the organization.

The Rocky Mountain Spiritual Fellowship, ironically enough given the book's beginnings, was leasing a Seventh-Day Adventist church in Boulder one day a month for their own Urantian service. They had no minister. Each week different members read from the book, sang, or delivered a message. Their only ritual was a remembrance of Jesus with bread, wine, or water, as *The Urantia Book* singles out this ceremony as legitimately left by Christ for his followers. "You can't equate it with the old paradigm of 'church,' " says Paula Thompson. "That implies something more ritualistic. Ours is more free-flowing and communal." The group also was trying to secure status as a nonprofit religious organization—a move that would have had the added advantage of helping them to circumvent the foundation's legal control of the very term "Urantia" and of the symbol of the three concentric circles. (That is, the Boulder group was playing Martin Luther to the foundation's papacy.)

The most utopian vision of such a church was given by the anticlerical Bill Sadler Jr. "I think there is a possibility of developing from this blue book a religion the like of which the world has never yet seen—a religion that's full of good humor; a religion which is full of the joy of existence; a religion which is totally devoid of fear . . . a religion which has nothing to do with any one day of the week; a religion which pervades the whole of a human life twenty-four hours a day. . . . This is a religion which you're good-natured about . . . you breathe it like you breathe air. You drink it like you drink water."

Founding such a church means going public. As the Anglican *Book of Common Prayer* elegantly phrases it, worship is "the public work of the people of God." Yet all *Urantia Book* readers aren't necessarily willing to be as public about their enthusiasm as Paula Thompson or Meredith Sprunger. Often, they're shy, or guarded, communicating vague embarrassment or suspicion. An important Urantian reader and supporter, for instance, is Lynn Davis Lear, who lives in Los Angeles and is the wife of Norman Lear, the producer of such fantastically successful TV shows as *All in the Family* and *The Jeffersons.* Though she has been quite active behind the scenes in the Fellowship, and has served on its general council, she's reluctant to publicly discuss her beliefs. As strong as the trend toward forming a church is, there seems to be an equally strong countertrend toward privacy and slow growth, especially after the mass suicide, in 1997, of the Heaven's Gate group, whose science fiction theology sounded to a few untrained ears similar to that of *The Urantia Book.*

"I'm just very private about it," Lynn Lear said to me in an interview. "I don't feel comfortable talking about it publicly. It's such a personal experience. I don't see it as a movement, really. I'm worried about the way in which it can be seen as involved with cults or fringe groups. Because there are all kinds of people who can read a book."

In April 2001, I was surprised to come across an article in *Publishers Weekly* titled "Religion, Philosophy, or Metaphysics?" featuring the relatively obscure *Urantia Book* along with such best-selling quasi-scriptures of sidebar religious movements as Ron Hubbard's *Dianetics,* generally considered "the Bible of Scientology," and *The Four Agreements: A Practical Guide to Personal Freedom,* by Don Miguel Ruiz, an updating of pre-Mayan Toltic and Mesoamerican spirituality published by a tiny Bay Area house that then had 1.3 million copies in print. *PW* reported that *The Urantia Book* was a work in the same genre that was also on a rising curve. Totaling a more modest half-million copies in print, *The Urantia Book* had jumped in sales by about forty thousand in 2000, an increase of 38 percent over 1999.

Having moved on, after 1997, to covering other spiritual movements, I hadn't been intimately involved in Urantian circles. So in 2001, I was inspired by the article to check in. Most of the news I heard was similarly upbeat, stressing rising book sales, or, as inside gossip, the boon of having Mo Siegel bring his corporate expertise in packaging and conflict management to the foundation in his new role as trustee. The only one of my interlocutors to sound a dissonant note was Matthew Block, the inquisitive academic type I'd first met at the Chicago reading group in 1997. He told me he'd been let go from his job in the reader services of the Fellowship in December 1998—due to financial difficulties within the organization—and had moved the following February to Glendale, California. "I'm less an apologist now than an appreciator," he added, cryptically.

I knew of Block's research into the possible sources of the *Urantia Book.* Indeed, I'd interviewed him on the topic in the Fellowship offices a few days after we first shared in the roundtable discussion of Paper 112. But his answers on that snowy afternoon always seemed to stress the oft-quoted caveat from the presenter of the last section of papers, whose title was given as the director of the Midwayer Commission: "As far as possible I have derived my information from purely human sources. Only when such sources failed, have I resorted to those records which are superhuman. . . . In many ways I have served more as a collector and editor than a narrator."

In 1997 Block sounded to me too much a spin doctor for all the book's many foibles to be entirely trusted. Whatever "human sources" he was identifying seemed to be only emboldening his worship of the book. "The important thing is that there's an ingenious treatment of these sources," he said to me at the time. "It is not by any means word-for-word plagiarism. It's not workmanlike paraphrasing. It's something I have not come across before. You can see that the mind that reworked this material is very acute, sensitive, and highly disciplined. . . . I definitely don't feel that it's a hoax." When I played back the tape of our conversation, however, I noticed lots of ellipses and possibly coded conjecture. Block's alignment with his arguments seemed unsteady.

Martin Gardner registered a similarly ambivalent attitude toward Block in 1995, in his scabrous *Urantia: The Great Cult Mystery*. Much of the evidence Gardner used against the "monstrous" blue book, leveling his numerous charges of plagiarism, came from his own following of Block's early research, particularly a four-page paper published in 1992 titled "A Bibliographic Essay on Some Human Books Used in *The Urantia Book*." He characterized Block in his book as "a young, devout, hopelessly naïve Urantian," concluding, mischievously, "You can be sure that by the time my book is published he will have, in his untiring search, found numerous other sources, and that they will strengthen, not diminish, his belief that the *UB* could not possibly have been written by human authors!"

Block had certainly found numerous other sources by the time of our most recent phone conversation: 125 source texts, and counting, showing up in a large portion of about 140 of the book's 196 papers. Just as significant was an openness I detected in Block's tone. I was intrigued enough to ask if I could visit him in his new home, which he was sharing with Saskia Praamsma. She is also a reader of *The Urantia Book* and is the editor of *How I Found The Urantia Book*, a collection of more than three hundred first-person accounts, self-published by Square Circles Publishing, a desktop-publishing company of which Praamsa and Block are president and vice president, respectively. After a few e-mails and phone conversations, as well as a reversal or two, Block agreed to meet with me.

I spent two afternoons with him in 2001 on a May weekend in

Glendale, in the San Fernando Valley. Glendale was once billed as "America's hometown," and it is still famous for its Forest Lawn Memorial Park, the inspiration for Evelyn Waugh's satirical novel *The Loved Ones.* These days, Glendale, hazy with a seasonal smog, is simply a suburb, population two hundred thousand, made up of long streets lined by jacaranda trees, stores, and Spanish-style houses or three-story apartment complexes with orange tile roofs built around a central court—such as the one where Block lived. Still boyish and wiry though now in his mid-forties, Block was dressed on both days of our interview in a black T-shirt, black pants, and black sneakers, and a digital watch with a silver band on his wrist; his black hair was cut short, his brown eyes were alert and whimsical, and his soft voice rose and fell melodically depending on his level of interest. Partly because of his small frame, I rarely escaped feeling that I was hanging out with that one bookish kid in high school who had taken an interest in arcane subjects, the class UFO expert or cyberspace explorer who preferred to stay in his room with the shades drawn.

The white stucco living room where we spent most of our time was comfortable. Most prominent was a large workstation with a computer and a printer, backed by shelves of books. Block worked here on the freelance editing projects that were sustaining his modest lifestyle; he spent many more hours using a word-processing program that allowed him to develop a two-column parallel format to segment and match lines from *The Urantia Book.* To order his own copy of sources he'd found in the library, he would log onto bookfinder.com, a vast used-book database. He was preparing a book of his discoveries to be published by Square Circles Publishing. We sipped coffee from blue ceramic mugs and pored over dozens of pages of two-column comparisons Block had printed for me. Between study sessions, Block told of his early infatuation with *The Urantia Book* as wisdom literature.

"*The Urantia Book,* which I found when I was eighteen, had a tremendous impact on my life," he began. "Parts of it were really delightful. It was exciting to open your mind and soul to this incredible universe and destiny. I was a troubled kind of teenager.

I was having difficulty making all sorts of adjustments. *The Urantia Book* was an inspiration. But you couldn't apply it. No one knew about it. It was a kind of formless thing. It hadn't been validated publicly. Nor had it been discredited in any way. It was in this weird kind of zone." Living in Philadelphia, the son of a Jewish father and a Roman Catholic mother, he'd first flipped through the book in 1976 at a metaphysical class his mother joined because of her interest in marketing New Age products. Besides the excerpts on the dust jacket and a more philosophical paper titled "Rodan of Alexandria," the passage that sold him was made up of twenty-eight statements in a section called "Morontia Mota," a series of aphorisms that he has described as "a welcome island of simplicity in a book full of dense paragraphs and intricate discussions." These inspirational sayings have since graced calendars and cards, serving as the *Urantia Book* equivalent of the Bible's Book of Proverbs.

Ironically, "Morontia Mota" was the first major section of *The Urantia Book* whose source he was to discover, sixteen years later. In "Morontia Mota," its designated presenter, "an Archangel of Nebadon," claims, before listing the maxims: "Not long since, while executing an assignment on the first mansion world of Satania, I had occasion to observe this method of teaching; and though I may not undertake to present the mota content of the lesson, I am permitted to record the twenty-eight statements of human philosophy which this morontia instructor was utilizing as illustrative material designed to assist these new mansion world sojourners in their early efforts to grasp the significance and meaning of mota." (In the Urantian system, humans, upon death, are transposed to "morontia," a level of reality between physical and spiritual realms, where they are briefed on "mota" or a higher mode of comprehending reality by a type of angel known as a "morontia instructor.") By chance, Block, while leafing through a friend's training manual for the Amway door-to-door sales force, in 1982, came upon a curiously familiar quotation from Robert Browning: " 'Tis not what man does which exalts him, but what man would do!" The line resonated for Block with "Morontia

Mota" statement 22: "The evolving soul is not made divine by what it does, but rather by what it strives to do." Block concluded that perhaps a saying of Browning's had been incorporated by the morontia instructor, or that in a moment of angelic inspiration the English poet had voiced a truth well known in the heavenly spheres. This single sighting was expanded in 1984 when Gard Jameson, a reader then living in the San Francisco Bay area and now a trustee of the foundation, identified fifteen of the twenty-eight statements by using a huge book of quotations, *Forty Thousand Sublime and Beautiful Thoughts,* compiled by Charles Noel Douglas, first published in 1890 and enlarged in 1904. Among several new names responsible indirectly for morontial bezels of wisdom were Goethe, Longfellow, and Disraeli. *The Urantia Book* promises in its foreword to include "more than one thousand human concepts representing the highest and most advanced planetary knowledge of spiritual values and universal meanings" gleaned from "God-knowing mortals of the past and the present." Block now assumed these men to have been verified among their number as well.

He and his fellow study group members in Chicago eagerly copied the new quotations in the margins of the "Morontia Mota" sections of their books. He wrote in an article in the September 2000 issue of *The Circular,* a magazine of *UB*-related news published with his roommate, "No one at that time knew or suspected that the authors of *The Urantia Book* had drawn copiously and systematically from a small number of previously published books to fashion whole series of papers. Having read the book's two acknowledgments regarding the authors' use of human concepts we understood that thousand of concepts had been drawn from thousand of humans. No one human, and no one book (apart from the Bible), could be responsible for anything but a miniscule amount of material used by the *Urantia Book* authors."

Block was eager to uncover the identities of these "God-knowing mortals," as well as to familiarize himself with the literature of the period—the intellectual wallpaper, as it were, of the era in which *The Urantia Book* appeared. "I always felt there was something opaque and impenetrable about *The Urantia Book*," he told me. "The terminology the book uses seemed pegged to an earlier time." This interest was galvanized in 1991 and 1992 when Kristen Maherra used computer technology to isolate all nonbiblical sentences and clauses with quotation marks around them, and to search various databases to find parallels. She was able to add John Keats, among others, to the growing list of "God-knowing mortals."

In the spring of 1992 Block accidentally found a number of books that set him off on a decade-long investigation. In a used-book store, he picked up *The Origin and Evolution of Religion,* by E. Washburn Hopkins, published by Yale University Press in 1923. "I bought it because it was inexpensive, and I thought that it would give me a sense of orientation about what was thought on the history of religion at the time of *The Urantia Book.* I eventually got around to reading it and was taken aback by the obvious parallels, beginning with the sequence of chapter titles. It appeared that its chapter titles were section titles of Paper 85, titled 'The Origins of Worship' in *The Urantia Book.*" Chapter II, "The Worship of Stones, Hills, Trees and Plants," corresponded to Sections 1 and 2, "Worship of Stones and Hills" and "Worship of Plants and Trees"; Chapter III, "The Worship of Animals" to Section 3, "The Worship of Animals"; Chapter VI, "The Worship of Man" to Section 6, "Worship of Man." And so on.

A friend who knew of Block's interest tipped him off that same spring about the annual Brandeis book fair in a Chicago suburb where thousands of inexpensively priced used books are put up for sale. Hoping to find his own copy, Block telephoned Gard Jameson for the title of his book of quotations. After an unsuccessful search at the bazaar for *Forty Thousand Sublime and Beautiful Thoughts,* he settled for another such book, titled *The New Dictionary of Thoughts.* Its copyright date, 1960, wasn't exactly suitable, but he thought the book might be helpful for comparison purposes. He left the sale with two shopping bags full of pre-1936 books on science, history, philosophy, religion, and sociology. The compilation of "thoughts" was low on his reading list, but eventually he started it. He discovered, on closer examination, that the volume was a revised and enlarged version of an original *Dictionary of Thoughts,* which had been compiled by Tryon Edwards, a descendent of the Puritan preacher Jonathan Edwards, and its copyright page listed a succession of copyright registrations, with a curious slew of them appearing in a ten-year period: 1927, 1931, 1933, two in 1934, and one in 1936. The next wasn't until 1957.

Block searched the authors' reference index to see if any of the quotations in Jameson's list were included and was pleased to discover that most of the stronger correlates were. He was especially surprised that most were located in the first several pages of this eight-hundred-page volume (in which quotations were arranged by topic). One was under "Accident"; several under "Action"; a couple under "Adversity"; one under "Affectation"; another under "Affliction." He started on page one to look for correlates to the twenty-eight statements; to his astonishment, within a few minutes he'd found the first four statements—never before identified—all on the first page. Such an occurrence was well outside the possibility of coincidence. And there was little doubt of their similarity. For instance, the quotation from the American author Margaretta W. Deland under "Ability"—"A pint can't hold a quart—if it holds a pint it is doing all that can be expected of it"—matched too closely the morontia instructor's "Inherent capacities cannot be exceeded; a pint can never hold a quart." (Block had never before considered the quaintness of such Anglicisms as "pints" and "quarts" making their way to the morontial realms.) Following just below, under "Action," the Eastern proverb "The acts of this life are the destiny of the next" became Urantia-ized as "The acts of today are the destiny of tomorrow." Most of the epigrams had apparently been lifted from the compendium's first thirty-five pages.

"I had a swirl of mixed emotions," Block told me. "One was delight at being able to penetrate *The Urantia Book's* opacity. The delight part was success. But then mixed in with that swirl was shock. Because I had never actually expected that I would find what I was finding. . . . Initially, there was this shock. But life goes on, and so you just keep going." Shock gave way to expertise, as Block became savvy at finding his way to sources: "At that point it was pretty much touch and go. But as I delved more deeply I looked at the bibliographies in the books I was finding and saw the interconnectedness of them. For instance, many of the science books at that time referred to some religious thinkers, and vice versa. I realized I was dealing in the main with writers in the twenties who knew each other. The books I found seemed tailored to the intelligent layperson. Plus, I already knew enough about *The Urantia Book* to screen out many sources. For instance, I knew there was nothing in the book about the Virgin Mary. . . . Eventually I would carry *The Urantia Book* with me to refer to if I came across a book that appeared somewhat similar." By the end of 1992 he'd found twenty source books.

Block's next step was to trace the more complicated appropriations of *The Urantia Book* in its voracious assimilation of a mounting pile of books on theology, archaeology, ancient history, biology, and chemistry. He had found *The Religion of Jesus* (1928), by Walter E. Bundy—Paper 196, "The Faith of Jesus," contains many of Bundy's exact wordings on how we must recover the religion *of* Jesus rather than the religion *about* Jesus. There was *Preface to Christian Faith in a New Age* (1932), by Rufus M. Jones (its title a reminder that "New Age" was not just a buzz phrase invented in the early 1980s)—almost every paragraph of Section 10 of Paper 195, "After Pentecost," is drawn from the last half of this book's discussion of Christianity's struggle to awaken to its spiritual mission in the face of modern secularism. There was *The Dawn of Conscience* (1933), by James Henry Breasted, from which Paper 95, "The Melchizedek Teachings in the Levant," borrows its analysis of early Egyptian social idealism and religion, including the teachings of Amenemope and Ikhnaton, the *ka* and the *ba,* and Egypt's influence on the Hebrews. And there was *Man Rises to Parnassus: Critical Epochs in the Prehistory of Man* (1928), by Henry Fairfield Osborn, which is the main source for the *Urantia Book* discussion of the successive human races in Europe from the Foxhall peoples to the Neanderthals, the Cro-Magnons, and the ancestors of the Nordics. Osborn's entire section on the Bretons is paralleled exactly in *The Urantia Book.*

Admittedly *The Urantia Book* doesn't seem to be trying very hard to disguise these sources. In *The Architecture of the Universe,* W. F. G. Swann, for instance, writes of chemical elements: "Starting from any one of them and noting some property such as the melting point, for example, the property would change as we went along the row, but as we continued it would gradually come back to the condition very similar to that with which we started. . . . The eighth element was in many respects like the first, the ninth like the second, the tenth like the third, and so on." In *The Urantia Book* this same sentence appears, only slightly revised, as "Starting from any one element, after noting some one property, such a quality will change for six consecutive elements, but on reaching the eighth, it tends to reappear, that is, the eighth chemically active element resembles the first, the ninth the second, and so on."

When Block moved to southern California, his research—again with the help of chance—began to close in inevitably on the figure of Dr. Sadler himself. For just seventy miles east of Glendale, toward Palm Springs, is the Heritage Room of the Del E. Webb Memorial Library at Loma Linda University. Its Seventh-Day Adventist archive includes a complete collection and database of Ellen White's manuscripts and letters, some written to the young Sadler. Here Block found articles and essays Sadler wrote for Seventh-Day Adventist periodicals, including the *Life Boat* and the *Youth's Instructor,* and the newspaper the *Review and Herald.* Block hunted for early inklings of Urantian concepts, and he soon found them. In an article from around 1900, for instance, Sadler writes that we each have a "fragment" or "portion" of God in us—a view not shared in Seventh-Day Adventist thinking but arguably a seed of the Thought Adjuster concept original to *The Urantia Book.*

In the archives Block also discovered the only copy of Sadler's long-lost first book, *Soul Winning Texts, or Bible Helps for Personal Work,* published in 1909, which Block and Praasma reformatted and republished in 1999. In this book of helpful biblical quotations for the personal evangelist, written by Sadler near the end of his involvement with Seventh-Day Adventism, Block found parallels with Part IV of *The Urantia Book,* in which Jesus undertakes his own "personal ministry" during his Mediterranean tour, in the company of Gonod and Ganid, before setting out on his public ministry in Palestine. In Sadler's first book, he recommends, for Christians faced with the question, "Why Don't I Have More Agreeable Work?" a verse from Ecclesiastes 9:10: "Whatsoever thy hand findeth to do, do it with thy might." When Jesus' friend Ganid is faced in Antioch with a fellow Indian who "felt he had been put at the wrong job," *The Urantia Book* records: "But of all that Ganid said, the quotation of a Hebrew proverb did the most good, and that word of wisdom was: 'Whatsoever your hand finds to do, do that with all your might.' "

After Block presented me with so much evidence, especially his new finds on Sadler, I pressed him to come clean publicly and acknowledge what I felt was clearly—much more so than five years earlier—the bottom line: Dr. William Sadler wrote *The Urantia Book,* possibly with the help of the inner circle known as the Contact Commission, or perhaps simply with his brother-in-law, Wilfred Kellogg; the contact personality was a ruse he invented to throw off the curious. But Block demurred. "It's true that I'm finding certain parallels between Sadler's works and material in *The Urantia Book,*" he said. "Sadler is one of the source authors. And his own writing is massaged and tweaked in much the same way as the other authors. . . . As part of my research in reading Sadler's books, I've looked at his bibliographies, and they indicate that some of the bibliography turned out to be source books. That's very intriguing, from my point of view." He added, parsing his words carefully, "I have no dogmatic resistance to the possibility that Sadler wrote the book."

Whatever the uncertainties of Block's public position, his literary genome mapping certainly spells trouble for *The Urantia Book.* Or perhaps not for the book itself. In shading in as well the original sections Block does reveal to us an author with a busy genius for metaphysical invention and poetic turns of phrase whose scam was at worst benign and at most visionary. (An open question, of course, remains the lawsuits for plagiarism that might have ensued had these discoveries been made fifty years ago, when the perpetrator and his "human sources" were all still alive.) As Block said, "It was written with artistry and a great deal of ingeniousness, and there's quite a bit of inspirational material in it." But for the professionals, the ecclesiastics of the foundation and their flock, the results may well be less delightful.

"*The Urantia Book* tells us very clearly that it draws on over two thousand human beings whose ideas embrace superior concepts from the time of Jesus to the time of indicting these revelations," Tonia Baney, executive director of the Urantia Foundation, assured me, responding to Block's latest research. "Matthew Block's research may very well identify the sources of ideas that perhaps were universal in some subjects, but as an example of what we have examined from what Matthew has made public, ideas encompassing five or ten chapters of a book are distilled into one page or one paragraph in *The Urantia Book.* Also the words are changed to reflect denser meanings and values. The wealth of subject matter in *The Urantia Book* is encyclopedic in its composition and in fact the book calls itself a composite work. . . .

"In the examination of the writings of Dr. Sadler it is very clear that he did not have the capacity to write *The Urantia Book.* He could not have cobbled together information regarding immensely diverse subjects, including the revelatory information, nor did he have the additional capacity to write in a highly literate form as does *The Urantia Book.* And I doubt that there was anyone living at that time who could have done so. . . . *The Urantia Book* stands on its own. If what you are telling me is that Matthew is trying to prove that Dr. Sadler wrote *The Urantia Book,* I simply do not agree with him."

When I returned to New York from Glendale, I revisited the reading group at the SoHo loft of Robin and Helene Jorgenson. Not much had changed since I'd attended five years earlier. That evening eight men and two women pulled together their black-leather-and-chrome office-style chairs into a circle to read in turn from Paper 148, "The Misunderstanding of Suffering—Discourse on Job," one of Jesus' supposedly lost discourses delivered to the apostle John. Except for occasional breaks to answer the doorbell, to pour a cup of coffee, or to pick up a cookie, everyone concentrated earnestly on the knotty question of why bad things happen to good people.

"The world's like a broken step," said Paul, an older gentleman who had a trimmed white beard and who was wearing a powder-blue button-down shirt.

"No," countered Robin, who had long gray hair and double earrings in each of his pierced ears, seizing on the carpentry metaphor, perhaps because he owns a construction business. "The step is broken because it was made from a misshapen tree. Or because of the bad plans of an irresponsible architect. . . . The important thing is that God is not punishing us personally."

For a few moments the readers allowed themselves a detour, trying to decide how the days of the week came to be divided into seven.

"The seventh day comes from where?" asked Nick, who was tall and black-haired, wearing a black "Massachusetts College of Art" T-shirt. "Why not eight?"

"Was the Chinese calendar based on eight days?" asked another reader. "The Hindu calendar?"

"*The Urantia Book* says that Adam and Eve just rested on the seventh day, and it came from there," contributed an Australian, visiting with his wife. "I always liked that, so I remembered it."

"What a good memory you have," complimented Robin's wife, Helene. She had red hair and was dressed in sharp clamdigger pants and tan pumps. "Well, that settles that!"

I was moved by the good-humored soul-searching, the digging for answers. Yet when I checked back with Block, he claimed that the section of *The Urantia Book* that was the inspiration for their talk was in fact drawn from four books: Henry Kendall Booth's *The Background of the Bible* (1928); Hastings's *Dictionary of the Bible* (the 1909 edition's article on Job); Julius A. Bewer's *Lit-*

erature of the Old Testament (1933); and the King James version of the Book of Job. In this section, Jesus also indulges in his *Urantia Book* habit of pre-quoting Saint Paul. His statement "Do you not comprehend that God dwells within you, that he has become what you are that he may make you what he is!" refers to 1 Corinthians 3:16 ("Know ye not that ye are the temple of God, and that the Spirit of God dwelleth in you?") and 2 Corinthians 8:9 ("Ye perceive the grace of our Lord Jesus Christ, that for your sakes He became poor when He was rich, that ye, by His poverty, might become rich"). Block also fairly highlighted for me the original bits in the distinction in Paper 148 between evil, sin, and iniquity, and in Jesus' meditation beginning "Do you not see that Job longed for a human God. . . ."

On June 3, 2001, I drove with Robin and Helene in their vintage 1962 white Cadillac to the Lenore Nature Preserve near Yonkers for a Urantian Sunday-morning worship service. It was organized by Les Jamieson, a forty-seven-year-old Panamanian-born musician and Web site designer who is actively involved with the Interfaith Council of Greater New York, where he represents the Community of Readers of *The Urantia Book.* Nearly two dozen men and women, including two Interfaith ministers, gathered among the rolling green hills, hummingbirds, and butterflies at eleven a.m. to plant gladiola bulbs, as well as red columbine, lavender, and delphinium seeds. They then regrouped in a nearby wooden gazebo, as two deer ran by. Jamieson read verses for reflection from *The Urantia Book,* sometimes to a guitar accompaniment. Lainey Sainte-Marie—the sister of folk singer Buffy Sainte-Marie, who performed with her group at an international Urantia conference in Vancouver in 1999—sang her own composition, "Calling All Altruists," and closed with a version of the Righteous Brothers' "Unchained Melody," with new lyrics: "Oh my love, my Father / I've hungered for your touch, your truth so divine."

Later in the week, I told Block about Jamieson's "Worship Service Plans." He returned to me his usual deconstruction, separating the original words from the borrowed ones. I told him about a passage of which Jamieson notably promised that morning, "This is unique to *The Urantia Book*," treating "truth, beauty, and goodness in a very profound way." Block typed back, "If Les means here that the *UB* is unique in speaking of truth, beauty, and goodness in a profound way, he's not correct. A major source of the *UB*—Harry Overstreet's 1931 *The Enduring Quest*—refers to truth, beauty, and goodness as 'The three great elementals' and devotes a chapter to each." I recalled one of Block's comments to me in Glendale: "In the past I've learned not to be rash in assuming that something is original to *The Urantia Book,* because then the very next day I find something."

Taking my own pulse during the worship service, I could predict the main problem the *Urantia Book* readers would face if Block's notions took hold. Though always a firm nonbeliever, I'd previously been kept entranced by the "what if?" possibility while hearing these papers from the celestials. Its imaginary writer-reader contract was always interstellar. However, the prospect of tracing Sadler's mixing and matching seemed less thrilling than those interactive sci-fi scenarios. The mystery of *The Urantia Book* shifted palpably from the book to its author and his unexplained motives. Was Sadler a sociopath using his detective skills to advance a hoax while playing Svengali to his own adoring drawing-room cult? Or was he a benign visionary trying to coat hopeful liberal Protestant notions with current scientific glamour for the greater good? Admittedly, the mental movie of Doc Sadler in his study late at night composing *The Urantia Book* did continue to hold some allure.

When Block and I finished our second interview, he took me into a small den in the rear of the apartment, where he kept his research materials. A double bookcase was filled with Sadler's books and rows of "human sources." "These are books that pertain mostly to Papers 99 through 103," he said, sweeping his hand across one shelf. "And here are some things I dug up recently from the Seventh-Day Adventist archives." Drawing one book off the shelf, he flipped to a photograph and said, proudly, "For instance, this is where Sadler went to medical school. It's called the American Medical Missionary College. This book came out in 1955, and Sadler's mentioned as a promising young man who'd been sent to Chicago to supervise the mission there."

Piled beneath sheets covered with Indian designs were more boxes of unpacked books. A collection of drawings, illustrations, and photographs was on the walls. An obvious joke was a mounted book jacket with the title *The Golden Rule: Know Your Source.* I asked about the unfamiliar subject of one faded photograph, whom Block quickly identified as David Paulson. "He was Sadler's colleague when he was a charity worker in the Chicago slums under the auspices of John Harvey Kellogg," he said. "He wrote a book called *His Name Was David.*" He added, with an understandable sigh, "Sometimes I feel like I'm wandering through a cemetery. All these people are dead. It's regrettable all this wasn't found out in the fifties. Then things would be different."

"This . . . this is a drawing of Sadler done by my roommate Sasha," he said. As he stood next to the pencil sketch of the full-faced, bespectacled, and enigmatic doctor at about age forty-five, based on one of the few available photographs, I realized that Sadler had found in the obsessed Matthew Block both his nemesis and his ideal reader.

"It's been an interesting process, having *The Urantia Book* for so many years and being mystified by my lack of knowledge of it," Block was saying. "Now I'm somewhat mystified by being overwhelmed with lots of new stuff. It's a complete and major turnaround in the sense of what I now have to work with."

In an obvious understatement, he added, "I imagine many people who were in my position as a devotee of *The Urantia Book* are going to feel the impact of this new information."

Two

Two Translations:
Deepak Chopra and
Gurumayi Chidvilasananda

Landing at two o'clock in the morning at the dusty, mosquito-infested Sahar International Airport in Mumbai—the city's name was changed in 1995, for nationalist reasons, from the Portuguese "Bombay"—I felt that I'd been pulled strongly toward an Indian destination for some time. Any traveling in spiritual America is filled with reminders of India: incense, yoga, meditation rooms, colored beads, New Age goddesses with Sanskrit names. The main shopping strip in Sedona, where I'd first heard of *The Urantia Book,* constituted a collage of advertisements for Indian-based concepts such as: chakra adjustment, kundalini workshops, past-life regression therapy, and lectures on "Cosmic Maya." I began to suspect that in order to really "get" Boulder, Colorado, or Ojai, California, or Woodstock, New York—or any other spiritual-friendly American town—you needed to have at least passed through the Indian sub-continent. In the importing and exporting of spiritual goods and services, India definitely has been a most-favored nation.

My plan in March 1998 was to trace to this fertile source the activities of two of India's current spiritual imports to America, Deepak Chopra and Gurumayi Chidvilasananda, both of whom have been influencing a number of followers, including some prominent names in entertainment, business, and fashion, and both in quite different ways. Chopra, the more exposed of the two, whose home base is now the Center for Well Being, in the San Diego suburb of La Jolla, was to be conducting a meditation workshop to which I was on my way; it was suavely titled "Seduc-tion of the Spirit." The workshop would be taking place in Goa, a beach resort and the twenty-fifth state of India, located a fifty-minute flight south of Mumbai on the Arabian Sea. My intention was also to somehow make my way to the home ashram of Guru-mayi, in the small village of Ganeshpuri, seventy miles northeast. Though I'd visited Gurumayi's main Catskills ashram, I'd failed to extract from devotees more than the vaguest of directions to her Indian ashram, with its 400 residents, about 150 of them Ameri-can. Less of a recognized name in popular culture than Chopra, Gurumayi was certainly the most active and intriguing of leaders offering a modernized version of Hinduism.

Being transported by bus into downtown Mumbai for the night, and then back again the next day to the Santa Cruz domes-tic airport for the flight to Goa, I saw the sorts of kaleidoscopic, excessive, and contradictory sights common to this financial capital of India. (If Delhi is Washington, D.C., Mumbai is surely New York City.) Its incessant percolating is quite unlike the torpor of much of the rest of the country: a boy with a stump leg begging for *baksheesh* from a passing three-wheeled auto rickshaw; the boysenberry-colored Haji Ali's Mosque rising dreamily at the end of a long causeway that stretches into the sea; cows meandering unharmed across intersections; "Go Cellular Now" signs plastered along the waterfront; carts full of lumber, chickens, vats of milk; a wall painting of the blue-skinned Hindu deity Krishna, juxtaposed with a bright red Coca-Cola advertisement. (The Coke connection was even more pronounced in Goa, where entire houses doubled as billboards, painted red, with the beverage's logo emblazoned on their sides.)

But there was also much subtle evidence of the daily, almost subliminal, and hardly self-conscious spirituality indigenous to the country. I saw children and adults asleep under blankets, three deep on sidewalks. But occasionally there would also be a *sadhu,* an itinerant "seeker," with a long, white, matted beard, sitting cross-legged in a trance on the sidewalk. In the bright sunlight of the next morning, I watched a man in a suit deep in meditation on the steps of an office building in the midst of the most incredible noise and traffic as red double-decker buses passed by. Construction workers on a high rise chanted in Sanskrit as they raised and lowered buckets of cement. Vendors' stands were stocked with coconuts, leis, and garlands of daisies and marigolds to be sacrificed at any of the city's many temples and shrines. Reproduced images of the more than 300 million Hindu gods and demons, visible on walls or through store windows—especially Krishna, Ganesh, Vishnu, and Siva—competed for space with posters for the more than nine hundred highly popular films produced yearly by the "Bollywood" Indian cinema.

Besides being the epicenter of worldwide Hinduism, with about 670 million followers or 80 percent of the population, and the home of Buddhism, with about 6.6 million followers, India has a large minority of Muslims (105 million followers), and is still a vital center of Sikhism, Zoroastrianism, and Jainism. Goa is an anomaly even in this busy religious tapestry. I finally arrived there the following afternoon, after enduring a harrowing bus ride to the Calangute Beach that took an extra hour because the main bridge was out. (Glued on the midnight blue bus's dashboard was a painted statue of the elephant-headed god Ganesh.) Along the way from the airport, I noticed that much more common than temples and mosques were the whitewashed churches set in the hillsides. The most famous of these is the Basilica of Born Jesus, in Old Goa, which contains the mortal remains of the missionary

Saint Francis Xavier; its vaulting arches and honeycomb of chapels are ornately decorated with gold leaf and painted with clouds. A third of Goa is Christian, reflecting the policy of the Portuguese, who, unlike the English, were as eager to spread Christianity as to make money from trade, and who controlled the province until its independence, in 1961. In their front ranks were the evangelical Jesuits, who poured in during the sixteenth century to try to check a perceived moral decline among expatriates enjoying a decadent lifestyle.

The appeal of Goa for Westerners in the past few decades has been the same uninterrupted stretch of palm-tree-fringed beaches favored by their hedonistic predecessors. Since the 1960s, this happy combination of sea, sun, and sand—and, until recently, the accessibility of ganja—has made the resort a continuously evolving scene for hippies, rock bands like the Rolling Stones, surfer dudes, stoners, and slackers. American and European free spirits, now in their forties and fifties, can still be seen hanging out in beach shacks drinking beer, or riding their motor scooters on the British side of the road, their tie-dyed shirts making them look like survivors in a land that time forgot. Raves are the current craze. They flourish on nights of the full moon, when up to five thousand kids—mostly visiting Western teenagers—gather on the beaches to take Ecstasy and groove to techno. According to one observer of the scene, raves actually began in Goa and have spread out globally from there. (Unfortunately, on the evening I chose to venture out, the moon was only a sliver, and the party hadn't yet begun: Indian women bearing large amplifiers on their heads were still making their way down steep passes to a thatched deejay booth set among a clump of tall palms.)

Deepak Chopra's "Seduction of the Spirit" workshop had taken place in Goa in 1997. It had also taken place in Asheville, North Carolina, and in November 1999 it would reconvene on the Gold Coast of Australia. The fee for Goa that year was $2,495, which included meals but not accommodations or airfare. Admittedly, Chopra is already widely available to the public through his exhaustive round of signings at chain bookstores, or his lectures— for which he can receive up to $50,000 an appearance—and his three highly successful PBS fundraising specials. The first of these, "Body, Mind and Soul: The Mystery and the Magic," raised $2.5 million for the network in less than six months. ("They love an Indian accent on American television," he told me wryly in La Jolla in 1997.) He has produced many of his own "audiovisual workshop" cassettes, including "Magical Mind, Magical Body"; the Time-Life video "Growing Younger—A Practical Guide to Lifelong Youth"; and "Journey to the Boundless," packaged by Nightingale Conant as "a life-changing seminar that frees you to realize your full potential." And he became a usual suspect on talk shows such as *Donahue*—taking Phil Donahue's pulse, for instance, and diagnosing him as a "romantic"—and *The Oprah Winfrey Show.*

In 1994, *Forbes* magazine described Chopra as "the latest in a line of gurus who have prospered by blending pop science, pop psychology, and pop Hinduism." *Esquire* portrayed him more gently, as "a personable charismatic man of handsome mien and beguiling voice who has mastered the rhetoric of enhancement." In October 1997, he was on the cover of *Newsweek;* its vaguely damning cover line was "Spirituality for Sale." Chopra's claims have extended along a continuum of plausibility from the modest dust-jacket promise of *Perfect Health*—"this book provides you with a personally tailored program of diet, stress reduction, exercises, and daily routine"—to the more challenging boast in his autobiography, *Return of the Rishi: A Doctor's Story of Spiritual Transformation and Ayurvedic Healing,* to have mastered "yogic flying" while a TM meditator: "I was sitting on a foam rubber pad, using the technique as I had been taught, when suddenly my mind became blank for an instant, and when I opened my eyes, I was four feet ahead of where I had been." (Chopra sticks by this story, and claims to have taught others to do it, including in an advanced-class tent in Goa, though I never witnessed the phenomenon.) Like Krishnamurti or the Maharishi Mahesh Yogi before him, Chopra has become the embodiment in the popular mind of all things spiritual and Indian.

"The Seduction of the Spirit" week, though, has a special reputation among Chopra's followers, justifying all the effort and expense, because he takes time there to literally teach hands-on sessions in meditation. It's the difference between hearing a fitness expert talk about the theory behind his practice, and spending a week working out with him. The set-up in Goa also allowed for a safe, protected, PG-rated Indian vacation, without the country's special rigors and challenges. The setting was more reminiscent of Chopra's signature terrain of southern California—though with more weeds and oil slicks—than anything in the tropical province of Kerala, in southern India, or in the jungles of Orissa, in the East, or at the mouths of the Ganges, where visitors to India might otherwise go.

Our meeting place, the Taj Holiday Village, was deluxe, resembling a Caribbean resort like Caneel Bay, on St. John, or Virgin Gorda. Located near the ruin of the seventeenth-century Portuguese Fort Aguada, the hotel is a member of India's largest chain and is a cluster of thirty-three butterscotch-yellow, umber, pink, and vanilla cottages with brown terra-cotta roofs, palm trees, banyan trees with downward-hanging roots, and a paramecium-shaped swimming pool. Cliffs wind down to uninterrupted sand beaches where guests nightly watch the huge, red sun disappear beyond the horizon. Its staff is colonial era in size. I watched one young man in a hotel uniform writing regularly in a small notebook; when I asked him what he was doing, he replied, "I observe." Labor is inexpensive in India, and his job was, apparently, to serve as a human surveillance camera, recording the habits of guests, and noting repairs to be made on the property. With 175 participants from twenty-three countries—many from America and Australia, few from India—the place was effectively transformed, from Sunday through the following Saturday, into an upscale New Age Club Med.

"I don't feel any jet lag at all," a woman from Denver was saying to her husband while they waited for their bags in the lobby of the resort's reception area. "It must have been the hour-long meditation we did on the plane."

"That, and the melatonin, perhaps," surmised her husband, a certified meditation teacher.

"Do you meditate once a day or twice?" a Scandinavian woman asked them.

"Twice. Twenty minutes in the morning. Twenty in the afternoon."

"Do you always use your mantra? Or are there times when you just let it go?"

Besides semiprofessional meditation teachers and "body workers," a more sophisticated term for "masseurs" with a special expertise, there were a number of traditional medical doctors: a surgeon from Baltimore, an obstetrician from Pittsburgh, a dentist from Oslo, a gastroenterologist from Delhi. I felt occasionally as if I were along for their busman's holiday. But there were plenty of others as well. I'd met Ryan Haddon, the daughter of seventies fashion model and L'Oreal spokeswoman Dayle Haddon. She appeared with her mother a few months later on the cover of *Town and Country,* and by the next year, she had had a baby, Jaden, with the actor Christian Slater. We first talked when I stepped off the back porch of my cottage into a coconut-dotted backyard as she was walking by. I recalled that I'd spotted her earlier on the bus using a postcard-sized photo of Gurumayi as a bookmark. "Yes, Gurumayi is my guru, and I'm actually hoping to stay for a bit in the ashram in Ganeshpuri after I leave here, though I haven't received clearance yet," she told me, giving me hope that I might have found a guide there. Walking down to the swimming pool, I met Michael Hegerty, a bass guitarist who played backup for Jimmy Barnes, an Australian rocker who had sold ten million records worldwide. Jimmy Barnes was accompanied on this trip by his beautiful Thai-Australian wife, Jane, a Chopra fan.

We began on Monday morning at ten a.m. with a scheduled talk by Chopra called "The Field of Infinite Possibilities." The setting was a chicly designed tent constructed on a cliff overlooking the sea; the primary ambient sounds were waves breaking, crows cawing, jet skis zooming. The tent poles were palm trees wrapped in saffron-and-white-striped cloth. Colored sheets with repeating mandala designs in red, green, blue, and turquoise were stitched into a flapping roof. Bamboo shades could be raised or lowered according to the encroachment of the ninety-degree afternoon sun. Pale orange and scarlet burlap rugs were spread on the ground. Seven purple banners were hung medieval-tournament-style on one side of the tent emblazoned with Chopra's "Seven Laws of Spiritual Success": "Pure Potentiality," "Giving," "Cause and Effect," "Least Effort," "Intention," "Detachment," "Purpose"; and on the other side, seven red pennants were devoted to advertising concepts from his latest book, *The Path of Love*: "Infatuation," "Passion," "Ecstasy."

Chopra was introduced by his longhaired, English-accented emcee Roger Gabriel, originally from Liverpool, a regular member of Chopra's team, aptly described by one journalist as "monkish." "Deepak and I have been working together since our early days with the maharishi," he said. "A couple of days into a meditation workshop, Maharishi would always ask, 'How many people don't like me this morning?' If hands shot up, he'd say, pleased, 'Good . . . something must be happening.'" After a drum roll of compliments and a buildup of anticipation, Gabriel introduced Chopra as "the magician himself." Murmuring "Thank you, Roger," in his richly nuanced Anglo-Indian accent, Chopra then appeared onstage. Short, compact, with thick black wavy hair, he had adopted the casually rich look of a successful Hollywood producer, sporting a cream-colored polo shirt, black jogging pants, and silver Nikes, a Krishna medallion tucked under his shirt. (When he was a child in New Delhi, where Chopra's father, Krishan, served as personal physician to Prime Minister Nehru, his mother used to read to him from the 220,000-line epic poem *Mahabharata* about his favorite god—and, arguably, role model—Krishna, who was mischievous, played the flute, and attracted lovers easily with his charm and beauty.)

"How do we access the soul?" Chopra asked rhetorically, after a cursory minute or two of pleasantries. "Through meditation. I meditate because it gives me great joy. The way some people sing in the shower. Or run on the beach. But also it's true that in my meditation I get amazing insights into things that I then write about. Much of my creativity I attribute to meditation."

Chopra's opening statement was reminiscent of a daytime talk show, a format familiar to him as a frequent guest. (His most recent public appearance on *Politically Incorrect* had been controversial. Particularly riling to the other guests had been Chopra's go-easy policy on Saddam Hussein: "You should treat him with ruthlessness, cunning, patience, and sweetness—but not cruelty.") This first morning he immediately displayed his knack for finding bumper-sized bon mots for communicating subtle realities: "Meditation is plastic surgery for the soul"; "The word 'enlightenment' means 'lighten up.' " Our goal that week was "getting in touch with our karmic software." (He seemed particularly entranced by metaphors drawn from personal computers.) He promised that the *sutras,* short messages about love or power, he would teach us during the week would "write the screenplay of your life." Within ten minutes, he had zigzagged from Einstein to Robert Frost to Saint John of the Cross to "one of my favorite authors, H. G. Wells," to William Blake to the *Rig Veda* to findings on "psychological stress and susceptibility to the common cold" in the *New England Journal of Medicine.*

He also had much to say that first morning in a rambling way about contemporary life and society, like those favorite high school teachers who never stuck too closely to their subject. "Today our children join street gangs because they're hungry for ritual," he digressed at one point. "I think the attraction of a gang is not so much the mayhem and violence, the suppressed rage in impoverished children who didn't get enough love. The prime attraction of gangs is that they involve ritual, magic, and initiation. It takes as much imagination to be a gang leader as it takes to be Ulysses. In our emotionally and spiritually bankrupt world, we've lost all that."

After a break, he confessed, somewhat but not entirely contradicting his avowed love of ritual, that "I personally feel that all organized religion takes you away from spirituality. This is true of Hinduism and Buddhism as well. Spirituality is supposed to free you. To give the experience of unbounded freedom. All organized religions do exactly the opposite. They're judgmental. They impose punishment. Every religion is fear-based." His personal solution to the poverty encouraged in India by some religious concepts—arguably bordering on "wishful thinking"—was something he called "spreading wealth consciousness."

Chopra's other lectures during the week included "Integrating Body, Mind, and Spirit," "The Mirror of Relationship," "The Path to Love," and "SynchroDestiny." This last was a concept he was developing at the time to explain the significance of chance events and meetings, a sort of pop updating of the psychologist Carl Jung's concept of "synchronicity." Chopra told, for instance, of one day when "The usual black town car that takes me to the airport didn't arrive. Instead, a yellow cab was sent. I thought, 'Hmmm, I wonder what the cosmic significance of this yellow cab could be.' " He kept spotting the color yellow that day, including a billboard for Celestial Seasons teas with yellow lettering, until he finally wound up sitting on the plane next to the tea company's publicity director—a chance encounter that led to talks of his doing an endorsement for their herbal products. Chopra's stand-up performances, heavy on anecdote and storytelling, were followed by sessions in which participants could step up to a mike to ask direct questions. The doctors seemed to have the most questions, especially about the relation of meditation to diagnosis, surgery, and the immune system.

"How can we apply the lessons of spirituality to diagnosis?" asked one earnest young American physician.

"The universe sends us only two messages—comfort and discomfort," Chopra replied, a bit simply. "Feel your body. Where does your awareness go? Your heart? Your feet? Your stomach? Go inside your body and feel any part that is asking for attention. We feel those parts of our body that are asking for our attention, either emotional or physical. We bring our awareness to them. And awareness is the same thing as spirit."

Chopra's manifest ability to think on his feet was obvious, as was the self-invention he was managing, the integration of his various backgrounds and personas. This encampment in Goa was a return to his roots, and a family affair as well. Chopra, born in 1946, was raised in New Dehli, his family were Punjabis from India's richest agricultural state, the Punjab. His wife, Rita, to whom he proposed during his college days at the All India Institute of Medical Sciences, from which he graduated in 1968, was accompanying him; when she had to leave the seminar a day early, they hugged and cried together. Their oldest daughter, Mallika, and her husband were present as well, though not Chopra's younger son, Gautama. His son had recently published, while a Columbia University senior, a Deepak Chopra–esque first novel, *Child of the Dawn: A Magical Journey of Awakening,* which was translated into thirteen languages; this was followed, in 1999, by *The Bulletproof Monk,* a comic book with a spiritual message that was optioned for a movie. Mallika lived in Delhi, where she'd been involved in creating MTV India; she eventually returned to the United States to found the Web site mypotential.com. Chopra's brother-in-law was attending the seminar, too; a former army officer, he reminisced during one question-and-answer period about his experiences in the war against Pakistan in the 1970s.

Chopra's medical pedigree is very respectable. His father was a prominent, British-trained cardiologist who was the dean of a local hospital and a lieutenant in the British army. Both Deepak and his younger brother by three years, Sanjiy, pursued medical educations; Sanjiy is now an associate professor at Harvard Medical School. "When I was six, my father passed his medical exams in England and my grandfather took me and my brother to the movies to celebrate," Chopra told me. "That night we woke up to the sound of women wailing, and discovered my grandfather was dead. They cremated him, there was a jar with his ashes, and he had disappeared. A few years later the same thing happened to Prime Minister Nehru. We thought Nehru was the most important person in the world. He was God. One day he had a stomach-ache, and my father went to see him. Then we heard on the radio that he had died. They took him for cremation, and the next day his ashes were in a jar and he had disappeared. These were very powerful experiences for me. I think I went to medical school to find out what happens to people when they die."

Chopra progressed from an Irish Christian missionary school and medical school in India to completing a $200-a-month residency in a community hospital in Plainfield, New Jersey; he then trained for several more years at the Lahey Clinic and the University of Virginia Hospital, and eventually taught endocrinology at a hospital associated with Tufts University and at the Boston University School of Medicine. Besides establishing a large medical practice in internal medicine and endocrinology, he was promoted in 1985, at age thirty-seven, to the post of chief of staff of the Boston Regional Medical Center, where he supervised doctors caring for three dozen patients in wards and a dozen in intensive care, and returned up to two hundred professional calls a day. As he wrote in *Return of the Rishi,* "My ambition was to equal or surpass my American colleagues." Unfortuately, side effects of his type-A career path began to include pots of coffee, packs of cigarettes, and a tumbler of Scotch each night to calm down.

In 1981, the Ayurvedic physician Dr. Brihaspati Dev Triguna gave Chopra a disturbing "pulse diagnosis," warning him of developing heart disease. In 1983, Chopra visited the headquarters, in Uttar Kashi, of the founder of transcendental meditation and guru of the Beatles, Maharishi Mahesh Yogi, and he began to diverge from the path of Western medicine adhered to so adamantly by his father. (Adding to Chopra's boyhood questioning, his father had insisted his grandfather call in a Western specialist and stop taking herbal cures for a heart condition two weeks before the old man died of a heart attack.) In the Maharishi, nicknamed "the giggling guru," whom Chopra finally met personally in Washington, D.C., in 1985, he found a spiritual father on whom to model himself, as well as products to believe in.

Not only did Chopra eventually become one of TM's leading teachers, he also became the number one salesman for the maharishi's line of Ayurvedic herbal cures. (*Ayurveda,* a Sanskrit word meaning "science of life," is a tradition of Indian medicine dating back thousands of years to sages in the Himalayas devising a complex pharmacology of herbs.) In 1985, Chopra became medical director of the Maharishi Ayurveda Health Center for Stress Management, in Lancaster, Massachusetts, and he was chairman and sole stockholder of Maharishi Ayur-veda Products International (MAPI) until September 1987, when the stock was transferred to the tax-exempt Maharishi Ayurveda Foundation. (MAPI is now called Maharishi Ayur-Ved Productions International.) In May 1991, he published, with two coauthors, a glowing assessment of Ayurvedic medicine in the prestigious *Journal of the American Medical Association.* (This article created a blot on his medical credentials, as he didn't reveal his link to the commercial Ayurvedic venture, and a rebuttal commissioned by the journal accused its authors of misinformation and deception. A $194 million libel suit was filed by Chopra against *JAMA,* but he later dropped the case.)

If the figures of father and guru could neatly symbolize the first and second segments of Chopra's life, Merlin the magician seems to be his choice in self-image for the third; hence Gabriel's introduction of him as "the magician" at the seminar, and Chopra's 1995 best-selling novel, *The Return of Merlin,* which he optioned himself as a TV miniseries. "When I was twelve years old I read Lord Alfred Tennyson's *Idylls of the King,*" he told us one afternoon, and quoted a few lines from memory. "I could recite the whole thing to you now if you wanted. Later, I went to Wales and Cornwall, which is Arthurian and Druid country. Somewhere along the way I came across where somebody had said that the word 'Druid' comes from *Dru Vid. Vid* is the origin of the word *Veda.* These words all come from the same Indo-Aryan roots. It fascinated me. Also when I look at the Arthurian characters, and all the characters built around Merlin, they're very similar to the characters in the great epics like the *Mahabharata.*" Using this etymology based on the unproven assumption of a universal primal language, he rationalized the magic act of his own complicated personal identity, which is at once Eastern and Western, doctor and *rishi,* guru and magician.

After leaving the maharishi's company a millionaire, though stung by the criticism from *JAMA,* Chopra turned to writing books and giving lectures, which helped transform him into a celebrity preaching a message of self-transformation. Fame suddenly came his way in 1993 when *Ageless Body, Timeless Mind* remained at the top of U.S. best-seller lists for nine months. Oprah Winfrey had invited him on her show for an hour to discuss "the physiology of immortality," leading to the book's selling 137,000 copies the next day. Having self-published his first book for $5,000, he has gone on to publish nearly thirty books translated into more than two dozen languages; to release a CD of songs of Rumi—the thirteenth-century Sufi poet—as part of a two-album deal with Tommy Boy Records; and to write a film script, "The Lord of Light," in which Satan escapes from hell in a ball of fire. Chopra's most recent book, published in September 2001 and coauthored with a Dr. David Simon, is *Grow Younger, Live Longer: 10 Steps to Reverse Aging.* The photograph used on the cover of *The Return of Merlin* was a defining moment in this transformation. "I look like a real author," he proudly told *Publishers Weekly.* "No stethoscope."

Part of the draw of the Indian "Seduction of the Spirit" theme vacation was to be close to Chopra. He is a surprisingly complex spiritual celebrity, and he proved able to mingle with guests without letting his aura slip too precariously, at scheduled book signings, in relating loose anecdotes, and in sitting down randomly at meals. "I experimented with LSD twice when I was in college," he indiscreetly confessed to us one morning. Perhaps because he was in India, he was particularly nostalgic and gossipy about Maharishi Mahesh Yogi, whom he described as "not an ordinary kind of guy that you'll meet on the street. Ever! He was never worried, he was never upset, he was never not joyful." He reminisced about bringing George Harrison back to India to reconcile with the guru, from whom the Beatles had parted on dubious terms after John Lennon accused him of having had sex with Mia Farrow. (Chopra assured me that the maharishi was celibate, in the traditional Hindu monkish fashion: "He'd literally shrink back if a woman even came near him.") "When George Harrison asked if they were forgiven," Chopra recalled, "the maharishi said, 'The Beatles were angels. I could never be angry with them.' I asked Maharishi later what he'd meant by that remark, and he said that FBI statistics showed that no crimes were committed in America during the hour of the Beatles' appearance on *The Ed Sullivan Show.* So they must be angels!"

The Indian underpinnings of Chopra's third incarnation as "the magician" became obvious as the week continued, especially given the setting. In La Jolla, Chopra was creating, in the guise of a day spa, a healing center based on the principles of Ayurvedic medicine he'd learned during his time with the maharishi, including *panchakarma,* or "purification and rejuvenation treatments," emphasizing sesame oils, herbal enemas, and deep massage. In the "Seduction of the Spirit" week in Goa, he was constructing a course of attitudes and techniques largely by translating notions from the *Vedas,* with added references to medical science and physics. The main source of these ideas are the most ancient of Hindu scriptures, introduced in India from roughly 1500 to 300 B.C.; their essence is the belief that all life and thought is a permutation of a single reality, which could be thought of as "Brahman," "God," "Consciousness," "Soul," "Nature," or "Self." This philosophy is presented in its most undistilled form in the *Upanishads* portion of the *Vedas,* the earliest of which were taught by anonymous sages or *rishis* to spiritual seekers, who wrote them down around the eighth century B.C. The rest of the volumes, some of which remain untranslated, contain prayers, hymns, rules of conduct, and instructions for the performance of rituals.

On arrival, we all had been given a course booklet with schedules and space for note-taking. Our foreheads had been marked with a *tika,* the stripes of colored paste worn by many Hindu adults, given in this case in much the same spirit as leis are draped on tourists in Hawaii. On the bright blue inside cover of the booklet was printed a hymn from the *Rig Veda,* a collection of ten books of Sanskrit hymns that is the most ancient of the *Vedas,* collected around 1000 B.C. This hymn was titled (or paraphrased, a bit clinically) as "The Spirit as Our Internal, Eternal Reference Point" and included the stanzas "Although my Spirit may go far away into all forms that live and more, / Let it come back to me again so that I may live and journey here," and "Although my Spirit may go far away to all that is and is to be, / Let it come back to me again so that I may live and journey here." This sense that all time and space are folded into one continuous consciousness was central to much of what Chopra said that week, and also to what he has written, as is hinted in a title such as *Timeless Body, Ageless Mind,* which sounds like a broad self-help claim about staying young and fit but could also be a rendering of Vedantic philosophy.

The heart of the "Seduction" event, and its main reason for being, was the practice of meditation. "We're going to start out with a little bit of intellectual understanding, even though that's not the point of this week," Chopra said on the first morning. "The most important part of the week, though, will be meditation." By the end of the week we were meditating up to four or five hours a day, practicing what Chopra, with a more scientific gloss, called "advanced psychophysiological techniques." To qualify, everyone first needed to receive a parchment card from an instructor with a personal and confidential "primordial sound" mantra concocted by computer and based on date and time of birth. This customized mantra consisted of a few Sanskrit words to be synchronized with inhalation and exhalation. (My own contained a conglomeration of words distractingly close to the English word "chipmunk.")

We spent most of the week sitting cross-legged in large white plastic chairs or lying on blankets, breathing carefully in and out, trying to slip into what Chopra called "the gap": the missed beat where bliss lies. For anyone who peeked into the tent, we must have looked like we'd been knocked out by a powerful bug spray. During breaks, marked by tiny chimes of a bell, tea was available, brewed from hot water, ginger, and mint leaves, and accompanied by bowls of honey. Mostly I was distracted by the pesky mosquito bites of my own thoughts: "What's for lunch?" "Why didn't Jane talk to me on her way in?" "What if that check hasn't cleared yet?" By Friday or Saturday, though, I'd experienced a few moments of what was described in the 1960s as a "natural high." At the end of one session, Chopra put his hand on my shoulder and murmured quietly, "Sometimes you just don't want to come out of it." Having breathed according to such regular patterns for so long, I found myself walking one afternoon toward the sea with a slow, steady gait and a warmth suffusing what Chopra called the "fourth chakra," the heart. According to Chopra, a Harvard clinical experiment in meditation had once described such limbering as "the relaxation response."

Much of the rest of our time was spent in a kind of summer camp, a global version of what the Chautauqua circuit in nineteenth-century America must have been like, with its revival tents, inspirational speakers, and hymn-singing around campfires. (Thanks to air travel, spiritual leaders are no longer confined to one hemisphere's spring and summer for their outdoor retreats.) There were yoga classes at 6:30 each morning as the sky turned from black to violet to blue. Our instructor claimed to be teaching us fresh techniques in isolating and tensing specific muscles, which she'd learned just a few months earlier from yogis in the Himalayas. Booths were manned every afternoon by a complimentary pulse diagnostician and a palm reader, and by a "Vedic astrologer" at 3,500 rupees, or about $100. (When I came across Chopra outside the tent and asked if he'd had his palm read, he replied, "No, I don't believe in all that. . . . But try the astrologer. He's very good.") Women could have their hands or feet temporarily tattooed with *mardi*—decorative henna stains lasting a week or two. Free Ayurvedic treatments of nose and eye drops and an application of *ghee,* or clarified butter, to the eyeballs were offered in a large infirmary tent. Breakfast, lunch, and dinner were smorgasbords of Goanese cuisine, an edgy mix of European, south Indian, and west Indian cooking: whole pomfret stuffed with red-hot spices, grilled kingfish steak in coriander, cauliflower mixed in a thick paste of curd, potatoes, and green curry, red papaya salad, coconut soufflé, chocolate pancakes, honey and ginger pudding, and *lassi* (water mixed with yogurt, salt, and fruit.)

Evening entertainers were usually locals playing sitar, dholak, and harmonium, or dancing a traditional Kathakali or Goan folk dance. One was an ancient soap opera in dance about Parvati's infatuation with Siva, the Creator and destroyer worshiped in the form of lingam—phallic stones rising from the ground that are often enshrined in Hindu temples. "Put on these blindfolds and lie peacefully on the floor and just listen," Chopra invited us one evening. We all stretched out next to speakers, like teenagers, to listen to a preview of his *Gift of Love* CD, which was about to be issued by Tommy Boy Records. It consisted of rap-like recitations of the mystical poetry of Rumi, and included cuts by Madonna, Demi Moore, Rosa Parks, Robert Thurman, Richard Harris's son Jared, and Chopra's son Gautama. The project had grown out of a "Seduction of the Spirit" week in Beaver Creek, Colorado, in August 1996, attended by a Rumi translator, Fereydoun Kia, who gave Chopra a copy of his translations from the original Farsi. "One day a young lady named Madonna picked up the manuscript when she was in my office in La Jolla," Chopra confided coyly. "She said, 'I love this poem, it really moves me.' I said. 'Well, why don't you sing it?' " Her admiration of the poem, "Bittersweet," led eventually to his spoken-word recording.

If all of these activities emitted the pleasantness of shipboard shuffleboard, after-dinner self-help exercises in "Subtle Body Clearing" from 7:30 on could be more tough going, at least for anyone not entirely comfortable with group therapy or meaningful consciousness-raising. We wrote down emotional issues that were disturbing us, and then burned the pages in a single fire, as an exorcism. On another evening, we paired up with a stranger who was instructed to whisper in our ear every fifteen seconds, "Who are you?" and then, "What are you doing?" (I was reminded of the scene in the unsuccessful 1997 movie *Sphere,* in which Sharon Stone types on computer to the alien she's contacted, "What are you doing?" The extraterrestrial types back, "We are travelers on a cosmic journey," to which Stone's partner quips, "Sounds like Deepak Chopra.") These nightly sessions climaxed with the mostly middle-aged participants dancing to "Get Happy," by Lionel Richie, or to Boy George singing "Hare Krishna." (Similarly Indophilic was that season's hit recording in India, "Govinda," by the British rock group Kula Shaker, with Sanskrit lyrics.)

Since Chopra based all his teaching and meditating on body-awareness exercises, the week fit neatly with a current trend toward vacations with a spiritual or therapeutic bent. By 1997, for instance, 46 percent of American spas were offering yoga classes. As Chopra told us on the second day, in his talk "The Law of 'Karma' or Cause and Effect," "The way to plug into the universal computer is through body awareness. What people call intuition comes from being tuned into the finest levels of intuition in the body. For most people these signals are in the area of the heart. There is intelligence in the heart. Besides being a pump, it's an intellectual organ." Of the maharishi, again, he recalled, "We used to have lines of people for hours waiting to talk with the maharishi. They'd tell him about all their many problems with love, with work, with health, with money. And when they'd finished, he'd simply smile and say, 'Feel the body.' "

On the final day, at a lunch of red-lentil dahl, okra, and date and fig ice cream in the "Beach House," the obstetrician from Pittsburgh neatly summed up the residual effects of our week. "On vacation I always want to be active," he said. "I have a whole checklist of activities I have to accomplish to feel good: running, fishing, hiking. Meditation turns out to be the perfectly relaxing vacation for me, because you're always doing something. It's very structured. But what you're doing is sitting doing nothing."

That Sunday afternoon Ryan Haddon and I returned to Mumbai. Happily for me, she'd invited me to go with her on her unscheduled trip to Gurumayi's ashram, Gurudev Siddha Peeth, and I'd quickly accepted. Ryan had lived in Ganeshpuri for two years after finishing high school nearly a decade earlier, serving as what those in the community loosely call a "*darshan* girl"— someone whose service is to attend to the guru during her public appearances. (*Darshan,* from the Sanskrit *darsana,* meaning "sight," is the term for an audience with or viewing of a guru, or even of a guru's seat, sandals, or photograph.) Ryan's adolescent devotion had been kindled in part by the TV actresses Barbara Carrera and Peggy Lipton, of *Mod Squad* and *Twin Peaks,* who'd first introduced her to Gurumayi.

Her own tentative plan as we prepared for the trip had been to remain at the ashram for an extended stay. I was looking forward to at least touring the grounds and buildings. However, our expectations were foiled by the more intense restrictions placed by Gurumayi, beginning in 1994, to establish her Indian ashram as an old-style *gurukula* with relatively few students, each of whom is required to set aside time each day for scriptural study, group chanting, meditation, and service, and where a visitor must fill out an application form several months in advance for a stay at least a month in duration. The guru's intention was to restore peacefulness and to check the tendency of the ashram to become a mere rest center for mostly American passers-through. Chopra's "Seduction of the Spirit" was kept manageable by its steep financial requirements; Gurumayi's ashram remained insular as a result of ancient traditions that could feel foreign, arbitrary, or even unfriendly to the uninitiated.

Nevertheless, we were invited on the phone by the woman in charge of visitors to spend a half day and have lunch. So we bought garlands of red roses and marigolds at a nearby flower stand in Mumbai as an offering, and hired a driver for the two-hour drive to arrive by 5:30 a.m. for the morning chant. Ryan brought along tapes of Brahmans chanting from the *Vedas* to play on the car's tape machine, a clue that inspired the driver to happily point out to us along the way a prominent temple to Ganesh, who'd certainly won the popularity contest for deities among Indian Hindus for his adorable elephant's head as well as for his promises of wealth and prosperity. The driver also stopped to pee in a ditch next to the side of the road where lots of trucks loaded with petrol were precariously parked. Though it was dark, the transition was obvious as we passed from the urban chaos of Mumbai into sparsely populated small villages of primitive huts fashioned from bamboo, mud, and straw, built along extended rice fields. The dry Indian plain was hot and dusty even in the early morning.

By contrast, the ashram glowed luminously and coolly; the marble floor of an outer courtyard was interrupted here and there by mango trees, and the gate was manned by two uniformed guards, and by the transplanted New Yorker to whom Ryan had spoken on the phone. The latter was tall, with gray-streaked hair and an intelligent and aloofly sophisticated manner. "Is your car waiting for you?" she asked, seemingly concerned that we might be planning to stay beyond the proscribed time limit. Wind chimes tinkled in the trees as we explained that our driver was hired to take us back in the early afternoon.

On the side wall of the entry courtyard was an imposing placard with a message of both welcome and warning from the trustees of the Shree Gurudev Ashram Trust, the charitable trust set up by Swami Muktananda in 1962 under the Bombay Trust Act of 1950 to handle his ashram's financial and legal affairs: "We welcome you all with great love and respect! This is an ashram, a place where *shrama,* fatigue, is destroyed. The ashram is not a tourist spot, a hotel or zoo. The ashram is for those who are interested in spirituality, in knowing the divine Self that dwells within. The ashram was founded by Swami Muktananda Paramahamsa in 1956, when his guru Bhagawan Nityananda gave him three little rooms on a small plot of land. Through the grace of his Guru and by his divine guidance, the ashram has become what it is today. The ashram is open to seekers who want to do sadhana and seva and want to attain peace. The ashram is for meditation and chanting." (The accusatory mention of the "hotel" and "zoo" seemed a bit jarring amid the peacefulness of the rest of the prose.)

We were then led past the placard through an archway between white stucco buildings to a central courtyard built by devotees in the late 1960s and distinguished by hanging arabesques, white lampposts in the nineteenth-century European style, palm trees, marble benches and walls, wooden doors with imposing bronze latches, frosted windows partly ajar, and amber lamps. The style was an evocative mix of Anglo and Indian. A sliver of yellow moon was visible in the geometric segment of dark sky. Roused birds shuttled above us between trees and windows while devotees, both Asian and Western, began to find their places for the morning chant on folded blankets and pillows, many wearing saris or white cotton pants, a few with cowls or hoods fashioned romantically over their heads. I was strongly reminded, as I had been on the beaches of Goa, of the legacy of those sixties kids who had both colonized and been subsumed by India three decades earlier. These were apparently their tidier descendants. (Indeed, faced with the phenomenon of extreme scruffiness among his young American followers, Baba Muktananda in 1975 began teaching that dressing well was a sign of respect, leading women to wearing skirts and dresses and putting on small amounts of makeup, and men to trimming or shaving off their beards—a comely, formal, and decidedly un-hippie style still prevalent in both the Indian and American ashrams.)

At dawn began the chanting of the sonorous *Gurugita,* the "Song of the Guru," a 181-verse poem that presents a dialogue between Siva and his consort, Parvati, on the nature of the universal teacher and of the guru-disciple relationship. Taken from a sixteenth-century text in the yogic tradition of this western Indian state of Maharashtra, the song was chanted by Swami Muktananda privately for years until he made its daily recitation "the one indispensable text" of the morning service, timed with the rising of the sun. Chanted in Sanskirt by this international mix of decotees, the hymn contained many lines; the parallel English translation signaled entry into a truly exotic and foreign realm of guru adoration further emphasized by the presence of the looming photograph of Gurumayi—who looked both statesman-like and glamorous, a synthesis of Indira Gandhi and Bianca Jagger—that was leaned into a throne against one wall of the courtyard and surrounded by flowers and burning incense sticks. A swooning introduction to the chant is the *"Sri Guru Paduka-Pancakam,"* or "Five Stanzas on the Sandals of Shri Guru." (A similar sentiment was borrowed from the *Yoga Taravali* by Madonna in a cut on her 1998 release, *Ray of Light,* in which she sings *"Vunde gurunam caranavavinde,"* meaning "I worship the gurus' lotus feet.") Feeling chilled from the early-morning air, and wrapped in a blanket as I sat on the stone courtyard floor, I had trouble concentrating on anything but my own sense of displacement. I tried to peek into everyone's hooded faces to discern if they were one of the Indians or one of the Westerners, young or middle-aged, tired, blissful, or simply cultic and zoned out.

As the chanting slowly wound its way down again into silence an hour and a half later, the devotees dispersed, a red dot, or *bindi,* now visible on many of the women's foreheads. Soon enough the efficient factory of an ashram could be felt whirring into motion— almost eerily smooth and perfect in its choreography. Breakfast was served from seven to eight in a large refectory named "Annapurna," in honor of the goddess of nourishing food. After breakfast, the residents began their different styles of *seva,* or "selfless service": tending the gardens, preparing flower arrangements, washing dishes, cutting vegetables for lunch, distributing milk to local village schoolchildren, translating Sanskirt texts, repairing buildings, cleaning the temple. I watched one young woman, on her knees, spend about fifteen minutes fussing adoringly in an outdoor courtyard as she festooned with garlands yet another enthroned photograph of Gurumayi.

Unfortunately, much of the ashram was off-limits for visiting. A line of demarcation was the doorway leading to the second-floor apartment where Gurumayi lives when she's in residence. Surprisingly, her quarters are situated very much in the middle of the action, making this a more intimate situation than her South Fallsburg complex. Off-limits too were the gardens that Muktananda had cultivated from scratch when Nityananda first offered him the three buildings in what was then the township of Gavdevi, a cluster of mud and straw huts. The swami made the sequestered landscaping sound positively Babylonian in his monograph *Ashram Dharma,* published by the SYDA Foundation, in which he gloated about "beautiful and rare trees, such as the white coral, white swallow wort, white beech, white oleander, and chtrika," as well as "eleven varieties of champa, twelve varieties of chameli, twenty-two kinds of jasmine, forty kinds of roses, twenty kinds of Nilgiri eucalyptus, Japanese bamboos, Zanzibar plantains, eighteen varieties of coconuts, one hundred and eight varieties of mangoes."

I *was* allowed into "the *samadhi* shrine," where Muktananda is buried in a manner fit for an honored Oriental figure, reminiscent in its simple yet rich and stylish manner of some of the more modest burial tombs of Ottoman emperors in Istanbul. (An ecstatic state sometimes defined as "ecstasy, trance, and communion with God," *samadhi* is also the name for a mausoleum where a holy man has been buried.) After Muktananda died, on October 2, 1982, his body was buried in the earth in seated meditation posture beneath a large flat white marble slab in the room where he used to receive visitors. His tomb is marked off by chains slung from silver pilasters topped with sculpted winged creatures. Facing the single entrance doorway, two elephant statues guard a marble font for holding the gifts, white roses, and other offerings, which are cleared away frequently by an attending devotee. On a far wall hangs a large color photograph of Muktananda in a cross-legged pose. As I sat with others against a side wall, practicing some of the meditative techniques I'd just learned in Goa, a steady supply of visitors entered the shrine, circled the tomb clockwise, then exited, bowed, or stayed to pray. The iconic portrait was the natural focus of everyone's eyes, and presumably of their higher thoughts.

During the late morning, while Ryan visited with some old friends from her days in the ashram, I ventured into the village of Ganeshpuri, half a mile away, to yet another burial shrine, that of Muktananda's guru, the grandfather of Siddha Yoga, Bhagawan

Nityananda, who died in August 1961. When Nityananda first walked into the Tansa Valley, still mostly jungle, in 1923, he was a tall, thin, loincloth-clad yogi from southern India with a reputation as a miracle worker. Over the decades, as Nityananda's fame as a holy man grew, devotees, especially from Bombay and south India, moved to the tiny hamlet then only known for its proximity to natural hot baths bubbling up from the riverbed. Gradually restaurants, rest houses, and flower stalls began to flourish, the economy of the town depending to this day on services catering to the many pilgrims to Nityananda's and Muktananda's burial shrines.

Nityananda's ashram, Kailas Bhavan, in the center of town, is preserved in the style of homes of Western celebrities, artists, and political leaders. This simple two-story building is mostly empty, with black-and-white photographs bringing Muktananda to life. Propped under the stairs where he often sat to receive guests is a photograph of him taken in that same spot forty years earlier; a similar exhibition is set up in his bedroom, which you can peek at through glass doors. One particularly telling photograph in the large entry hall shows a middle-aged Nityananda with full belly, dressed only in a skimpy loincloth, lounging with apparent disinterest as a trim, youthful Muktananda stands worshiping him reverently and adoringly, with palms pressed together. (Muktananda—who once described himself as having "wheels for feet" because of his early appetite for crisscrossing India on foot—possessed a sharp eye for holy men. Another of his favorites was Zipruanna, in the village of Nasirabad, in northern Maharashtra, who would lie naked all day on a heap of garbage, eating whatever passersby offered.)

Today Ganeshpuri is a busy Indian village organized around a town square filled with thin dogs, old men with poles for canes, a few crippled women, children occasionally suffering from skin diseases, vendors selling magnets in the shape of different Indian deities, brown cows, and a number of ficus trees. Several favorite devotional spots are on its edges. Most prominent is the small burial shrine of Nityananda, much less imposing than the ashram's own commemorative temple, Turiya Mandir, with its life-size statue before which a ceremonial "waving of the lights" is regularly performed. Yet it was to this burial shrine that Muktananda's body was brought in procession in an open vehicle during his funeral to face for the last time the grave of his guru as bereaved devotees, many of them Westerners, chanted "Om Namo Bhagavate Nityananda." The burial shrine of another of Nityananda's disciples, Swami Dayananda, who in his heyday used to ride into town carried on a palanquin, is nearby. An obscure, ancient shrine to Siva walled in rock and housing a rough natural linga stone on which drips a steady trickle of water, predates the other shrines; its constant *abhiseka,* or ritual bath, is considered a blessed phenomenon by the villagers. (As is common in many small Indian towns, a local family has taken over the care and virtual ownership of the temple since the eighteenth century, receiving a small pension for this service from the government.)

After visiting the primitive temple of Siva, I asked our driver to take me the few miles to Vajresvari, the market town on the other side of the ashram where Muktananda first settled when he came to the Tansa Valley region. Here on a prominent hill is the more elaborate temple to the local *devi,* the goddess Vajresvari, the "goddess of the thunderbolt," who is credited with intervening with Siva's consort to catch a destructive thunderbolt in midflight to save the town from destruction. The temple was a favorite of Muktananda's, who lived briefly in an adjacent hut. Gurumayi annually brings the devotees of the ashram to pray in its central courtyard, which is open to views of the surrounding volcanic countryside and, to the north, the dramatic Mandagni Mountain, named after Agni, the fire god. A devotee told me that the temple was in disuse when Muktananda arrived and that he smacked one of its lion statues on the head and said, "It's time to wake up," to signify his desire that worship of the local goddess be resumed.

Located, like many Greek temples, on a high promontory, the main sanctuary is reached by a steep flight of Lourdes-like stone stairs, lined with villagers on their way up or down. I carried my own packaged tray of sacrificial offerings—kernels of sugar, a coconut, daisies—purchased in the hectic town square below. In an inner sanctum behind a brass rail two attendants did the sacrificing for me while they faced brightly painted statues of the goddess which had been restored in the eighteenth century by a local ruler, Chimaji Appa, to celebrate his victory over the Portuguese. The attendants cooked the bits of sugar, cut the coconut in half, stripped the stems of their petals, and casually handed me the remains in a blue plastic bag. I exited through an amalgam of stone walls painted luscious colors—lime green, ochre, red, blue, yellow—and was reminded of the sensuously painted walls of the destroyed houses of Pompeii, or the bright red and turquoise murals of Crete's Minoan palaces. But here the environment was still heavily trafficked, a sturdy and delectable setting for daily life rather than a museum of artifacts.

When I arrived back at the ashram, the round of morning routines was winding to a close. At 11:15 everyone was invited into the temple to sing the *Rudram,* a song to God in his awe-inspiring and fearful form, and at 11:50 the *Siva Arati,* a chant in which God the Destroyer is honored. Local men, women in saris, and kids just out of school showed up for the noontime service, then casually departed, like parishioners in a small Mediterranean village. Lunch was served from noon to one, with two lines: spicy and nonspicy. Ryan and I chose to eat on the talking side of a wall of windows curtained off from those eating in silence. Kathleen Parrish, a poised American woman about fifty years old, joined us for lunch. Parrish was then in charge of the PRASAD Project— "Philanthropic Relief, Altruistic Service and Development"—the charitable services of the worldwide organization responsible in the Tansa Valley for an eye camp and a mobile hospital. (Marty Cannon became the program's executive director in 2000, after a thirty-six-year career with a Fortune 100 company.) Parrish mentioned David Kempton, the son of journalist Murray Kempton, whom I'd met once at the ashram in upstate New York. The director of their nonprofit educational center, the Muktabodha Indological Research Institute, he had been staying at the ashram just a week earlier and was now traveling around India. This news

reminded me that the ashrams—particularly those in South Fallsburg and Ganeshpuri—were commuted between quite frequently
by the more committed or affluent devotees of the order, and so
were in quite close contact.

After lunch, our somewhat overly attentive supervisor showed
us to the front gate as the strong afternoon sun seemed to melt
everyone into submission and slow motion. I felt saturated with
an excessive amount of devotional input, not simply from the
ashram, which I had expected, but from the two villages, where
there seemed to be some new shrine, temple, holy rock, or holy
person to worship at every turn, and where so many of the inhabi-
tants seemed busy, not with jobs as in New York City, where I'd
come from, but with an endless round of praying and sacrificing
either for superstitious reasons or from simple piety. It was like
visiting a busy mall of shops with more praying than buying, or
stumbling into a complex celebrity system built around the ineffable quality of holiness rather than of beauty, financial power, or
entertainment-industry fame.

"Even though I'm living in La Jolla and I'm so involved with
Deepak, Gurumayi will always be my guru," Ryan was saying on
the ride back to Mumbai, as she tried to work through the question of spiritual allegiances, especially after not having been
granted the right to stay over at her former home. "She changed
my life. I was with her constantly for two years, and then one day
she said, 'Ryan, it's time to go to college now.' That's something
my mother had been trying to get me to do, and I was totally
unwilling. When Gurumayi told me to, I did. It's not the karmic
moment for me to stay here, I guess. But I love her. She's the real
thing."

Playing on the tape machine was Ryan's choice of inspiration
for the return trip, a recording of a talk titled "God Is Your Constant Companion," given by Gurumayi in upstate New York
before she departed for her 1995–96 world tour to California,
Mexico, and Europe.

"Wherever we go, the guru's grace is present," Gurumayi's
lilting voice promised with its alluring Indian accent as we passed

teetering trucks on one-lane roads with traffic zooming blindly in two directions. "Therefore, we can never really leave each other. Nothing can separate us. . . . Wherever we go, we are surrounded by God's grace and by the guru's love."

My traveling companion's attraction to both Gurumayi and Chopra, as well as her accompanying anxiety about the meaning of the differences between them, was understandable. Gurumayi tends to remain steeped in a mystical atmosphere that is sometimes difficult for Westerners to penetrate, and can remain all the more obscure because of a guarded secretiveness now kept up between the ashram and the outside world by her and her followers. Of course, her very status as a guru, or "enlightened being"—an incarnation of pure divinity—creates a daunting existential distance between Gurumayi and everyone else. Chopra is a much more accessible type, as he tries to reconcile the traditional and the scientific in a spiritual marketplace that often overlaps with a potentially lucrative entertainment industry. To some, though, this very accessibility is suspect and transparently self-serving.

Colorful and intriguing as these two may be, they are certainly not the first Hindus to have attempted to colonize the West. Hindu philosophy was already familiar enough to an interested few by the middle of the nineteenth century, especially through early translations of the *Upanishads* and the *Bhagavad Gita,* to permeate the New England Transcendentalist philosophy of Ralph Waldo Emerson and Henry David Thoreau. As Emerson wrote of the "Over-Soul" in his essay, "History": 'There is one mind common to all individual men. Every man is an inlet to the same and to all of the same. . . . Of the universal mind, each individual is one more incarnation." When Emerson's poem "Brahma" appeared in the *Atlantic Monthly* in 1857, he was amused by the puzzled reaction of many readers. "Tell them," he said, "to say 'Jehovah' instead of 'Brahma' and they will not feel any perplexity." Indeed, the first Hindu teacher to travel publicly to America,

Protap Chunder Mozoomdar—a representative of the reformist Brahmo Samaj movement in India that was trying to make connections between Hinduism and Christianity—delivered his opening American address on September 2, 1883, in Emerson's widow's front parlor, in Concord, Massachusetts.

True flash and public excitement awaited the World Parliament of Religions held in Chicago a decade later, in 1893. Mozoomdar and several other Hindus addressed this first international conclave between representatives of Eastern and Western religions. Their talks, however, were eclipsed by the presence of the far more charismatic Swami Vivekananda—nicknamed "the Hindoo priest" by the press—who'd been a disciple of the late Bengali saint Sri Ramakrishna, who was known for carrying his mystical desire to merge with the goddess Kali to the extreme of cross-dressing. Vivekananda was such an instant celebrity that afterward he toured the United States for two years lecturing on the universality of all religions; eventually he founded, in 1894, the first Hindu movement in America, the Vedanta Society. His visit to America even sparked a Broadway play, *My Friend from India,* about a group of social climbers who dressed their barber as a Hindu sage so they might break into high society. Returning to India in 1895, he organized the scattered disciples of Ramakrishna and convinced two of them, Swamis Abhedananda and Turiyananda, to lead the Vedanta groups already formed in New York City and San Francisco. Their legacy would eventually include the Vedanta Society in Hollywood, where Aldous Huxley and Christopher Isherwood apprenticed themselves. Isherwood—who translated there in the 1940s *The Bhagavad Gita, The Yoga Aphorisms of Patanjali,* and Shankara's *Crest-Jewel of Discrimination*—told in his disarming memoir, *My Guru and His Disciple,* the story of his devotion to the chain-smoking saint of the center, Swami Prabhavanada, who died in 1976 on the seventy-fourth anniversary of his own teacher Vivekananda's death.

One by one various Hindu holy men followed Vivekananda's lead and were soon joined by American converts with Hindu names. Swami Rama Tirtha, a young mathematician-turned-monk, arrived in 1902 and lectured on Vedanta for two years, including a visit to the White House to meet President Theodore Roosevelt. That same year, Baba Premanand Bharati, a Bengali disciple of Sri Chaitanya, began a five-year stay during which he organized the Krishna Samaj, leaving behind disciples who carried on in his memory into the 1980s. William Walker Atkinson wrote thirteen books on Hindu teachings under the pseudonym of Swami Ramacharaka, beginning in 1903 that are still in print. Pierre Bernard, who went by the alliterative moniker Oom the Omnipotent, invented the scandal-ridden Tantrik Order of America. The most successful Hindu of the era, though, was Paramahansa Yogananada, who arrived in 1922 to attend an interfaith conference, stayed on in California to found the Self-Realization Fellowship (SRF) for teaching his path of Kriya Yoga, and, in 1946, published his popular *Autobiography of a Yogi*. When he died, in 1952, Yogananda's body reportedly lay in state in an open coffin for twenty days without showing any signs of decay.

Jiddu Krishnamurti gave an otherworldly face and voice to Indian spirituality from the 1920s through the 1980s. His spiritual career got off to a brilliant start when he was discovered in 1909 as a ten-year-old Brahman in Andhra Pradesh, north of Madras, by Annie Besant and the former Anglican clergyman Charles W. Leadbeater of the Theosophical Society. They declared him the long-awaited Lord Maitreya, or "World Teacher," an incarnation of divinity along the lines of Krishna or Christ. Krishnamurti lectured throughout most of the 1920s on behalf of the society, which held that the spiritual destiny of humanity was in the hands of such "masters," who transcended material existence and lived on a higher plane. In 1927, after settling for health reasons in Ojai, California, he upset the organization's cosmic plan by abruptly renouncing his messianic role and beginning a career as an independent teacher with a pan-religious, or even postreligious, point of view. He renounced any affiliation to caste, nation, or religion and taught that humans must reject all authority and become their own guru. Engaged in the 1980s in a dialogue with scientists, especially physicists, Krishnamurti completed shortly before his death, in 1986, *The Ending of Time*, cowritten with David Bohm, a professor of theoretical physics at Birkbeck College at the University of London. (Since Kirshnamurti's death, Chopra, with a similar interest in the interface between science and spirituality, has become one of the main supporters of the Krishnamurti Foundation in Ojai.)

The development of Hinduism as anything other than an elitist option in American religious life had been seriously checked since 1917 with the passing of the Asian Exclusion Act, which was directed mostly against Japanese and Chinese Americans but included Indians as well. A few years later, as a result of a lawsuit brought by Bhagat Singh Thind, an Indian Sikh, the Supreme Court punitively ruled all Indians ineligible for citizenship, an act that also revoked the citizenship of some who had already received it. A popular spin on this legally supported racism was a bestselling book in 1927 that viciously attacked Hinduism, *Mother India*, by Katherine Mayo. The repercussions of these laws in a public prejudice expressed in editorial pages and popular fiction only grew worse during the intense anti-Japanese sentiment of World War II.

Nevertheless, a thin line of Hindu teachers continued to squeeze past the restrictions and set up outposts, engaging in a kind of reverse missionary work—though without the same need to count bodies, since Hinduism is not strictly a proselytizing religion and is passed officially only through birth. Among those who founded movements upon which modern American Hinduism was built were A. K. Mozumdar (Messianic World Message); Swami Omkar (Shanti Ashrama); Sri Deva Ram Sukul (Dharma Mandal); Rishi Krishnananda (Para-Vidya Center; Sant Ram Mandal); and Swami A. P. Mukerji (Transcendent Science Society). Particularly because of its vague adoption by the Theosophists and its teachings on reincarnation, Hinduism became blurredly associated with occultism, spiritualism, and, eventually, the New Age.

An important plot point was the eventual repeal of the Asian Exclusion Act with the 1965 Immigration and Naturalization

Act, similar in spirit to the Civil Rights Act passed just a year earlier. Suddenly immigration quotas from Asia were on a par with
those of Europe, and the number of Indian immigrants jumped
dramatically, resulting in the so-called "brain drain" as thousands
of Indian professionals, doctors, and scientists left for the United
States. This phenomenon included Chopra in July 1969, when he
emigrated to New Jersey for his medical internship, filling gaps in
a hospital staff depleted by the Vietnam War. A spin-off of this
new demographic was a resurfacing of Hindu gurus in popular
culture. The Maharishi Mahesh Yogi, who'd received a bachelor's
degree in physics at Allahabad University, seemed to appear from
nowhere when the Beatles discovered him lecturing in a London
hotel in August 1967. He taught transcendental meditation—a
form of Japa Yoga, yoga relying heavily on the use of mantras,
he'd learned during several years in seclusion in a cave with its
founder, Guru Dev. He was soon endorsed by Clint Eastwood,
Mike Love of the Beach Boys, Mia Farrow, and Merv Griffin, and
his face was included in the bouquet of celebrities on the album
cover of *Sgt. Pepper's Lonely Hearts Club Band.* In addition to the
fully accredited Maharishi International University, in Fairfield,
Iowa, the maharishi eventually opened universities in Washington, D.C., and Moscow, and now claims for his organization three
million members worldwide, with close to a million in the United
States alone.

Swami Satchidananda, who was also popular with the emerging counterculture movement, gave the invocation at the Woodstock Festival in 1969, and still quietly teaches his own version of
Integral Yoga at his ashram, Yogaville, in Buckingham, Virginia.
Sai Baba, easily recognized by his bright red robe and Afro hairdo,
and said to be able to manifest objects from his hands or mouth—
gemstones, clocks, sacred ashes, photographs of himself—rated
highly enough to have his portrait hung in the Hard Rock Cafe in
Manhattan. He claims to be a reincarnation of Sai Baba of Shirdi,
who died in 1918; the first Sai Baba was worshiped as a divine
avatar by both Muslims and Hindus and was reportedly able to
appear in two or more places simultaneously and to effect miracu-

lous healing. The Hare Krishna movement, begun in New York City in the mid-1960s as the International Society for Krishna Consciousness (ISKCON) by Srila Prabhupada, was positioned prominently when its members with shaved heads, dressed in saffron robes and playing drums or tambourines, began passing out flowers and religious texts at airports and on street corners, their chant "Hare Krishna" making its way into the 1968 mood musical *Hair.* In 1998, the organization, now claiming three million followers worldwide, opened a six-million-dollar temple in India. It is replete with life-size robots designed by technicians from Disneyland and Hollywood that are mobile from the waist up and act out scenes from the *Bhagavad Gita* and other ancient Hindu texts. Sales at their boutique, Govinda's, opened in 1983 in west Los Angeles, doubled in 1998, with customers buying forty-dollar pashmina scarves, and Sharon Stone buying saris to upholster her dining-room chairs.

The sixties sympathy for Hinduism, and for meditation and Vedantic notions in general, has since been given credence and global importance by the phrase "consciousness movement." Indeed a movement of attitude as much as of place, the phenomenon wasn't confined merely to America. As Chopra recalled, "When I was in medical school in India, the hippies were there, and the Beatles were there. We in India were growing up with the same ideas. People think that the sixties came and then went away. They didn't. They just evolved into the nineties. What happened was that the press focused on the young people of that generation. Then the press took their attention away from them. Now they're focusing on them again. But these people have been evolving, growing, and maturing. It's the same generation that's calling the shots in industry, in Hollywood, in the world of creativity and writing and music. They've gone through an evolutionary process. But they've never lost their interest in the ways of spirituality. They may have been distracted here and there." Certainly the great majority of those at Chopra's seminar in Goa were middle-aged baby boomers who had come of age during the 1960s.

The press did continue to focus on the more colorful Hindu leaders. When the teenage guru Maharaj Ji, of Divine Light Mission, made his tour of the United States in 1971, he mixed visits to Disneyland and horror movies with sessions with prospective disciples. Another favorite on the North American continent was Bhagwan Shree Rajneesh, who ran ashrams in the mid-1970s in Bombay, Poona, and Montclair, New Jersey. He moved his entire operation in 1981 to a sixty-four-thousand-acre ranch in Oregon, later called Rajneeshpuram, where he continued to teach a variation of Tantric practice involving indulgence in anger, violence, and sexuality supposedly leading to an abandonment of these guilty pleasures. Known in the press as "the swami of sex," he became notorious for his machine-gun-toting bodyguards and a fleet of twenty-one Rolls Royces. In conflict with nearby townspeople and police, Rajneesh was finally deported to India in 1985 for violation of U.S. immigration laws, and he died there five years later. The American Dr. Frederick Lenz—a disciple of Bengalese-born meditation teacher Sri Chimnoy—drowned mysteriously near his four-acre Long Island retreat in 1998 after having set himself up as a guru named Atmananda, then Rama, and finally as the ninth incarnation of Vishnu; he had attracted more than nine hundred followers in several cities until charges of financial improprieties and sexual misconduct weakened his attractiveness.

While these assorted saints and other characters have passed before the public consciousness like bit players in a vast and richly textured Bollywood movie, a more historically significant story was taking place much more quietly all across America. For by the 1990s, the immigrants who took advantage of the initial repeal of the Asian Exclusion Act had raised a new generation of children, who were both Hindu in religion and American in culture. Harvard religion professor Diana L. Eck looked at this coming of age of a new force in national life in her article "The Mosque Next Door," in *Harvard Magazine* in September 1996. She wrote about the first class at Harvard to be comprised of 5 percent south Asians, recalling, "In the spring of 1993, when that first class graduated, I slipped into the balcony at Memorial Church for the

Baccalaureate service and sat with the families of Mukesh Prasad and Maitri Chowdhury, the first marshals of the Harvard and Radcliffe graduating classes that year—both Hindus. Maitri recited a hymn from the *Rig-Veda* in ancient Sanskrit. It was a new Harvard. It had happened in four years." Fitting this same profile, Chopra's son graduated from Columbia University four years later, in 1997.

The presence of Indians is no longer remarkable or exotic in America, and neither, increasingly, is the presence of Hindu temples. In Ashland, Massachusetts, the Sri Lakshmi Temple was consecrated in a ceremony in May 1990, in which the waters of the Ganges were mingled with water from the Mississippi, the Colorado, and the Merrimack Rivers. At the Sri Venkateswara Temple, in Bridgewater, New Jersey, priests have performed the sacred thread ceremony, or *upanayana*. A ten-foot bronze statue of Vivekananda was unveiled in 1998 at the Hindu Temple of Greater Chicago. Hindu temples have been configured in a former watch factory in Queens, a former YMCA in New Jersey, and a former Methodist camp in Minneapolis. There are now even several multimillion-dollar Hindu temples in North America, including the Sri Venkateswara Temple, in Pittsburgh; the Bharatiya Temple, in the northern suburbs of Detroit; the Sri Meenakshi Temple, south of Houston; the Mangal Mandir, in Washington, D.C.; and the Ganesha Temple, in Nashville. Surprisingly, the archconservative *shankaracharya* of Sringeri empowered a woman (Lakshmi Devi Ashram, Jewish by birth) to found the first American temple to the Divine Mother in Stroudsburg, Pennsylvania. Rajarajeswari Pitha, a popular summer camp for Hindu kids, is located nearby in the Poconos.

To travel in America nowadays is to travel through regions Hindu, Muslim, and Confucian, as well as the traditional three, Protestant, Catholic, Jewish. In a sense, these world religions are treated as denominations rather than as obscure or fearsome cults. And leaders such as Gurumayi or Chopra, who fix themselves within ancient Hindu teachings, are listened to less as alien freaks—which was often the impulse behind the interest shown in the first "Hindoo priest"—and more as public preachers. Ironically, few of their American followers are either Indian-born or Hindu, yet they're increasingly able to cross denominational lines to reach large audiences, in the tradition of such religious media types as Archbishop Fulton J. Sheen, the Roman Catholic personality with his own *Life Is Worth Living* TV show in the 1950s, or Billy Graham.

My own first meeting with Gurumayi Chidvilasananda had been at her Shree Muktananda Ashram, in South Fallsburg, New York, on September 10, 1995—two-and-a-half years before my visit to her ashram in India. The occasion was a special 5:30 a.m. chanting of the *Gurugita* before Gurumayi's upcoming world tour. I was brought as a guest by Philip Baloun, a party planner who began his career decorating parties for Elton John and Halston at Studio 54 during the 1970s and has gone on to cater to such clients as Mercedes and Sid Bass, Betty Knight Scripps, David Koch, the trustees of the Museum of Modern Art, and *Time* magazine. A Roman Catholic increasingly disillusioned with parish life in New York City under the leadership of the conservative cardinal John O'Connor, he was first taken by a friend in 1994 to a Siddha Yoga satsang, or "spiritual fellowship," held, ironically, in the basement of the Jesuit St. Ignatius Loyola Church, on Park Avenue and Eighty-fifth Street.

"They showed a video that night of Gurumayi speaking," Baloun told me as we drove to South Fallsburg. "Just a short, sweet thing. I thought, 'What an incredible woman, and what an incredible amount of knowledge she just gave me in fifteen minutes.' I thought she was so hauntingly attractive, and so intellectually stimulating and clear. She was even funny, making me laugh at myself. After that experience, I became a video addict. I started going to any program in New York City that had a video of Gurumayi, either the SoHo Center or the Manhattan Center. I used to look into the program and call them up and say 'Is there a video tonight?' All I really wanted was to see a video." (The "SoHo

Center," later renamed "The New York Center," is a weekly meeting held in the fur district on West Twenty-ninth Street; the Manhattan ashram has been housed since 1976 in a brownstone on West Eighty-sixth Street that had previously housed a Russian children's school.)

Baloun captured in his approach and attitude the profile of a dutiful follower of Siddha Yoga and Gurumayi. Hinduism itself—as an ancient, extraordinarily complex religion of the subcontinent of India, a country that, according to a recent Gallup survey, ranked highest in the world, followed by the United States, in the number of its citizens believing that religion is "very important"—impinged only slightly in our talk on the drive up. Baloun's focus of devotion, or *bhakti,* in Sanskrit, was this woman herself. Indeed, that season you could walk up Madison Avenue and see her colored photographs stuck by devotees in the windows of several fashion shops. Along with this idealized love for someone who's made truth beautiful—an important nuance, perhaps, in explaining the numbers of her followers drawn from the fashion industry—Baloun, like other devotees, seemed drawn by the practice of meditation, the emptying the mind of distractions so that a sense of a calmer, more meaningful life could begin to grow.

"I'd been doing a lot of work on myself through therapy and reading," said Baloun of his state of mind when he first encountered Siddha Yoga. "I'd gone to a few evenings at Unity, which is Eric Butterworth's group meeting at Lincoln Center, sort of the power of positive thinking linked with a Christian concept. But I was looking for a meditation practice to center myself in some way." Gurumayi's followers use CDs of her speaking or chanting as an inspiration to be played while they sit, burn incense, and allow their minds to slow down in a directed manner. Baloun often popped them in his Jeep's tape deck. (By 2000, the "Solo Series" of Gurumayi's chanting alone included nine titles, with a two-volume set titled "Sweet Dreams.") He and her other followers seemed mostly drawn by a person who'd impressed them as embodying enlightenment, and by a comforting practice, an antidote to the centrifugal forces of modern busyness, rather than by any philosophical formulation about the nature of the material world as real or unreal *(maya),* both of which have been argued by Hindu philosophers over the centuries.

If my guide's initial contact with his guru was through a videotape, mine was with the woman herself as she presided motionlessly, on the morning of the farewell *Guragita,* in an orange monk's robe rumored by at least one ex-follower to have been designed by Versace. (Her clothes, I was assured by a spokesperson, are in fact handmade at the ashram.) The room to which I'd been brought in the darkness was the converted ballroom of an old hotel in the foothills of the Catskills, the Gilbert; the hotel had fallen on hard times, like many hotels in the region, and had been bought in 1979 by Siddha Yoga Dham Associates, or the SYDA Foundation, a financial trust organized by Swami Muktananda in 1975. The Gilbert had been renamed "Anugraha," or "Descent of Grace"; the entire ashram was named Shree Nityananda Ashram. Its name was changed again by Gurumayi after Muktananda's death, in 1982, to Shree Muktananda Ashram. The hotel was situated centrally within the two hundred fifty square miles of Sullivan and Ulster Counties known as "the Borscht Belt" (or, more grandly, "the Jewish Alps"), where Jewish families, numbering up to a million people a summer during the peak years of the 1950s, had escaped the sweltering heat of New York City to be entertained by their favorite stand-up comedians. The hotel's entrance from the street was now guarded by statues, or *murtis,* of the celestial musicians Jaya and Vijaya. Enthroned on its front lawn like a friendly character from Disneyland was a statue of Ganesh, as well as a bronze, four-armed dancing Siva Nataraj statue, in front of which burned a musky ceremonial log fire. (Approximately two dozen Buddhist centers have also proliferated during the same few decades, enough so that the area has been nicknamed "the Buddhist belt." Most prominent are the Zen Mountain Monastery in Mount Tremper, the Karma Triyan Dharmachakra in Woodstock, and the International Dai Bostasu Zendo at Livingston Manor.)

A disconcerting first stop in the predawn was a sort of customs office located in a trailer near the main hall. Here I stood in a long line of arrivals with flashlights who'd found their way stumbling up from the parking lot under the starry sky, their breath condensing in the bracing autumn air, filling out forms and having their photographs taken. These three-by-five black-and-white snapshots were then processed and clipped onto a plastic-coated identification badge that could be marked by blue or red stars to indicate *seva* completed or courses purchased. This information was saved on computer, the photograph scanned, and the next time I visited it would be called up on screen and a new badge printed out, making the ashram singularly sophisticated in its airport-style high-tech security.

The chanting was already beginning as we were led by an usher down the slope of the front half of the hall named "Muktananda Mandir," to a spot on the green-carpeted floor where we could place our pillows and blankets: men on one side, women on the other, Indian-ashram-style. The large hall was mostly dark except for the vague pulsing violet luminescence of its walls—actually painted celadon green—caused by four racing stripes of neon blue in the ceiling, and by the dull glimmer of nine ostentatious cut-glass chandeliers hung in rows of three. In the rear half of the hall were nine rows of plush dark blue movie-theater-style chairs. As the sun began to rise, its pale yellow light was admitted into the hall through double rows of windows on either side.

The back wall of the auditorium was taken up with a lit shrine built around a large painting of Muktananda as a thin young man, its effect heightened on both sides by large chunks of crystal. (The ashram's main reception hall also includes, on display, a huge unprocessed outcropping of pink crystal.) Along one side wall nearby was a row of sepia-toned photographs of Indian holy men of modern times: Siddharuda Swami, who died in 1929, from whom Muktananda received his mantra, *Om Namah Shivaya;* Ravi Avadhoot; Alkotkot Swami; Zipruanna, of garbage-heap fame; Hari Giri Baba, an eccentric in the village of Chalisgoan who impressed Muktananda by conversing Saint Francis–style with pebbles and the wind; Ranchoo Bapuji; and Sai Baba of Shirdi. On a facing wall were illustrations of Indian women saints: Garji; Sakhubai; Rabia; Mirabai; Janabai; Akkamahadevi, a twelfth-century south Indian poetess whose renunciations included walking the streets nude; and Lalleshwari, who fled an indifferent husband and a vicious mother-in-law in fourteenth-century Kashmir to learn Tantric practices, and likewise was said to occasionally go without eating or dressing.

The focal point of Muktananda Mandir was unmistakably the triple archway at its front that framed a raised dais on which was set a low gold upholstered armless chair for the guru, and on the wall behind, a gold-framed picture of Muktananda looking a bit like a jazz musician in an orange ski cap, an orange robe, and a red dot on his forehead. Over the archway was gilded the mantra of Siddha Yoga: *Om Namah Shivaya* (meaning "I worship the God within"). Elegant side tables held framed colored portraits of a capped Muktananda and a bare-chested Nityananda, and a digital electric clock. The slowly unwinding and escalating chant was being led by men and women sitting cross-legged before low mikes on either side of the dais, some playing sitars, others two-sided mridang drums.

The entire location was wired with sophisticated sound and video systems. The covers of two TV screens inset in the front wall were folded back, revealing their inlaid Sanskrit/English messages in gold lettering: "The Guru Is the Root of All Action" and "Only He Who Obeys Can Command." These small blue screens were complemented by two larger screens set higher up on the front wall. The ceiling of the ballroom had been transformed into a busy complex of colored spotlights and sound-system speakers. A video camera was set up on a central ramp leading down to the guru's chair for projecting her image onto all four screens. Along part of the back wall was constructed a long rectangular control booth, where producers could communicate with their point people, who were wearing headsets. This positioning of the event somewhere between a real three-dimensional experience and simulcast television—a familiar trompe l'oeil trick borrowed from sports events—imbued the chanting of this centuries-old *Gurugita* with some of the slick seductiveness of the electronic age and mass media.

A few minutes after we'd begun to fall into the chant's rhythms, Gurumayi processed slowly down the central ramp to take her seat. "They say that she's taken on Baba's walk," Baloun whispered to me. She did seem to be walking with the limp of an old man, one hip slightly akimbo. This jarred with the rest of her projected presence, with her high cheekbones, neatly cut black hair, straight shoulders, almond skin, and the exotic, shifting beauty of her face, vaguely reminiscent, on that particular morning, of Raquel Welch. Once Gurumayi took her position cross-legged and yogic on the golden seat, she held her pose with hardly any movement for the next several hours, appearing to be some new and successful hybrid of a saint and a high-fashion model. It was as if she didn't need to speak, her posture advertising an entire philosophy of detachment and self-discipline in its singular poise.

At about seven a.m., the chant ended. The hall had filled by then with about fifteen hundred devotees, many of whom had been rocking back and forth or swaying their arms in the air, visibly excited. Nearly all then lined up for *darshan,* a process lasting almost four hours, during which devotees kneeled before Gurumayi's throne as she tapped their shoulders or heads with a wand tipped with peacock feathers. This ritual is particularly important in Siddha Yoga because of the belief in *shaktipat,* in which a guru literally can transmit her energy, or *shakti,* to anyone, sometimes causing dizziness or other physical symptoms, and often credited with provoking long-term life changes in those affected. *Shaktipat* can also supposedly be induced at increasing degrees of separation by simply seeing her image, hearing her words, or being in touch with someone who's been in touch with her.

"What time did you wake up this morning?" the guru playfully asked me from her throne when it was finally my turn to kneel near her and be swiped with the wand of feathers.

"Four o'clock," I answered, unsure of where the question was heading.

"When do you usually go to bed?" she laughed.

"At around one, but I'm not feeling too bad," I answered, enjoying our instant intimacy.

"Have you visited the temple yet?" she asked, pleasantly enough. When I answered, she commanded, much more definitely, "Visit the temple." Before I had time to explain that I had no idea which temple she meant, Gurumayi had redirected her peacock wand, and her attentions, to the person kneeling on her other side.

As I was walking off, one of her assistants followed after me and pressed a few Hershey Kisses in silver wrappers into my palm. "*Prasad* from the guru," she said, referring to the gift of candy. Later a few devotees who observed the action came up to tell me how impressed they were—and that I should be too—that I had received this special attention.

I returned to the South Fallsburg ashram on several other occasions, for the Siddha Yoga meditation retreat on "The Splendor of God, the Joy of Fearlessness and Blessings," taught by Gurumayi, and transmitted worldwide via satellite, on December 28–29, 1996; Gurumayi's New Year's message in 1997; the celebration of her forty-second birthday, on June 24, 1997; "First-Timers Weekend," on May 29–31, 1998; the global satellite chanting course, "Everything Is Attained through Chanting," on June 20, 1998; and the presentation of a children's pageant based on the *Mahabharata,* on the afternoon of July 10, 1998. Although I was never allowed to interview Gurumayi—the formal rule is that she will only speak to writers for in-house publications—I did see much of her in action and in meditation, and came to know many of those both currently and formerly within her orbit of influence, as well as those committed to making the SYDA Foundation successful.

I came gradually to have a wider sense of the scale of the Catskills ashram; it is made up not only of the Gilbert but of two other converted resort hotels as well. The Windsor, bought in 1983, was turned into dormitory and office space and renamed Sadhana Kutir, or "House of Spiritual Practices"; the former

Brickman Hotel was bought in 1986 and revamped as a large dormitory and residential complex known as Atma Nidhi, or "Treasure of the Soul." In 1985, construction was begun on the glass pavilion known as Shakti Mandap—a Crystal Palace version of the gigantic revival-style tents Muktananda taught in across the country and in India. Muktananda himself planned and oversaw the construction of the lavish pagoda temple to which Gurumayi had directed me—filled with candles, bright light bulbs, which were pink, frosted, and Candyland-like, and fragrant with flowers—honoring Bhagawan Nityananda (a.k.a. "Bade Baba," meaning "Elder Baba"), who presides in the form of a gigantic gold statue, his sculpted round belly ballooning out. Quiet trails and walkways have been built leading up from forests surrounding the buildings to an expansive hilltop, Mount Kailas. A manmade lake, Lake Nityananda, was constructed at considerable time and expense. The cumulative effect is of ashram-meets-country-club-meets–Epcot Center. The entire 550-acre operation—paid for initially in cash because of Muktananda's dislike of loans and debt—has been reported to have an estimated market value of over fifteen million dollars. (In one story about Muktananda's thriftiness, he ordered daily prayers said and a coconut waved ceremoniously to placate a much-valued, if dilapidated, air conditioner threatening to break down in another Catskills hotel rented for a summer in the 1970s.)

Because the SYDA Foundation is a nonprofit religious organization, no financial statements need to be made public. However, all of the courses, housing, and Atma Cafe vegetarian meals carry a fee, and the bookstore sells a long list of books published by their own press, CDs, cards, videotapes, audiotapes, photos of the guru, meditation pillows, oils, shawls, incense burners, statues and commemorative coins, and a correspondence course—all of which can be ordered by phone, through a catalog, or on Amazon.com. The fee for a two-day intensive session is generally $400; the cost of a single room, $101 per day, including three meals; or space in a dorm, with meals, for about $40. On a busy summer's weekend the ashram can reportedly raise more than a million dollars. In 1989, revenue from the South Fallsburg bookstore alone was $4 million. One devotee from 1979 to 1989 estimated she spent more than $20,000 on food, housing, courses, and products at the ashram. Contrary to unsubstantiated rumors of secret bank accounts in Switzerland, however, a foundation spokesman assured me that "all revenues we receive are put back into our organization to further our work in the form of operating and capital expenses." American dollars help keep meditation classes appropriately priced in poorer parts of the world as well, such as Poland or India.

The scope of the organization is best experienced at Gurumayi's annual New Year's address, where she traditionally debuts her positive, increasingly simplified message for the entire year. In 1997: "Wake up to your inner courage, and become steeped in divine contentment." In 1998: "Refresh your resolution. Smile at your destiny." In 1999: "A golden mind, a golden life." In 2000: "Believe in love." In 2001: "Approach the present with your heart's consent. Make it a blessed event." For several years these New Year's celebrations alternated between South Fallsburg and the Wyndham and Riviera Hotels in Palm Springs. The New York–Los Angeles axis is always especially evident during this week, and, with about two thousand people attending, not only are the numbers of followers apparent, but also the inner lining of Hollywood celebrity—unkindly nicknamed by some as "trophy devotees"—for which Siddha Yoga has become known. (The Los Angeles Center of Siddha Yoga on Bundy Drive, where the Hollywood contingent meets, was previously a microbrewery and restaurant owned by Wolfgang Puck.)

The 1997 New Year's celebration at South Fallsburg often had a very "bucks up" feeling to it, with one guest driving up in his new black Mercedes four-wheel-drive wagon, and other devotees accessorized with cell phones, Prada bags, Monolo Blahnik shoes, and Hermes scarves. Dennis Quaid and Meg Ryan—who have since separated—and their son, Jack, were always ushered to a spot down front for the chanting. Gillian Anderson of *The X-Files* mistakenly believed she recognized me in the lobby: "Are you an actor? Oh, sorry. I thought I knew you from L.A." Among those who came to chant in the New Year were Joan Osborne, whose "One of Us" was in heavy rotation that year on Top 40 radio stations; Alfonso Cuarón, the director of *Great Expectations;* Andre Gregory, the theater director and subject of Louis Malle's film *My Dinner with Andre;* the model and artist Ann Duong, whose *seva* included dishing out oatmeal at breakfast; best-selling self-help author Barbara D'Angelis; and actor Christopher Lawford. Reading aloud a list of the nearly two dozen cities on six continents to which the event was being broadcast live by satellite was Bill Cosby's former TV wife, Felicia Rashad. Lulu sang a modified version of "To Sir with Love," dedicated to her guru.

These recognizable celebrities were only the visible representatives of an entire roster of well-known names who've been associated with Siddha Yoga over the years since Swami Muktananda first came to America in 1970. This list has included Jerry Brown, John Denver, Diana Ross, Isabella Rossellini, James Taylor, Don Johnson, Melanie Griffith, Carly Simon, William Hurt, Stephen and Kimberly Rockefeller, Mica Ertegun, Sting, Betty Buckley, hairstylist John Frieda, style editor Ann Jones, and entrepeneur Matthew Melton.

The actress Marsha Mason told *Vanity Fair* in 1987 that Baba Muktananda inspired her to make the radical changes in her life that included, but did not cause, her divorce from Neil Simon. Don Johnson and Melanie Griffith are both devoted followers. (Their daughter Dakota's middle name is Mayi.) At the 1998 chanting intensive, supermodels Naomi Campbell—back from the ready-to-wear shows in Rajastan in March—and Christy Turlington were both participating, dressed in Indian-style pants and tunics. With homes in New York, Paris, London, Milan, and Hong Kong, Joyce Ma, the wealthy Asian fashion retailer and publisher of her own magazine, *Joyce,* often chooses to spend time at the South Fallsburg ashram, as does Suze Orman, author of the best-selling advice books *The 9 Steps to Financial Freedom* and *The Courage to be Rich: Creating a Life of Material and Spiritual Abundance.* Tamerlane Phillips, a devotee and the musician son of the

Mamas and the Papas' John Phillips, told the *New York Post* in October 1998 that Shree Muktananda Ashram was "the St. Tropez of ashrams," and that Gurumayi "travels like Queen Noor. She has exquisitely beautiful Indian girls who sit next to her on her throne and who wear $5,000 saris." He also credited his guru in the same interview as being "better than AA or NA. . . . If it weren't for her, I'd have died and been reborn as a flea on a Mexican water rat." (The gossip column further informed its readers that "Gurumayi is more in vogue right now than ever. Indeed many followers like to carry a wallet-sized photo of the guru with them.")

In *Daughters of the Goddess: The Women Saints of India,* Linda Johnsen addressed the chic surface of this most publicized segment of Gurumayi's scene. She explained, "It occurs to me that many of us yoga students are children of Sarasvati, the goddess of wisdom. We forget to acknowledge others who may be children of Lakshmi, the goddess of prosperity. Almost every other ashram I have visited in the United States is struggling month to month for its financial survival. At the Siddha centers, however, it is not unprecedented for wealthy celebrities to make million-dollar donations. Gurumayi honors beauty and wealth, and they pursue her wherever she goes. . . . Most Western yoga students are oriented to the ascetic traditions of yoga, and may be unaware that other types exist." Indeed, several rooms in the South Fallsburg ashram feature pre-Raphaelite-looking devotional paintings of the goddess Lakshmi, portrayed as standing nimbly on a lotus, coins flowing freely from her right hand.

Certainly, though, on New Year's Day, 1997, the more general impression was of all sorts of people, on all sorts of career and life paths, making their way up and down the narrow hallways of Anugraha, chanting in Sanskrit to calm themselves as they waited in line for hours that morning to get into the main hall, or into other meditation rooms, cafeterias, or buildings equipped with video monitors to handle the overflow. Most were well dressed, and in suits or long skirts and hats—a conservative dress code strongly encouraged by Gurumayi—and the effect was of Easter Sunday at the Cathedral of St. John the Divine. I met, among them, a nun, a housekeeper, a cook, a hairstylist, a butler, a book-seller, a dancer, and an advertising copywriter. While forming an extremely varied group, most of Gurumayi's followers are college educated and middle-aged, though there's been an effort to attract teenagers and young people to the ashram with its camp-style atmosphere during the summer months.

The main body of Gurumayi's address lasted just over an hour. While much of her content seemed lifted directly from the feel-good prose of self-help writing, her delivery was by no means ordinary. Like a brilliant actress or statesman, she communicated her words with personal commitment, seduction, charm, charisma, and power, carrying her willing audience along with her. She sat on her throne before a clear Plexiglas stand that supported her text, wore an orange, saucer-shaped pillbox hat to match her robes, and gestured allusively with her long fingers while expertly working three different camera angles. (For instance, she silently mouthed the words "Thank You, Baba" directly into the camera after revealing her inspirational New Year's slogan.)

"As you welcome 1997, you must realize that it holds a message at every moment," she said. "A playful dog you meet might convey a message of joy and fearlessness that allows you to solve a very difficult problem you are facing. A weed beside a footpath can hold a message. The deep sorrow in the heart of a friend may hold a message for you. There may be a pebble in your shoe that is annoying you yet its presence may be a message. The sight of moonlight streaming through a window might hold a message that reminds you of the infinite splendor of God. Listen to the messages that life provides."

After the camera lights dimmed, signifying that her formal talk was no longer being beamed around the world, she spoke extemporaneously for about fifteen minutes. On her mind that morning were attacks on the Internet from former Siddha Yoga devotees, ex-swamis, and even a former trustee, who left after becoming disillusioned by various scandals. There was apparently a reference to her as a "wild woman" that seemed to have particularly caught her attention. "I *am* a wild woman," she exclaimed, breaking out in almost self-deprecating gusts of laughter. "I'm on fire. Who wants to follow a woman on fire?" The previously sub-dued and reflective congregation broke into enthusiastic applause at this audacious challenge. She had quite obviously hit a high note of daring and spiritual confidence.

Adding extra impact to her rhetorical question was the truth that Gurumayi wasn't just any saint on fire, she was a *woman* on fire, and a woman on fire inviting followers. The spectacle of a female religious leader is a bit more traditional in India than in America. Besides those prototypes framed on the back wall of the Muktananda Mandir, there are a cluster of living ones: Sri Ma of Kamakhya, who resides at the Devi Temple she's founded in Napa, California; Anandi Ma, who oversees kundalini centers in Antioch, California, Woodbury, Connecticut, and Portland, Maine; Ma Yoga Shakti, who is the spiritual director of ashrams in Bombay, New Delhi, Calcutta, Madras, New York, and Florida; and Meera Ma, a nearly silent incarnation of the Divine Mother living near Frankfurt, Germany, who's been adoringly portrayed in Andrew Harvey's memoir, *Hidden Journey,* and Mark Matousek's *Sex, Death, Enlightenment.* Certainly *devi,* or goddess, worship is quite common in Hindu practice, and the energy credited with creating the world, *shakti,* is feminine energy. And yet, in daily life in India, of course, lower-class women tend to have tightly cir-cumscribed rights: arranged marriages are still the norm rather than the exception, with the women in these cases having no property rights, and domestic violence is common.

Female religious leaders have risen up over the centuries in America as well, again usually as exceptions: Ellen G. White, Mary Baker Eddy, Mormon hymn-writer Eliza Snow, spiritualist and feminist Victoria Woodhall, Pentecostal healer and twenties radio evangelist "Sister Aimee" McPherson, and Anne Hutchin-son, the free-thinking Puritan who was an inspiration for Hester Prynne, in *The Scarlet Letter.* To discover influential contemporary women preachers in America requires a stretch to Marianne Williamson; Science of Mind minister Louise L. Hay; the conser-vative Roman Catholic nun Mother Angelica, with her own Eternal Word Television Network broadcasting from Irondale, Alabama; or—standing either behind or in front of her man—the born-again Christian Tammy Faye Bakker.

"I think in one sense it's irrelevant that Gurumayi is a woman, but in another sense it's obviously very important at this point that there's a powerful, authentic spiritual leader who's a woman," says Swami Durgananda, formerly the journalist Sally Kempton, who has been a monk of the Siddha order for more than fifteen years. "This is the era of the emerging woman, isn't it? So it's important to women. I think of the way Gurumayi is given to taking care of everyone as displaying classically feminine energy . . . all that nourishing and caring. She is definitely having an enormous impact on people's ideas of what a woman can do."

But Gurumayi's coda to her address was daring not just in its invitation to trust a woman at the control of this sizable religious organization, but also in its brushing ever so lightly over the topic of dissension, conflict, and scandal so much under the surface of the SYDA Foundation—that is, she alluded to its dark side. For the history of this worldwide network of ashrams is a fascinating tale of East meeting West and sometimes misunderstanding it, with quite negative consequences; of the kinds of mad power struggles common when charismatic spiritual authority is attempted to be passed down from generation to generation; and of the difficulties in reconciling glamour and holiness. The phenomenon of Siddha Yoga can seem like those two-way drawings that, when looked at from one angle, portray a beautiful young woman, and from another, an old hag. Or like the experience of Young Goodman Brown, in Nathaniel Hawthorne's short story, who wanders into the woods at midnight to discover all the upstanding citizens of Salem involved in devil worship, awakens the next morning to find everyone back in their minister's robes and Sunday-school garb, and finally winds up schizophrenically unable to discern anymore which version is real.

While Siddha Yoga traces its lineage directly to the god Siva, the historical movement is exclusively a twentieth-century event. Its three leaders have been Nityananda, whose birthdate is unknown but who died in 1961; Muktananda, who lived from 1908 to 1982; and Gurumayi, born in 1955, who briefly, and awkwardly, shared the guru's seat from 1982 to 1985 with her younger brother, who became named Nityananda as well. Besides being strong characters themselves—"not your typical Joe," was one devotee's first impression of Muktananda—these three successive gurus instructively present, in a kind of time-lapse photography, the quick, adaptive changes made by this brand of Hindu spirituality as it grew from a local to a global event.

Bhagawan Nityananda was a classic Indian *avadhuta,* meaning "shaking off"—it's the term used for those beings who've shaken off ordinary convention and seem to be living on another planet of consciousness entirely. The equivalent of a primitive, or naif, Nityananda's nonmonastic name, meaning "one who is always in bliss," was given to him by his followers as a kind of nickname. The facts of this ecstatic, mostly silent renunciant's origin are only sketchy. He was raised by and perhaps was the son of domestic servants in the house of a Brahman lawyer named Ishwara Iyer in Qualandi, in the province of Kerala, in southern India. Among the constraints Nityananda shook off were clothing; he usually walked about clad only in a precariously loose loincloth. Because he owned nothing and had no visible means of support, the police occasionally tried to arrest him—once for forgery. His sense of organization was extremely laissez-faire, and his few teachings were delivered in such cryptic terms that not everyone could understand what he meant. As Swami Muktananda wrote in *From the Finite to the Infinite,* "If he ever spoke, he might say two or three words, and those three words were enough for a person's entire life. . . . He was beyond your rules, beyond your customs, beyond your disciplines. Siddhas live a strange life." (Focusing on his oversized hands and feet, some of the trippier American converts in the 1970s used to contend that Nityananda was actually an extraterrestrial—hence his obscure origins and encoded teachings.)

At Chopra's seminar in Goa, a businessman from Mumbai told me of having paid homage to Nityananda when as a child he visited him with his parents and hundreds of other Indians, who revered the old man lying blissfully for all to see in his stone house. "Nityananda just had this otherworldly air about him," he told me. "He was rare. I've never encountered anyone else quite like him. Muktananda was another creature entirely. He operated much more in this world." Indeed, Muktananda's biography is more straightforward, his behavior consistent with that of the wave of colorful Indian gurus who arrived in America in the 1970s. He was exceptional and possessed enormous energy and eccentricity, but he was certainly not incomprehensibly alien.

Unlike Nityananda, Swami Muktananda came from a wealthy landowning family in Mangalore, near the coastal region of Karnataka State in southwestern India. Named Krishna at his birth, on May 16, 1908, his early wanderings in search of enlightenment took him to Hubli, in northern Karnataka, where he studied and chanted the mantra *Om Namah Shivaya* at the ashram of Siddharudha Swami. In the mid-1920s, he became a monk of the Sarasvati order, receiving the religious name Muktananda, meaning "bliss of spiritual liberation." In 1930, Muktananda began his period of wandering, carrying the traditional water bowl and staff of the spiritual seeker. In the mid-1940s he professed himself a disciple of Nityananda's, and on August 15, 1947, he received *shaktipat* through the medium of his guru's sandals. In his autobiography, *Play of Consciousness,* written in twenty-two days in 1969, he describes receiving a zap of grace as he gazed into his guru's eyes while holding these sandals: "I stood there, stunned, watching the brilliant rays passing into me. My body was completely motionless." The force being with him, he was then eventually settled by Nityananda in the three-room house that is now Gurudev Siddha Peth. This, along with Nityananda's sticking his hand, unobserved, down Muktananda's throat while on his deathbed in August 1961, Muktananda interpreted as establishing him as a successor to a lineage, though some have disputed his assumption.

To whatever extent Siddha Yoga derives from the primordial god Siva, or from the *avadhuta* Nityananda, the path as it's currently understood was, if not invented, then at least colored in

and fulfilled by Swami Muktananda. Beginning with the seemingly irrational force of nature of Nityananda, Muktananda soon
assembled a coherent philosophy, a streamlined attitude toward
initiation, and, eventually, a worldwide Siddha Yoga organization.
(The term "Siddha" refers to any of a group of semidivine "per-
fected ones" first mentioned in the Vedic *Puranas.*) The philosophy he revived as the metaphysical basis of Siddha Yoga was
Kashmir Shaivism, an eighth-century school of northern Indian
thought that incorporated Tantric and Buddhist influences and
adopted a monistic metaphysical position similar to that of non-
dualist *(advaita)* Vedanta. (Perhaps because of Kashmir's proximity to Tibet, the Tantric elements in Kashmir Shaivism sometimes resemble those in Tibetan Buddhism.) While Vedantism,
especially as outlined in Shankara's eighth-century *Crest-Jewel of
Discrimination,* emphasized the material world as *maya,* or illusion,
Kashmir Shaivism emphasized the reality of material phenomena
as masks, or versions of *shakti,* the creative energy of the universe.
The fine line of distinction between these two schools is primarily
attitudinal, Shaivism being perhaps slightly more playful, plural-
ist, and bodily, though both—of all the twenty-seven schools of
metaphysical thought in India—rest most simply on the assumption of a single divine force behind creation. As S. Ramachandran, an eighty-two-year-old Indian devotee of Muktananda's,
explained to me: "In Kashmir Shaivism, you are an actor on a
stage. All the world's a stage, as Shakespeare himself says it."

The main event in Kashmir Shaivism is the awakening of
kundalini, which is divine energy stored at the base of the spine
that is often depicted as a snake uncoiling until it reaches the
crown of the head and disperses enlightenment. Traditionally this
awakening, such as Muktananda experienced while holding Nityananda's sandals, was only achieved by yogis after years of renunciation and ascetic practices requiring great self-discipline.
Muktananda's modern innovation was to fast-forward the process
of purification, claiming that he could effect such an awakening in
anyone instantly by a word, touch, look, or thought. His rationale
was that he had been instructed by his guru that the world was in

such a state of emergency that hasty and extreme measures were required. His mission, as he explained it, was to spark a "meditation revolution."

Muktananda's reformatting of an ancient practice had great immediate appeal in America, which he first visited on his initial world tour, in 1970—a three-month sweep through Italy, France, Switzerland, England, Australia, Singapore, and the United States, including long stays in New York City, Los Angeles, and San Francisco. Muktananda's advance man in America and Australia for this first tour was Baba Ram Dass, the former Harvard psychologist Richard Alpert, who'd collaborated on early LSD experiments with Timothy Leary. "Baba Ram Dass would basically sit at Baba's feet and say 'Tell me about all the Siddhas,' " recalls longtime devotee Melynda Windsor. "He was like a little kid around Baba."

To help make possible an ensuing, and much more elaborate, second world tour, which lasted from February 1974 until October 1976, Werner Erhard, the founder of est, was tapped. A series of psychological assertiveness-training seminars popular especially in California at the time, est—begun in 1971, modified and renamed the Forum in 1985, and the basis in turn of the current Landmark Forum—combined alternative spiritual practices with a seductive philosophy of success. Promoted with an advertisement featuring a photo of Erhard—born Jack Rosenberg, the ex–used-car salesman fashioned his new name from those of atomic scientist Werner Heisenberg and economics minister Ludwig Erhard—the slogan for the seminars was Know and Understand Yourself and Others. Est attracted more than a half million people, including John Denver and Yoko Ono and enough members of one film company to earn it the nickname "Werner Brothers," and was the basis of Tom Wolfe's defining "The ME Decade" article in *New York* magazine.

In 1973, Erhard traveled to India in hopes of meeting an authentic spiritual master whom he could present to his est students as a living model of an enlightened being. A friend of his, Don Harrison, who was managing a Siddha Yoga ashram in Piedmont, California, near San Francisco, suggested he visit Ganesh-puri. Fascinated by his experiences at the ashram (which he visited at least once with Diana Ross), Erhard was moved to buy five round-trip tickets to America for Muktananda and his entourage; he also set up several lecture programs where he introduced Muk-tananda to est students in Honolulu, San Francisco, Los Angeles, Aspen, and Manhattan. As these early alliances are officially summed up by Swami Durgananda in her official history of the Siddha Yoga movement, "Erhard and est provided a springboard that helped introduce Siddha Yoga into the mainstream of Ameri-can consciousness. Yet just as Swami Muktananda remained inde-pendent of those whose help he appreciatively accepted during his first tour, so he remained independent of Erhard and the others who came forward to help facilitate this one." (The need to main-tain distance follows perhaps from a scathing *60 Minutes* exposé on excesses in Erhard's personal life in 1991, after which Erhard dis-appeared from the scene.)

On this second tour, Muktananda stayed for ten months in Oakland during 1975 and 1976, presiding over the conversion of a run-down dive hotel frequented by hookers in miniskirts and boots, the Stanford. Located in an industrial neighborhood in north Oakland predominantly filled with low-to-moderate-income families, this first Western Siddha Yoga residential ash-ram was remade by devotees into an immaculate retreat for what has become the largest surrounding lay Siddha Yoga community in the world. A segment of the local population involved to differ-ent degrees with Muktananda were actually members of the Black Panther Party. One leader, Ericka Huggins—whose husband had been murdered on the University of California at Los Angeles campus in 1969 and who was herself imprisoned for two years in New Haven, on charges later dropped—met Muktananda in 1979 and felt transformed: "When I was on trial everyone was yelling 'Free Ericka!' " she recalled to me. "All this fighting I did for free-dom, Baba embodied. In his presence I felt entirely free. Freer than I did the day I walked out onto the New Haven green with-out handcuffs." She soon returned with friends, schoolchildren, and other Black Panther leaders, including Huey Newton, who met Muktananda several times. "Huey was very taken with Baba," said Huggins. "He was charismatic and wise, but he knew there were some things he needed to change. Being around Baba highlighted that for him."

During this second world tour, when Swami Muktananda resided for a few months in the spring and summer of 1976 at the Hotel De Ville in the Catskills, a spectacle was created by yogis driving up from New York City to experience his rumored powers of instantaneous transformation. "New York had a lot of serious yogis at the time," recalls Melynda Windsor. "These yogis were austere-looking, with long hair. They'd been standing on their heads in closets for God knows how long trying to awaken their kundalini. Then they heard there was this little guy dressed all in red up in the Catskills who could do it. We gathered on the first morning of the intensive meditation workshop in the old De Ville's nightclub, with windows floor to ceiling, and watched Muktananda and Gurumayi, who was his translator at the time, walk across this dandelion field from his house. As soon as the yogis saw him, they took off like rockets, having all these *kriyas,* making all these wild noises." (A *kriya* is an involuntary spasm during which blocks to the flow of kundalini supposedly snap loose.) Another devotee, California trust-and-estate lawyer Janet (Sushasini) Dobrovolny, tells of an African-American gentleman, now a devotee, who claimed he experienced *shaktipat* when Muktananda, a complete stranger, walked up to him at a bus stop on San Pablo Avenue in Oakland, California, and simply hugged him.

Poet and playwright Arnold Weinstein encountered Muktananda first in a devotional picture he spotted on the wall of the actress Barbara Harris's apartment in 1975. "He looked to me like a cross between Dizzie Gillespie, with the hat, and Taj Mahal, the great blues singer," Weinstein recalls. "I said to Barbara, 'Where's he playing?' She said, 'Oh, he's playing at 92nd Street.' She took me up there to an intensive for about twenty people at about ten dollars a head, and I just sat there and listened to him and fell in love with him. I brought the painter Larry Rivers to meet him. Everybody who met him, loved him." Weinstein went so far as to write a musical version of Muktananda's life, *Play of Consciousness,* with music by William Balkam, performed in workshop at the Manhattan Theater Club in 1979. (After a performance, Muktananda asked Weinstein, "Am I going to Broadway?")

The mid-1970s were historically the comet's tail of a hyperactive ten years of experimenting in America, and some devotees' experiences were more "out there" than others. One memorable tale of *shaktipat* is told by the photographer Joe Lalli: "I went to a Diana Ross concert at Forest Hills Stadium in the seventies. As she was singing, this light came out of her. I thought, 'Wow, it's the Bob Mackie gown.' But then I felt the light go into my heart chakra and explode, and I felt high. The next day I opened the *Daily News* and there was a picture of Diana Ross in a white Indian robe, her hair pulled back, no makeup, on the ground in the lotus position sitting next to this man. The caption read 'Diana Ross with Spiritual Master Swami Muktananda.' The article reported that she'd flown straight from India to Forest Hills, Queens, for this concert." Lalli left Siddha Yoga in the early 1990s, as he felt the movement had become "like a Protestant church, the men in suits and their wives in dresses, all very formalized. It had become the polar extreme of Nityananda, who was *avadhuta* and had no regard for social convention."

Others had less tabloid introductions to the contagious power of kundalini. Swami Akhandananda, originally Daniel Bauer of Seattle, Washington, with whom I spoke one morning in a seminar trailer behind Atma Nidhi, first met Muktananda as a teenager, in August 1974, when the swami came to stay at the home of family friends. (Tall with piercing blue eyes, Akhandananda's secret nickname among some of the more lighthearted members of Siddha Yoga is "Hunk-dananda.") Akhandananda was familiar with Asian culture, as his architect father and mother had spent time teaching English in south India during the 1960s. "I pulled my hair back in a ponytail, got some flowers from the garden, put on my best Indian-print shirt, and walked up the hill to meet him," Akhandananda recalled. "Baba was sitting very casually in this living room in a floppy chair, very animated, totally engaged with everything around him. I came before him, and he asked where I was from. After I'd given him my flowers, which had wilted, he motioned for me to sit in the room where about fifty people were gathered. 'He doesn't look like a saint,' I thought to myself, because he was moving around so much and wasn't at all spaced out. I had the sensation when I met Baba, though, that he knew everything about me. There was this totally unconditional love I felt coming from him. I just sat in that room for the rest of the afternoon, barely able to look at him. Then I came back a couple more times."

This sensation of love was powerful enough for Akhandananda to move into the Oakland ashram in April 1976, after graduating from high school. He worked at a series of jobs, including cook, carpenter, and electrician, and as a member of the crew preparing for Muktananda's third and final world tour (August 1978 to October 1981). He also gradually desired to be ordained as a monk, including taking the vows of poverty, chastity, and obedience. This wish was realized in April 1982, when he was included in the last of four groups of renunciant *dasanami sannyasa* monks of the Sarasvati order initiated by Muktananda in Ganeshpuri between 1977 and 1982. At that time there were sixty-five monks, of whom fourteen were women. (By 1996, their numbers had dwindled to twenty-five swamis, five of them women; Gurumayi has yet to replenish the order.)

"The ceremony was like a rebirth," remembered Akhandananda. "We went into the Tansa River at two o'clock in the morning to make our ablutions. Under the stars, in the early-morning darkness, we took our final vows. Then we started walking toward the Himalayas. After taking seven steps, they call you back for the sake of humanity. Baba then gave us our orange robes, our monastic names, and blessed us." Not regretting his choice of such a chaste life, Akhandananda says, "The love of God you can directly know is even greater than you can experience in a relationship. Of course, if a person doesn't have that experience, and they've been culturally conditioned for something far different ever since they were old enough to watch TV, then they'll find this concept difficult."

Even more important for the continuity of Siddha Yoga than the monks were the two successors Muktananda put in place as double gurus on May 8, 1982: Malti, now Gurumayi, a round-faced Hindi girl with a long braid who was the daughter of a Bombay restaurateur, and who served as Muktananda's translator after she arrived at the ashram in 1973, when she was eighteen; and her younger brother by seven years, Subhash Shetty, renamed Nityananda. This flurry of ordinations and promotions proved critical five months later when, soon after returning from a trip to Kashmir with his brother-and-sister successors, Muktananda died of heart failure in Ganeshpuri on October 2, 1982. Thousands of mourners lined the single road between the ashram and Ganesh-puri as his body was carried in procession through the town and eventually sprinkled with camphor, salt, and sandalwood for its final burial in his *samadhi* shrine.

The next several years in Siddha Yoga were marked by a few of those crises in a minor key that greatly tested the durability of the organization Muktananda had put in place—numbering thirty-one meditation centers internationally by the time of his death. The first was an article titled "The Secret Life of Swami Muk-tananda," written by William Rodarmor and printed in *CoEvolu-tion Quarterly* in 1983. Its author accused the deceased swami of having regularly had sex with young female devotees, and he quoted SYDA Foundation ex-trustee Michael Dinga, claiming the guru kept a special gynecologist's table with stirrups in South Fallsburg for such occasions. These accusations were revisited to even more devastating effect more than ten years later by Lis Har-ris in an article titled "O Guru, Guru, Guru" in *The New Yorker,* in November 1994. She claimed to have interviewed about a hun-dred ex-devotees, ex-swamis, and ex-trustees, and found corrobo-ration for the charges. The only curious fillip is that a common detail in the stories of the women interviewed was that the guru never ejaculated, and many agreed that the experience therefore was "not exactly sex."

The publishing of this story, twice, has been a kind of depth charge in the history of Siddha Yoga, and is certainly partly responsible for the eventual cutting of the number of committed swamis by more than half. Yet finally the entire incident has remained as a kind of floating anxiety rather than a definitive deal breaker. It's become a cosmic version of "he said, she said." Muktananda's followers who don't want to be swayed have their own subjective impressions to cherish. As Janet Dobrovolny told me: "I knew from my own connection to Baba, especially one time when he held me close, that you could attribute many things to him, but not sexual desire." Likewise Swami Durgananda feels that "Part of being in Baba's state—and in my experience of him it was completely *intrinsic* to Baba's state—was the fact that he existed only to help people. For Baba Muktananda to be engaging in behavior that was selfish or personally motivated is a contradiction in terms."

The only other exit sign in sight for believers has been marginally theological, based on the conjecture that his behavior was actually a version of esoteric Tantric practice, a corollary of the Eastern spiritual practice based on a number of sixth- to twelfth-century mystical Hindu and Buddhist scriptures describing a range of practices—including controlled ejaculation—for attaining exalted states of enlightenment and awareness. But Tantric scholars tend to dismiss such explanations. As Robert Thurman, professor of religion at Columbia University and a follower and scholar of Tibetan Buddhism, told *The New Yorker*, "This kind of behavior should not be legitimized by calling it Tantra. The occasional shocking incident, even in legends, demonstrates exactly the degree to which such behavior stands against the tradition."

If the debate over sublimation and spiritual growth was subtle, the struggle between brother and sister over the guru's seat was much more in the face of all devotees. For no sooner had the rumors of Muktananda's sexual dalliances been thoroughly raised, disputed, and disseminated than Gurumayi's brother, Nitya-nanda, in October 1985, admitted that he had broken his own monastic vows between the ages of nineteen and twenty-three by having sexual encounters with six different women. This announcement led to what seemed a voluntary resignation after an intensive in Ganeshpuri that month, and an anointing of Guru-mayi as sole head of the lineage on November 10, 1985. "I was at that intensive in Ganeshpuri where her brother had dropped out of sight for the ten days before," one ex-follower told me. "All of a sudden at the very end of the weekend, Gurumayi entered the hall wearing those dark sunglasses, looking extremely fierce, and fol-lowing about ten feet behind her was Nityananda, dressed in blue. You could hear people gasp, then muffled sobs, then stunned silence. It was an absolutely unbelievable, shocking moment."

However, in February 1986, the *Illustrated Weekly of India* printed an article in which Nityananda claimed he'd been forced out, and soon afterward he showed up in Bombay in his orange robes again to resume his former spot. The SYDA Foundation blocked this move, and these days he maintains his own very scaled-down ashram, Shanti Mandir, in Pine Bush, New York. It is not far from Gurumayi's much grander operation, though the two reportedly haven't seen or spoken to each other since July 1986. His principal aide at Shanti Mandir, Devayani, was one of his controversial six lovers.

In characterizations of Nityananda, drawn from those around at the time, he does come across as a bit of a guru without a cause. "He was a kid who wanted to hang out with the girls, and drive around in cars," one ex-follower put it bluntly. "You could see it was all going to his head." Others have more evenly remembered him for his good humor, sweetness, and love of playing the drums. Whatever the missteps and confusion at the time, the party line, as put by Swami Akhandananda, is basically that "There's an old saying in India, 'You strain your water before you drink it, and you test your guru before you accept him.' That was one of the deeper lessons of that whole period. It wasn't easy. But it made everyone much stronger."

At the time, however, the vitriol and acting out surrounding the affair could amount to overkill. "They were all gossiping and hissing," said one ex-follower of the swamis' announcements about Nityananda in South Fallsburg in March 1986. "You began to realize that they could twist anything. There was no dignity around how they handled it. It was all ugly." "The center leaders asked us to return all pictures of the brother so they could be burned," another ex-follower, from Boston, told me. "Well, those pictures cost us fifteen bucks a pop, and when you brought in a whole pile of them, that could be quite an investment going up in flames. They were basically trying to rewrite history." Certainly the tone of Gurumayi's "Message from Gurumayi to All the Devotees of Siddha Yoga" circulated by the foundation seems startlingly sharp and occasionally petty, as in her characterization of a vacation taken by her brother: "At this time I was in Los Angeles in April 1985. When he called me on the phone I asked him, 'How hard have you worked so that you feel the need to relax for two weeks?' When asked, 'What do you do all day long?' he replied, 'I drive around.' (Not a bad life for this Guru!)" She admitted in this public memo to ordering her brother's tires slashed to prevent his leaving the ashram, and to having given him "a few slaps" with Muktananda's walking stick to try to "wake him up from his fantasy world."

The New Yorker reported an escalation of events, amounting to a vendetta apparently at least partly overseen by George Afif, a confidant and unofficial guard of Gurumayi's at the time, who was shadowed by the dubious record of having pleaded no contest to a misdemeanor statutory rape charge in California in 1983. One incident in Ann Arbor, Michigan, in August 1989, reported in the magazine as well as in the local Ann Arbor *News,* involved the kicking down of the door of the visiting Nityananda, pushing aside of his followers, and throwing of skunk scent on his walls by a group of men, at least some of whom admit to having been devotees of Gurumayi's. "I was part of the good-cop team against the brother," says Dan Shaw, an ex-devotee, now a psychotherapist in private practice in New York City, who served on Gurumayi's tour staff from 1985 to 1992 and as her director of public programs and intensives. "We were the spokespeople who rallied the devotees, spread rumors about him, tested allegiances, reported whoever was shaky. . . . Gurumayi wanted all of us to call her brother 'Fatso' whenever we referred to him in private. . . . George Afif was head of the bad-cop team. He had a kind of gang who would go to meetings, disrupt things. Gurumayi had her brother stalked and harassed all over the globe, everywhere he went, for seven years. This harassment didn't stop until the *New Yorker* story came out." (In response to my request for information about Afif, a spokesman for the foundation e-mailed me that "Several years ago he left the ashram to be with his family in Lebanon.")

"There's so much that needs to be acknowledged on the dark side that just isn't apparent when you go to the ashram," an ex-follower who was a member of the inner circle until 1994 said to me. "If they'd just come out, speak the truth, and say, 'This is our past,' the way the Catholic Church is at least trying to deal with the suffering caused by their priests who engaged in sexual abuse. But in Siddha Yoga, no one has done that. Siddha Yoga appears to be a huge dysfunctional family with a long history of secrets, denials, and cover-ups. At the center is the guru, who has betrayed the *dharma* of right action toward her own brother. Over all these years, she hasn't reconciled with him. It's very sad."

For those many followers who were entirely left out of some of the creepier behind-the-scenes machinations, the problem had been more simply the disparity between the length of the *darshan* lines of the two gurus, and the trickiness of devoting themselves in meditation to two living, breathing icons. "I brought my mother up to the ashram for Mother's Day," recalls Joe Lalli. "She's from Queens, so she's got this whole other perspective. She said, 'That brother's living in the shadow of that sister. She's so elegant. She's got class. Him, none.' I said, 'Mom, don't say that, he's the guru.' She said, 'He's not gonna last. Who's gonna follow him?' We went up to meet Gurumayi at *darshan,* and when we were walking away she called my mother back and gave her a white orchid. That did it for my mother. It's like one of these cliché miracle stories. For three weeks the orchid was on her bureau, with no water, and was just perfect."

Over the past decade Gurumayi has obviously been working to keep the spotlight off some of the more Old World–style intrigues—that is, she's been modernizing. She has also, apparently, been realizing, whether consciously or not, that a guru in America must adhere to some of the purity of style expected of a Christian saint. Unsubstantiated rumors over the past few years have been confined more to the order of her having had plastic surgery on the tip of her nose, jaw, and cheekbones, or having had her hair cut by a hairdresser at the John Barrett salon on the top floor of Bergdorf Goodman's, or having sent a shopper to purchase expensive jewelry at Van Cleef & Arpels. Her public makeover has included an increasing sophistication in her telegenic presentations. And she has pared down Muktananda's occasionally theologically dense talks, which were punctuated by his singing Sanskrit verses from Scripture, to what one follower described to me as "manageable bite-sized pieces." ("Sound-byte-sized pieces" might be an even more accurate description). She consolidated her position effectively enough to be named by the Honolulu-based monthly magazine *Hinduism Today* as one of the ten most influential international Hindu leaders of the last decade.

"Sometimes Gurumayi's exceptional discipline and commitment is so obvious that people miss it," says Janet Dobrovolny, defending her against those who insist on seeing her as somehow fraudulent, a poseur. "The most obvious test of Gurumayi and her greatness is to watch her sit for seven hours in perfect posture without really moving. She's done that year after year in front of thousands of people. They don't realize that what she's just done is really amazing."

One of the more intriguing members of the inner cadre, and perhaps the most compelling present-day spokesperson for Siddha Yoga, is Swami Durgananda. Her profile seems to some that of a female, late-twentieth-century Hindu version of Thomas

Merton. In *The Seven Storey Mountain,* Merton told of his rejection in the 1940s of the life of a New York writer and intellectual to go off and devote himself to the solitary practice of a contemplative monk, far from the round of magazine bylines, competition for publication, and heated conversations in late-night bars and restaurants.

The afternoon I visited with Durgananda (her thundering name means "the Bliss of the Divine Mother") in a very functional conference room at the South Fallsburg ashram, she was dressed in an orange robe; her sunglasses were set to the side, and she wore a fashionable wristwatch. Her blond hair was cut straight, and her pale blue eyes were clear, focused, and appraising. When she spoke, she had control of the sorts of ironic edges, the invisible quotation marks, mastered by other women who, like her, graduated from Sarah Lawrence or had become equally engaged in the ambiguities of the *Play It as It Lays* terrain of Hollywood in the late 1960s and early 1970s. But her sophistication was ventilated by an apparent directness and openness about her own pursuit of ultimate joy and happiness.

Durgananda had recently reappeared on the radar screen of the New York literary world on the occasion of the funeral of her father, the iconic *Newsday* columnist and *New York Review of Books* writer Murray Kempton. The funeral was held on May 8, 1997, at St. Ignatius of Antioch, the Episcopal church he'd attended later in life. Both Durgananda and her brother David, who'd also been devoted to Siddha Yoga for twenty years, came down from the ashram to take care of their father in his last months. Their devotion, clarity, and healthy demeanor were much commented on. And of course the mystery of "Whatever happened to Sally Kempton?" was tantalizingly raised again, if not exactly solved. Among those at the funeral who'd been a friend in Hollywood was the writer John Gregory Dunne. "When I knew her in the late sixties, she was bright, extremely attractive, tall, lissome, and lithe," he commented to me. "As a job category, monk is not one I would have picked out for her. She just didn't seem the type. When she went off, I thought it was just a phase. I was obviously mistaken."

"There was a whole group of people for whom my becoming involved in Siddha Yoga had been a sort of mythological event," Durgananda said. "Somebody in your world leaves everything and goes off to a monastery. It was like that. . . . And then there were people who had issues about spirituality, especially involving a guru, with all the ideas the uninformed have about that. They tended to think it was about giving over freedom and autonomy to someone else."

She traces her spiritual inklings as far back as her childhood in Princeton, where she was born in 1943; her father was Anglican, her mother Jewish, and she was the older sister of three brothers. Experiencing her first flash of religious curiosity at age twelve, she was quickly disillusioned: "I conceived this tremendous desire to have a religious experience, so I began to go around to all the churches in Princeton, but they were all hopelessly dry and hideously impossible to connect to." Instead she studied world religions with a woman in the neighborhood her mother chose to call a "mystic," and she "spent an enormous amount of time doing what I now realize was meditation—sitting and staring at the sky, staring at a tree for three hours, staring at the moon. But I didn't call it meditation. I didn't think of myself as religious. I thought religion was for goody-goodies."

Her search soon gave way to the typical adolescent trope of "losing touch with my inner being and becoming utterly involved in peer values"—though hers was in the not-so-typical bohemian style being played out at the time in downtown Manhattan, a mere train ride away: "I had about as many adventures as I could, given the fact that I was a somewhat fearful middle-class girl. It was the usual late-fifties stuff—I'd run away from home with a friend and hang out in Village coffeehouses and jazz clubs, meeting the kind of people you met there, reading bad poetry, wearing black, reveling in the varieties of adolescent pain." This style of acting out was interrupted, or at least deepened from style into substance, when she went away to Sarah Lawrence College and began submerging herself in the philosophical works of Plato,

Spinoza, and Kant. It was the study of philosophy that opened up for her "questions of meaning such as 'Who am I?' and 'Why am I not happy?'"

As the daughter of a famous journalist, and possessing an intellect given to perfectionist standards, Kempton struggled with her own writing, and even more especially with the success that came to her so easily straight out of college due to a series of fresh, acerbic pieces she wrote for the *Village Voice* in 1964 on then-underexposed topics such as drugs, hippies, and homosexuals. "I was quite successful at it, almost within minutes," she told me. Her most direct hit was an article published in *Esquire* coolly dissecting her relationships with men, including her husband, Harrison Starr, the producer of Antonioni's *Zabriskie Point,* whom she divorced in 1970, the year her piece, "Cutting Loose," subtitled "A private view of the women's uprising," appeared in print. The popular essay alternated between candid confession: "I used to lie in bed beside my husband after those fights and wish I had the courage to bash in his head with a frying pan"; nifty stab wounds, such as her reducing her father to someone "uncomfortable with adult women"; and acute feminist analysis: "I became a feminist as an alternative to becoming a masochist." But it was the last line of the piece that gave a clue to what would be next: "Women's liberation is finally only personal. It is hard to fight an enemy who has outposts in your head."

Back on West 11th Street in Manhattan, with an advance for a novel, Kempton became more and more concerned with the outposts of suffering in her own head, describing the painful contours of which had proved her strongest subject as a writer. Perceiving the limits of feminism and psychoanalysis as cure, she turned, in May 1972, to Arica, a secular consciousness movement begun by Oscar Ichazo and taken up by many intensely intellectual counterculture types. "I'd used up most of my advance, so for three months I spent eighteen hours a day writing, trying to finish the book before I ran out of money," Durgananda recalled. "When I wasn't writing I spent a lot of time just sitting with myself, and it was then that I began to see how out of control my mind was. From what I could see, the unhappiness I experienced was largely the result of the fact that I couldn't keep my mind from running down negative channels. I started looking for some sort of technology to bring my mind under control. I sensed that this was the way to get back in touch with an experience of joy."

Moving back again to Los Angeles to stay briefly in a "house" of Arica trainers, she was convinced by friends in 1974 to meet Baba Muktananda, who was staying in town at an Italianate mansion in Pasadena that had been used as a set for the movie *Chinatown.* She walked in skeptically, in the planning stages for an article that she eventually published in *New York* magazine in 1976 titled "Hanging Out with the Guru." However, by the time the article appeared she'd already passed through the looking glass, having changed her point of view from that of observer to believer, moved as she was that day, and on subsequent days, by her experience of Muktananda. Whatever her problems with father, boyfriend, and husband, here was a male figure with a different sort of authority eliciting in her a quite different response. And in place of dwelling on negative emotions in the fashion of psychoanalysts, he simply advised: "Let them go."

"There were about a hundred people there, sitting on the floor," she recalled of that first meeting. "At first glance it seemed like the usual early-seventies spiritual scene—American boys in orange lungis passing bowls of chocolates and this little group of girls in saris who'd just come from India. In the midst of it all sat Baba in his orange clothes and dark sunglasses, radiating this huge field of loving energy. For a minute I could actually sense him taking in all the scattered energy in the room, all the feelings people carried—the cravings, the desires, the irritation, the sadness, the excitement—filtering them through his own body, transmuting it all so that it flowed back as love. My own inner state—by which I mean my ability to be aware, to be present, to feel love, to feel connected to my own energy—accelerated from zero to sixty in fifteen minutes. There was a feeling of vast energy and at the same time a sense of protection. I walked away from there with an open heart, and the feeling didn't go away." Her reaction that night in bed was, "Oh, God, it's all true what those creeps were saying." She described the experience as "filling my body with the feeling I associated with intense romantic love," and described Muktananda as "the least spaced-out person in the room, a practical, solid presence." Three months later, she joined Muktananda's tour in Denver, taking on the work of press liaison, and eventually of cutting and pasting her guru's talks into book form.

These gatherings in the 1970s were much more intimate than the later auditorium-sized venues of Gurumayi's, with Muk-tananda having time to wander around touching everyone, and giving personal advice. "Everybody had hair down to their waist and was into 'go with the flow,'" Durgananda recalls. "Baba was teaching the disciplined life. You'd come to him with your fuzzy thinking and your spaced-out conclusions and he'd sort of force you to get one-pointed and clear. It didn't last very long because that kind of thing never does, but it was quite divine to be there because you got to see him interacting with hundreds of different kinds of people." After several trips to India, and a gradual adop-tion of a yogi's lifestyle, Durgananda took the vows of a *sannyasin* monk in 1982, in the same ceremony as Akhandananda and Gurumayi.

She has managed to keep to her path in spite of all the diffi-culties of the early 1980s. Of the charges of sexual abuse leveled against Muktananda, she maintains personal skepticism, having called them "laughable" and "ridiculous" in print, though she did walk a razor's edge of interpretation, reminiscent of the legal pre-cision of a Hillary Clinton, when she spoke to me, carefully and haltingly, of the subject, making clear in later correspondence with me that her statement referred to gurus in general and not specifically to Baba's alleged actions. "It's true that certain scrip-tural texts, especially texts of high Vedanta like the *Avadhuta Gita,* but also the *Bhagavad Gita,* say that an enlightened being has no need to follow the same rules of conduct as an 'ordinary' person, because he or she is understood to be operating from a completely different level of understanding, from a state of pure love, selflessness, attunement to the higher will," she communicated to me by e-mail. "Nonetheless, there is also a tradition that such a being follows the *dharma,* or social code of conduct, of society in order to serve as an example. In the *Bhagavad Gita,* Lord Krishna says though he has no need to perform actions of any kind, still he acts in the world in order to set an example to others, 'since people follow the example of the great.' "

She has also dealt head-on in her own mind with the problem of the deposed guru Nityananda: "My experience of Gurumayi's brother was that he was a delightful young man through whom vast amounts of *shakti* flowed, but who never seemed to me to have the qualities of a guru, the qualities I'd seen in Baba and which I saw in Gurumayi." Her argument is basically that the lineage confers power, as the office of president might be seen as adding wattage that is diminished when the term is completed. "The will of a master like Baba is very powerful. He is able to direct the flow of the *shakti,* the spiritual energy of the lineage, in a certain direction. So he can say, 'Let the power of the lineage flow through that nineteen-year-old boy when he sits on the guru's seat,' and his intention will focus the lineage-energy in such a way that people will experience kundalini awakening through that person. The guru can empower someone, but then the person has to hold the state he or she has been given. If the person doesn't keep up his practice and his discipline, then the state won't stay with him."

Currently Durgananda spends much of her time at both the Indian and South Fallsburg ashrams, teaching intensives on the basics of meditation; she has written a long, historical essay on Siddha Yoga for a definitive tome published by the foundation, *Meditation Revolution,* designed to give the movement some historical and theological depth. Her experience of Gurumayi as guru, or enlightened being, has been of a "God-is-in-the-details" person:

You never see Gurumayi rushing, for example. When you watch her you see that when she walks or talks she's always coming from a very centered place. You sense a depth and stillness about her. When you're in a room with her, it often feels as if time were flowing differently. There's a clarity. Your senses are heightened. You become instantly self-aware—you see your motivations and your feelings and your thoughts in a kind of high relief. It's as if her presence activates the inner witness in people. . . . And at the same time being around her is like being in a very deep well of love. Love is her context. It's in the atmosphere around her. She's also extremely light and funny and enjoys herself enormously. She really seems to have a better time than anybody I know. . . . Over the years I've had many experiences around Baba and Gurumayi, experiences of having my inner state uplifted, transformed, from a state of relative contraction and separation to a state of love and clarity and unity. It's happened so often that I've come to take it for granted that my state of being is affected by theirs.

As for Durgananda's decision to look for happiness—sparked by a conversation with a friend in 1972 in which she heard herself making the unorthodox remark, "I always thought you were supposed to be happy"—she claims to have found at least the variety of happiness that is separable from day-to-day ups and downs and reversals, primarily through meditating for at least an hour a day: "If you shake up a Coke bottle, it gets full of bubbles and fizz. But if you just let it sit for awhile, the fizz dies down and you can drink the Coke. It's the same with the mind when we're thinking or taking in a lot of stimulating input. It gets agitated, fizzy. When we sit for meditation, if we just sit quietly for a while, the fizz will settle. The inner static calms down on its own if you just give it time. That's when meditative states arise."

Of her sacrifice of romantic, and married, love—the very stuff of the traditional feminine mystique—she also claims to have become quite adjusted. "By the time I gave them up, I'd pretty much tasted them," she told me, almost nonchalantly. "I saw their limitations for me. Couple relationships are a great part of the path for many people. For me, they tended to be obstructive. Of course, any choice you make in life has its pros and cons. When you give up partnership relationships you also give up a certain kind of intimacy. But you gain a lot of freedom, and you also experience a wider, less exclusive form of love."

Working some of the same theological territory as Gurumayi, and coming as well from an Indian cultural background, Deepak Chopra has created a spiritual atmosphere for his sympathetic readers and followers that feels quite different from Siddha Yoga's. The single most important difference in mood and emphasis is his avoidance of the central role of guru. By dispensing with the charged relationship of a divine teacher and worshipful student he has also done away with much of the shadow side of gurus and ashrams, including sexual scandal, murky transfers of power, and financial impropriety, as well as with some of the deep and more irrationally compelling stuff of religious tradition. That is, while Chopra may have followers, he doesn't have a Swami Durgananda who is absolutely obedient and dependent on him for grace. And while he's controversial, he's relatively scandal-free.

"Deepak is a visionary, but he's not a guru," says Gayle Rose, a former CEO of his for-profit organization, Infinite Possibilities. (The organization's name was taken from a phrase used by Krishna in the *Bhagavad Gita*.) "He's never claimed to be enlightened himself. A guru tends to devote his entire life to spiritual experience. Deepak is more of a messenger. There's no one on earth who can speak the way he can. Some people ask for pictures of him to put on their wall. He would *freak* if we ever sold a picture of him. Rather, he starts from a very scientific perspective. He's unattached to guru tradition."

Chopra revealed to me that he'd thought at length about his departure from the ways of his own guru, Maharishi Mahesh Yogi, who introduced a scientific perspective to TM yet remained removed from ordinary humans by claiming to be an enlightened being. The maharishi's solution was halfway between the Indian tradition and Chopra's own entirely secular operation. "If you talked to somebody who's involved with one of these guru movements, they might superficially admire what I'm doing, but they would still treat what I'm doing as not deep enough," Chopra explained. "The way their psychology works, they need a guru. It's like a dependency. In the West for thirty or forty years now one guru after another has come, been embraced, put on a pedestal, had an image created, and then the image is defiled sooner or later by scandals and rumors. But the hard-core people aren't affected by that. I personally think that the problem isn't with the guru but with the people who set them up. Also, in India, you don't question the guru's paradoxical behavior. A lot of these scandalous things could be happening in India as well, but they don't care."

Unlike most Americans, Chopra grew up with the guru system as a part of life. He describes his mother as a "shopper," who entertained different gurus for different occasions. His family did maintain one family guru, as did most Indian families, who was supported and passed on: "Just as you pass on family heirlooms, you passed on the guru, too." When he was in medical school, his professor performed EKG experiments on gurus deep in meditation. "As recently as five years ago, I went to Rishikesh with an Indian friend who's now a professor at MIT," said Chopra. "We went to this house, and in the twilight you could see an old man sitting naked on the veranda. My friend, who is normally a very sophisticated Harvard Bostonite, ran from the car and prostrated himself before this guru. That's how he'd been raised as a child, and it brought back to him whatever emotions were associated. This guru was ninety-five, and half senile. But to my friend he was God."

In place of this ancient system to which he'd been exposed in its old-fashioned and completely indigenous form as a child, and in a more Westernized adaptation as an adult, Chopra has come up with his own two revisions, or updatings. Instead of an ashram he has put together a hybrid of a medical clinic and a day spa based on the principles of Ayurvedic medicine, the Center for Well Being. And using ancient Vedic texts—many of them untranslated or poorly translated—he's spun a series of best-selling books in the self-help genre. "All my books are based on Vedanta," he admits. "There's not a single one of my books that hasn't borrowed from the Vedanta, and I'm talking about twenty-three books including fiction, including *The Return of Merlin.* Whatever I've written, you can find in one of the *Upanishads.*"

He developed the basic blueprint for the Center for Well Being in the late 1980s at the maharishi's Ayurvedic center in Lexington, Massachusetts. The center was located in the Thayer Spring House mansion, formerly belonging to the Vanderbilt family's East Coast banker, and provided space for twelve patients in a beautiful, opulent, and intimate setting, with no TV and no phones. The treatments were standard *panchakarma,* purification and rejuvenation treatments of oils, massage, enemas, healthy diet, and yoga—or "neuromuscular integration," as it was labeled. Chopra's picture was on the cover of *Harvard Magazine* for his work in Lexington, and he soon began to attract some of the celebrity clients he's become known for. Calvin Klein, for instance, was an early guest.

One of those who sought Chopra's help after seeing the *Harvard* article was Gayle Rose. She was, at that time, living in Nashville, and was married to Michael Rose, the chairman and CEO of Holiday Inn Worldwide, with whom she had three children, and from whom she was divorced in 1995. A former Miss Tennessee, Rose was suffering from a rare and inexplicable case of cardiac arrhythmia. "When I finally went to Deepak, the first question he asked me was, 'Are you happy?' I wondered if he really meant it. I said, 'I don't know.' He said, 'Soon you will.' " She attributes her eventual cure to Chopra. "There's one medical category of stress-induced ventricular cathocardia," explains Dr. Stephen Bieckel, who served as CEO of Chopra's Infinite Possibilities from 1995 to 1996 and is a neuroendocrinologist trained at Rush Medical College. "That's probably what Gail had. When you see the kinds of rhythms she had over and over, and to have been in the intensive-care unit, and then have the condition go away, that's pretty remarkable. In a clinical study, though, it would be very hard to prove or disprove that what happened to her was real." Since that experience, Rose had been committed to Chopra's cause, occasionally even as a business partner.

Another key player has been Dr. David Simon, the medical director and co-founder of the Center for Well Being. A neurologist and practitioner of TM since his days at the University of Chicago medical school, Simon became chief of staff of Sharp Hospital, a large medical complex near San Diego. In 1993, he invited Chopra to become executive director of the Sharp Institute for Human Potential and Mind/Body Medicine. "When we invited him he wasn't really well known," says Simon. "Then he went on Oprah Winfrey's show and became an overnight household word. He hadn't even arrived here yet and we were overwhelmed with thousands of calls, every day." This interest eventually led to the opening of a treatment facility called the Center for Mind-Body Medicine, which charged $1,125 to $3,200 for its week-long "purification program." Chopra also began marketing seminars, books, and herbal products through Quantum Publications, a company owned by him and his family. Most of these products were distributed under the brand name "Ageless Body, Timeless Mind." His private treatment center was briefly relocated to a wing of the L'Auberge Del Mar Resort.

In October 1996, the Center for Well Being relocated its headquarters to 7630 Fay Avenue, in La Jolla. This area is nicknamed "the Monte Carlo of California," and is known for its curving beaches, palm-lined promenades, million-dollar homes designed by important architects such as Frank Lloyd Wright and Irving Gill, and a cluster of high-tech research-and-development companies attracted by the facilities of the University of California at San Diego, the Scripps Institute of Oceanography, and the Salk Institute, designed by Louis Kahn. A particularly futuristic enclave in La Jolla is Michael Graves's Aventine complex. Far humbler is the two-story stucco building housing the center, where on my first visit I observed a teenage girl roller-blading by commenting to her friend in perfect *Clueless* diction, "What is it? A cult or something?"

The center's interior communicates friendly wealth and somewhat unfocused luxury rather than cultic intensity. At a front reception desk with a fashionable glass mosaic top, American Express cards are swiped regularly as clients show up for a la carte facials and massages, or for more committed three- or seven-day Ayurvedic treatments. (The three-day rejuvenation program costs $1,250; the unabridged seven-day version, $2,900.) Adjoining the reception area is the usually sun-dappled Quantum Soup Cafe and Infinite Possibilities Bookstore, where all of Chopra's books and tapes, related books on religion, health, and spirituality, and a rack of bottled Aveda scents are on sale. From a nearby creamy gold-and-butterscotch hallway filters the sound of splashing water from a fountain of Ganesh.

The center is laid out in blocks of organically colored rooms, each with a specific function. Guests who've signed up for complete programs follow itineraries that lead them all week through green hallways filled with sconces, cast-iron columns, and alabaster lamps, which lead to a bank of sterile examination rooms; an insulated meditation room, stuffed with gold brocade pillows; the food court; the library, with its Brompton sofa and Victorian milk-glass floor lamp; and the *panchakarma* treatment rooms, each seductively named after one of Chopra's laws of spiritual success. All of the center's textured interiors, which rely mostly on sea colors or sunset pinks and amber, were styled by Paulette Cole, partner and creative director of New York's ABC Carpet and Home.

When I followed the Ayurvedic regimen at the center for a week in March 1997, my fellow dozen or so "patients" were all women except for one buff young gym owner from Aruba. He was attending with his mother, who had just arrived from a Tony Robbins seminar in Denver, where she'd walked on hot coals. (Tony Robbins is another La Jolla resident.) The women were as mixed in type as the cast of any murder mystery or plane-crash movie: a Turkish woman from Istanbul and her daughter in her early twenties; an actress from Los Angeles; a manager of a lodge in Billings,

Montana; a health-food-store owner from Jackson Hole, Wyoming; and two lady friends from Las Vegas. Most of them simply complained of being "stressed out," but a few had medical issues, such as the businesswoman in the software industry who had been diagnosed with breast cancer: to her great disappointment, the doctors at the center advised her to go forward with the operation her own specialists had recommended. (Fitting this general profile—four years later—were Ruth McCourt, forty-five, and Paige Hackel, forty-six, two friends taking separate planes from Boston on their way to the Center for Well Being on September 11, 2001. Both were killed when their planes were separately commandeered by the terrorists who crashed into the World Trade Towers. Hackel, who'd recovered from drug and alcohol addiction, was described by a friend as "deeply spiritual.")

To arrive at treatments appropriate for various ailments and tendencies, a consultation was set up on the first day, after yoga class, with a staff of doctors, to decide to which of the three doshas, or body-mind types, we belonged: Kapha (solid, stable, earthy), Vata (quick, changeable, airy), or Pitta (intense, sharp, fiery). Crucial to this decision was a detailed questionnaire about quickness of temper, condition of skin, and eating and sleeping habits. Each of these types carries its own dietary requirements (Kaphas thrive on red-lentil dahl, Pittas on spinach soup), treatments (Pittas require rose and jasmine, Vatas orange and clove), and life lessons (unbalanced Vatas tend to snap, Kaphas to withdraw). In practice, the doshas quickly became retreads of the astrological signs; they were continuously the stuff of leading questions among the guests: "What dosha are you?" My doctor concluded that I was tridoshal, or a mixture of all three, her diagnosis bolstered with traditional medical instruments: stethoscope, blood test, cholesterol count.

Each afternoon's regimen of *panchakarma* treatments was carried out by a staff of young, centered types in white smocks, beginning with an *abhyanga* massage, in which the full body was kneaded from head to toe five times in succession as oil was worked into the tissues. *Udvaranta,* exclusively for Kapphas, involved a massage of the heart area with a paste made from more than twenty ingredients, including garbanzo and barley flour. "Vital touch" massage enlivened "marma points," which follow the basic map of Chinese acupuncture points. I was apparently in need of all things oily and rich. In *shirodhara,* a treatment for madness in India, warm sesame oils were dripped over my forehead for a half hour until I went into a mental orbit, imagining I was thinking someone else's thoughts. (A woman at the laundry? A soldier?) In *pizichilli,* for seventy minutes two attendants simultaneously massaged and poured over me more than a gallon of oils—blended from sesame, almond, and sunflowers and slowly heated in a Crock-Pot—until I resembled a human candy bar. A young woman who looked like Siddhartha, with severely chopped black hair, prayed over and touched different spots on my quivering body, which was covered in a light cotton sheet, as part of an energy-balancing treatment concentrated on the third eye, the heart, and the stomach.

Bastis, herbal water-and-oil-based enemas, elicited nervous giggles from just about everyone. These are gentle, noncolonic treatments for elimination and cleansing, or for nourishing the reproductive or immune systems. One is expected to rest with them for fifteen or twenty minutes, but I found myself more than once in a bathrobe, compromised, hurrying through the hallway, my hair slick with sesame oil or wrapped in a turban, passing other vulnerable guests on my way to the nearest rest station. For a surcharge of $115 there was the center's popular "bliss facial," which combines the usual needle in the nose to root out blackheads with foot rubs of Tibetan paste. My facialist was an ex–fashion model with blond dreadlocks who snapped her fingers and whooshed her hands over my chest to discharge "blocked energy." "You're going to go on a trip now with Deepak, and I'm going to be right here with you," she whispered while slipping a cassette into a boom box and handing me a round hand mirror to stare at my face. Chopra's voice then led me into an examination of my own skin, eyes, eyebrows, lips, and nose. "Now put the mirror aside," his undulating voice instructed eventually. "Close your eyes and feel the bones, ears, eyelids." "All is illusion," he concluded, having magically spun a cosmetic facial into a post-Einsteinian sermon, explaining that the face actually consists of constantly changing molecules and electrons existing at the subatomic level.

This very southern Californian style of pleasurable, if sometimes overly tender-minded, thinking was carried through to even more exaggerated effect at a special event one evening, during which Jill Eikenberry and Michael Tucker, of *L.A. Law,* presented their findings—seminar-style—on how they'd saved their marriage through the practice of Tantric Yoga. Eikenberry explained how she and Michael had come to find and appreciate her "sacred spot." Key to their entire enterprise, apparently, was her "fountaining," a noun turned into a verb to describe one of their breakthrough practices. She clarified for us that "orgasm is not an event, but an ongoing state of being." It was a session of very adult entertainment. But then Chopra himself had boldly stated his own belief in the compatibility of sex and spirituality in three rules in an article titled "Does God Have Orgasms?" in the January 1997 issue of *Playboy* magazine: *"Sex is itself spiritual, because flesh and spirit are one; God is in every orgasm; the creative energy of the universe is sexual."*

The cumulative effect of these Americanized Ayurvedic treatments and lessons was somewhere between harmless and beneficial. As Dr. Bieckel told me at the time, "At the center we're trying to break down the distinctions between looking at your health as different from looking at your life." Much of the advice was common sense, like Grandma's voice, repackaged: early to bed, early to rise; chew your food slowly; smell the flowers. We were urged to be in bed before 10:30 every night; to be up by 6:00; to walk barefoot on the beach daily; to avoid television and tabloid newspapers; to breathe deeply and bring our attention back to ourselves whenever stress and anxiety began to surface. Whatever directive there was for someone to become a follower of Chopra's Ayurvedic path—in the way that you could be a dutiful follower of Siddha Yoga by daily chanting of *Om Namah Shivaya* or keeping postcards of Gurumayi on your bureau or dashboard and tapes of her inspirational talks playing as you drive—simply involved following, upon your return home, these basic rules of sleep, diet, exercise, and meditation.

Where Chopra has come under attack and scrutiny, though, has been rather in the shadier, crosshatched gray territory where New Age–style positive thinking could be construed as definite medical claims. Chopra has purposely not transferred his license to practice medicine to California, leaving any actual diagnoses to practicing doctors on his staff and thus protecting himself from any disgruntled, litigious patients. Yet still he can provoke ire. "If you take a medical oath and then give up your license, that's a major statement coming from a physician," said Dr. John Renner, who died in 2000 following emergency heart surgery, but in 1998 was still a family physician in Independence, Missouri, and president of the National Council for Reliable Health Information. "It's as if a major surgeon gave up performing surgery in order to heal through finger painting. Well, his prior expertise in surgery shouldn't affect the way we judge him as an art therapist. . . . The public is made up of patients with different illnesses. The first question to be asked of someone who's offering up a cure is what the cure *doesn't* deal with. Is it good for breast cancer? Is it good for AIDS? When I meet someone who says they can operate on any part of the body, I take them off my list of 'recommended physicians.' And that's basically what he's doing. . . . By not being licensed anymore, he's insulated himself from the rest of the medical community so that he's not held accountable." (Listed as well on "Nonrecommended Sources of Health Advice" posted online by a member of the board of Renner's National Council for Reliable Health Information was Andrew Weil, M.D., a graduate of Harvard Medical School who argues for integrating Western medicine and alternative medicine in his most recent best-selling books, *Spontaneous Healing* and *8 Weeks to Optimum Health*.)

"Deepak Chopra is the most dangerous man on the planet," concurs James Randi. Known as "The Amazing Randi," a MacArthur Fellow and the author of numerous books debunking psychics and frauds, he is perhaps Chopra's severest and most hyperbolic critic. "He sells quackery. He sells medieval medicine dressed up misleadingly in the terminology of modern science and medicine with all this talk about 'photons' and 'quantum physics.' Now, he's an M.D., so he knows better. He knows what he's saying doesn't make sense. But he's becoming a multimillionaire by playing dumb. It's all feel-good stuff. My mother used to say 'Go take a nap, you'll feel better.' And I did feel better. But she didn't say she was an Indian guru with a Ph.D. Why should we pay huge amounts of money for someone to tell us what our common sense tells us already?"

As Chopra pushes into the field of entertainment and away from medical practice, the more exempt he is from charges of malpractice or scientific misrepresentation. His increasing success, however, continues to bother those for whom spirituality and wealth don't properly coexist, or for those who see his spirituality as commercialism disguised for personal gain. This is one of the main resentments directed against Gurumayi as well, and is a topic on which Chopra is particularly passionate. "In India, too, this thing was so hammered in: that if you want to be spiritual, you can't be rich," he complained to me. "You see how poor India is. That's a good example of it." Comfortably escaping the karma of his homeland, Chopra has estimated that his various businesses have made him between $10 million and $15 million a year—not all of which he keeps, since he's known to be a lavish donor to charities.

Chopra stresses, however, that getting rich is not his top priority. "I do not take any income from the Chopra Center, nor do I take any income from the workshops I give through the center whether these workshops are in San Diego or elsewhere such as the workshop you came to in Goa," he wrote to me. "Since the center has always lost money I have subsidized its activities over the years and poured in several million dollars to keep it going because I believe it is a practical expression of the things I teach in my books. I do not believe in savings because I believe that wealth is a state of consciousness and not the amount of money that you have in the bank. Therefore I have always spent what I have earned trusting that I can create the amount of money that I need when I need it. So far this philosophy has worked. My promoters cover my travels. I travel first class and stay in first-class hotels but all this is taken care of by the people who invite me. I live in a very comfortable home in La Jolla but it is by no means extravagant or lavish. I drive a four-year-old Range Rover. Most of my physician friends including cardiologists and plastic surgeons live a much more lavish lifestyle than I do."

Chopra's favorite crystallization of his teachings and interests these days is titled "SychroDestiny—Enlightened Leadership for Personal and Professional Success," an exclusive three-day seminar costing more than $5,000 per person and limited to about thirty participants, with whom he shares his notions in talks and awareness exercises. It's sort of his advanced class, his Eagle Scouts group; it is made up of proven disciples both of Chopra's message and of worldly success, since only the most elite seekers have the time and cash to attend such an event. I participated in a session in October 1998, with a former film-studio head; the founder of a record label and independent-film production company; a twenty-something actress about to appear on an episode of *Beverly Hills 90210;* a businessman controlling a significant amount of stock in Disney; a producer for New Line Cinema; the wife of the CEO of a major video-rental chain; a Broadway singer and dancer; a Scottish entrepreneur specializing in theme parks; a health-care professional from Boston; two filmmakers documenting Chopra for public television; a young composer of music for video games, from Vancouver; and a venture capitalist who spent much time on his cell phone or reading *The 22 Immutable Laws of Marketing.*

Each morning at 7:30 our group gathered in the comfortable main room on the first floor of the center. Chopra scribbled lists on an overhead projector in red and blue Magic Markers, quantifying the "Qualities of Spirit" or "Characteristics of Self-Actualized People," and he spoke so fast and so extemporaneously that even the more studious types were hard put to write down notes quickly enough in their "SynchroDestiny Handbooks." We sat in a semicircle of chairs, Navajo blankets, and tan pillows in a beige-carpeted room outfitted with candles, an Oriental gong, tall green plants, alabaster ceiling lamps, a CD player, a carved Indian wooden chest, and, on the wall, a large colorful *thangka* painting by a young Tibetan artist being promoted by Chopra, Romio Shrestha, from Katmandu.

"This lecture really began to incubate in Colombia twelve years ago," Chopra explained. "I was having dinner with the CEO of Avianca Airlines. Just that day there had been a crash of a commuter airliner, and it was on the television stations. He'd been interviewed about whether the plane had been properly checked before, and what had happened in the air control tower. He said to me, 'You know, whenever anything like this happens, it's a conspiracy of improbabilities. Whatever could have gone wrong, went wrong.' Well, in the spiritual world there are also these conspiracies of improbabilities. These are what we are going to learn to pay attention to this week. Whenever there's a pattern interrupt in the field, that's when we should pay special attention. Be alert to the conspiracy of anything that breaks the pattern." Chopra, in his black polo shirt and sweats, and silver-black Nikes, went on to relate this "conspiracy of improbabilities"—and, by extension, "Synchrodestiny"—to all the various chance meetings and coincidences meant to be significant if the universe is as meaningful and magical as Chopra preaches: "When you start to experience synchrodestiny consciously, it's what is called in Christianity 'the state of grace.' "

In practice, the SynchroDestiny seminar was a sort of cosmic networking session. "Everyone here has a karmic connection, or you wouldn't be here," he told us. "It would be very magical if in the next two days we can discover what the connection is. Because that karmic connection is significant." Each participant was then paired with a stranger and given a day to find out their "karmic connection." During the evenings, we cast our fortunes using the ancient Chinese book of fortunes, *I Ching,* as well as tossing Celtic runes. During sessions we wrote down troublesome thoughts and shared them with a partner. On the last day, we enacted a ritual of retrieving a stone from a central pail while silently investing it with "intention"—that is, making a wish. A class portrait was taken that final morning by a professional photographer and mailed to all the participants two weeks later.

Over the three days Chopra gave six talks: "Understanding Conscious Energy Fields"; "Understanding Cosmic Connections"; "Making Use of the Conspiracy of Improbabililites"; "Understanding the Role of Inner Dialogue"; "Using Emotional Turbulence to Our Advantage"; and "Using the Organizing Power of Intent as Structured in Spirit." Because of the disproportionate Hollywood presence in the room, there were many analogies to the world of spirit drawn from TV, movies, and big business. One of the producers present asked, for instance, "Why is it that nine people are making movies about the Dalai Lama. For a hundred years nobody wanted to make movies about the Dalai Lama." Chopra answered, "Because sychrodestiny is a manifestation of the suborder of being."

Chopra also used as one of his many examples of spiritual warriors the founder of Sony, Masaru Ibuka, whom Chopra claimed would consider a proposed business deal by swallowing an herbal pill and seeing how it felt when digested. "He would literally swallow the deal," explained Chopra. "That's a ritual. Ritual traps your attention. In the corporate world that's what's missing. You use the ritual to step outside the condition, to step outside the box." Having been asked by a group of NBC television executives just a week before to give a talk to help with their ratings drop, he said he'd advised them, "Start an in-house course on mythology." (The talk was then linked in the *Washington Post* to the firing of many of those same top executives the following week.)

More revealing of the concocted magic behind the wizard's curtain was my one-on-one conversation that weekend with Chopra in his office, when we talked about the Vedic underpinnings of his enterprise—the subtext, as it were, of his best-selling prose, the Sanskrit between the lines. Chopra relaxed behind a large wooden desk, on which rested a metal statue of a Hindu goddess and a huge blue Webster's dictionary. The room was comfortably filled with Indian rugs and hanging tapestry. Chopra pointed to the top shelf of a bookcase on the opposite wall, where there was a row of small, handsome hardbound books containing portions of the *Vedas.* "It's like a gold mine for me," he said. "Here's this immense amount of literature that is very poorly translated in English. And 99.9 percent of humanity is totally unaware that it even exists. In India also there is a great deal of misconception about it. I felt I was in the lucky position of taking some seemingly esoteric and far-out literature and making it mainstream."

"There is a bookstore in New Delhi on Barakhamba Road," he went on, "which has enough books to fill a library on every single aspect of Vedic literature. Most of the books are in Hindi, which I can read. Some have very poor English translations. I go and buy books from India, and then I put that material in my own language. A lot of stuff in there is totally junk. But there are some kernels of wisdom too. So you have to be selective in what you pick out. If you look at Vedic literature, a lot of it is homophobic, it's sexist, it's ethnocentric, it's bigoted. I just ignore that and look for what I want." He did pull down one of a series of thin commentaries on the *Vedas* that certainly looked remarkably in format like his *Seven Laws* series: small, easy-to-read, divided logically into answers to numbered questions.

Peter Guzzardi, his editor at Crown, and "the godmother to my whole career," his longtime agent in Washington, D.C., Muriel Nellis, have been crucial to his literary success. However, one recent deal, for *Lords of Light,* a "thriller for the millennium" published in 1999 by St. Martin's Press, was handled by Robert Gottlieb, then at the William Morris Agency. The rationalization for the switch was that the new genre of science fiction was not covered under his contracts negotiated by Nellis with Crown, an imprint of Random House. Persistent rumors that such output could only be explained by the use of ghostwriters were denied by one of Chopra's freelance "editorial team," who insisted nervously on anonymity when he spoke to me. "I can't talk about the internal dynamics," he said. "I know it makes it seem there's something sinister, and there's actually not. It's not any kind of sham. I'd say that it's basically editorial work, but I'm not allowed to even say that. It's not his rule. It's the publishers. They regard Deepak as a brand. He's an important author, and a celebrity, and they try to protect him."

For Chopra, Vedantism—the essence of the sources from which he's drawn—constitutes a sort of inside track of spirituality for those seekers who've been around. "The classical traditional Judeo-Christian idea of God is basically a dead white male floating somewhere in space, and we're not happy with that anymore," he said. "So then people look at Buddhism, and it's very sexy. It's built on compassion. There's no personal God. There's reincarnation. There's basically more humanity. So it satisfies people even more. Then you go deeper to Vedanta and it's quite abstract and can take you to lofty heights of intellectual gamesmanship. So if you're intellectual and you're smart, or think you are, you'll want to go beyond Buddhism into that. In the end, I can tell you, none of them has the answers. But Vedanta is certainly more sophisticated than anything else." Chopra is expecting a spirituality of freedom and enlightenment to take hold in the future on a mass-market scale, as perennial ideas become "seeded so fast in the collective psyche" as to reach critical mass. "In the past, spirituality gave enlightenment to a few luminaries, and we honor them in history books," he said. "But today that knowledge can immediately feed the collective psyche. Never before did we have that ability."

Still, Chopra retains some of his fascination for and adherence to the tradition. He told me excitedly that after an upcoming nine-day trip down the Nile planned for that December—trailed by a camera crew—he would be going off to the north of India near the Himalyas to receive the blessing of the *shankaracharya* of Jyotirmath, the current leader of the strain of Vedantism expressed by the seventh-century Shankara in his *Jewel-Crest of Discrimination.* Shankara's was the linage of nondualistic philosophers to which the Maharishi Mahesh Yogi eventually belonged, and so Chopra's acceptance amounted to a seal of approval and a healing of a theological Oedipal split. "He's like the pope," Chopra explained to me of the *shankaracharya*. "I kind of broke away from all of them and went on my own. And now they're saying, 'Oh, you're one of us.' So it's nice to be invited into the fold—not that I'm going to do anything differently."

Having met only once, Gurumayi and Chopra would probably not enjoy being compared, and Chopra declined to comment directly on her rather than on the general phenomenon of gurus in America. For disciples of Siddha Yoga, though, Chopra tends to be discussed around tables at Gurumayi's Atma Cafe as a lightweight New Age phenomenon, a doctor, but certainly someone incapable of direct transmission of *shakti*. For Chopra's usual followers, a portion of whom are doctors and scientists, the Siddha Yoga tradition has been saturated in ancient superstition. That both are Vedantists in their metaphysical orientation—Gurumayi through the Kashmir Shaivist tradition as taught by Swami Muktananda, Chopra through the Shankarite philosophy espoused by Maharishi Mahesh Yogi—is a largely submerged and only dimly understood factor for most of their American devotees or readers and supporters.

Where they merge in experience, rather than theology, is in the general perception that celebrity and power somehow raise the visibility of both. In Chopra's case, his celebrity support is even more easily underlined, as so many famous names have been listed as advisors—Demi Moore, Naomi Judd, George Harrison. Others of his devotees have included Michael Jackson, Michael Milken, Linda Gray, and Olivia Newton-John. Donna Karan, with whom he's often seen in paparazzi photos, used Chopra's *Gift of Love* as runway music for her fall 1998 fashion show. Madonna was rumored, when I was at the center, to be one of those sailing down the Nile in mid-December on Chopra's yacht of a barge.

Chopra has also attracted some powerful businessmen to his brand of spirituality. Considering sharing fiscal responsibility briefly for Infinite Possibilities with Gayle Rose, for instance, was Ray Chambers, a tall, handsome, preppy-appearing, sometimes exceedingly shy philanthropist, who made most of his fortune in mergers and acquisitions in the Wesray Corporation, begun in 1979 with his partner, William E. Simon, former secretary of the treasury under President Nixon. In an effort to revitalize his hometown of Newark, Chambers has backed a mentoring program for underprivileged youth. He has also funded, with $12 million, the Newark Arts Center, which opened in October 1997, and is the leading partner in a consortium that purchased the Nets basketball team in December 1998 as part of a larger plan to build a sports center in downtown Newark. Though he has never entered into a definite business relationship with Chopra, his interest in his teachings led him to fly Chopra and George Harrison to India to meet with Maharishi Mahesh Yogi, and he bought an apartment on the beach in La Jolla to be able to conveniently meet with Chopra and attend more events at the center. (A condo-style "community" in southern California has increasingly become one of Chopra's wishful themes.) Evidence of Chambers's involvement with others as a sort of spiritual businessman was the acknowledgment in Don Miguel Ruiz's *The Four Agreements:* "I am also abidingly grateful to Ray Chambers for lighting the way."

Why such Hindu-based, Indian spiritual leaders as Gurumayi and Deepak Chopra should animate a scene peopled with an above-average number of celebrities is, in the end, a mystery. In its colorful panoply, though, there is something of a Bollywood film about their intentional communities, whether at the ashram or in a tent in India or on a yacht going down the Nile. No heaven is busier, after all, than the Hindu firmament. Perhaps Hollywood, with its celebrity system and star-making industry, is not so far in temperament from that of this heterodox Indian spirituality that finds no single god, but looks rather for the numinous in personal charisma, beauty, and, above all, holiness, wherever and whenever expressed. The American manifestation of this sensibility is of course mostly confined—excluding immigrants and their families—to those self-selected ones who are open to the foreign and exotic, and who are generally more traveled than the poorer

Indian devotee who is only unawaredly rather than self-consciously costumed or cinematic.

A few weeks after the SynchroDestiny seminar, I talked with Chopra on the phone. I told him of my luck in having one of the people who'd attended the event offer me a ride from a small airport near San Diego to the Morristown Municipal Airport in New Jersey on his private Gulfstream-IV jet—outfitted with panoramic windows, tan leather seats for eight, and a separate cabin for viewing videos.

"Oh yes, I saw you, actually, at the airport," Chopra revealed, sounding pleased by evidence that we were indeed linked by our synchronous destinies, with a little help from his seminar.

Then he added, "That is definitely an example of simultaneous actualization of information from the submanifestation of being in different space-time locations. I love it!"

Becoming clearer to me in Chopra's upbeat tone of voice that morning—and during the course of all of our conversations and experiences over a year and a half—was the manner in which for him, and perhaps for other Hindu imports as well, the exotic beauty of the temple carvings and numinous power of the gods and goddesses could also be felt, in those making the *Entertainment Weekly* "Year's 100 List" or the Forbes 500. "Karma" could be enfolded with "networking." And events associated with the noble battlefield on which Krishna poured out the secrets of the universe in the *Bhagavad Gita* might very well be relived on a private airstrip.

Three

"Silence Is Spoken Here":
Trappists and Trappistines

"What are you doing here?" a young guy wearing a Levi's jacket and a black Harley Davidson cap, with a skull and rose tattooed on his forearm, asked reasonably enough. He was trying to see over my shoulder to two sisters, both twisted with laughter, almost falling off their bar stools.

"I'm going to the Abbey of Gethsemani," I answered him.

"What's that?" he yelled back, with little apparent interest.

Even though I was obviously a misfit in this tacky cocktail lounge attached to a flatly standard Holiday Inn in Bardstown, Kentucky—located southwest of Lexington, in "Blue Grass Country"—I can't say I wasn't thoroughly enjoying myself sampling several shots of Heaven's Hill, one of the favorite local whiskies. I'd stopped by the bar at the suggestion of the motel desk clerk, who took pity on me when I'd checked in a few hours earlier. "It's Sunday, so our cocktail lounge doesn't open until 7:30," he told me conspiratorially. My imaginings of a quiet neon-lit place with a single jukebox and a few accidental tourists fell far short of the raucous party into which I'd quietly slipped.

On a teeny stage raised only a foot above the shiny linoleum floor was playing, nonstop, an energetic ZZ Top–style band. The band members, with long hair and electric guitars, cranked each of their numbers louder than the last, raising the ante by feeding their enthusiastic, if unfocused, crowd what was obviously their signature tune, which they replicated at least three times that night: Alice Cooper's 1972 hit, "School's Out." By now I'd real-ized that these weren't tourists after all but rather locals in their twenties and thirties dipped deeply in a cultural dye of motorcy-cles, MTV, metal rock, video games, and body art. The noisebox of a room, with its low acoustic ceilings and reddish beer signs on every wall, was jammed with biker types in leather jackets smok-ing cigars or shooting pool, and young women mostly with streaked blond hair and multicolored fingernails. Their temporary clubhouse was charged with the electricity of pickups, though by the time I left, stopping by the front desk to order a wake-up call, the crowd was noticeably denser and no one seemed to really be hooking up.

Promptly at eight o'clock the next morning, September 14—the Feast of the Triumph of the Cross, according to the Roman Catholic liturgical calendar—my cab arrived to make the twelve-mile ride south to my true destination, the contemplative Trap-pist monastery of Our Lady of Gethsemani. All signs of last night's remake of *The Wild Ones* had vanished by the time the cab, a white Chevy driven by a middle-aged woman named Becky, with a large wooden cross hanging solidly from her rearview mir-ror, pulled into what was now a sun-dappled, serene, and peaceful parking lot.

"I just took someone from here to Gethsemani earlier this morning," she informed me in a sweet tone of voice as we pulled out, her round face reflected in the long strip of a mirror. "You'd be surprised how many people my husband and I drive there. We've taken hundreds of people over the years. A lot of them are repeats. They come back every year on their vacation for a week. They make a reservation the day they're leaving for the next year. Same time, same place. . . . It's hard to get a spot, as I guess you know. There's a long waiting list."

Becky went on to provide twenty minutes of tour-guide-style information as we drove through a landscape of rolling hills, dark green trees, and limestone cliffs, taking Route 31E from Bardstown and eventually making a left on Route 247. With very little prodding from me, she filled me in on a number of subjects: the various distilleries for Maker's Mark or Jim Beam that offer free daily tours; the probable influence of limestone-filtered water on the strength of local racehorses' legs; the annual videotaping of the gold bricks in Fort Knox; the Confederate state's legacy of Knob Hill, Lincoln's boyhood home; the importance of Bardstown as the location—along with many other early-nineteenth-century structures—of Federal Hill, the mansion that inspired Stephen Foster's "My Old Kentucky Home."

"Have you ever been to the monastery before?"

"Yes, briefly, twenty years ago," I answered weakly, glancing out the window to avoid having to tell the story.

"Have you read Thomas Merton?" she fast-forwarded. "He was the most famous monk ever at Gethsemani. And a wonderful writer."

"Yes," I answered, spinning the word out enthusiastically.

I had of course read Thomas Merton—a common reference for nonbikers in these parts, I soon discovered—beginning, as had most of his readers, with *The Seven Storey Mountain* (or *Elected Silence,* in England), first published in 1948. This perennially popular autobiography was a tale of radical conversion, a sort of modern Saint Augustine's *Confessions,* tracing Merton's transformation from an unruly undergrad at Clare College, in Cambridge, from which he was expelled (for fathering an illegitimate child by a chambermaid, a fact left out of the account) to a poet and writer among a sophisticated set of students at Columbia College in the mid-1930s that included the painter Ad Reinhardt, the novelist Herman Wouk, and the poet John Berryman, to a teacher of English literature at St. Bonaventure College, in Olean, New York, to, finally, a monk at Gethsemani, which he joined as a postulant on December 10, 1941, at the age of twenty-six. The title of his book was a jazzy evocation of the seven terraces of Dante's Mount of Purgatory, where the seven deadly sins are gradually purged, fitting in with his sense of the monastery as an institution for transformation. "The monastery is a school—a school in which we learn from God how to be happy," he'd optimistically written.

Merton's account, which he'd been ordered to produce while a novice as an act of obedience by his abbot, Dom Frederic Dunne, was edited by his Columbia classmate, Robert Giroux, then a junior editor at Harcourt Brace & Company. It went on to be a surprise "sleeper," selling millions of copies, including paperback editions and translations. The buzz surrounding its publication was intense, though Giroux received one piece of hate mail complaining, "Tell this talking Trappist who took a vow of silence to shut up!" During his lifetime, Merton continued to publish parts of what he seemed to consider a continuing autobiography in poems and essays, and he kept extensive private journals and notebooks and corresponded with many friends and colleagues, including Boris Pasternak in Russia, Czeslaw Milosz in Poland, Abraham Joshua Heschel at the Jewish Theological Seminary in New York, and Canon A. M. Allchin at Canterbury. The subjects of his subsequent books—which Becky, my taxi driver, hadn't read—were almost dizzyingly diverse and occasionally uneven. There were biographies of saints, *The Last of the Fathers: Saint Bernard of Clairvaux and the Encyclical Letter "Doctor Mellifluus"* (1954); monastic history, *Guide to Cistercian Life* (1948); mystical theology, *The Ascent to Truth* (1951); studies of the psalms, *Praying the Psalms* (1956); and of the Desert Fathers, *The Wisdom of the Desert* (1960); essays on Oriental religions, *Mystics and Zen Masters* (1967); and on contemporary problems such as war and racial injustice, *Faith and Violence* (1968). As he'd complained to a religious sister: "People are now convinced that I secrete articles like perspiration." Merton died in Bangkok, Thailand, on December 10, 1968, the twenty-seventh anniversary of his entrance to the monastery. He was electrocuted by a faulty wire from an electric fan at the Oriental Hotel, where he'd just given an address on "Marxism and Monastic Perspectives" to a conference of Asian monks and nuns.

The unspoken answer to Becky's earlier question was that besides having read about Gethsemani in high school in Merton's book, I had visited for three days in the summer of 1976, days that remained mostly as a sunny blur in my memory. At that time I was in the middle of an unusual six-month stint as a member of a group called the Trees, an experimental semimonastic community of eight to ten young men and women affiliated with the Cathedral of St. John the Divine in New York City. We lived in a three-bedroom apartment on West 110th Street, one bedroom with bunks for the men, one for the women, and the third for the chapel, where we emulated the monastic daily offices of prayer. The group supported itself by visiting monasteries, convents, and churches across the country in a big old school bus, nicknamed "Athanasius" for the stalwart fourth-century church father. We performed a "musical meditation" titled "The Christ Tree," which was a presentation of the psalms using liturgical theater and world instruments such as harps, gongs, Mexican prayer wheels, sitar, clarinet, and shenai. A recording was issued by Pomegranate Records in 1975 in which the monks of Gethsemani were thanked in the liner notes, and it included a portion of them singing a free-fall chord. By the end of the summer of 1976, the Trees, inspired mainly by a charismatic leader named William "Shipen" Lebzelter, disbanded, and all of us went our separate ways.

While my first visit with the group to Gethsemani came at the tail end of their existence and didn't include performing for the monks, the impact of their earlier visits was still palpable. It was less than a decade after Merton's death, and with the sentiments of the 1960s and the church reforms of Vatican II still fresh, the monks had formed a romantic attachment to the group as embodying a life of free-spirited ministry they felt they perhaps should be emulating. In return, the group imagined the monks to be spiritual astronauts of the highest and most rarified order. From such misunderstanding and mutual fascination, a bond of friendship had been formed. On that first visit I had met Brother Mark, a postulant who had been a disciple of Swami Satchidananda, and Brother Lavrans, who built a hermitage where he painted icons for the chapel; both eventually left. Abbot Timothy was still in charge during my second visit (he had just been installed as abbot on my first visit), and his sympathetic memory of the Trees helped him agree to let me visit this time and talk with many of the monks, as well as to share in their traditionally off-limits life. (His title taken from *abba,* Aramaic for "father," the abbot is the community's elected leader and ultimate arbiter, if not enlightened despot.)

In the two decades since my brief visit, I had thought back on the community many times. Gethsemani had become the embodiment, in my memory, of a most compelling road not taken. Certainly there were several times when the option of simplifying life to such an extreme recurred as an attractive alternative— especially in hard times, whether financial, vocational, or personal. My conversations with a few of them during my initial visit fed an adolescent fantasy of delving into the mystical truth with a fellow seeker or even guru. And yet Gethsemani had also been crucial in helping me decide that I was, in the end, more suited to secular life, especially since I'd visited during the 1970s, when so much of the social change and sexual liberation occurring in the outside world was attracting even the monks, and their own medieval lifestyle was being updated with more conversation, more secular contacts, and less Latin. That is, they seemed to be converging with the very society I might have considered abandoning. More than the average number of monks during that decade were "jumping over the wall," as these exits are gingerly referred to within the community.

I knew that the monastery to which I was returning was altered, more pared down. The charming milking of the blue-ribbon herd of purebred holstein-friesian cows I'd witnessed had been discontinued as a money-losing enterprise, with the making of cheese, fruitcake, and fudge remaining as the sole monastic industries. In 1976 there were about a hundred monks. Now there were seventy. An official cutoff age of forty-five for novices was being ignored; new monks tended to be older, or once married, or leaving a career, some even with grown children (the Sunday before I arrived, a sixty-year-old recovered alcoholic, divorced, with children, had taken solemn vows). The average age of the monks had climbed to sixty-four, and only one out of ten of all novices was expected to endure long enough to be buried in the cemetery on the small hill to the west of the church, with its rows of two hundred seventy identical white iron crosses marked only with a monk's religious name and the date of his death. "The past year or so has marked a low ebb in people knocking at the door," Abbot Timothy admitted to me. And he added, compellingly, "But we're not here to keep an institution going. We're here to lead honest lives." (The situation reflects the Roman Catholic Church generally, in which, according to the Center for Applied Research in the Apostolate at Georgetown University, the number of diocesan priests in the United States declined by 15 percent from 1965 to 2000, to 30,607, and the number of nuns and brothers by more than half, to 79,814 and 5,662, respectively.)

New, too, as Becky had pointed out, were the high numbers of those wanting to visit on retreat, both at Gethsemani and at monasteries across the country. When I visited in 1976, the guest rooms were mostly empty, and visitors a bit of a surprise. Now there was a new retreat house with comfortable rooms equipped with private showers, light gray wall-to-wall carpeting, and air-conditioning, and it was booked out as much as a year in advance. St. Joseph's Abbey, in Spencer, Massachusetts—the largest of the Trappist monasteries, with about eighty monks—currently has a policy of only allowing reservations for a minimum of three months in advance, and when I'd left my name on a waiting list and missed a call from the guest master, I'd lost my space. When a journalist for *Time* magazine working on a well-meaning summer piece about vacationing at monasteries in August 1998 called an abbey in Vermont with twenty-nine guest rooms and a waiting list of a year, she was told, to her surprise, "Please don't mention our name. We're overwhelmed." The decline in those willing to commit to a monastic life has been equaled only by the rise in those wanting to visit, taste, and sample. This paradox of rising and falling public interest was probably the greatest shift in the mood of the place. The abbeys were simultaneously dying and trending up.

"Since 1995 there's been an upsurge in popular interest in monastic spirituality," *New York Times* religion reporter Gustav Niebuhr told me in 2001, shortly after returning from a visit to the Abbey of the Holy Trinity, in Utah. "Being inside a Trappist monastery is about as countercultural as you're going to get. But people have also more recently been looking for what they think of as authentic spirituality. There was a lot of experimentation that went on in the United States in the sixties through the eighties. Now there's more of an interest in time-honored spiritual practices. The Trappists are looked at as being authentic, stable. There's a certain amount of literature, too. At the Abbey of the Holy Trinity, you walk in the door and turn to the left and there's a little library full of spiritual classics. You can read Saint Theresa of Avila, Thomas Merton. People who are looking for a sense of spirituality are often readers."

The greatest peak in the Abbey of Gethsemani's popularity had indeed been around the time of the publication of Merton's *Seven Storey Mountain,* though the book's impact couldn't be isolated from the general revival in Roman Catholicism and the monastic life after World War II. Following the war, many *Saving Private Ryan*–type soldiers who had served in the army, navy, and marines repeatedly rang the rope bell at its front gates, some still in uniform, upset enough by what they'd seen to seek permanent sanctuary. The number of committed monks at Gethsemani alone, which had been 63 in 1935, rose to 80 in 1945, peaked at 157 in 1950, then dropped back down to 68 by 1995.

This shift in numbers was not entirely an approval or disapproval rating, however. Beginning in the 1940s, Gethsemani, which had been the first permanent foundation of the French Trappist order in the United States, had to siphon off its numbers to cope with overcrowding. During the most intense period of jamming after 1947, when the monastery was filled with seventy novices—as opposed to one novice, during my visit in 1998—a makeshift framework was built in the cloister courtyard. It was covered with a huge tarpaulin, filled with straw mattresses, and used as a temporary dormitory for fifty monks, many of whom still tell stories of their boots freezing to the floorboards overnight during the bitterly cold winter months.

The new foundations formed to cope with this expansion were called, with a unisexual twist, "daughter houses." In the Trappist filial tradition, monasteries are bound in a kind of obedience to their founding house, Gethsemani itself being the daughter house of the Abbey of Melleray, in France, from which its founding forty-four monks sailed in October 1848. All six of Gethsemani's daughter houses are still operating: Our Lady of the Holy Spirit, in Conyers, Georgia, founded in 1944; Holy Trinity, near Salt Lake City, Utah, 1947; Our Lady of Mepkin, in South Carolina, 1949; Our Lady of Genesee, in upstate New York, 1951; Our Lady of New Clairvaux, in northern California at Vina, 1955; the monastery of Miraflores, near Santiago, Chile, 1966. In total there are now twelve Trappist men's houses in America, and five Trappistine women's houses, with about six hundred monks and nuns altogether. Internationally, 4,350 monks and nuns are living in the order's 162 cloistered monasteries on 6 continents, the growth areas being in the Far East and Africa. (The graph of falling numbers in America is parallel in all the daughter houses. Holy Trinity, founded when the abbot sent thirty-five monks into Mormon country in Utah to build a quadrangle of Quonset huts and establish a farm in a mile-high valley, had as many as eighty resident brothers in the 1950s. By 2001, the community numbered twenty-two, many of them elderly.)

Merton's own first glimpse of Gethsemani, charged with the romance of his search for the grail of his identity, took place when he arrived for an Easter retreat late one evening in April 1941. He wrote in *The Seven Storey Mountain* of his ride from the former Bardstown train junction: "Then suddenly I saw a steeple that shone like silver in the moonlight, growing into sight from behind a rounded knoll. The tires sang on the empty road, and, breathless, I looked at the monastery that was revealed before me as we came over the rise. At the end of an avenue of trees was a big rectangular block of buildings, all dark, with a church crowned by a tower and a steeple and a cross: and the steeple was as bright as platinum and the whole place was as quiet as midnight and lost in the all-absorbing silence and solitude of the fields. Behind the monastery was a dark curtain of woods, and over to the west was a wooded valley, and beyond that a rampart of wooded hills, a barrier and a defence against the world." This "us-against-them" dividing of monastery from world was crucial for the young Merton's attraction, as for many of the monks during that time of political and economic crisis. (Merton himself was not involved in the war, since he had been classified "1-B," or noncombatant, because of problems with his teeth.)

My own return took place on a sunny morning under a broad Kentucky sky; the monastery was clearly etched rather than shrouded in mystery. As we approached in Becky's Chevy along the curving state highway, the complex of buildings registered at first as a kind of citadel, most of its four-story walls the blanched-white shade of farmhouses in the French countryside, the pitched roofs tan and green, a tall tin-covered church bell tower dominating. From old black-and-white photographs, and from Merton's description of his own arrival, I could picture the elaborate architectural frontispiece dismantled decades ago that used to be a visitor's first impression, with its lettering over the doorway to the old guest house spelling out in Latin *"Pax Intrantibus"* (Peace to All Who Enter Here), a statue of the Virgin Mary enshrined above in a niche, and a bell rope for summoning the guest master. Now, however, the entrance square was wide open.

"Have a good visit," Becky sang out, dropping me at the end of a long sidewalk leading down toward the entrance. "Here's my card. Call me if you need a ride back. But I'm sure one of the

brothers will take you. . . . Have a good retreat. Be sure and look
at the sign on your way in." The "sign" she was referring to was a
plaque on the wall next to the door to the guest house quoting, in
English, from Chapter 53 of the *Rule of St. Benedict:* "All guests
who present themselves are to be welcomed as Christ."

The reception area to the new guest house, extensively renovated in 1988–89, turned out to be as accommodating as a hotel
lounge. Behind a long, angled wooden counter sat a large man in
an automated wheelchair volunteering as a lay helper to register
guests and assign rooms. I was pleased to discover that due to an
overflow I'd been given a room in the more "authentic" old south
wing now used for administrative purposes, rather than in the
thirty-one fully modernized suites. I quickly took advantage of
the opportunity to use the single available phone booth, since
phones, televisions, and radios are excluded from the cloistered
areas. (Emerging from that same phone booth a few days later, I
met a potential postulant, who remarked a bit peskily, "I thought
you came here to get away from telephones!") Holding my room-
assignment slip and a towel, I crossed back over the entrance
square, through an iron gate with the words "God Alone" etched
in its stone lintel—a motto that could be referring either to dedication only to God or to dedication to God alone, in solitude.
(Again from Merton: "So Brother Matthew locked the gate behind
me and I was enclosed in the four walls of my new freedom.")

My room on the third floor was large, like a school principal's
office, with well-waxed stone floors, cinderblock walls painted
white, and a fluorescent ceiling lamp. (Fifteen extra rooms for men
had been set aside in this wing within the monastic quadrangle
rather than annexed, like the guest house.) The furniture consisted of a single mattress on a metal frame, a desk, a chair, a
wooden clothes closet, a floor lamp, and a sink wedged in the corner with a shelf and mirror above. On the wall behind the bed was
nailed a modern abstract wood cross (the horizontal slat longer
than the vertical) with dry palm leaves stuck behind from Palm
Sunday. Through big double windows covered in white venetian
blinds I could look into the inner courtyard, or *preau,* with walk-

ways and a splashing fountain providing a mollifying European sound effect. (When its wooden gazebo was done away with during renovation in the 1960s, the current guest master, Father Matthew Kelty, wrote a bit acidly in *Liturgical Arts* that he found the new courtyard "strangely urban," reminding him of being "back in Detroit or downtown Boston.") A singing version of *The Psalms* from the Paulist Press and *The New American Bible* (Saint Joseph edition) were on the desk. A sheet of "Biblical Readings for Office and Mass" and a listing of the times of the prayer services had been slipped under the door.

During my week's retreat, extended beyond the usual five days by the abbot's permission, I came to gradually have a sense of what Merton slyly implied was actually a monastery subordinated to a cheese factory. Begun rather humbly by monks from Melleray, in western France, this Nelson County farm was originally purchased to import a monastic influence to the Midwest; this was encouraged by Bishop Flaget of Kentucky when the United States was divided by Baltimore's Bishop Carroll in 1808 into the four Catholic dioceses of Boston, New York, Philadelphia, and Bardstown—the last a response to so many Maryland Catholics immigrating to the region beginning in the 1780s that it became known as "the Catholic Holy Land." Its original group of French monks arrived in open wagons and lived in log cabins, farmed the land in their woolen habits, and began to build, with two million bricks burned from clay at the site, the abbey buildings, on a knoll above a creek that wound through the property. Today those monastery buildings, when seen across the fields, are impressively enormous, though somehow out of all context in time and place, seeming more like a page from *Les Très Riches Heures du Duc de Berry* than a Kentucky lodging.

Of course the American countryside was marked with many hopeful utopias during the same period as Gethsemani's founding. As Ralph Waldo Emerson wrote to Thomas Carlyle in the 1840s of the communitarian impulse astir in the country at the time, "We are a little wild here with numberless projects of social reform. Not a reading man but has a draft of a new community in his waistcoat pocket." The historian Sydney Ahlstrom backed up Emerson's observation in *A Religious History of the American People:* "The United States was the Promised Land for both American and European communitarian planners, and the antebellum half-century was their great seedtime. . . . [S]ix score of them were actually founded, a few dozen of them became celebrated through transient successes, and, if we include Mormonism, one became a major American cultural force." Among the transient successes: the Shakers, or the United Society of Believers in Christ's Second Appearing, brought to this country from England by Ann Lee Stanley in 1774; Jemima Wilkinson's Society of the Public Universal Friend; German pietistic communities like the Ephrata Community in Pennsylvania and the Hutterites; sectarian utopian communities such as New Harmony, in Indiana, the Oneida Community, in western New York; Hopedale, near Milford, Massachusetts; and Brook Farm, outside Boston. Among these utopian communities in the "antebellum half-century" were arguably Gethsemani and New Melleray, founded near Dubuque, Iowa, from their mother house of Mount Melleray in Ireland in 1849. But the adherence to an ancient tradition perhaps saved these two monasteries from the fate of their contemporaries, that of having become quaint utopias lost.

The Abbey of Gethsemani, after all, is designed according to a monastic blueprint dating back to the fifth century, its mighty fortress almost entirely focused around its central cloister square. The abbey church is located in the west wing of the monastery quadrangle; in the north wing is the chapter room, where the community meets every Sunday morning for an address by the abbot, and on Thursday evenings for more informal discussions about the business of the house; in the east quadrant is the refectory, or dining hall, where each monk has a designated place at table, according to his date of entry; on the south wing's ground floor are the offices of the abbot, and on its upper floors the fifteen rooms, including mine, set aside for men only. (The guest house alternates biweekly between men's and women's retreats.) The monks' residences are on the second and third floors of the north and east wings, along with a tailor shop, music-listening room, photo and dental labs, and a scriptorium with a censored local *Courier Journal* daily newspaper. (Although sports and entertainment articles and racy ads are clipped out by Brother Guiseppe, the abbot told me he suspected that "the sports page has an underground movement.") A brown brick infirmary annex to the north of the abbey contains fourteen rooms for aged and sick brothers. Outbuildings in the fields to the east include a library, a cheese and fudge factory, a bakery, and a garage. (The monks sell more than one hundred thousand pounds of their mild, aged, or smoked Port Salut cheese annually and have been increasingly successful with fruitcakes and fudge spiked with Kentucky bourbon.)

Beyond the confines of the low white stucco walls surrounding the enclave stretch thousands of acres of rolling fields, farmland, forests, lakes, knobs, mountains, and streams, as varied and pigmented in shades of green and brown as a topographical model. About three hundred fifty acres of row crops and one hundred acres of hay were still being cultivated, the monks were tending a large vegetable garden behind the enclosure walls, and a forest of approximately fourteen hundred acres of woodland once cut for lumber was being reforested. Most of the lands—fitting, perhaps, for a contemplative monastery—were simply lying fallow and unkempt. Following a dry summer, the grass was yellow and brown, the mountains were silhouettes of blue on the horizon, and the Queen Anne's lace and purple and gold weeds were high. Once past the wooden shrine, with its sign *"Maria Benedici I Nostri Campi"* (Mary, Bless Our Fields), on the other side of Monk's Road, most of the farming structures were partly abandoned skeletons: a tin shack, a barn, a silo, and a water tower, one of which had been described in a poem by a monk as "Ocean breeze green / Serene as a cucumber peeled." Woodpeckers screeched from the trees, while meadowlarks made sweeter music.

Almost immediately after my arrival, I was alerted by the ringing of the bells, a signal that draws everyone into the heart of the Trappist regimen of prayer and the antiphonal chanting, in two-week cycles, of all one hundred fifty Old Testament psalms. The monks come together seven times a day for these services: vigils (meaning "watching"), a forty-five-minute service beginning at 3:15 a.m. that includes chanting of the more harrowing and warlike of the psalms, referred to as "the raging psalms" by some of the monks; lauds (meaning "praise"), a twenty-five-minute sunrise service at 6:45 a.m., which introduces melodic organ music and leads into a daily community mass, followed by breakfast; terce, a ten-minute service to mark the beginning of the workday, at 7:30 a.m.; sext, a ten-minute service at noon, followed by the main meal; none, a ten-minute service at 2:15 p.m..; vespers (meaning "evening"), a twenty-five-minute service at 5:30 p.m., followed by supper; and compline, a twilight service beginning at 7:30 p.m. which ends with monks and guests alike lining up to be sprinkled with holy water by the abbot following the singing in candlelight of the *Salve Regina,* a haunting hymn to the Virgin Mary. It is said to have been written by the monk Herman the Little in the ninth century, and crooningly ends "O clement, O loving, O sweet Virgin Mary." These services constitute a merry-go-round of regularity that sets both the internal and external rhythm for the entire community. Participation allows any guest access to the peculiar time zone of the monastery, though a certain amount of jet-lag-like symptoms famously overtake those not used to rising at three in the morning.

That first day, the bells were calling me to the brief sext at noon. The bells then continued to mark fifteen-minute intervals throughout the day, except during "the Great Silence," from 7:30 p.m. to 3:15 a.m. I proceeded through a maze of halls and staircases directly to the guest balcony; the squeeze of getting there was completely reversed by the almost shocking first step into the vast, white, weightless, stripped-down sanctuary with its slits of pale glass windows arranged in geometric shapes, brick walls painted white, and exposed timber buttresses rising fifty feet above the floor. On a dais at the front, the altar was simply two vertical blocks of black granite topped by a horizontal slab and lit from above by a spotlight. Behind the altar, the starkest of thrones has been fashioned from six flat planes of polished oak.

In Merton's time, the church had been a Gothic showplace of Old World ornamentation, plaster and lath arches, fake vaulting, and deeply hued Munich stained-glass windows. In 1962 the architect William Schickel was given a charge to renovate this elaborate interior in a radical 1950s architectural style known as "brutalist." The stark, minimalist result in which the monks now prayed was successful at least in finding a contemporary diction in which to translate a purist medieval aesthetic, rendering it simultaneously futuristic and traditional. During the Middle Ages this order's monasteries had been similarly unadorned, with unplastered walls, towerless churches, and windows displaying only colorless patterns. An affinity between modern minimalism and the traditional Cistercian style was reaffirmed when John Pawson, the British architect known for his austere projects, including the coolly spare Calvin Klein flagship store on Madison Avenue, was chosen in 2001 by the Cistercians Sept-Fons, based in Central France, to design a monastery in the Czech Republic. He'd been making his own aesthetic pilgrimages for ten years to the twelfth-century Cistercian Abbey of Le Thoronet in Provence. "I think that recent events have made the creation and support of points of stillness and reflection in our world more relevant than ever," Pawson wrote to update me on his project soon after the September 11, 2001, attacks on the World Trade Center. "One doesn't need to subscribe to any conventional faith to feel that monasteries are one form these vital points of stillness might take." He added, "In a world in which isolation becomes the ultimate luxury, it is inevitable that the monastic cocoon acquires a sort of exoticism."

As the monks began to quickly straggle into their places in facing choir stalls, they, too, looked both old-fashioned and simply modern. Dressed in white robes with hoods, a sleeveless strip of black cloth, a scapular, worn over the robe, their waists cinched with thick black leather belts, they were apparently the inheritors of useful round-the-clock all-purpose formal wear. The only tip-off that they were contemporary Americans was their shoes: an assortment of Reeboks, Birkenstock sandals, even black cowboy boots. While tonsures were no longer a requirement, most of the men were shorn, some bearded. A few required walkers, one a wheelchair. The character lines in their faces lit evenly in the bright sunlight, they obviously held great interest to those looking down from the rear balcony—not only retreatants, but also a busload of tourists. As one brother told me: "Americans are curious. They want to come and gawk at us. Monks are always a good show. The problem is how to preserve what little privacy and solitude we have left."

The monks are a very all-American cross-section. Nationally, they range in age from their twenties to their nineties, with educational backgrounds from high school to medical school. Past jobs have included soldier, concert organist, pilot, accountant, doctor, lawyer, barber, jeweler, postal worker, and college professor. They are sons, uncles, and cousins, even twins, parents, and grandparents. If there has been any one quality drawing them to a contemplative life, it would be, in the guest chaplain's opinion, introversion. "Most monks are probably on the introverted side," he told me. "In Western culture, if you're not an extrovert, you should become one, or you won't make it. Here all the business is interior, internal. I often say to a young man when he comes here, 'Do you want to spend the rest of your life making fruitcake?' If he doesn't understand, he doesn't belong here." Interestingly, few monks come from broken families; the breakup of their first family perhaps ruins for other people this particular ideal of community.

If the structure of the monks' day is set by the hours of the services, the structure of their lives is established by their three solemn, perpetual vows: stability, to remain in the enclosed community for life; fidelity to the basics of monastic life, including poverty and chastity; and obedience, to the abbot and the rule. To be allowed to take the path leading to these final vows, each candidate must first be evaluated by a vocations director, take a psychological exam, and make several retreats at the monastery over the course of a year. Received into the community, he then must spend his first six months in street clothes as a "postulant," after which he is clothed in a white novice's habit and admitted to the novitiate for two years. He then takes temporary vows, marked by putting on the black scapular and the leather belt. For three or more years, up to a maximum of nine, a monk may renew these temporary vows before making his final assent. Ordination to the priesthood may follow later.

The monks submit themselves to *The Rule of St. Benedict,* written by Benedict of Nursia for the monastery he founded in Monte Cassino in 529 that later became the chief house of the Benedictine order. Twice a day at Gethsemani I heard readings from his sixth-century how-to manual, which begins with the poetic invitation, "Listen carefully, my son, to the master's instructions, and attend to them with the ear of your heart." The *Rule* outlines a life of private and communal prayer, inspirational reading *(lectio divina),* manual labor—"When they live by the labor of their hands, as our fathers and the apostles did, then they are really monks"—and doing the work of God *(opus Dei)* by performing the Eucharist, or mass, the central Christian sacrament. The last of Saint Benedict's seventy-three brief chapters ends, promisingly, "Are you hastening towards your heavenly home? Then with Christ's help, keep this little rule that we have written for beginners. After that, you can set out for the loftier summits of the teaching and virtues we mentioned above, and under God's protection you will reach them. Amen."

The Trappist version of this Benedictine life has been filtered through an eleventh-century French reform known as the Cistercian order. The Cistercians, or "White Monks," named for their unbleached, uncolored white robes, split from the Cluniac order, or "Black Monks," because of dissatisfaction with the easing of Benedict's *Rule* at many of the more than one thousand Cluniac monasteries, which were known for lavish ritual and liturgy and where the brothers often prayed in fur-lined jackets and ornamental garments. The highest profile among these Cistercians, who founded their new order at the Abbey of Citeaux in 1098, was their third abbot, Bernard of Clairvaux, who was a mystic, a preacher—most famously on the Song of Songs—and a nobleman who campaigned for the Second Crusade across northern Europe (a career move not much admired these days) and directed the founding of sixty-eight new houses before his death, in 1153. In their own spare liturgies, these monks used only unembroidered vestments of light linen, wooden crosses, and iron candlesticks.

A further and even more severe reform of the order took place in the seventeenth century at the monastery of La Grande Trappe, led by the Abbot Armand Jean de Rancé, responsible for the Order of the Cistercians of the Strict Observance (O.C.S.O.), known popularly as "the Trappists," demanding strict silence and a vegetarian diet. Some of de Rancé's bracing rigors were still in play when Merton arrived at Gethsemani: monks weren't allowed to shave themselves; sleeping quarters were dormitories rather than cells; to prepare for ordination to the priesthood a brother had to kiss the feet of all his brothers at dinner and beg for food on his knees with an outstretched empty bowl; self-punishment for mistakes in choir involved prolonged kneeling, and rapping knuckles on wood; and the monks flagellated themselves weekly with small, knotted whips. Such gestures helped provoke one popular criticism of Cistercian life as "Christian masochism."

These rigors are being greatly soft-pedaled these days, especially for guests. After sext, I descended for the main meal of the day, in the guest refectory. Sitting with the other retreatants, most in their fifties or sixties—more than one looking to me like John Updike—I ate iceberg lettuce, rainbow pasta with tomato sauce, and tapioca pudding set out on a cafeteria tray while listening to a tape of Merton lecturing the novices on the mystical poetry of Rainer Maria Rilke. "Rilke is the most fantastic poet of this century," Merton was saying in his dry, witty clarinet of a voice. In the main refectory the monks are read to aloud during their silent meals; the literary fare, following a requisite excerpt from *The Rule of St. Benedict,* is anything from a biography of Bernard of Clairvaux to Stephen Ambrose's *Undaunted Courage,* about the Lewis and Clark expedition, or Paul Roberts's *History of the American People.* In the guest refectory, the male guests sat at two rows of tables and gazed out in one direction, through a wall of windows, toward cedar trees, squirrels, low stone walls, tumbling cumulus clouds, and a blond ponytailed local worker—looking much like the young men I saw at the Holiday Inn—sitting obliviously on a rock smoking a cigarette.

Breaking through this usually anonymous blur of other guests, in a short subsequent retreat I took the following spring, was the movie actor Ethan Hawke, recognizable from his roles in *Dead Poets Society, Gattaca,* and *Great Expectations.* He was accompanied by a longhaired, Kurt Cobain–like friend, who went hiking with him in the surrounding hills. Hawke's wife is Uma Thurman, the daughter of Robert Thurman, and Hawke brought along his father-in-law's latest book, *Circling the Sacred Mountain.* But he confessed to another guest—an ex–Gethsemani monk turned Tibetan Buddhist who'd brought along the same book— that he'd decided not to read the book, Thurman's account of a trip to the Himalayas, but to "leave everyone behind" and just concentrate on being in the monastery. There were some whispers in the guest house, a couple of forced handshakes. Word even reached the monks, and I saw one of them staring at Hawke as he exited mass one day. Another monk checked with me to ask which one was the actor—"the young guy in the T-shirt?" I confirmed this, but then caught him staring, a bit starstruck, at the wrong young guy in a T-shirt.

During that same week, a fellow retreatant became fixated on my having been invited by the brothers to sit in choir with them. "You'd make a great monk; I'm praying for you," my middle-aged, excessively enthusiastic fan from Ohio assured me. "You are thinking about it?" he added, hopefully. Not wanting to let him down, I answered, "Well, I think about it, sure." My answer was apparently sufficient, for the next time he saw me his expectations had already increased. "You've got a lot of love and a lot of vigor in you," he stopped me in the hall to whisper. "They'll probably have you doing all the work. . . . I'm praying for you." I slunk off feeling like a complete fake.

After lunch that earlier September afternoon, I walked up a flight of stairs to the renovated guest library, where a sign on the main table cleverly warned, "Silence is spoken here." This small-town-style library carries only religious and spiritual books and magazines, but adjacent to it is a screened porch where guests can look out over a Stations of the Cross pathway on the grounds below, or read and smoke—though the monks are, of course, encouraged not to smoke. At the far end of the reading room, Father Alan Gilmore, the guest master, had just returned from lunch and was rustling through papers in his office. A first-generation Irish American in his mid-sixties from Cincinnati, Ohio, Father Alan belied, in his communicativeness, the notion of all monks as introverts. He also turned out to be an important history lesson himself. Having entered Gethsemani in 1955 after serving in an army artillery division in southern Germany, he'd lived through the transition in Cistercian life during the Vatican II era of the 1960s, which was probably as important, and as disorienting for many, as the historical reforms of Bernard of Clairvaux or Abbot de Rancé. Particularly transforming in his own life had been the dismantling of the medieval Cistercian two-class system of dividing educated choir monks, known colloquially among the brothers as "the saints," from farming lay brothers, or "the bums."

"I entered as a lay brother," recalled Father Alan as he settled behind his desk, friendly and a bit rough around the edges, like a blue-collar monk, almost a Friar Tuck figure, his white hair and beard cropped short.

We lay brothers were mostly oriented to working. We weren't considered as monks at the time. We wore brown habits rather than white ones and lived in separate quarters. A lot of those who entered with me were still teenagers. I was twenty-five. Some were in charge of the work areas, but they were only sixteen or seventeen years old. They were always trying to find faster ways to do a job, which is difficult when you're not allowed to talk. Or they'd drive a jeep without knowing how to drive. I was accepted with sixty-four others that year, and there are only two of us left. For many centuries, though, the term for the lay brothers in Latin was *conversi,* or converted ones. They weren't teenagers. They had undergone a conversion and were drawn to this type of life. If I'd known beforehand that the failure rate, or whatever you want to call it, was that high, I might have figured 'What's the use?' But thanks be to God, I've been here forty-two and a half years. The two years I spent in the army seemed a lot longer than the time I've been here.

Begun as an innovation to keep large monastic farms operating in the Middle Ages, and to allow for the difficulty of illiterate monks singing offices in Latin, the final result of the lay brothers class had become an increasingly archaic-seeming caste system, especially when Latin was done away with as the sacred language of the mass. Before Vatican II, nearly everyone who joined the choir at Gethsemani eventually became a priest; for lay brothers, choir wasn't a part of their lives. When the monks were praying, the lay brothers would stop in the fields, like Muslims pausing during the workday to bow toward Mecca, to recite their simple Paters and Aves—ten of each. The only time the two groups came together was for Sunday mass and every evening at compline, when the lay brothers sat in the rear under the guest balcony and weren't allowed to sing. Monks worked four hours, with the remaining time for reading; lay brothers worked eight. When this division was done away with by decree of a general chapter of the order's abbots in 1964, lay brothers were encouraged to take part in the divine office and even to study for the priesthood. "There were ten of us who started as students of philosophy and theology, and three of us were ordained," recalled Father Alan. "One of them thought he could never be ordained here so he left and became a secular priest. Another brother was ordained a priest at the same service I was ordained a deacon. After a year he left and got married. He lives in Kentucky. I'm the only one of the ten who's still a monk here."

The reaction to these changes among the lay brothers was often more disgruntlement than liberation. After the decree, most of the lay brothers left Gethsemani, creating the biggest crisis in the order in this century. Indeed, the number of committed monks dropped by one third between 1960 and 1970. "I think the changes after Vatican II took a lot of the starch out of the lay brothers," one choir monk explained. "Most left. I think they really loved the old lifestyle. They had very deep values, a real sense of camaraderie, and probably more solitude than we did. The old work routine must have functioned as a prayer form for them. Agriculture, working in the fields, gave them an immense sense of God at work in the universe. The brothers shared that. Most of them were macho guys. They really dug the penances and the sacrifices. Their work was affirming. Their self-esteem got a constant boost. . . . They kept this place going, just as lay brothers made the first Cistercians into commercial wizards in medieval times."

There was also a general consternation among other monks, who left as the order became modernized and increasingly unfamiliar. Many felt betrayed, as they were deprived of the absolute capsule of solitude and medieval contemplation for which they'd originally signed on. "Vatican II stripped down that wall people were hiding behind," another monk explained to me. "They changed some of the formulas and chants and prayers. Gregorian chant used to be very soothing to hear for hours a day. Now you could no longer hide behind the poetry of Roman Catholicism to sustain this vocation. Nor would you be able to simply hide out with your various personality problems. A lot of the brothers were terrified by what was happening. They were forced into the modern dialogue. Their attitude was, 'I didn't come here for this. I have no intention of talking to anybody about my past, or working this thing out. As far as I'm concerned I left my past on the beaches of Normandy.' "

A monastery might seem to be its own planet, lost in time and space; it's often disconnected from the rest of the world, whose news reports, films, and values it rejects—the monks made news themselves by turning on a TV in the infirmary to watch the World Trade Center collapse on September 11, 2001, something they had not done for the Vietnam War, the Kennedy assassination, the *Challenger* explosion, or the Oklahoma City bombing. But surprisingly, trends seem to register just as strongly within the monastery's walls as without—that is, the 1960s were every bit as convulsive for monks as for everybody else. Within Roman Catholicism, the Second Vatican Council, of 1962 to 1965, was the new wind that toppled old rituals throughout the church: the mass was mandated to be said in the vernacular rather than Latin. The priest had previously said mass with his back to the congregation; now he turned around to face the people. Members of the congregation were invited to read portions of the service previously reserved only for the priest. In effect, these changes brought the Roman Catholic Church closer to many Protestant denominations. But for monks, Pope John Paul XXIII's call for *aggiornamento,* or coming to terms with the times, required an even more intense identity crisis, since they had been so bound up with the notion of the blessedness of radical separation from the world.

Again, Thomas Merton's was the voice that most clearly articulated the meaning of these changes for monks. The man whose heart had been in his throat when he first glimpsed Gethsemani as hidden behind "a barrier and a defence against the world" wrote of his own shake-up at the corner of Fourth and Walnut Streets, now marked by a commemorative plaque. During a visit to downtown Louisville on March 19, 1958, to oversee the printing of a new postulants' guide, Merton recorded his illumination in his journals, published as *Conjectures of a Guilty Bystander* (1966): "In Louisville at the corner of Fourth and Walnut, in the center of the shopping district, I was suddenly overwhelmed with the realization that I loved all those people, that they were mine and I theirs, that we could not be alien to one another even though we were total strangers. It was like waking from a dream of separateness, of spurious self-isolation in a special world, the world of renunciation and supposed holiness. The whole illusion of a separate holy existence is a dream. Not that I question the reality of my vocation, or of my monastic life: but the conception of 'separation from the world' that we have in the monastery too easily presents itself as a complete illusion: the illusion that by making vows we become a different species of being, pseudo-angels, 'spiritual men,' men of interior life, what have you."

Merton's voice carried, and not only in the world where he was a widely read author, but also in the monastery where he increasingly had taken on posts of influence and importance in spite of his steady petitioning of the abbot, Dom James Fox, to be allowed to retreat to a private hermitage in the woods. He was finally allowed, in 1965, to retire to a hermitage, but only after four years as junior master and ten as master of novices. As a result of Merton's years of institutional service, many in leadership positions in the monastery had been novices under him, including Abbot Timothy Kelly, Guest Master Matthew Kelty, and Junior Master Paul Quenon. John Eudes Bamberger, who is now abbot at the Abbey of the Genesee, studied under Merton when he was junior master. The influence of his Vatican II–era ecumenism and openness permeates subtly even today.

Yet some who knew Merton caution against making him the embodiment of all ideas liberal and reforming. He had come out of the old-guard Cistercian belief in life being solitary. Robert Imperato, who had been a Gethsemani monk, Brother Mark, from 1968 to 1976, after having been a disciple of Swami Satchidananda's, was struck in his one meeting with Merton and in discussions with those who knew him by Merton's solitariness in spite of later notions of him as all-embracing. "I remember John Eudes Bamberger telling me 'I went it alone, and Merton went it alone,' " said Imperato, now professor of religion and dean of arts and sciences at St. Leo College, in Florida. "They weren't really endorsing friendship. It was the tough-guy approach to monastic life. There was a book in the library at Gethsemani with the title *American Tough*. I always saw the Trappists as 'American Tough.' Somehow friendship was soft. They wouldn't let a friend of mine, Brother Gabriel, take final vows, and he went somewhere else. I always thought it was partly because he was just too friendly. There's always a lot of talk about Merton and friendship. But I think that people have overvalued friendship in Merton's life. Remember that solitude is the dominant note with him. I don't know how intimate he finally was with anybody. The life there is much more solitary than any of us ever experience elsewhere."

When I spoke with Abbot John Eudes a few months later at Genesee, he concurred, at least insofar as Merton was concerned. "Many people thought they were closer to Merton than they were because he was so sympathetic with them," he said. "But his sympathy didn't necessarily mean that he was engaging himself. He actually had difficulty doing that, I think. And that was part of his suffering, his anguish in life. He was a very loving person. He was easy to like. But I never had the impression he was intimate with me. That was a big part of his way. He had a great need for contact with people. He really liked them. But he had an even deeper need for something transcendent. And I don't think anybody really got there for any length of time. That was my impression. . . . But there's some of that in anybody who's a monk. Why else would you live this way?" Bamberger interestingly compared Merton on the basis of sheer presence—"a sort of nimbus around him"—to only two other men he'd met in his life: the poet Robert Lowell and an obscure senator in southern France, where Bamberger had worked while secretary general of the Consilium Generale, from 1969 to 1971.

Walking later that afternoon through the lobby of the guest house, I was serendipitously given another opportunity to understand Gethsemani's social history when I ran into Brother Joshua Brands, the monastery's archivist and cellarer, and the third superior in the community after the abbot and the prior. Trained in archival work at Saint Mary's College in Kentucky, Brother Josh, as he's known, was a good-humored middle-aged monk who had been enthusiastic in organizing the monastery's collection of rare manuscripts and papers, and in putting together a recent illustrated history, *The Abbey of Gethsemani: Place of Peace and Paradox,* written by Dianne Aprile for the centenary celebration on December 21, 1998. He was in the reception area saying good-bye to a friend. Knowing of my project, he said, "When we were doing the centenary edition, I took Dianne around to meet some monks and sat in on her interviews. It was fascinating. Since we don't speak casually, we really don't know anything about our brothers on that level. Who they are, where they came from, what drove them to come here."

When we were left alone, I began to discuss with Brother Josh my previous trip to Gethsemani, and particularly Brother Lavrans Nielsen, whose hermitage I'd visited. I remembered Lavrans as tall, fair, balding, and large-boned, with a goatee-style mustache and beard, an intense blue-eyed gaze, and spare, big hands. Born in Brooklyn of Scandinavian background and baptized as Donald Anthony, he'd entered the community in 1957, at age twenty. A self-taught artist, his haunting icons, executed in the Greek and Russian styles, now dot the walls of the new guest rooms in small reproductions, so any visitor's memory of Gethsemani is colored by Lavrans's art. During his time at the monastery he made grand liturgical banners in felt that hung over the abbey altar on feast days; linoleum block prints for community Christmas and Easter cards; woodcuts, engraving, and calligraphy for the new English liturgy texts; and abstract oil paintings in light colors, often multilayered and three-dimensional. In 1970 he exhibited his paintings at the J. B. Speed Museum, and in 1975 at the Swearingen-Byck Gallery, both in Louisville. In 1976 Brother Lavrans left the monastery and moved to Atlanta, where he continued to paint in the abstract expressionist style. He died of AIDS in 1991, at age forty.

In a homily entitled "Remembering Lavrans," delivered on August 30, 1991, Father Matthew Kelty recalled Lavrans as following Merton's lead in folding art, contemplation, and a hermit's

solitude into the Cistercian vocation: "His assignment one season was to operate the vacuum machine that drew the air from
plastic sacks of quartered cheese rounds and sealed them. It was,
of course, a monotonous routine that would drive a man like
Lavrans into a state of high exasperation. This went on, for the
work had to be done, until he began to break out in large, ugly
boils. So a halt was called, and the brother in charge made a bold
move and offered a deal to Lavrans. If he would milk cows each
morning—no favorite among city monks—and do the chores that
went with it, he could have his afternoons for his art. Lavrans
seized the opportunity. This was the first time any monk had been
given official work time for something like art." To work on his
paintings, he moved first to a gristmill within the cloister and
then to his hermitage outside the cloister built for him by a
friend.

"Would you like to see the hermitage?" asked Brother Josh,
who'd known Lavrans and the community intimately while living
in Kentucky during the 1970s. "It's sad what's happened out
there."

Our vehicle was a little green go-cart. Brother Josh drove,
wearing a battered tan baseball cap. There was not much metal
between our seats and the ground, so we felt every bump
thoroughly as we passed through the "Enclosure" sign to the
monks-only lands behind the cloister. We passed the various outbuildings, as well as a few monks waving to us, their white robes
billowing in the breeze, eventually making our way into a less cultivated, woodsy area where tree branches scraped against the front
of the cart. Finally we shifted into a noisier low gear to make the
final climb up a hill until coming to a sudden stop in front of the
hermitage.

"Wow, it's so overgrown," I said. What happened?"

The brown brick hermitage was intact but dilapidated, wildly
overgrown by weeds, obscured by bent trees, its door hanging off
the hinges, windows broken. When I'd visited in 1976 the most
striking aspect of this angular building was its glamour; it had
resembled a sleek suburban ranch house, or a Fire Island beach

bungalow, hardly the humble shack of a stereotypical gaunt hermit. Its insides now were mostly empty except for a half-filled bottle of copper-colored Jim Beam whisky left on a wooden kitchen table. Lavrans's vast garage-like painting studio was filled with trash and had apparently been used recently by local teenagers. Its last resident, Father Chrysogonus Waddell, a choirmaster trained at the Philadelphia Conservatory of Music who'd devised a new plainchant to accommodate the English vernacular, had vacated the place years earlier. I remembered Brother Lavrans telling me that the tragic death of a fellow monk who'd fallen from the roof during construction cast a continuous shadow on his heart. From appearances, the shadow had seeped into the place itself. I couldn't help feeling the pang of loss at so much romance and spirituality mixed together in this place in such a potent fashion. (Underlining his loner qualities, Lavrans, by the time he left, was saying the simple Paters and Aves with a group of lay brothers who met in a separate chapel, never having adapted to the new one-size-fits-all choir service for all monks in English.)

The condition of his abandoned hermitage was emblematic, hinting at two developments that marked Gethsemani during the 1970s as the brothers tried to assimilate post–Vatican II experimentation. The first was the hermitage movement. This innovation could be credited to Merton, who petitioned Dom James Fox and the general Cistercian order for years to allow him to sequester himself in total solitude and silence. To rationalize this desire, he searched for historical precedent, finding his strongest case in the Desert Fathers of Egypt and Syria in the third and fourth centuries, especially Saint Anthony, who left the sophisticated metropolis of Alexandria in A.D. 285, gave away all he owned, and secluded himself in a cave in the desert. Such caves were soon filled with as many as nine thousand men and women. Merton enlivened this tradition by translating many of the koanlike sayings of these early Christian hermits in *The Wisdom of the Desert,* published by New Directions in 1961. Gradually Merton realized his ambition, as he spent from 1965 to 1968 in and out of one or another version of a hermitage, including "St. Anne's," an abandoned tool shed, and culminating in his own full-time white cinder-block cabin with its flat roof and casement windows, open porch, logs piled high by the side of the house, and hand-built cross in the yard.

This hermitic movement peaked at the time Lavrans left his hermitage and Gethsemani, in 1976. There were then three other monks occupying hermitages on monastery property: two former abbots, Dom James Fox and his successor, Father Flavian Burns, as well as Father Hilarion. Two other monks, both priests, had moved abroad: Father Matthew Kelty to a hut in New Guinea, where he stayed for ten years, and Father Roman Ginn to Mexico, for nineteen years. One older monk, Father Alfons Berg, lived as a hermit within his own monastery cell. By 1998 there were only two hermit monks left—Father Roman, who'd returned from Mexico to a small cottage, and Father Hilarion, who lived in a larger trailer in a wooded area. Merton's old hermitage was available for all the brothers to take a week's retreat annually if they wished.

The dying down of hermit fever was partly the responsibility of Abbot Timothy Kelly, who has always openly identified himself as being "antihermit." "I believe in the *possibility* of a hermit," he stressed to me in his office one morning. "But I think it's a very extraordinary type of response to the Gospel. For most of us, community is necessary for our self-knowledge. It helps us to recognize our own limitations. Hermits tend to become a little strange. I think it's a life you can go bad on, get a bit funny. A lot of things can happen." One incident that helped turn the community against hermitages was an attack on a Saturday night in April 1977, on James Fox, in which two men from nearby New Hope, Kentucky, broke into his hermitage and severely beat and terrorized him.

A sidebar to the seventies hermit movement was an attempt within the community to propose various hermit colonies, or alternative experiments in communal living. One of the more popular proposals was for a grange across the valley in Keith Hollow; it was seriously debated by Father Flavian's council in 1972 and was supported by eight brothers, including Father Alan, who wished to live more poorly and radically. The notion was to set up a back-to-the-land-style community by building log cabins without electricity or simply sleeping in tents, echoing various utopian communes being founded in America at the time. Another of its supporters was the current junior master, Brother Paul Quenon. "We wanted to live poorer than we live here," recalled Brother Paul. "But when Abbot Timothy was elected in 1973, he let it be known that he was opposed to the idea. He said we were just like a bunch of kids who wanted to set up a tent in the backyard. He said if you want to leave home, really leave home." Their monastic version of Thoreau's Walden Pond experiment eventually died.

In February 1999, when I visited for two days at the New Melleray Abbey, in Iowa, the abbot told me about similar failed attempts in his own monastery during the same period. "The first thinking after the Vatican Council was small, simplified communities of four or five people," recalled Dom Brendan Freeman. "We had one farmhouse in Belleville, Illinois. The monks wore a simple blue denim habit. They really wanted to get back to the earth, including baking their own bread from wheat, with everything organic. But they found that living together in such close quarters was very difficult. It fell apart. We started another in Brooksville, Mississippi, that lasted for eighteen years. There were several such communities started by Trappists around the country. But none of them survived. We soon learned, again, that we needed some sort of structure. An institution like this can carry a lot of people, but if you're out there trying to live with four or five you have to work really hard to pay the expenses. Why do that? You don't need to come to a monastery to do that. There's some advantage in joining forces, sharing out the work on a large scale." The solution at Melleray was to begin making Trappist caskets in 1998—the business became profitable by May 2001 when they sold twenty-three in one month.

The monastery's creation had taken place in the 1840s during a time when utopian communities were popular in America, and the urge for hermit colonies in the 1960s and early 1970s shared similarities with that earlier communal movement. During those two decades, thousands of intentional communities appeared in response to the countercultural impulses of an anarchic "hippie" youth movement. Many, such as Haney, a mountain commune in Oregon, or Arroyo's in the Sierra Nevada mountains, were on the West Coast, or near Woodstock, in upstate New York, like Skiara. Many of these communes were at least superficially affiliated with Eastern spirituality of the sort that later became a fascination of the New Age movement—the Rada Krishna Temple of monks founded by Swami Bhaktivedanta in a storefront in Haight-Ashbury, and Santa, or "the Farm," started by a Yoga teacher in the foothills of the Sierra Nevadas. Some were political camps of Vietnam War draft resisters, such as the Peace and Labor Commune, in San Francisco, and the Resistance Commune, at Stanford University. All eventually disbanded, their demise almost predestined by a dislike of any authority that wasn't charismatic or informal. (The Book of Acts, describing in the New Testament the communal sharing of goods, peace, and love in the early church, was the Christian text most popular with these communards.)

But Lavrans's career as a monk was not only emblematic of various attempts to reinvent the Benedictine life after Vatican II, but also of the challenge to monastic life of the sexual revolution, which was moving full speed ahead in the culture at large. The vow of chastity had always presented challenges, as far back as those Desert Fathers tempted by hallucinations of beautiful women visiting their isolated caves. (Chastity is a virtue in the Christian tradition. There is the example of Jesus remaining unmarried, and celibate Saint Paul, who, in 1 Corinthians 7:8, urges "To the unmarried and the widows I say that it is well for them to remain single as I do.") But the 1970s in America are remembered in part for the growth of the women's and gay liberation movements. Certainly, for any gay monks who'd chosen a life of closeted solitude during a time of repression, this option of openness might well have caused new doubts. I remembered Brother Lavrans telling me somewhat nostalgically of the Greenwich Village he'd left twenty years earlier, and I'd sensed in his telling the conflicts he was experiencing and the lure of living on the outside. As I'd heard the story at the time, later in that year he put on a pair of Wellington boots and blue jeans and took a plane back to New York City, where he went directly to Ty's and other gay bars on Christopher Street, undoubtedly a culture shock given the dramatic changes from the far gentler, bohemian period he'd known there in 1957. Either on the plane or at a bar, he met someone from Atlanta with whom he then lived unsuccessfully for a period of time. Whatever the details, Abbot Timothy confirmed that sexual liberation played a part in Lavrans's decisions. "With Brother Lavrans that was very much involved with some of his choices," the abbot told me.

"Because we've just been through an age of sexual liberation, it's most un-American to be celibate," the Benedictine monk Remy Rougeau wrote to me shortly after the publication in the summer of 2001 of his novel, *All We Know of Heaven,* about life in a Trappist monastery much like the Canadian Abbey of Notre Dame des Prairies, where he spent six years in his early twenties. "Sexual expression is *the* ultimate freedom. And celibacy is construed as a form of repression. One may as well live in China as join a Cistercian abbey. But, of course, popular perception isn't necessarily welded to truth. Sexual expression doesn't always liberate people. Celibacy is not inevitably repressive. In fact, if people understood how celibacy, freely chosen, is superbly liberating, we'd have no shortage of monks and nuns."

The monk currently most involved with the touchy subject of monasticism and homosexuality is Matthew Kelty, whom I visited later in the week in his guest chaplain's office down the hall from Father Alan. Kelty's own story is quite unusual. Born in a suburb of Boston in 1915, his reputation in the monastery was that of being "eighty-two going on thirty-nine." Spry, tough-talking, and sassy, Kelty still flavored his talk with an Irish accent, especially in his popular meditations for guests each evening, in which he quoted Ezra Pound and Gerard Manley Hopkins, among dozens of other poets. Kelty led an earlier life as a priest of the more evangelistic Divine Word Society, including missionary work in New Guinea, until he entered Gethsemani at the age of forty-five in 1960. "I remember the day he arrived," Father Alan told me. "I was in charge of the guest refectory at the time. He was the only customer here for Friday lunch, and it was fish. He was sitting there with his legs folded, shaking his foot, reading a newspaper. I've never seen anybody do that before or since." In spite of his age, Kelty became a novice under Thomas Merton and in later years became Merton's confessor. Father Matthew still took a walk through the woods every morning, wearing an orange coat, a big black hat, and cowboy boots, and carrying a shepherd's crook.

Adding to his eccentricity is Father Matthew's position as the only openly gay monk at Gethsemani—he's not only open, but he keeps a rainbow-colored mug at his place in the refectory. He accepts his homosexuality without engaging in sexual acts, a nuance that allows him to survive publicly as a priest of the Roman Catholic Church. His published essay on the subject is titled "Celibacy and the Gift of Gay" and is theological rather than autobiographical, though it is derived, he writes, "not just from what was read, but from what was lived." When I spoke with Father Matthew he explained his nearly original position on gays as prime candidates for sustaining and renewing monasteries. "Gays make the best monks, in my opinion, because they're already on the road to a life integrating the masculine and the feminine sides," he said to me in his brogue-inflected voice. He was sitting behind his desk, which was piled high with poetry anthologies. "They don't need a woman to awaken and arouse their feminine side. They already have it. All they need is guidance, direction, companions, and a reason. The reason would be God. The companions would be your brothers under a rule and an abbot. And you've got a beautiful life of peace and work and prayer. There have always been monks and nuns in every society because there have always been men and women to whom the route to integrated personhood is not necessarily marriage."

In an essay in *Harper's* magazine in September 1998 titled

"Beyond Belief: A Skeptic Searches for an American Faith," the author Fenton Johnson, who'd been raised near Gethsemani, let slip another amusing bit of the monastery's gay history. As a child, Johnson's father, who delivered the monastery's bourbon for the production of fruitcake, used to invite some of the brothers home on special occasions for a meal. "One brother was fond of a grass skirt someone had sent my mother from Hawaii," Johnson wrote. "When the moon was right and the whiskey flowed he donned the skirt and some hot pink plastic leis, then hoisted my mother to the tabletop and climbed up after her. There she sang 'Hard Hearted Hannah' ('the vamp of Savannah, G.A.!') while her partner swayed his hips and waved hands in mock hula. Later he launched into Broadway tunes, warbling in falsetto with his arms thrown around one or more of his brethren. . . . Brother Fintan, my namesake, was a baker who made elaborate cakes for each of my birthdays until I was five. Then he left the monastery and disappeared from our lives, for reasons I would not learn for many years." The ex-brother returned to dinner at the Johnsons' several years later with his male lover.

Less frivolous and amusing was a memory of Robert Imperato's of an incident that today might be classified under the category of sexual harassment. "I did blow the whistle on one gay man who came on to me while I was there who was in a position of authority," revealed Imperato. "It scared the hell out of me. I have nothing against gays, but not in a situation where the claim is to be celibate. He was active sexually. They stepped in and had him go to counseling, and he finally left the monastery. That was not at all common, though. Basically I'd have to say that there really is this God thing going on at Gethsemani. I feel that God is alive and well in some monasteries, and that's one of them. I was certainly getting a lot of love and support from God there." Indeed, contrary to fantasies among many outsiders that monasteries must be made up entirely of gay men, the incidence of gay sex in Trappist monasteries seems, as Imperato said, "not at all common." The total gay population, as with some other ethnic and socioeconomic indicators (not racial, however, since most American monks are Caucasian), seems finally to be a reflection of the cross-section nationally—between 5 and 10 percent. "[Being gay] is taken in about the same light as my being color-blind," Matthew Kelty wrote to me. "Even that is too much. For I sometimes talk about my vision. No one seems interested in my orientation."

No matter what the decade, monks' lives have always been fraught with conflict, mostly because of the vow they find even more demanding than celibacy—obedience. Abbot Francis Kline, of Mepkin Abbey, entered Gethsemani as a novice in 1972 and was bracingly honest in sharing with me his own agony during his formation when we talked in South Carolina in October 1998. "I had always been at the bottom of the community in work," he recalled. "I was always wrapping cheese. They gave me time to study. Gethsemani was always a funny place, though. If you studied, you weren't considered one of the guys. It meant you weren't pulling your weight. It's very subtle. But I used to get all the shit jobs, pouring coffee in the guest house, milking cows. I went to Rome to study from 1980 to 1984, and when I came back I said to Abbot Timothy, 'I'm coming back for the summer. Can I have a different job?' He said, 'If you don't like it, just leave.' So it wasn't easy. But that's monastic life. Then all of a sudden in 1986 everything changed. Just overnight. One morning the abbot came up to me while I was typing orders for cheese and said, 'You'll be ordained a priest, and then you'll become novice master.' Just like that." Kline was eventually recruited for the job of abbot at Mepkin in 1990.

"If a monk leaves, it's almost always over the issue of obedience," Remy Rougeau wrote to me. His novel turns on the denouement of a Trappist monk leaving for just that reason. "Rarely is it because of celibacy. I remember once, when I had housekeeping duties, I was ordered to dust furniture with a dry cloth. I was only pushing the dust around. So I went to the abbot and asked for some Pledge, or lemon oil. He told me to use water. I argued with him. Water, I said, would ruin the finish. But he insisted, penny-conscious and pound-foolish. The water did ruin the finish. But obedience has been fortuitous for me as well. About ten years ago, I was told to become a beekeeper, and I thought I would die. But I quickly learned to love it, and it's one of my favorite things in the world. Bees are endlessly fascinating. The purpose of obedience, of course, is to keep the community together. We can't all go and do as we like."

This vow is perhaps toughest for creative types like Merton, Lavrans, and Rougeau. "The rule of Saint Benedict devotes a whole chapter to this issue of artists in the monastery saying 'They are to practice their craft with humility,' " Rougeau continued. "But can you imagine a Philip Roth, an Andy Warhol, or a Mikhail Baryshnikov practicing their craft with all humility? Artists are egoists. Yet at the same time, the abbey should not have to orbit around these people. A monk must learn humility. The only way a writer-monk or painter-monk remains in monastic life is if being a monk is more important to him than art."

Most of the life at Gethsemani for both the committed monk and guest is made up of a steady rhythm of community prayer and inspirational readings that constantly return everyone to "the God thing," with either manual labor or walks in the woods as meaningful pauses. Vigils, the most difficult of these communal gatherings, testing stamina and dedication each morning, is the most memorable, a spiritual litmus test. I managed to arrive at vigils each morning at 3:15 a.m., eyes burning, throat congested, after a quick stop in the lavatory, which was permeated by the smell of shaving cream and Old Spice, with a kitsch John Paul II mug left resting on a counter by Brother Rene, who lived on the floor. Making my way into the semidarkness of the sanctuary's balcony I would soon enough hear the signal knock on wood by the abbot, after which all the monks would turn to face the front of the church as the cantor broke the Great Silence (in effect since eight o'clock the night before) by singing "Oh Lord, open my lips," to which everyone would join in, either sweetly or froggily, "and my mouth shall declare your praise." During this forty-five-minute service, the longest of all the offices, the choir monks would then make their way through long readings from Scripture, chanting antiphonally some of the rockier psalms. For example, from Psalm 3: "You hack all my enemies to the cheekbone, / You break the teeth of the wicked."

Following one pair of morning services—vigils and lauds—I ate a breakfast of cornflakes and an orange in the only dining room where talking is permitted, located down the hall from the guest refectory. My companion was Geshe Thubten Tandhar, a Tibetan Buddhist monk who was staying in the cell next to mine. Following the example of the Dalai Lama, who'd twice visited the monastery because of his affection for Thomas Merton, Geshe Tandhar fit in well with the ecumenism displayed among the monastery's three thousand annual guests, only a quarter of whom are Roman Catholic, with many Jews, Buddhists, and even nonbelievers mixed in. Dressed in scarlet and gold robes and wearing sandals, Tandhar, who has taught at the Universities of Indiana and Wisconsin, spoke with me in his low, broken, occasionally difficult-to-understand English of his many years at Namgyal, the "personal attendant" monastery in India of His Holiness the Dalai Lama, from whom he'd received various teachings and lectures for a quarter century. He spoke too of his reactions to a week among these contemplative Trappists, referred to once by Swami Satchidananda as "Christian yogis."

"I noticed in some lines of the chanting they asked for God to hate their enemies," he said, puzzled. "I'm Buddhist, so I don't believe in a Creator God. In Buddhism we never ask anybody to hate. We certainly don't ask Buddha to hate anyone. Of course, we don't pray as Christians do. The monks here look very serious. They never smile. In our monastery there is smiling. Almost all the time is spent in sitting, chanting. There are many young people as well in our monastery, sometimes eight or nine years old. . . . But I do see humble, holy Christians here. In India we often grew up seeing only Christians who were missionaries. But these aren't necessarily representative of most Christians. They are often more aggressive, or they're trying to make converts. It's like Gandhi, who thought Englishmen were so horrible because of the ones in India and how they behaved when given power. But when he went to England he was surprised to see that the regular English people at home were quite sympathetic."

Geshe Tandhar was sensitive to the ambivalent reaction his presence in choir provoked among a few monks. On his first day, he innocently came forward to receive the wafer at the Eucharist, and needed to be turned away, as the ritual is reserved for committed Roman Catholics only. But mostly the response of the Trappist monks was accepting, a sign again of the continuing influence of Merton, who, shortly before his death, in 1968, had visited the Dalai Lama in Dharamsala. "I came here because the Dalai Lama came here to visit the grave of Thomas Merton," Geshe Tandhar said. "This is very special for the Dalai Lama to do this. It is very rare—of all the many graves in the world to visit that he chose to come to Thomas Merton's grave. And he asked to come here. It was at his initiation. . . . Of course, there was some question among Christians of what it means to have a Tibetan Buddhist here. But the reverse is also true."

Most responsible for this openness to Eastern spirituality as well as for a general mood of moderation and middle-of-the-road acceptance at Gethsemani recently had been Abbot Timothy Kelly. (In April 2001, Abbot Timothy was replaced by Abbot Damien Thompson. In his late sixties, Abbot Damien is described as a "very Marine-like guy who's actually gentle and firm and kind," and he is expected to serve until age seventy-five.) Given the medieval vertical structure of government in the abbey, the abbot always sets the tone for the entire community, making as he does so many of its decisions. Abbot Timothy had managed to steer a course less extreme than either of his two predecessors— Dom James Fox, whose abbacy lasted from 1948 until 1967, and Father Flavian Burns, whose reign was much shorter, from 1968 to 1973. Dom James—a graduate of Harvard School of Business Administration and briefly an inspector of corporate tax returns for the U.S. Treasury Department—presided as abbot over a boom period of expansion, rebuilding, behind-the-scenes fundraising, and the involvement in the destiny of the monastery of such

Roman Catholic celebrities as Bishop Fulton J. Sheen and Clare Boothe Luce. His attitude could be grand, final, larger-than-life. When, for example, he secretly had a bomb shelter built and a few monks protested that they shouldn't be saved at the expense of schoolchildren in Lousiville, he ended the debate by snapping, "The Lord needs us!" His successor, Father Flavian Burns, who eschewed the title "Dom," and wore no ring or pectoral cross, was far quieter. He acceded easily to many of the more radical requests of the monks, including giving away millions of dollars' worth of the endowment built up under Dom James to various orphanages and charities, even one in Chile. If Dom James had veered too far to the right, Father Flavian reacted by swinging to the left.

Abbot Timothy, however, successfully managed to govern from the center for twenty-five years. Born in 1935, in Canada, he entered the monastery in 1958 against the strong protests of his parents. He made simple vows in 1960, the year of his father's death, solemn vows in 1964, and was ordained a priest in 1965 before leaving for Rome for two years of theological study. Friendly, with short-clipped white hair and round glasses with transparent frames, he still speaks with a Canadian twang, and smiles easily. (He's smiling as well in a photograph popular among the brothers of him on skates wielding a hockey stick.) "Twenty-five years ago when I started, I knew exactly what to do and how to do it and how everyone else was supposed to do it," he told me on the Sunday morning when we talked; we sat in facing armchairs in his large, church-style office on the first floor of the building where I was staying. "Now I no longer have the vaguest idea." He described his style of leadership self-deprecatingly as "benign dictatorship."

The best clue to the drift of Abbot Timothy's choices could be read between the lines in his discussion of what he saw as the legacy of his novice master, Thomas Merton. "Earlier there was an almost athletic aspect of doing everything as hard as you could, as fast as you could, pushing the limits all the time," he said. "Merton kept saying that it isn't a matter of doing all these things and then God is going to reward you. Asceticism and discipline are meant to make you free to receive God's gift. He would preach discipline with that subtle distinction, which did have an effect, I think." This point was made as well by James Fenton in his essay "Beyond Belief": "Thomas Merton's greatest achievement may lie not in his books but in his lifelong, largely successful battle to shift the focus of the Trappists, from penitence and asceticism to the preservation and enhancement of the sacred."

The brother I met who seemed to most vividly personify the new style of monk both envisioned and in a sense fashioned by Merton was Brother Paul Quenon, a poet and photographer who entered Gethsemani in 1958, when he was seventeen. He is from West Virginia, and earned a master's degree in systematic theology at Catholic Theological Union in 1977. He is currently junior master, which earns him a place on the abbot's advisory house council. Wiry, alert, and clear-eyed, with a close-cropped salt-and-pepper beard, Brother Paul has found a way to live a rougher life without the benefit of a special grange or hermitage. Each night he sleeps in the corner of an open woodshed. He swims in one of the property's thirteen lakes three or four times a week into early October. And he regularly hikes to the top of nearby Knob Point.

We had a pleasant enough talk with each other in a room used for storing communications equipment. But I was aware of a certain reserve, a reserve characteristic of most of the monks when you first speak with them—the palpable residue of their solitude, perhaps. As he had said to me of his own novice master, Merton, "There was a kind of distance, it was hard to pin him down, but at the same time he was bubbling over with enthusiasm and wit and sarcasm and insights and ideas." Brother Paul's reserve burst when we were walking down the wide steps of the administrative building. I happened to mention that my birthday fell on January 31, the same as Merton's. (Merton describes himself in the first sentence of *The Seven Storey Mountain* as born "on the last day of January 1915, under the sign of the Water Bearer, in a year of a great war, and down in the shadow of some French mountains on the borders of Spain.")

"You have the same birthday as Father Louis?" he asked, obviously touched. (Father Louis was Merton's spiritual name within the community.)

"Would you like to go for a swim?" he asked almost immediately afterward.

"I didn't bring a swimsuit," I answered.

"We don't use swimsuits here," he answered, simply.

I accepted, and soon we were crossing the highway, making our way through high weeds and saplings to a secluded lake surrounded by sycamore trees, the surface inkily reflecting the golds and deep blues of a late-September afternoon. After a strenuous swim in the cool water, we stretched on nearby rocks and discussed theology like two teenagers full of ideas, before pulling on our jeans and T-shirts again. We gathered fresh persimmons from the ground and headed back to vespers, which was scheduled to begin in five minutes.

During our return through the woods, Brother Paul began talking about how his life—and these swims—fit into his personal vision of the monastic life. With his emphasis on nature and creativity, the sort of monastic life he described was not only more convincing as a choice for a modern man, but was also the embodiment of an asceticism that might be described as positive rather than negative, embracing rather than denying. Perhaps it is the solution to survival toward which the entire Trappist enterprise might be reaching.

"I sleep outdoors every night," he told me, crunching twigs and dried weeds under his L.L. Bean hiking shoes. "It's a wonderful thing. The lumber shed is open. But in the wintertime, I'm snug as a bug. I have a nice goose-down sleeping bag. It may be fifteen above and I wouldn't know the difference. I'm quite comfortable. I wake up, see the stars, and hear the owls. I like solitude. I like being where there's nobody around. It's a little bit scary to me. But I'm used to that. I'm open to whatever stray dogs might come along, or rabbits, or bats. But I like all that stuff. I'm not living like a street person. If I were sleeping outside in New York City I'd be very vulnerable. But nobody's going to take my sleeping bag here."

"They say, 'Oh, you're an ascetic,' " he continued, obviously carrying on an often-rehearsed dialogue with himself as we recrossed the highway, climbed the hill, and neared the wooden gate; the bells began to toll for vespers, and the sun cast long purple tree shadows across the lawn. "Well, I'm not an *ascetic.* I'm an *aesthetic.* . . . That's more of what I'm up to."

If Brother Paul Quenon is further exploring a lifestyle first tried by Merton decades ago, the most startling innovation has come from a quarter of Trappist life that didn't even exist in America when *The Seven Storey Mountain* was first published—Trappistine monasteries for women. No mention of such an option was made in his influential spiritual autobiography, and many women readers who were attracted to the life and spirit sketched by Merton had no idea that there was historically a place in Europe within the cloisters of the White Monks for them. But the first women's house in America was established soon thereafter. It was Mount St. Mary's Abbey, in Wrentham, Massachusetts, founded by thirteen nuns from Glencairn, Ireland, in 1949. The community's "father immediate"—the required sponsor linking them to the male hierarchy of the church—was the abbot of St. Joseph's Abbey, in nearby Spencer, Massachusetts.

Over the next four decades Wrentham gave birth to three of her own daughter houses: Our Lady of the Mississippi Abbey, near Dubuque, Iowa, founded in 1964; Santa Rita Abbey, in Sonoita, Arizona, founded in 1972; and Our Lady of the Angels monastery, in Crozet, Virginia, founded in 1987. The fifth American Trappistine house, Redwoods Monastery, in Whitethorn, California, was founded in 1962 from Nazareth, Belgium, and since the 1970s its sisters have exhibited the unorthodox looseness popularly associated with California by dispensing with their traditional white robes, black scapulars, leather belts, and black veils to adopt the secular clothes of their neighbors, except in choir, when they wear their white cowls. ("We were always jealous of the sisters at Redwood because they have hoods on their cowls," one Midwestern sister confided to me of their feelings about the California Trappistines. "We can't wear hoods because our veils get in the way. But we love cowls with hoods.")

Noticing the naturalness of the metaphor of daughter houses when applied to women rather than men, and the prominent place of the *Salve Regina* sung to the Virgin Mary every evening before bedtime, I'd begun to vaguely suspect that there were elements within Cistercian life that were more welcoming for women than for men. However, that might even be seen as a fulfillment of the Cistercian tradition. Clues were in the early writings, beginning with Bernard of Clairvaux's extreme devotion to the Virgin Mary, which had a current, American, almost feminist ring. ("Jesus' Father has breasts," Bernard wrote in one particularly ecstatic moment.) For the men of the Trappist order, Thomas Merton expanded the horizons of their vision by looking back to the Desert Fathers, the medieval mystics, and eventually other global religious traditions—Zen Buddhism, Sufism, Eastern Orthodoxy. But he never deeply explored the place of women's spirituality in his own tradition, and, in fact, their growing presence and appeal did not register strongly within American Catholicism until a few years after his death. (He did, however, visit Our Lady of the Redwoods monastery on his way to India and Thailand.)

Perhaps in response to this emphasis on men, some of the Trappistine sisters I spoke with strayed from the cultic devotion to Merton's writing loyally expressed over and over again at Gethsemani and at other men's houses I'd visited. Nearly all of the men I spoke with seemed to have been moved to become monks in part by Merton's books, or, at least, were sustained in their spiritual life by his writings. But among the women, I heard more independent opinions. "I'm not a big fan of his writing," one sister admitted to me. "I've always found his tone too *argumentative*. I guess it was the times. The issues he was discussing were debatable and urgent. But now I find myself saying, 'Stop arguing. . . . Just live it.'" Many of the women were inspired instead by Saint Therese of Lisieux's spiritual autobiography, *Story of a Soul,* first published in

1899, two years after she succumbed to tuberculosis at the age of twenty-five. (Merton, too, was a devotee of Saint Therese, and was carrying a relic of hers with him at the time of his death. Like *The Seven Storey Mountain,* the autobiography of this obscure nineteenth-century French Carmelite nun was written under obedience and sold millions of copies worldwide.) The book's message is simple: We needn't fear God nor do exceptional deeds to please Him, as He loves the simplest soul as much as the greatest church father.

My suspicion that the Trappistine communities were budding, and that they were perhaps more connected than their brothers to what was going on in the surrounding American culture, was confirmed for me, in February 1999, when I visited Our Lady of the Mississippi, located seven miles from Dubuque on a 585-acre estate overlooking the Mississippi River at an intersection of Wisconsin, Illinois, and Iowa. The men's monastery down the road, New Melleray Abbey, fit the pattern of Gethsemani: its impressive four-story limestone neo-Gothic citadel was built in 1868 in the Pugin style. It was reduced to housing thirty-seven monks averaging sixty-eight years of age, down from 160 (much younger) monks in 1960. The monks' consolation tended to be the historical long view. "There was a purging after Vatican II," explained the abbot, Dom Brendan. "It might have been distressful to see the numbers dwindle. But the ones who stayed were staying for the right reasons. They found happiness in this approach to life. They didn't feel this tremendous lack of fulfillment the other guys probably felt. The Vatican Council was wonderful, because truth and life came out of it."

But Our Lady of the Mississippi—created when Wrentham was overfilled with seventy-two nuns living in a house built for sixty—continued to grow. The number of nuns went from the thirteen foundresses who arrived on October 18, 1964, to a maximum of thirty today. The week I visited, five sisters were leaving to found what would be their own first daughter house, which they were building on the island of Tautra, in Norway. The Trondheim Fjord would become their new Mississippi, and herbal soaps, they hoped, their new means of support. The site is not far from the Klosterruiner, a Cistercian monks' abbey that survived some 330 years, from its founding in 1207 until its destruction in 1537 during the Protestant Reformation. In the last few years leading up to this expansion at Our Lady of the Mississippi, the average age of the sisters had been holding steady at about fifty—nearly twenty years younger than the median age at New Melleray. No solemnly professed sisters had yet died or permanently left the community. And the attrition rate among postulants and novices had been 50 percent, compared with the 90 percent dropout rate in the men's houses. (These numbers reflect the general situation in the Roman Catholic Church, in which nuns currently outnumber priests two to one.)

"Mississippi and Wrentham are flourishing," said Dom Brendan. "Santa Rita doesn't have that many. Redwood doesn't. The one in Virginia is new. But these two are definitely thriving. I think they just have a good community life, and an appeal. You see a lot of young women. It's attractive. You come to these other monasteries and see a bunch of old men. Who knows what the future might bring in mixed communities? We have a huge church here. There's the coed, experimental Pecos Benedictine monastery in New Mexico. But that won't be happening among the Trappists anytime soon." Part of the advantage of the women's houses, in all fairness, is that they are relatively new and haven't sustained the same vertiginous climbing and then plummeting in numbers that the men's monasteries have experienced. Their incremental growth has been happy and positive without being overwhelming. (Growth has also been stronger in these cloistered communities than in other more liberal women's orders. The American nun population reached its peak of 181,000 in 1965; ten years later, their numbers had dropped to 135,000; in 2000 there were roughly 84,000, with a median age nearing seventy. In Latin America, however, religious life for women is still a growth industry.)

In other respects they are very much like any other Trappist community. Iowa is certainly a classically Trappist out-of-the-way location, with lots of undeveloped land and few large cities. During my stay in Our Lady of the Mississippi's guest house, usually reserved for visiting family members, I had the rare gift of a radio, which I tuned in to the local news every noon. The content was almost entirely weather reports threatening snow, and the updating of negotiations with the federal government concerning the plight of family farms. As seen from a plane, the terrain between Detroit and Dubuque—a diocesan center with a population of sixty thousand known a bit exaggeratedly among Catholics in the region as "the Rome of the Midwest"—is brown, hilly, and divided so regularly into quadrangles of corn and soybean fields that it resembles a sheet of accountant's ledger paper.

While Our Lady of the Mississippi lacks a grand citadel in the Old World style of Gethsemani or New Melleray, its simpler presentation is not dissimilar from that of smaller men's houses I'd visited over the past year. The Abbey of the Genesee, for instance, is located on the old Chandler farm in upstate New York, thirty-five miles south of Rochester, and its twenty-two hundred acres of forest, ravines, hills, and creeks includes a collection of barns, a stone house, and a rambling wooden guest house from the 1850s, as well as the cloister, with cells for its forty monks, and an adjoining, highly mechanized modern bakery. Mepkin Abbey, in the low country of South Carolina along the banks of the Cooper River, is likewise a motley collection of smaller buildings as well as a chicken farm spread over three thousand acres of the old Henry and Clare Boothe Luce plantation, with the donors' burial place on the property marked by a marble headstone with a live oak carving. While its entrance is a grand antebellum avenue lined with Spanish moss–covered oaks, the mansion of what was once a slave-driven tidewater plantation was dismantled before the monks arrived in 1949, because of termite infestation.

Our Lady of the Mississippi is a part of the Stampher estate, its main building a two-story tan stone home, built in 1952, with a brown shingle roof, dormer windows, stone fireplaces, green wooden shutters, and tastefully appointed carriage lamps. The broad circular driveway completes the effect of an idyllic made-for-TV home. Yet when the property, advertised in the *Wall Street Journal,* was first visited by the buyer, Father Matthias Kerndt, of New Melleray, he wrote to the abbess of Wrentham that he saw in the elegant country home "a convent ready to go," and the purchase was quickly completed. The living areas simply needed to be transformed into monastic spaces: refectory, dormitory, chapter room, parlor, wardrobe, and chapel. The front porch was walled in as a visitors' parlor and divided in two by a concealing grille, which was a pre–Vatican II requirement for nuns, adding an unintentionally harem-like mystery to these enclosures. Its wet bar was transformed into a confessional. On the bluff below the house, the Hickory Hill Farm includes 214 tillable acres as well as a tree farm that produces eighty-five thousand Christmas trees each year.

The sisters have since transformed the property with a cottage industry. In May 1965, a white, prefab building was delivered and assembled with the help of some of the monks from New Melleray, who'd already laid the foundation. This candy factory is now the operations center of an industry that ships thirty tons of creamy caramels and four tons of mints annually from September through December. The caramel recipe is said to have originally been given to their mother house in Wrentham by a Greek candy maker. A separate chapel was dedicated on May 3, 1968, simply built with facing wooden choir stalls, stone altar, red brick walls, brown tile floors, pipe organ, clear windows, and a guest chapel with five pews at a right angle from the altar so the nuns remain out of view, another leftover from before Vatican II. (I was invited by the nuns to read the lesson on Ash Wednesday from Paul's Letter to the Corinthians, and so had the opportunity just once to face them from the lectern in their off-limits zone.) There is a brick addition at the rear of the nuns' enclosure now, which contains cells for thirty, since the main house was filled to capacity in the early years and sisters slept together in dorms converted from its bedrooms. Stone House, an old country farmhouse at the bottom of the hill, is unreachable on snow days except by vehicles with four-wheel drive. It also has been renovated for guests, and there is a retreat house and a cabin a few minutes' walk from the cloister.

What most set off Our Lady of the Mississippi from men's houses I'd visited was its special energy. The men's houses are institutions from another time that seem to be offering an alternative to modern life both quaint and strangely futuristic. They are touching and paradoxical, as they seem to be withering on the vine at the very moment they are again reawakening interest, if not commitment, in the general population. The women's communities seem more contemporary, without in any way being lax in their fulfillment of the Cistercian regimen of seven prayer offices a day, divine reading, and manual labor. At Our Lady of the Mississippi, they do receive a daily news summary from yahoo.com printed out by the abbess, and their menu of entertainment includes five feature films a year and weekly educational videos chosen by the video committee. (The monks at the Abbey of the Genesee see only one feature film a year—*Driving Miss Daisy, Chariots of Fire*—and get their weekly news only from a diocesan newspaper and *U.S. News & World Report.*) At Our Lady of the Mississippi, the dividing line between cloister and world seems dotted rather than solid.

I noticed the liveliness of the nuns almost immediately when Sister Carol Dvorak, the guest secretary, met me at the Dubuque airport. Her graying brown hair was stuck under a short, black veil, her white habit was covered in a thick green ski jacket, and I could see she was wearing black stockings with brown loafers. "I thought that was you," she said in the flatly musical *Fargo* accent that many of the sisters had, especially those, like Sister Carol, who were raised in Iowa. Sister Carol was a slight, peppy woman in her early sixties who seemed a couple decades younger, due to her almost girlish manner. She led me out to a battleship-gray van owned by the community. Her relationship to the vehicle was a bit awkward. "Do you know how to drive?" she asked, half offering me the keys. "When I drive with someone I get distracted." I declined, but a few miles down U.S. 52, I wished I hadn't, as we flew past a state trooper while we were doing eighty miles an hour.

Sister Carol turned to me and smiled as she said, "The abbess lectured us just last week on speeding." But I was used to such driving from contemplatives. When Merton's literary secretary, Brother Patrick Hart, dropped me at the Louisville airport, I watched as he took off with an extremely comic flourish of noisy lurches and sudden, screeching stops.

We went by New Melleray to deliver a tray of little sandwiches pierced with toothpicks and festooned with green pickles left over from Sunday's party for the departing foundresses. Sister Carol drove for another twenty minutes before turning left onto Hillans Road at a sign for the abbey. "I think that's the most beautiful sight in the world," she said, gesturing toward the view over the icy Mississippi River and farmlands dotted with occasional silver silos beneath faded blue skies. She stopped to show me a "prairie patch" of indigenous grasses being cultivated by one of the sisters. We then drove down a steep hill past a white wooden barn with green shingle roofs and a cupola, in front of which were piled round bales of hay wrapped in clear plastic. Peeking from the stalls of yet another barn—which the sisters were now leasing to local farmers—were Black Angus cows. Shifting gears, we then drove through a creek with water splattering around us like a full-service car wash and up a hill opening out onto more swerving brown, tan, gold, green, gray, copper, and white fields.

Many sisters were out doing chores that afternoon. One stood stranded by her tractor because she hadn't brought the key. "Do you have an extra key on your ring?" she asked, coming over to our vehicle. When Sister Carol told her no, she complained, "Shoot! I guess I'll have to go back to get it." Then she added another "Shoot!" for good measure. When we'd driven back up the hill to the main road past the English country house and the candy factory on the way to the guest quarters, more sisters in regular street clothes were proceeding in one direction or another. Many of them waved as we drove past. They were bundled up for winter, but I caught flashes of sweatshirts, flannel shirts, colored socks, and bandannas accessorizing their habits, as well as running shoes and Birkenstock-style sandals. When we arrived at the single-story guest house covered in white aluminum siding, a hefty-looking sister waved at us. She was pulling a blue Toyota pickup truck into the garage, located between one wing with three separate studio bedrooms, a kitchen area, and a full bath and my own more homey wing.

Along the way Sister Carol told me some of her own story. Born in 1937. Attended an all-girls Catholic academy in Cedar Rapids. Became a Sister of Mercy, practicing nursing and social service, and teaching French in college. In her twenties decided to become a contemplative rather than an active sister, but the mother general of the Sisters of the Mercy put her off, saying, "You don't have a contemplative vocation, just a devotion to Therese of Lisieux." Finally entered Our Lady of the Mississippi in 1968, when nuns still lived six to a dorm room, flagellated themselves every Friday after vigils with knotted ropes, and used sign language to speak with anyone besides the novice mistress or the second superior. Her many official hats now also included novice director, librarian, temporary secretary to the abbess, and porteress, answering the phone and the door.

"I don't think any of us is a feminist, strictly speaking," she said, in answer to my question about her feelings on women's social issues. "But some of the sisters are more aware and self-sufficient. The monks used to help us a lot with the machinery and maintenance. Now we're trying to do that ourselves. Some of us have fought hard for inclusive language in the offices. We haven't totally succeeded in the liturgy, but sisters on the liturgy committee are working on changing the language." The abbess later admitted to me that they'd come under criticism from women she characterized as "from Chicago, the University of Chicago," who'd been on retreat and were upset that God was still referred to in their services as "He" rather than "She" or some other admixture of pronouns. Still, the bottom line is that expressed simply by Lucy Kaylin in her *For the Love of God: The Faith and Future of the American Nun:* "Although some would balk at the characterization, being a nun seems inherently feminist: This rigorous and communal life fosters a self-reliance and interdependence among women in spite of the patriarchy that oversees it."

"Will you be coming to compline later?" Sister Carol asked as she dropped me off. "We'll leave the night light on for you in the guest chapel."

The half of the guest house where I was staying was quite different from the cells I'd stayed in at other monasteries. I found myself in a mini-home, with bedroom, bathroom, living room with working fireplace, and eat-in kitchen. Two picture windows looked out on a brown snow-flecked landscape, white birch trees, and vast amounts of gray-blue sky. Unlike other monasteries, where one would eat in cafeteria-style refectories, Our Lady of the Mississippi leaves its guests to prepare their own food. My refrigerator was stocked with staples: bacon, chicken, eggs, cold cuts, sliced cheese, peanut butter. The one low bookshelf next to a walnut rocker in the beige-paneled and-carpeted living room was filled with Catholic standards by Merton, Nouwen, Hans Urs von Balthasar, as well as a few surprises, such as Kahlil Gibran's *The Prophet,* Elie Wiesel's *Night,* and a picture-book encyclopedia, *Birds of America.* What I'd discovered to be the most important item in more rural monasteries, where you need to walk from guest house to chapel in the dark, was a long metal flashlight that rested on a window ledge next to a "Thank You for Not Smoking" sign.

Unfortunately, contrary to the freer spirit that blows through Our Lady of the Mississippi—their church having been built on a pre–Vatican II blueprint—the nuns were heard but not seen as they chanted the psalms. Visible to the guests were the raised sanctuary stage with its granite altar, an orthodox icon of Mother and Child, and a wooden, rustic sculpture of an outstretched hand holding a candle, the reserved sacrament, the bread and wine used in the Eucharist. Father Jim, the white-haired chaplain of the community, who's in his eighties, performed the mass at 5:00 p.m. on weekdays in purple vestments and with a walker. Father Jim is a former abbot of New Melleray and now lives in his own cabin on the property. The conclusion of compline was a bit haunting, after the nuns sang the *Salve Regina* to the candlelit icon of the Virgin Mary. At Mepkin Abbey in South Carolina, guests sit in choir with the monks, and the *Salve Regina* often features a guitar accompaniment since their abbot, the musically inclined Father Francis Kline, graduated from Julliard. Then the guests line up with the monks to be sprinkled with holy water before retiring for the night. At Our Lady of the Mississippi, I stood alone at the guest steps to the side of the altar as the abbess, visible only in silhouette, her head covered with some sculptural headpiece draped in a cowl, came to the side railing to sprinkle me with holy water. In the near dark, she seemed an unreal figure out of a Grimm brothers tale.

The nuances of all these Trappist and Trappistine communities make the metaphor of mother houses and daughter houses especially apt. They seem as similar and different as parents and children. Of the daughter houses of Gethsemani, the Abbey of the Genesee offers the most traditional option. Their abbot, John Eudes Bamberger, embodies the attitude of "American Tough" that Robert Imperato felt so essential to the older Trappists: a sign outside Genesee's cave-like cedar-and-oak chapel reminds guests that mass is for Catholics only; the brothers rise for vigils at 2:25 a.m., an hour before the monks at Gethsemani. Mepkin Abbey, by inviting guests to sit in choir and eat in the refectory with the monks, offers a more flexible version of monastery life. Likewise, among the women, Wrentham is most traditional and conservative in look and manner. ("We founded three daughter houses in equal parts sorrow and joy," the Abbey of St. Mary's reports on its Web site, along with its current healthy tally of five junior professed and six novices.) Redwoods, one hundred miles north of Cape Mendocino, on the westernmost point of the state of California, is the most experimental. Our Lady of the Mississippi has a Midwest character, especially as explained to me by its abbess, Mother Gail Fitzpatrick. "The Midwest moved pretty quickly in its churches and religious houses after Vatican II, much quicker than the East Coast, not as quickly as the West Coast," she told me. "The Midwest in Catholic matters steers a pretty forward-looking course, but pretty mainline. Whereas in general the East Coast is conservative and the West Coast is far-out."

Our Lady's temperament has also been colored by other factors. The original foundresses were unusually young when they first arrived in Iowa. Their average age was twenty-seven, and only three sisters had been in the order more than ten years. The group was a mix of former lay and choir sisters, a distinction erased just before the group departed Wrentham. They were accompanied on this first trip by Mothers Angela and Benedict from Wrentham, and by Dom Thomas Keating, their father immediate from Spencer, who in recent years has become well-known as a monk of the Snowmass monastery near Aspen, teaching a meditation practice he calls "the centering prayer" in seminars and on a series of cassettes. ("Well, the centering prayer is really just Merton's notion of prayer redone," a monk of Gethsemani claimed to me a bit brusquely.) Timing was also important for the Mississippi foundation. Their cutting loose at this moment made it much easier for them to make changes so they experienced little of the turmoil of other communities about the elimination of the lay class and they switched to an English liturgy long before their mother house. As Mother Gail told me, "We went to the English liturgy very quickly, and that became a problem in our relationship with the mother house. That was part of the trauma of our foundation."

The woman in the community who probably knows the most about this period is Sister Columba Guare, a cousin of the well-known playwright John Guare, who has written many plays and screenplays, among them *Six Degrees of Separation.* As the first abbess of this new community—a post Sister Columba held until 1982 when she stepped down—her vision was perhaps the most crucial in shaping Our Lady of the Mississippi. Sister Columba has blue eyes, white hair, and flawless ivory skin, and the day we spoke she was wearing a knitted black sleeveless sweater over her white habit, dark blue stockings, and brown leather sandals. She told me her own story and the history of her community. We sat, as in all of my interviews at Our Lady, in the visitors' parlor, the converted porch with its rosy wall-to-wall carpeting, two facing wooden rockers upholstered in green, a small ticking clock and a large pink candle on a small walnut table, two high windows with wooden shutters, and a print on the wall of an early Renaissance "Annunciation" painting.

Born Peggy Guare to an Irish Catholic family in Montpelier, Vermont, in 1926, Sister Columba entered Mount St. Mary's Abbey in Wrentham, as a Trappistine postulant, in 1951, when the monastery was only a year and a half old. "My friend Rita had put her application in and was going down to visit at Wrentham and asked me if I wanted to go," she recalled. She had thought only vaguely until then of becoming a Sister of Mercy. "I said, 'Oh, I'd love to go.' Well, the minute I saw the sisters walking out to the barn to shovel the manure and take care of the cows . . . oh, that really spoke to me. Rita was a very fastidious person, so it didn't appeal to her at all." At first they wanted to send her to Ireland because the monastery had no extra rooms, but Archbishop Cushing in Boston intervened on her behalf, and she entered that May. "In those days you just went in cold," Sister Columba recalled.

> The first thing that surprised me was that the monastery was light inside. It was built around a courtyard. I had this idea that it was going to be dark and gloomy. But the life was very hard. We didn't get enough sleep. We didn't get enough to eat. I was skinny as a rail. We worked out in the fields. We milked cows, tended the garden. But I really loved it. There were a lot of young girls there, which helped. There were about twenty in the novitiate when I entered. So it was a big crowd. I persevered through thick and thin and finally made my vows. Then in 1960 the community had grown so much that they were looking for another place to start a monastery. The site chosen was Argentina because the monks had gone there. Mother Angela, who was the abbess, took me with her to Argentina. We were offered a site. But we were

always under the aegis of the monks in Spencer. The next spring, a year later, the abbot resigned, and the new abbot at Spencer, Thomas Keating, wasn't willing to take on a new foundation in Argentina. So we had to wait.

By 1961, however, Mother Angela renewed her campaign, sending letters to all Trappist abbots in America informing them of the community's need to expand. A response came from New Melleray Abbey, and the abbess replied with a suggestion that the sisters needed "a farm with charm." Property was purchased about twenty miles from New Melleray in January 1963, and plans were drawn up by an architect for a building that was too expensive and had no windows, only skylights and murals of the outdoors painted on the walls. The abbot general of the order rejected the plans, commenting dryly, "With this system, the architect will divide the community into two groups—those who will become saints, and those who will go crazy." Then Father Jim saw an ad in the *Wall Street Journal* for the Stampher estate. Mother Angela and Sister Columba, who had already been chosen as superior-to-be of the new community, were in Citeaux, France, at a meeting of abbesses, when they received the real estate brochure. They arrived in Iowa to view the property on July 14, and closed on the deal two days later. By October 21 the foundresses—who'd left Wrentham in their black traveling cloaks as their sisters waved from the infirmary windows—moved into the guest house for two weeks while modifications were made to the main house.

Over the next decade, the sisters outgrew this new home as well and launched a fundraising drive to build an entire cloister. By late winter of 1979 the building was nearly completed, but the final cost came to $750,000—almost twice the original estimate of $400,000—and funds were insufficient to complete the project. Having tried everything, Mother Columba put an ad in the *Wall Street Journal* with the plea, "Nuns Need Help." Soon afterward more than $240,000 was received, most of the money coming from Reverend Leo L. Henkel, an Illinois priest and friend of the abbot of New Melleray. The *Wall Street Journal* capitalized on this supposed modern-day miracle of advertising by running an accolade for itself in *Advertising Age* titled "An Inspirational Story" and quoting a UPI report: "Mother Columba would like to thank God—and the *Wall Street Journal*—for helping her abbey survive its financial crisis."

As she tells the story today, the miracle sounds a bit less like the plot of a sentimental 1940s Hollywood movie. A pivotal character in the placing of the ad had been B. J. Weber, a local high school rugby player described by one sister as having been "a hippie and down and out in many ways" from nearby Dubuque; he had showed up at New Melleray Abbey one afternoon to buy bread and wound up being converted to Christianity after one conversation with Father Jim and then in further visits with the monastery's hermit, Father William. He became friendly with the nuns when Father William was elected community chaplain. As Sister Columba recalled, "With Father William came B.J. and his dog." Weber eventually graduated from the University of Dubuque theological seminary without ever joining the Roman Catholic Church or becoming a priest. After six years of living in the community, he moved to New York City at the suggestion of Sister Columba, who sensed that "B.J. would be good at working with young kids. So I told him, Why don't you go to New York to Covenant House?"

One of Weber's contacts when he moved to New York City in 1979 was an old rugby friend who was writing for the *Wall Street Journal.* "So that's how there got to be an ad," said Sister Columba. "Actually, it only brought in about $40,000. Not an awful lot. We got people who called but didn't follow through. At the very end, we'd exhausted all our resources, so we were going to have to stop. The bank called and said there was a priest with bonds amounting to $100,000, which would get us over the hump. I talked to the priest, and I said, 'Is it because of our ad in the *Wall Street Journal?*' He said, 'No. I did see the ad. And it almost made me change my mind.'" B. J. Weber went on to become a licensed pastor of the Manhattan Church of the Nazarene, working from 1979 to 1984 as a self-supporting missionary out of the Lambs

Club near Times Square, helping street people, prostitutes, and drug addicts. In 1984 he founded the New York Fellowship, a free-form interdenominational ministry to Wall Street bankers whom he takes on yearly retreats to New Melleray and Our Lady of the Mississippi; his ministry also includes: professional athletes, at-risk city kids, diplomats, and public officials. His most high-profile personal ministry has been as chaplain to the New York Yankees, and he has spoken at Sunday-morning chapel services for the Mets, the Giants, and the Jets.

I visited with Weber one afternoon in the New York Fellowship offices on Gramercy Park. Describing himself as having been "kind of like the nuns' mascot" during the 1970s, Weber attributes much of his spiritual direction in those years, and now, to Mother Columba. "She changed my life," he said, stretched out on a blue upholstered couch in his office following a counseling lunch with a retiring pro-football player. "Here was this woman who was receiving me and loving me, like a mother. I had a great mom. But Columba was a spiritual mother who really directed my life in a very key way. Once you put yourself in the hands of a spiritual director, you have incredible opportunity for experiences, but also you're confronted with your weakness, your lying, your bullshit, by absolute, rigorous honesty, which is demanding. She was, and still is, a source of wisdom and intimacy and vulnerability and fondness and remembrance. My children were baptized at the monastery." The father of two boys, Weber has been married since 1980 to Sheila, who serves as associate director of the fellowship.

With those active years as abbess and hands-on spiritual director to Weber and others during a historically disruptive time, Sister Columba, like many contemplatives in their seventies or eighties, expresses a kind of wisdom that is more commonsensical and even irreverent than might be expected. Older monks and nuns, at least among the Trappists, tend to be wry, and sometimes giddy, but rarely pious. As Sister Columba looked back on her experiences—including having spent several years after she stepped down as abbess setting up a hermitage and orphanage in the mountains of Bolivia with Father William, who has since left the order and married—she was both frank and upbeat. "We try to be careful about the people we take," she said.

> You have to be a self-starter in a life like this. Once the novitiate is over, you're pretty much on your own. You have to be something of a scholar, you have to have some interest, and be a reader. A life of prayer can be pretty dismal. You just go and sit. And the next day you go and sit. It isn't that all these lights are flashing. It's not a lot of fun. And you have to be faithful to that.
>
> What happens is that your life deepens, and it gets turned upside down, too. All the things I believed in so heartily when I first came about saving all these souls, and doing penance and making my way to heaven. Well, that gets all turned upside down. But so many theologians think the same thing. If you go on with your childhood faith, it's not really faith. It has to be challenged. I think you get to the point where you say, "I don't know." And I can't know. And nobody can know. I guess belief keeps me here. I guess I believe in love, whatever that is. That whatever this being . . . you can't even call God "being," you don't know what to call it . . . but love is the force, and everything we see and experience is an expression of this love. Behind you, behind me, behind who we are as a people is the love that called us forth. It's that love that's going to receive us back. But how it's going to be, I just can't imagine.

Her frankness about the emptiness as well as the fullness of her life came back to me when I later read Mark Salzman's novel *Lying Awake* (2000), a tour de force in which the author imagines himself in the life of a nun who writes poetry, secluded in a contemplative Carmelite monastery outside Los Angeles:

After Solemn Profession, however, rites of passage in the spiritual life suddenly thinned out. For seven years she watched as the cloister got smaller and the silence got bigger. She was a bride of Christ, but still had not met her Spouse, and the farther she traveled inward without finding Him, the more aware she became of His absence.

> *I am like a desert owl,*
> *like an owl among the ruins.*
> *I lie awake and moan,*
> *like a lone sparrow on the roof.*

The hour concluded with a sigh. The Sisters filed out of choir in order of seniority, with the oldest Sister at the front of the line and the youngest taking up the rear. Sister John kept pace with the veil in front of her, thinking, *I've been walking behind Sister Angelica for thirteen years. Only our deaths will change the order. Or if one of us leaves.*

Later that afternoon, I returned to the visitors' parlor to meet with Mother Gail, the current abbess. When I rang the bell in the foyer, a sister working as porteress popped her head through a portal. "Mother Gail's in a pretty high-powered meeting about the foundation in Norway," she informed me. "I'd hate to interrupt. But just a minute. Have a seat." After some rustling she opened the door from the other side, allowing me back into the sunlit sitting room. I was met there about five minutes later by Mother Gail, an obviously intelligent woman in her early sixties. She had white hair pushed back behind her black veil, big blue eyes, and wore knee-high black stockings and sandals. She kept an alert, knowing, and kind expression throughout our talk, which was less about the essential spiritual issues currently on Sister Columba's mind, and more about matters of building a community of women, especially in an America focused increasingly over the last twenty-five years on feminine identity and self-determination.

Having entered Wrentham at what is now the unusually young age of eighteen, in 1956, Mother Gail came as a foundress to Our Lady of the Mississippi when she was still only twenty-four years old. Like many presidents of women's colleges affiliated with men's universities across the country, she has dealt since being elected abbess in 1982 with new decisions presented by the changing status of women. And like many of those women presidents, she tends toward a "separate but equal" policy. "I'm not sure that a completely mixed community would be ideal," she said. "It complicates life immensely if you're trying to lead a celibate life. I think the charism of men and women is complementary periodically. But on a day-to-day basis I think we'd do better to live our life fully as women. A women's monastery tends to facilitate women being able to handle every aspect of their lives they physically can. Which means they have to develop talents which aren't normally women's talents—financial, mechanical. And men in the same way develop talents in cooking, housecleaning. When they don't, it's a mess. It's really bad. In a dysfunctional men's community, you can walk in the door and tell. But where there's a healthy community of men or women they can develop their complementary gifts." She added, somewhat circumspectly, "What I'm saying isn't coming from feminism. It's coming from observation."

Of course, women have always had a place in Cistercian life, and, as in the church generally, that place has sometimes been more prominent than in the rest of society. There have been houses of women since the early years of the order. Tart, the first house of Cistercian nuns, was founded around 1120. Indeed, while there were about four hundred Cistercian men's monasteries in existence in Europe by 1300, there were eight hundred women's monasteries, from Switzerland to Cyprus, Spain to Syria. Alongside the famous male centers of spirituality of the twelfth century, Clairvaux, Villers, Himmerod, Heisterbach, those of the nuns were also developing: Parc-aux-Dames la Ramee, Florival, Aywieres, Nazareth, la Chambre, and Val-des-Roses. The intensity of the women's monasteries' spiritual life is witnessed by their first generation of spiritual biography and mysticism: Saint Lutgarde, Saint Alice, Beatrice of Nazareth, the three Idas (of Louvain, Novelle, and Leau), and the saints of Helfta—Mechtild of

Magdeburg, Mechtild of Hackeborn, her sister Gertrude, and especially Gertrude the Great. (Without belonging officially, these last three have been identified with the Order of Citeaux by their spirituality and observances.) Catherine Bosa, a later well-known Cistercian sister who became the wife of Protestant reformer Martin Luther, has been predictably made less conspicuous.

At the heart of the Cistercians' distinctive spirituality were not only women, but also an adoration of the feminine aspect through both Jesus and Mary. Andrew Harvey, in *Son of Man: The Mystical Path to Christ,* includes the Cistercians in a "largely forgotten tradition within Christian mysticism—that which worshipped Jesus directly as the Mother. . . . This tradition runs underground from the Greek fathers (who may have been surreptitiously inspired by Gnostic sources) to a group of Cistercian mystics of the twelfth and thirteenth centuries—Guerric of Igny, Bernard of Clairvaux, and Isaac of Stella—through to its consummate expression in the visions of women mystics such as Marguerite of Oingt, Mechtild of Magdeburg, and—especially—the wisest and greatest of all the 'mother' mystics of Christianity, Julian of Norwich."

The enthusiastic Marian devotion of Bernard of Clairvaux was well known enough to be memorialized by Dante in *The Divine Comedy,* in which the Cistercian abbot is awarded perhaps the most glorious job in the entire epic—introducing the poet to the Virgin Mary, the ultimate beatific vision in which human, romantic love is revealed in its essence as eternal and divine, and feminine in form. In Canto XXXII, the penultimate canto of *Paradiso,* the transfigured Bernard of Clairvaux tells Dante: "Look now on her who most resembles Christ, / For only the great glory of her shining / Can purify your eyes to look on Christ." Few men contributed more than Bernard to the cult of the Virgin, which spread over Europe in the twelfth, thirteenth, and fourteenth centuries, leaving its mark in the hymns, paintings, sculpture, and architecture of Western Christendom. The multiplying lady chapels of this period were mostly a response to the teachings of his series of sermons on the Gospel text of the Annunciation (*"Homilae super Missus est"*), seven prime-time sermons for the feasts of Our Lady, and the sermon on her nativity. And so all Cistercian abbeys are named for *Notre Dame,* Our Lady.

The first house of Trappistine women was La Val-Sainte, founded more than six hundred years later, in 1796, under the sponsorship of Dom Augustine de Lestrange. The house came about when a disparate group of religious women sought refuge in Switzerland during the French Revolution with some Trappist monks who had recently fled France. This feminine version of the Cistercians' strict reformation then experienced a worldwide expansion, along with the men's houses, in the nineteenth and twentieth centuries. Indeed, since 1970 there have been twenty-one new women's Trappistine foundations and one incorporation. At the general chapter meetings of the late 1980s and 1990s the women were given greater strength constitutionally within the order, so that abbesses now take part equally with the abbots at general chapters, vote equally for the abbot general, and have laid down the principle that a woman could be elected as the leader of the entire order. In most other orders of the Roman Catholic Church, the men's and women's chapters are separate, with the men remaining as the final legislators. In this sense, the Trappists are the most forward-thinking in gender balancing. They are putting into practice the words of Pope John Paul II in his statement "On Women," words which many women within the church grumble about as being hypocritical, given the pope's adamant opposition to women priests: "Woman has an indispensable contribution to make in establishing a culture capable of harmonizing reason and feeling, for providing a concept of life which would be open to the idea of mystery."

"For so many years the women had no voice at all except through the abbots who legislated for them," said Mother Gail. "The voice of women is now being heard and respected. Many abbesses are now making visitations and giving retreats at houses of monks. That's very significant. They realize that the nuns have a gift to offer. It's different, because by and large we don't have the same level of higher education. That's not going to be true across the board, but basically. The men have always been the teachers, the preachers, and the truth-givers. Now they realize that higher education isn't necessarily what's most important for someone who's going to come in and give a retreat. There's something else."

This percolation of change within the church has interestingly been paralleled in popular culture in the last fifty years by the fascination with nuns, and priests, too, though hardly and barely at all with monks. In 1959, Audrey Hepburn was nominated for an Academy Award for her depiction, in *The Nun's Story,* of a sister in the Belgian Congo who rebels and leaves her order. More light-hearted portrayals were made in the 1960s by Debbie Reynolds, in the true story of the Belgian sister Ann, torn between God and a recording contract in *The Singing Nun* (1966), and Sally Fields as Sister Betrille, a nun in a Puerto Rican convent gifted with the ability to fly, for eighty-two episodes, in the 1967 ABC sitcom *The Flying Nun.* (Her headdress was a version of that of the Daughters of Charity, a French community founded in 1633, with dramatic points protruding nearly a foot from either side of the head, earning the sisters the nickname "God's geese.") A group of East European Catholic nuns were helped in building their chapel in the desert by an unemployed construction worker, Homer Smith, a role for which Sidney Poitier won an Academy Award, in the 1963 film *Lilies of the Field.* In the 1990s, Whoopi Goldberg played a Vegas lounge singer hiding out in disguise as a choir director in a convent in *Sister Act* (1992), and Susan Sarandon won an Oscar for best actress for her portrayal, in *Dead Man Walking* in 1995, of the Louisiana nun Helen Prejean, who became the first female spiritual advisor for an inmate on death row. On Broadway, the governess in *The Sound of Music,* played by Julie Andrews, was a disillusioned novice from a convent; more farcically, *Nunsense,* which opened at the Cherry Lane Theatre in 1985, was a musical comedy about "The Little Sisters of Hoboken," staged as a fake benefit revue to raise money to bury the last four of fifty-two nuns killed by botulism. The British nun Sister Wendy Beckett has become a cult figure for her televised art tours. Among recent novelty items capitalizing on the almost kitsch appeal of nuns are wind-up toys such as Nunzilla; the popular hand puppet known as the "Boxing Nun"; and "Warrior Nun" comics with illustrated sisters in slit skirts and thigh-high boots.

Mother Gail envisions a place for nuns as well in contemporary life though with a different emphasis perhaps and without the laugh track. "I think monastic life corresponds to something that's innate in human nature," she said. "I really wanted to get married and have a family. It's very attractive to me. But I knew that it wasn't going to be enough. Some of us have this drive to the ultimate. The active living out of the Gospel can change with the culture. The face of apostolic life can change radically, and I think it is right now. Women can do a lot of things in the world and still have a regular life and family. But monastic life goes back even pre-Christ. It corresponds to something in nature. Women who are drawn to it have to go to that level. They can't just live on the surface of happiness. They have to go deeper."

During the rest of the week I saw in operation the sisters' self-sufficiency and the cost of the freedom of contemplation. Their earliest incarnation as farmers was tied into a dependence on their brothers down the road, especially Brother Placid, who began in 1967 to oversee the harvesting of their soybeans, corn, and hay, and the planting of an orchard of apples, peaches, cherries, and plums. After Brother Placid left the abbey, in 1985, the nuns decided to rent the farmland rather than continue the work of cultivation by themselves, though three large vegetable gardens are still maintained by the sisters, some haying is done, and a woodlands conservation program is underway. In charge of these activities was the monastery's farm manager, Sister Sherry Pech, who also kept a kiln in a cabin on the property.

Their current center of financial self-subsistence is the candy factory, where I was taken on tour by Sister Rebecca. She had entered the monastery twelve years earlier, at the age of twenty-seven, after growing up in San Antonio, Texas, and working at a well-paying job at an insurance company in southern California.

She had adjusted well to the community, though she admitted that her successful past in the secular world was at first a psychological impediment. "I felt like a hypocrite the first few months I was here," she told me. "I just felt that I'd done too many things to measure up to the purity I saw around me. But gradually I came to see that we were all in this thing together in pretty much the same way. I grew more into the reality of life in community."

As I was visiting off-season, the production lines were mostly empty. I saw an empty copper caramel bowl; machetes for cutting candy; a hot kettle for the chocolate; a statue of the Blessed Virgin Mary sharing shelf space with jars of citric acid, used for cleaning. The 1940s-era factory equipment was imposingly industrial in appearance. "These can be real heartbreaks when we're busy," Sister Rebecca told me. "When they break down, we can't get parts very easily anymore." On the walls were signs reminding the sisters of their ultimate vocation: "Embrace Each Moment in Simplicity"; "This is a House of Prayer." The factory also included a prayer room, where the workers gathered for breaks. "We come here to refocus and not get too absorbed in our work," she told me.

I was told that visitors must step carefully while walking through, during the crucial time before the Christmas holidays, as the sisters are wielding cleavers with foot-long blades, hefting eighteen-by-thirty-six-inch sheets of hardened caramel from room to room, or emptying vats of hot light or dark brown viscous liquid lifted from the flame at the precise time and temperature (after forty-five minutes, when the liquid reaches 245 degrees Fahrenheit) into table-height, cot-sized, inch-deep cooling trays. On two occasions, once in the 1980s and again in the 1990s, the abbey, which sells its product by mail order and online, decided to boycott Nestle (then its principal chocolate manufacturer) because of the company's violation of World Health Organization human rights agreements. They finally settled instead on Van Leer chocolate, of Paterson, New Jersey, the hometown of Sister Kathleen O'Neill. Their output now includes vanilla, honey, and chocolate caramels, fudge, penuche, and green and chocolate mints.

On the afternoon before I left the monastery, after a week's stay, I visited with Father Jim, chaplain of the community since 1980, in his two-room cabin a ten-minute walk down the road from the cloister. Born in 1913, he entered New Melleray Abbey as a veteran of World War II, during which he'd served on a navy cargo ship in the Pacific. Father Jim embodied the rising and falling curve experienced by that generation in monastic life. Having liked the navy regimen, Father Jim looked to the monastery "as a kind of support group," being unwilling to work in his family's banking business in Iowa. He created a successful enough groove for himself at New Melleray, learning to weld, to cut, and to put up breaching for boilers, and eventually he was elected abbot in 1964. But in the middle of the upheaval created by Vatican II, he had a nervous breakdown, or what he now sees as a "breakthrough." "We had a self-study in 1967," he recalls. "We brought in experts to help us learn to communicate every morning in groups of fifteen or twenty, eyeball to eyeball. You know in those days nobody ever looked at each other. Many good young men left. I discovered just how uptight I was, how angry I was, but how unaware I was of it." He eventually stepped down as abbot and reintegrated himself as an ordinary brother in the community.

The tumult of those days seemed far behind as I talked with the genial Father Jim, who had recovered successfully from bypass surgery in 1994. The main room of his small cabin was piled high on every surface with books, magazines, a magnifying glass, a phone, an answering machine, manuscript pages, and photographs. The golden sunlight of the late-February afternoon exposed all the motes of dust filling the room as crows cawed in the trees visible through the low windows. A sister would come to pick him up once a day to drive him to the chapel for mass; otherwise he observed most of the services by himself in his overstuffed armchair by his wide wooden desk. The arrangement struck him as ironic, since, as he put it, referring in part to his life amid twenty-eight women, "I thought I was going to give up everything by becoming a monk, and here I got everything back."

This surprising turn of events seemed to him crucial in his

own healing, and indicative of the direction of the healing of the monastic life so rife with conflict and doubt just thirty years earlier. "Coming to a life like this, you have to have a pretty good idea of who you are and what you want," he added. "But that wasn't so true before Vatican II, and that's why a lot of young men left. They had the opportunity to find out who they were. Now when young men enter, they have to ask themselves, 'Am I mature enough to live the celibate life?' "

A product of that earlier, challenging period, B. J. Weber remembers Father Jim's very brokenness as a source of the humility that inspired his own Pauline conversion on December 16, 1973, when he met him for the first time. "I had a ponytail, a 'Free Angela Davis' pin, and a pocket full of drugs," Weber recalled.

> Father Jim greeted me with, "Hey, you look interesting. What are you all about?" We started talking. I accused him of being a colonialist, imperialist pig because of his association with the Catholic Church. Then we went and had coffee and had this three-hour exchange about faith, God, sin, and the issues of life. I remember him reaching into his black-and-white habit and pulling out a green New Testament and turning to Hebrews 11:1, which reads, "Faith is the assurance of things hoped for, the conviction of things not seen." . . . That meeting was God's timing. No one can bring another person to Christ. They can only lead him towards Him. But there was this shadow of Christ in Father James, through his own humiliation, his own insufficiency, as it were. I was convinced of the deep conviction of the reality of faith in his life as he was willing to receive such a young man. He was fifty-nine at the time. I was twenty-six. That night I went home and said a prayer. I repented as best I knew how at twenty-six years old. I went home to this woman I'd met in Greece who I was living with—my sort of personal

recreation center. Poor thing, she just wanted to please a man. I told her I had to move on.

On the afternoon I visited him—twenty-five years after his life intersected with the young rugby player's—Father Jim was particularly proud of a finger-painting composition, which he'd taped on the wall, done by a sister. The first impression was of a rising swirl of light green thumb strokes undulating against a pastel background of orange, red, and blue daubs. The green dynamo, though, was obviously made up of a blurred, rising cyclone of women's forms. "I call that picture 'Women being freed from the bondage of matter,' " he said, proudly. "From Genesis on, woman has been considered matter. And matter has been considered alienating and evil. Saint Paul preaches disciplining of the body to let the spirit rise. But we know today that matter is energy that's ever evolving upward. . . . That green up there in that picture is a heart. We need to integrate the masculine and the feminine in an inner marriage, and we need some people to do that, to dedicate their life to celibacy to recognize that that has to happen *within* us. We need the feminine dimension in our lives to balance us off."

Father Jim then reached for one of the many text-heavy, graphics-free magazines piled nearby. He looked through one for a letter printed from Dom Bernardo, the Argentinian abbot general of the Cistercian order. Quoting fragments aloud as his interest grew and then losing them under his breath as his interest fell, he shared with me a few buzzing phrases: "Anthropology must be about man-woman humanity . . . from a masculine-centered approach to a human-centered approach . . . from duality to unity . . . we're not spirit in body, we're incarnated spirits." He then summed up, "Our abbot general says we're all mystics, we're all called in some way. . . . But we've been one-sided on the rational, masculine all these centuries." (Of a variation on this confluence of the masculine and feminine, fewer than 7 percent of nuns have been estimated to be lesbians by Sister Jeannine Gramick, who has done studies and counseled lesbian nuns. This number is comparable to the percentage of lesbians in lay life.)

Just then we were interrupted by Sister Kate Mehlmann, the tall, thin infirmarian, who joined the community in 1984 after having worked as a nun with the Sisters of St. Joseph, in Chestnut Hill, Pennsylvania. She'd stopped by unexpectedly in her pickup truck on her way up the road to the cloister. "Oh, excuse me, I didn't know you had company," she said as she stepped in, the screen door slamming behind her. "Here I am thinking . . . but of course you don't need wheels. We already had mass this morning." Father Jim invited her in, and it was decided that she would give me a lift to the guest house to collect my bags. I helped Father Jim, with some effort, out of his chair as he insisted on showing us to the door, which was rattling from the wind. As we said goodbye, Sister Kate was drawn quite willingly into the end of our discussion about men, women, and the Trappist life.

"I just feel women are more in touch with feelings and relationships, and I think that's an important part of being in a community," she said, and Father Jim nodded his head in agreement. "I'm not here for any one person. And I don't need them. I rely on God. But I do need them, too. Because community to me, especially in monastic life, really is the core of who you are, and then that is taken into prayer and the Eucharist. I think interrelationship helps our community remain healthy."

Rumbling back up the sunlit road in her truck, Sister Kate kept returning to this theme, almost vexed. Listening to her express her thoughts, I realized that the true antiphonal chant at the center of Trappist life these days has become the call and response between the men's side of the choir and the women's, the issues in some way as well related to the transition from what Brother Paul termed "asceticism" to "aestheticism"—that is, from suffering to joy and happiness, or from crucifixion to transfiguration.

"I mean with the brothers, they don't even celebrate their *birthdays*," Sister Kate complained in a tone of pitched disbelief, as if that pointed omission just sadly said it all. "That's the day they were *born,* and they don't celebrate. Now, celebrating each other's birthdays is interrelationship." We stopped in front of the guest house, and Sister Kate added, almost as a sympathetic yet honestly nurturing afterthought, still obviously caught up in the debate: "And when's *your* birthday?"

Four

The Best Little Cathedral in the World: The Cathedral of Hope, Soulforce, and Jerry Falwell

"What is the passion of architecture?" Philip Johnson asked musingly as we talked one July morning in 1999. We were in his minimally appointed offices on the thirty-fourth floor of the Seagram Building, the bronze-with-brown-tinted-glass slab at Park and Fifty-second Streets, built in 1958 in the International Style by Mies van der Rohe, with Johnson as his associate.

"It seems to me architecture has to be a spiritual passion," he went on, answering his own question. "I know I'm not supposed to use that word, 'spiritual.' And I can't use the word 'religious' either. Architects as a group are businessmen, technicians. If anything, their buildings are technologically important rather than spiritually important. It's all about having the biggest this or the biggest that. They say, 'We have the biggest fan.' But they're not saying, 'We have the greatest work of art.' The only people you can rouse to appreciating a work of art in architecture in America these days seem to be the ministers."

At ninety-three, Johnson was still recovering from heart surgery two years earlier, but his appearance in a blue pinstriped suit, gray hairs bristling electrically around his head, was as put together as his glass-walled office. Its black fiberglass armchairs upholstered in black vinyl, designed by Charles Eames, were positioned at a trestle-leg conference table; two posters of Johns and Rothko paintings he'd recently donated to the Museum of Modern Art were displayed on the white walls; and floor-to-ceiling windows looked out at 885 Third Avenue, the so-called "Lipstick Building" of red-brown and pink ellipses he'd completed in 1985. Johnson's voice was a little more frail than the last time I'd heard him speak, at a celebratory dinner in honor of his ninetieth birthday, at MOMA. Yet just as he'd emerged from what he described to me as "the amnesia" of his subsequent operation by designing a doghouse—he'd built it on the property of his Glass House, in New Canaan, Connecticut, and had been photographed sitting on top of it for *House and Garden* magazine in the spring of 1999—so he was continuing with architectural projects as humble as a lap pool for a gentleman with multiple sclerosis and as ambitious as a museum in Milwaukee and a vast estate in the Negev in Israel.

The project that I was interested in discussing with him, and about which I'd already interviewed him for a cover story in *Out* magazine in 1996, was his design for the Cathedral of Hope, to be built in Dallas by the city's local branch of the Universal Fellowship of the Metropolitan Community Church (UFMCC, or MCC). The UFMCC was founded in West Hollywood by Troy Perry in 1968. It could most simply be described as a gay denomination, but prefers to bill itself as a *Christian* denomination "with an outreach to gays and lesbians," and it has grown to include more than three hundred churches in sixteen countries, its membership in 2001 totaling more than forty-two thousand members. The largest MCC congregation by far is in Dallas, with three thousand members. It has an average Sunday attendance of twenty-two hundred at its four services, which are held in the current cathedral, a thirty-four thousand-square-foot, nine hundred-seat white stone church on twenty acres near Dallas's Love Field; the church was dedicated in 1993 and is already too cramped. The grander cathedral-in-progress had just begun in earnest during the month I spoke with Johnson. The construction of its seventy-eight-foot bell wall contained an electronic registry of the names of those dead from AIDS. It was being positioned in the spiritual marketplace as a "psychological cathedral" for all gay men, lesbians, bisexuals, transgendered persons, and their fellow travelers by its pastor, the Reverend Michael Piazza, who had been busily trying to raise the $25 million estimated for its construction.

On the morning I talked with Johnson, $10 million had already been raised. He and his partner, Alan Ritchie, had been commissioned to design the cathedral in 1995, and its building phase was clocked at an expected twenty-four months. Just the week before, Johnson had convinced Elizabeth Taylor to sign on as a sponsor. "She gave us her blessing," he told me. I knew from inside sources that Piazza had been cultivating a wealthy Dallas woman known for her philanthropy, whom Piazza had accompanied on a private plane to Las Vegas to try to woo. On the same trip was another prospective donor, the wife of the original Exxon leaseholder for Texas and Oklahoma. Johnson seemed to know all the most intimate details of this fundraising drive. He reported to me that the congregation's largest donor had died of AIDS the week before, and speculated that Piazza's plane trip to Vegas might have raised them $10 million. "But it will take lots of five millions," Johnson added. "You can build it. But with a building that size, you have to be prepared to keep up the fabric." He'd also agreed to take part in a fundraising dinner that fall at the Glass House for what Piazza breezily described to me on the phone as "thirty-two of the richest people in America." A surprising boost came from the generally conservative *Dallas Morning News* in an editorial stressing the potential civic luster of such a building: "In truth, Dallas' best shot at having a religious building that draws the world's attention to this city again is the Cathedral of Hope, which is being designed by Mr. Johnson." As Reverend Piazza puts it: "This will be the most photographed building in Texas, maybe after the Alamo."

For Johnson to be the master builder of such a politically correct sanctuary is a bit ironic. Although he has lived with his current partner, David Whitney, since the mid-1960s, he didn't publicly discuss his homosexuality until the publication, in 1994, of Franz Schulze's biography, *Philip Johnson: Life and Work,* which in a sense "outed" him. When he first attended a service at the Cathedral of Hope in July 1995, Reverend Piazza introduced him to the congregation with the words: "Please welcome the architect of the future sanctuary of the Cathedral of Hope, Mr. Philip Johnson. We are also glad to welcome his spouse of thirty-six years, David Whitney." Johnson confided to me afterward, with what sounded like a hint of elitism, "I'd never heard the word 'spouse' used that way before. I'm so out of touch with the gay world."

The only quote from the *Out* article that seemed to give the minister of the Cathedral of Hope real pause, and that forced him to do some explaining to his relentlessly politically correct congregation, had been Johnson's comment that "I'm not a gay activist. But I like to work. I'd work for Stalin." Johnson tried to soften the effect of that admission when I spoke with him in 1999, by explaining, "That was really a misquote from the architect Richard Neutra, who said, 'Who's this man Hitler? I hear he builds a lot of buildings.' " Johnson then went on, characteristically playing the part of the most senior bad boy alive, about his personal choice of aesthetics over politics: "I wonder if I would like to work for a bigoted church. A Christian-right kind of church." But when I pressed him as to whether he'd build a church for Jerry Falwell, he finally balked: "I can't believe it. . . . I'd have to draw the line there."

Johnson's brand of aesthetic spirituality is as complex as his attitude toward gay liberation. Manifesting a lifelong agnosticism—"I'm not a believer of any kind"—he also claims that "Religious space is the only thing worth being on earth for," and his repertory of religious architecture over the decades has included the Kneses Tifereth Israel synagogue, in Port Chester, New York; the Roofless Church, in New Harmony, Indiana; the Crystal Cathedral, in Garden Grove, California; and the Chapel of the University of St. Thomas, in Houston. (The building of the synagogue was particularly complicated morally, as Johnson's most distressing public gesture was a flirtation with Nazism that went as far as a journey undertaken in 1939 at the invitation of the German Propaganda Ministry to follow the Wehrmacht during the invasion of Poland. In a letter to a friend at the time, he wrote, "We saw Warsaw burn and Modlin being bombed. It was a stirring spectacle.") Consistent perhaps with his almost Wildeian emphasis on surface at the expense of content, Johnson claims that all of his buildings are somehow spiritual, including his nuclear reactor in Rehovot, Israel. "It's spiritual," he said. "Look at the shape of it. I make anything I do a spiritual building."

In a career built on controversy and self-reinvention, Johnson has been at different times, and occasionally simultaneously, a purveyor of modernism, neoclassicism, postmodernism, and deconstructivism, and his personal styles have included fascism as well as Upper East Side elegance and mainstream celebrity. In this context, his stance as the discreet, if not formerly closeted, homosexual and avowedly agnostic architect of a gay Christian cathedral might not be so impossible to assimilate. And certainly as architect, the inspiration of spiritual structures for him seems as visceral as his sexuality; an inkling of his vocation first occurred in 1919 when he visited Chartres as a thirteen-year-old with his mother. The intensity of the experience was repeated when he visited the Parthenon and the Byoanji Temple in Kyoto, buildings that he claims moved him to tears, still an important critical indicator to him in architectural matters.

"If I don't burst into tears when I walk into the Cathedral of Hope when it's finished, I'll be very disappointed," Johnson said. He raised the ante for himself by a comparison with the structure he currently admires the most, the worked-titanium-shelled Guggenheim Museum, in Bilbao, Spain, designed by his friend Frank Gehry. "I know that Bilbao is an important religious building because I burst into tears when I walked in. Just by the architecture alone. Bilbao is a museum. But take the art away, it wouldn't stop me from crying."

As unlikely as the pairing of architect and project in this case is the partnership formed for its completion between Johnson and Michael Piazza. A strawberry-blond, blue-eyed ex–Methodist minister born in Statesboro, Georgia, in 1954, Piazza earned his master's of divinity from the Candler School of Theology at Emory University. He is as open about his gay lifestyle as Johnson has been coy and guarded, and equally as enthusiastic in the pulpit about the connection between his spirituality and his decidedly liberal politics. If Johnson has repressed any part of himself during his lifetime, Piazza would mark the return of that repressed shadow material. A similar odd couple as collaborators, of course, had been Johnson and the Reverend Robert Schuller, the white-haired "Hour of Power" Dutch Reformed minister for whom Johnson designed the Crystal Cathedral, a telegenic church built from ten thousand panes of mirrored glass arranged in the form of a four-pointed star, located near Anaheim, California, and completed in 1980. But Johnson doesn't detect much similarity in personality between these two men. "Schuller's an extrovert and a manager, and Michael's a nice kid," he told me. "But of course Schuller would be Michael's role model. He's a success. Schuller once said to me, 'It's all about the names on the mailing list, Philip.'"

Nevertheless, the link between Johnson and Piazza *is* Robert Schuller, whom Piazza models in his ideals of church growth and in his understanding of the function of architecture in facilitating such growth. Piazza first heard of Philip Johnson at a seminar on building megachurches held at the Crystal Cathedral. "Schuller brought in pastors from the large churches all over the world," Piazza recalled for me at dinner in Dallas in 1995. "One of the things Schuller said during the seminar was that the greatest churches in the world haven't been built yet. What Christianity will be like will be determined by those churches. Not by denominations. Denominationalism shaped Protestantism in America.

But it won't in the future. What Americans value in Christianity will be powerful, influential churches like Jerry Falwell's Thomas Road Baptist Church."

Schuller told the pastors the story of the genesis of the Crystal Cathedral, how he'd been traveling in the fall of 1975 on a flight from Finland to New York City, when Mrs. Schuller showed him a photograph in *Vogue* of the Fort Worth Water Garden, a five-block landscape project designed by Philip Johnson. Neither of the Schullers had ever heard of Johnson and assumed he was a landscape architect. But a week later Schuller saw Philip Johnson listed in a different magazine article as one of the world's ten leading architects. He was in the market for an architect since Richard Neutra, the architect of Shuller's previous and now outgrown "twenty-two-acre shopping center for Christ," had died in 1970. He stopped by the architect's offices without an appointment on his next trip to New York City and spoke with John Burgee, Johnson's partner at the time. The meeting at which he'd proposed hiring the firm for the $10 million project ended with Schuller, who'd hardly glanced at photographs of the team's work, asking Burgee, "Do you think I will have a spiritual experience with Mr. Johnson?" and Burgee answering, "Oh, absolutely." Having relayed a version of this anecdote to me, Piazza added, "When we walked outside after he told the story, my predecessor in Dallas, who now works at the MCC denominational offices in Los Angeles, said to me, 'One of the parts of the story that Schuller never tells is that Philip Johnson is a gay man.'"

This overlooked bit of information was all that Piazza needed to begin to retrace Schuller's steps, and to put in play some of his aggressive methods in approaching and beginning to engage Johnson. Schuller had first been put off by a misunderstanding since the firm's secretary thought Schuller was looking for a job rather than offering one and avoided giving him an appointment, causing him simply to show up. Piazza, likewise had not been put off by a polite thanks-but-no-thanks note from Johnson explaining that he was too old to undertake the building of a church, and balking at the notion of being categorized by the public as a crusader for gay rights. Piazza simply brushed the note aside and instructed his assistant to call to make an appointment with Johnson.

"I just got on an airplane and went up and met with him," he recalled. "Philip came in and said, 'I'm sorry I can't do this project though it's intriguing to me. But tell me about the church.' Well, that was all the invitation I needed. I spent about twenty-six minutes without taking a breath telling him about the Cathedral of Hope. I explained that the cathedral's goal is nothing less than to reclaim Christianity from the fundamentalists. I told Philip Johnson all of this, and he was just sort of stunned. In the end he said, 'How could I not do this? I've been looking for something like this to be the apex of my career, and this sounds like it's it. After all, you can't build skyscrapers all day long.' "

Piazza also reenacted for me one of the more brazen plot points in the earlier negotiations with Schuller: the rejection of Johnson's initial set of plans. While sitting at Johnson's regular corner table in the upstairs Grill Room of the Four Seasons Restaurant, which the architect had designed in 1959 as a consummately elegant American restaurant in the Seagram Building, they'd shown Schuller the first set of plans, and he complained, "Why are you restricting yourselves? There are no restrictions. I want a *great* idea." He said that he wanted a glass church, inspired perhaps by Johnson's own Glass House, and by the two glass walls of his present Neutra building, which gave him a feeling of being open to the outdoors. When Johnson asked skeptically whether he really wanted to look out on a parking lot, Shuller had answered indignantly on behalf of his southern Californian congregation, "I want God in the cars, because that's where *they* are."

"My whole feeling about religious buildings is that they're primarily enclosures," Johnson told me. "My first design for the Crystal Cathedral was very different. I did this one at Schuller's insistence. But you have to remember that Schuller is an Iowa farm boy who was born on the back of a truck. So he didn't mind looking out on a parking lot. Still, if you go inside the Crystal Cathedral it's very much about the shifting clouds and sky. Similar to my Glass House, which isn't about the house, it's about the land around the house. These glass buildings are more like music stands. When you go in a concert hall you don't look at the music stand. You listen to the music."

Johnson's first plan for the Cathedral of Hope was rejected as well. His vision of the enclosure at first was nearly subterranean, catacomb-like. As he'd originally explained the plan to me at its inception, "I have an idea that there will be a forest of columns. There may be 154. They may be raised columns so they hang from the ceiling and stop above the ground at twelve or thirteen feet. They're going to be like strings of light. So I think it will give a very mysterious sepulchral light. We're restricted by not being able to go above sixty feet because of the flight pattern of nearby Love Field. So I have to do a horizontal space. The mosque at Cordova is 35 feet high with 252 columns. But you see in Islam they pray, they don't need a Michael. They do have an Imam, but they don't need to watch him. The question is how to get a feeling of spirituality and glory for three thousand people when you're down low like that."

Reverend Piazza and the building committee were underwhelmed by the subtlety of such a structure, which was reminiscent of the flat, airplane-hangar-like adobe chapels of the Penitentes in New Mexico. Using the clout of having Philip Johnson as architect, they finally persuaded the Federal Aviation Agency to roll back the restrictions on height in the area to allow them to build up to sixteen stories, which would make the cathedral by far the tallest building in the area. "It didn't accomplish what we wanted to accomplish," Piazza said of the first, rejected design. "We wanted this building to accommodate a few thousand people. But more than anything else we really wanted to captivate people's imaginations and to be a symbol for our brand of Christianity. We wanted a powerful symbol that while Falwell and Robertson are one kind of Christianity, there are others, and here is one. They've been the most visible form of Christianity. We had to do something to be just incredibly visible."

The current model for the Cathedral of Hope calls for a mammoth and definitely quite visible structure—a sort of massive iceberg rising and cresting. The finished version is planned to be 282 feet in length with an extra 159 feet of adjacent arcade area and to be taller, at 117 feet, than the Notre Dame Cathedral. A prospectus from Philip Johnson and Alan Ritchie's firm promised that "The new cathedral will seat 2,200 and inspire the same sort of awe as the great Gothic cathedrals." Crucial to its effect is Johnson's turn, in his old age, to an expressionist style, which is seemingly the antithesis of the modernism of his once beloved International Style. Eschewing straight walls and right angles, the rough model for the cathedral is wavy-walled and wedge-shaped. Its white concrete walls tilt to the left and to the right, until, at a point over the sanctuary, they soar. (Richard Lippold, the sculptor who created the suspended sculptures of bronze rods in the Grill Room of the Four Seasons, has been contacted as well to design a hanging over the altar.) The floor plan resembles a pattern quiltmakers call "the drunkard's path;" and the proposed doors resemble wind-torn flaps in a carnival tent. This warped yet elegant hulk collapses upward toward an overarching point, a curved rather than perpendicular spire, poetically reminiscent of anything from a dinosaur's fin to the tip of a Mohawk haircut.

Historically, the expressionist style echoed in the design can be traced back to the drawings of Hermann Finsterlin, known in the twenties in Germany for his series of unbuilt architectural follies with biomorphic contours. A contemporary of such modernists as Walter Gropius and Marcel Breuer, Finsterlin was ironically rushed more quickly into obscurity through Johnson's championing of these severe formalists. Johnson was, of course, not only an architect but also the influential Museum of Modern Art architectural curator during the 1930s. The first signs of a further shift in Johnson's own style—by 1984 exemplified by the postmodernism of the AT&T Building, with its Chippendale-style pediment—was his experimenting with an architecture of shapes and forms rather than with Euclidean lines and angles. This shift could also be seen in a 1993 model called "the Berlin Fantasy" for an iconoclastic structure rejected in favor of a more standard business center for the Estée Lauder cosmetics firm's offices in Berlin. In 1994, Johnson designed a much smaller version of this "Fantasy" as the gatehouse on his own property in New Canaan. But he always presents these architectural notions as directly indebted to the work of the artist Frank Stella and to Frank Gehry, with whom he had collaborated on an expressionist-inspired house for Peter Lewis in Lyndhurst, Ohio.

"Bilbao influenced me," Johnson said of the Guggenheim Museum, which opened in October 1997. "I was already going in that direction. But what Frank did was to make it great. He's the first one to bring architecture into the twenty-first century. It's modern architecture but with a small 'm.' But you can't make an -ism out of it. You can't use any of those words to describe this style—'postmodern,' 'neomodern,' 'deconstructivist.' No label sticks. What we're doing now is completely free and based on shapes." The Cathedral of Hope—he allows that this is "a very good title for a building"—would draw a significant amount of attention to this unlabeled style as well. (Ignoring Johnson's insistence against rationalizing architecture, the spin posted on the cathedral's Web site interpolated much into the building's post-Euclidean shapes: "It's reasonable to strike an analogy between Johnson's wavy, mutable forms and the mission of this church. Individuals and society are in a constant state of reformation. They share a stake in maintaining an attitude of openness to new forms, new values, and the twists and turns it may take to reach them. How mad, how ironic, that the great formalist, in his 90th year, should serve the cause of social reform!")

Even without the architectural glamour and attendant A-Gay support Piazza seems to hope for, the Cathedral of Hope is a curiously compelling phenomenon—full of surprises and the most unlikely juxtapositions. I visited twice, once over the weekend of the third Sunday of Advent in December 1995, the second time during a week culminating on the fifth Sunday of Easter, in May 1999. Although these visits were separated by more than three and a half years, the tenor of the place, and the earnestness and emotional authenticity of those involved, was fairly consistent.

Even Johnson, with his tightly wound sophistication, commented on the palpable spirit he'd experienced during his single introduction to his new clients en masse. "I was just amazed by the congregationality of the place," he said to me. "I don't know how in God's name they do it. And Michael's not a charismatic speaker like Schuller. He's not a revivalist sort. His impulses are much more Church of England. Maybe it's partly a persecution problem. Gays aren't as persecuted up here. And those people really use that church. Even during the week it's full. There are always people wandering around."

My first visit took place during the week before Christmas. My impressions were mostly of high-contrast moments. The charge of making such a traditional holiday somehow their own drove the congregation to excesses. Most excessive of all was a Christmas pageant I witnessed in the main sanctuary, which had been made over into a sort of regional theater. The pageant was a complex musical comedy about a workaholic gay man, Bill, who arrived onstage carrying a red Neiman Marcus bag indicating last-minute Christmas Eve shopping. He quickly revealed himself to be Scrooge-like in his dealings with his current companion, a single father. Enter Beatrice, a lesbian who resembled the television personality Roseanne, who led Bill past a scrim of twinkling stars on a journey to Christmas past to loosen him up. There were plenty of jokes about Garland and Streisand along the way. Bill got a laugh by remarking, "Christmas without Neimans? That's blasphemous." The finale was a living creche suspended midstage in which the baby Jesus was born to two women—artificial insemination finding its historical antecedent in the Immaculate Conception—as lasers crossed, a smoke machine worked overtime, and the candle-holding audience sang "O Come, All Ye Faithful" and "Silent Night, Holy Night." These disco liturgics were intriguing, but it was also perhaps too easy to exit with a feeling that cast, crew, and congregation were unwitting figures of fun. (For instance, as audience members were seating themselves, I heard one young man remark about a handsome couple seating themselves up front, "There's Greg and Mrs. Greg du Jour.")

On my second visit, which occurred just as Dallas was preparing to descend into the usual heat spell of its summers, I entered much more into understanding how—to answer Mr. Johnson's question—they do it, and why the church is full during the week, and certainly fuller on Sundays than most of the churches in the United States, including such icons of worship as Riverside Church or the National Cathedral. (Only the top 1 percent of American churches attract one thousand worshipers each Sunday morning; 75 percent count fewer than one hundred each Sunday.) I also came to understand the crucial role played by the culture of Dallas in the personality of the Cathedral of Hope. A stereotypical guess might be that a gay cathedral would have its best odds for success in a liberal city such as San Francisco or New York City, where the citizenry is prepared for such a hybrid concept, a pushing of the denominational envelope. But indeed the peculiarities of Dallas, and of a Southern Baptist culture, have much to do with the success in sheer numbers of the Cathedral of Hope, and indeed of a membership making up almost 10 percent of the entire global congregation of the Metropolitan Community Church, which has only been holding steady and perhaps even dwindling in the past few years. The Cathedral of Hope has become the unlikely source as well for positioning spirituality as central rather than fringe in a gay liberation movement generally viewed over a half century, especially since the seminal Stonewall Riots of 1968, as purely legal and left-wing political.

The entranceways to the current Cathedral of Hope are unimpressive and out of keeping with the grandness of its name. Access is either through a shopping center on Inwood Road, or through the parking lot of a steak house on Cedar Springs Road that allows the congregation a few extra parking spaces on Sunday morning before opening for brunch. It is set on the northern edge of Oak Lawn, Dallas's traditionally gay and lesbian zip code, and shadowed regularly by low-flying planes landing at nearby Love Field—the older Dallas airport, from which John F. Kennedy's body was flown on Air Force One after his assassination. The current cathedral is a standard white stone structure rising in its main chamber to a height of fifty feet, having only six years earlier cost the congregation $3.5 million, the sum raised mostly by its own purchasing of church bonds. "None of the church bond companies would work with us because their biggest clients are evangelical churches," recalled Piazza, who was hired as senior pastor in 1987 after serving at an MCC church in Jacksonsville, Florida. "We finally found one gay employee of one church bond company, but essentially we had to buy our own. None of the companies doing capital funds development for churches would help us."

Nevertheless, given the congregation's humble beginnings and the subsequent quadrupling of their growth since Piazza's arrival, this building is for them, in Piazza's pump-up-the volume portrayal, ". . . a miracle. They just have to walk into that space to be overwhelmed. They are worshiping in a space that beat all the odds." Indeed, when the Dallas chapter of the MCC was formed, on July 30, 1970, only an initial group of twelve gathered at a private home in Dallas. Their first service was a sort of house party. By the end of the decade, membership had grown to five hundred. Within two decades this accumulating group moved their services from a network of private homes to a gay bar, then to an abandoned private hospital built in the Spanish style, on Ross Avenue, to a Church of Christ building on Reagan Avenue, and finally to a two-story office building on Maple Avenue (memorably trimmed in hot pink with low ceilings and Levelor blinds, a space designed for 280 that managed to accommodate an average weekly attendance of 650).

The spirit of the services do convey a lively sense of what Johnson observed as "congregationality," which could only have been built up through a shared history and, probably, a certain amount of adversity. For their September 1997 issue, *D* magazine in Dallas commissioned Reverend George Exoo—the so-called "Church Man," whose critiques of church services are broadcast by WQED-FM public radio in Pittsburgh and printed in various city magazines nationwide—to visit the main houses of worship in Dallas and rate them on a scale of one to five stars. At five stars, the

Cathedral of Hope outstripped such stalwarts as First Baptist Church, Dallas (four stars), and Highland Park United Methodist Church (three stars). The Church Man's rave review of the Cathedral of Hope concluded, "Here I found worship that wrenches tears from dry eyes (my eyes anyway) and sends the rush of energy up the spine. This spiritual vibration is one I can never predict, and no amount of planning can force. It's worship with a capital 'W.' "

For the eleven o'clock main service on May 2, 1999, I took my place early in the balcony, glad to be able to observe a more ordinary Eastertide service as opposed to the pre-Christmas special four years earlier. I shared my narrow space with a bank of technical people, volunteers from the congregation who were operating video equipment for live simulcast on the two screens at the front of the sanctuary and who were in touch by walkie-talkie or earphones to backstage types elsewhere in the building. As I leaned into a corner with my pad and pen, a middle-aged man who'd been bent over a control panel for sound and light walked over and immediately shared a surprise with me.

"I'm straight," he said, with almost no buildup. "That's right. You'd be surprised how many straight people are here. And then there are gay men married to gay women. So I've given up trying to figure it out. My wife and I came here first because our daughter is gay."

Yet camouflaged straights or married gays aside, the message being blasted through the medium of the architecture and decor of the Cathedral of Hope remained very much that of gay pride and gay spirituality in the service of a rainbow-flag God. At the front of the clean, tidy, and expansive tan brick sanctuary, a bas-relief cross rose thirty-two feet high, flanked to the left and the right by stained-glass windows cut with the words "Hope" and "Esperanza" as well as with colorful religious iconography. There was an Easter lily, a dove of peace, an African *kente* cloth— jarringly mixed with emblems of the sexual liberation movements of the 1970s—a lambda sign, an iris (a symbol of lesbian sexuality), and male and female symbols interlocked to signify gay, lesbian, and straight combinations. Beneath the cross, an altar was set with six white candles burning in brass candleholders, and sprays of chrysanthemums and carnations were arranged in vases on either side. A few steps beneath the altar, a pink triangular pulpit evoked the badge worn by homosexuals incarcerated in German concentration camps during World War II.

Spreading out in a fan from the altar area were rows of wooden pews with forest green padding that the members of the congregation were now rapidly beginning to fill. Men made up about three quarters of the congregation. Most of them were middle-aged, preppy, dressed in jeans or khakis, polo shirts or checked cotton shirts, often wearing glasses. Three leather daddies were seated together, one in a black T-shirt advertising the "Inquisition" motorcycle club—a reference that seemed slightly unfortunate. There were also a good number of women with clean-cut style: tan pantsuits, pale blue dresses, paisley vests. With lots of children running around, the impression could have been of a family-oriented heterosexual community at prayer. Piazza and his partner of two decades, Bill Eure, have two daughters, one by adoption and one by artificial insemination, and the congregation has baptized hundreds on at least half of the Sundays of the year. Less preponderant, in spite of the bikers, were some of the more obvious subculture touches of leather, Levis, or bodybuilding evident in such gay-friendly Manhattan Episcopal congregations as St. Mary the Virgin or St. Luke's in Greenwich Village. As Piazza put it, differentiating his congregation from the blue-collar constituency in the majority of most other MCC congregations, "Dallas MCC is young, yuppie. The BMWs are parked in the parking lot. It's a starched-shirt professional crowd with credit-cards-charged-to-the-max kind of phenomenon."

Although services had already taken place on Saturday night and earlier in the morning, the pews were soon filled with a capacity crowd of about nine hundred. A fourteen-piece band of trombones, sax, clarinet, trumpets, piano, drums and cymbals, electric guitar, and cello was tuning up. A signer for the deaf had taken his place at the front of the congregation and was already moving his fingers, communicating with three rapt followers in the front row. The band, sounding very much like a percussive-friendly high school band, played "Holy, Holy, Holy" to warm everyone up for the entrance hymn. The clergy processed to the altar in red vestments, following behind a bronze crucifix lifted high by an acolyte in black robes just ahead of the choir in their white robes. The effect was very much that of a virtual Sunday-morning service in a suburban American Methodist church, circa 1962. In keeping with liberation and radical ecumenism, nostalgia seemed to be in the air, along with the fragrance of Easter-season lilacs near the doorway and the touching dissonance of volunteer choir members singing a tad off-key. (Since services are now broadcast on cable television, the singers are self-selected from those who don't fear being outed or losing a coaching or teaching job from the exposure.)

To say that the service evoked Methodism is only to place the cathedral impressionistically somewhere in the middle of the spectrum of Protestantism, with the humanity and historicity of Jesus stressed more than his transcendent divinity. The sermon is given equal importance with Communion, which is interpreted more as a memorial or a "love feast" than an actual mystical transubstantiation of the bread and wine into the body and blood of Christ—the central liturgical belief of Catholicism, Eastern Orthodoxy, and so-called "high church" Episcopalianism. There was no prayer book. The hymns and the readings were printed out in each week's program, a collage of borrowings from the various Christian traditions intercut with readings from Scripture. A dutiful member of this congregation would generally express his spirituality by attending this church service on Sundays, joining a smaller group for prayer and Bible discussion that might meet once during the week, and, perhaps most importantly, standing up publicly for gay rights. The social gospel of mercy and justice—Jesus' protecting the adulteress from being stoned, or throwing the money changers out of the temple in Jerusalem, for instance—would be his or her essential standard for right action and right belief rather than any theological arguments about the Trinity or Incarnation.

The service that morning followed a traditional mainline Protestant format, except that two verses of the entrance hymn were sung in Spanish, "Santo, Santo, Santo," in honor of the Cinco de Mayo holiday. A lesson was read from 1 Peter 2:4–11, on Christ as the rejected cornerstone, and the gospel lesson was Matthew 5:13–20, on the disciples as "the salt of the earth." The choir performed "High and Lifted Up," a traditional hymn popular with evangelicals that I'd often heard sung at services of the Promise Keepers, the men's Christian movement that is decidedly conservative in its attitude toward homosexuals. A blond female minister wearing white robes and a gold sash read a pastoral prayer. Everyone rose at a certain point and greeted each other by first name, with handshakes, exuding a backslapping fellowship. During the singing of the Gloria, two or three pairs of arms were raised by congregation members, signifying in evangelical body language the sensing of the presence of the Holy Spirit.

Reverend Piazza then walked across the green marble dais to deliver his sermon from the pink triangular pulpit. Every bit a pro, he showed the same alertness to laugh lines as he had in the previous two services I'd attended, the evening before and earlier that morning. With a freckly, pink-faced insouciance, his round glasses reflecting the sunlight, he seemed made for TV, though he had claimed to me that he felt "there's no lower form of life than a televangelist." The title of Piazza's sermon was "A Bodacious Lifestyle," an installment in a series on this topic—a series a bit less popular, I was told by a congregation member, than his previous one, "Lenten Lessons from Country Music." The sermon was aided audiovisually by slides flashed on the flanking giant video wall screens: a shot of students fleeing Columbine High School, from the cover of *Newsweek;* a still from a *Simpsons* episode in which Homer's devout neighbor informs him, "We were away at a Christian camp, where we were learning to be more judgmental"; candid snaps of parishioners working at a flea market in the parking lot the previous Saturday. The slide show was an intermediate step in trying to develop a rapid MTV-style running commentary on the sermons, in the hope of attracting more of a constituency of the souls Piazza and his staff tended to describe, in a cliché, as "Generation X."

"Robin Leach used to have a TV series called *Lifestyles of the Rich and Famous,* in which we were voyeurs of how those we envy live," Piazza began, with the usual minister's reliance on pop culture as a way to connect. "A couple of weeks ago, due to the generosity of a friend of this church, I was invited to fly on a private jet with some of the rich, if not so famous, residents of Dallas. Now, that's a lifestyle I could enjoy. I mean, the plane actually took off on time! You and I know a great deal about the lesbian/gay lifestyle, and the media has given us repeated lessons on how the rich and famous live, but just what is a bodacious Christian lifestyle, and what does it mean to be holy in our world in our day?" At that moment, the English, Greek, and Hebrew words for "Holy" *("Hagios," "Qadosh")* flashed on the video screen, and Piazza began to work his way through his sermon.

Piazza's final extended metaphor was of the Cathedral of Hope opening an optical shop. "I saw one in L.A. whose name we could steal," he chuckled. "It was called 'Specs Appeal.' " He imagined a shop that would sell divine glasses, so that, "When you look through these glasses, you see all the beauty and wonder God sees in each person. You know the amazing thing about these God glasses? They even work when you look through them at the person in the mirror." He concluded with the sort of affirmation and God-loves-you message that more than any other is the essence of the MCC theological agenda, and more than any other is presented by them as the rejection of the fundamentalist campaign against "the homosexual lifestyle." Indeed, the very use of the eighties-speak word "lifestyle" for his series' title, as with so much of the language used by Piazza in conversation and in his sermons, is in a sense a linguistic taking-on of right-wing Christianity. The only line in the sermon that drew applause was a call to sue Jerry

Falwell every time a gay teenager committed suicide because of the homophobia of his church.

After the passing of a bronze offering plate by a young man in a blue suit with a shaved head, what followed was the single innovation of the denomination that has some theological and liturgical substance, as opposed to simply gender politics. This was a Communion in which partakers can gather with a ministering server in small family groups of twos or threes. The lead-in to this segment was provided by a lay helper and two women ministers, who extemporized a pop invocation over the elements of bread and wine as the organist—a close-up of his hands blown up on the video screen—played a rendition of "You'll Never Walk Alone." The lay minister attempted to update an invitation to Communion by saying, "And now, when you go down to Hunky's for that hamburger, or when you sip that Coke, remember. . . ." Mona West, the cathedral's director of spiritual development, on the lay minister's right, added, "So hear those familiar words, retrace those familiar steps." Mary Warejka, director of publicity, moved in from the other side like a backup singer and softly explained into the mike, "The table is ready. You don't need to be a member of this church or any church to come and share in this community."

Congregation members, many of them misty-eyed, walked forward across the cool, gray stone floors alone, or in couples or small groups, as a line of helpers offered bread and wine at the front of the sanctuary. There was lots of hand-holding. I saw two men in tight cowboy jeans and pointed boots, like two Marlboro men, taking Communion together. A blond woman and a brunette were locked in an emotional embrace as a woman server gathered them in her arms. There were boy-girl combinations, too. Piazza's and Eure's two daughters, in matching black-and-white checked skirts and shiny black Mary Jane shoes, had already skipped out. Eventually the organ pealed and the congregation joined together with hands linked and arms held up toward the sky. The eleven o'clock Sunday service at the Cathedral of Hope concluded with the singing of a specially tailored gay hymn, which included the verse: "Once we were not a people, God's people now are we, / A gay and lesbian people, a new community."

Coffee hour in the adjoining dining hall was lively. A young woman serving coffee remarked to a longhaired man in a blue plaid shirt in front of me, as he was tapping Cremora into his cup, "You have beautiful eyes." Another male helper laughed as he said something about "barking up the wrong tree." A landscape architect from Fort Worth told me at length of his painful breakup with his longtime companion of a decade or so. One gentleman in a yellow-and-white checked shirt came up, much like the straight dad in the balcony, and, largely unprompted, praised Michael Piazza profusely. "I think he's the Saint Paul of the gay churches," he told me. "Just like Saint Paul took what was there and gave it shape and appeal, so Mike Piazza is doing right here at the Cathedral of Hope."

My curiosity about whether Piazza really did have a Pauline-style visionary agenda led me to schedule a weekday lunch with him at Biernat's, a Dallas restaurant with an urban, polished look which had a moderately priced menu and big black booths. More relaxed than usual, given the off-hour liturgically speaking, Piazza revealed himself to be almost unsettlingly aware of the possible effects of his stylistic choices on the members of the Cathedral of Hope. Just as he'd calibrated the impression he wanted to make by the architecture of the new cathedral, so he seemed to be going about the design of the services of the church in a way akin to a club owner building a better mousetrap to attract more customers. Especially surprising was his awareness of nostalgia and sentimentality as a possible attraction for middle-aged gay churchgoers. He seemed quite comfortable with what sounded at times like the Disneyfication of worship.

"We've been very conscious that our market has been post-churched people," Piazza told me over a deluxe chicken Caesar salad.

Those people like me and maybe you who grew up in church and got disenfranchised or disenchanted and now are in a place where they're coming back and reclaiming it. This whole nostalgia thing, the *Brady Bunch* and all those remakes . . . we were ahead of the curve on that. We tapped into the nostalgia of people so that if it looks like, feels like, smells like what they remember church as being, they'll come. But if they went back to those same churches today they'd be stunned how dull it is. We've tried to jazz it up a bit and make it exciting and relevant and a little more contemporary. But with enough nostalgia to attract post-church people.

Now what we've got to do, though, is make a major shift. I'll be forty-five in July. We really qualify as a post-church generation. But the next generation, the Gen-Xers or whatever you want to call them, are an un-church generation. Especially gay and lesbian folks. In the church I grew up in they never said the word "homosexuality" or "gay." They didn't say the word "sex," period. It didn't come up. You sort of knew what they would say if it had. In this generation it has come up a lot for them. They've come through a time when the church has been the enemy. Where they were bashed or at risk for being bashed. The media church was always out there bashing them. So they don't have a sense of nostalgia for church at all. Not even a little bit. We've got to figure out a way to reach them. That's the next challenge, I think, for us.

After lunch, Piazza drove me back to the cathedral, where he wanted me to meet with Mary Warejka, the director of publicity who'd helped at the Invitation to Communion Sunday, and who was currently most responsible for developing a ministry to young people, especially through cable television and the Internet. A student at Bright Divinity School, a Disciples of Christ seminary at Texas Christian University, Warejka was certainly "alternative" in her self-presentation; she sat at her computer monitor dressed in a gold T-shirt, blue jeans, and sneakers, her long hair tumbling freely. Her most recent project had been a thirty-minute infomercial produced over the course of two years to be broadcast by WGN-TV, which the station was not going to air until the Cathedral brought a lawsuit against them. Included in the compromise allowing its airing was a title change from "Holy Homosexuals" to "A Cathedral of Hope" and a blurring of the image of evangelist Pat Robertson to make his face unrecognizable. She was also involved in developing a "virtual church" on the cathedral's Web site, which she proudly claimed had scored nine thousand hits in April.

But Warejka's greatest passion was "6:16," the Gen-X Sunday service held at 6:16 p.m. on Sunday nights, and the attendant development of a ministry to gay and lesbian teenagers and the twenty-something age group. In her appraisal of the current Cathedral of Hope services, she shared Piazza's interpretation, though with the harsher edge of someone younger and less invested. "The main Cathedral of Hope service is liturgical, or traditional," she said. "It's for the gay or lesbian who wants the church they never had. Boomer services are very polished, like a show. But our Gen-X service is designed for people who don't want traditional church or who don't necessarily even call themselves 'Christians.' I find it hard to believe that church in the future will look anything like church looks today. We Gen-Xers like diversity. We don't like institutions. . . . The pastor at the last church I was at thought the Gen-X service was just a party. He was a total boomer pastor. His attitude was, 'When are you going to *do* something?' "

I did visit the 6:16 service, held in a recreation room, and the structure of the service was far looser than even the folk Masses of the 1960s. About thirty-five young gays and lesbians sat casually around tables piled with nachos and salsa, which were the Communion elements of the evening, meant to be nibbled at will. A computer monitor displayed the screen saver, "Welcome to 6:16. Your spiritual highway." Chris Wynn, a talented young musician with long brown hair and a goatee, wearing jeans and wire-rimmed glasses, sat at a black piano and played songs of his own composition. His opening number was "Lessons in Breathing," an expression of adolescent angst that began, "I could use a few lessons in breathing / I could humble myself and give in / And all the while pretend it's not me who's needing / A sanctuary where I can fit in." His sister, Tina Wynn, the youth chaplain, then led a meandering discussion about Columbine High School and youth violence, guns versus no guns, and so on. By the time lemonade and iced tea were brought around, the "service" had wound down to random chatting among those who happened to be sitting nearest each other.

My own neighbor at table, Joseph, who worked a McJob at the main offices of Budget Rent a Car, had been to a service that morning at White Rock, a gay fundamentalist church on the east side of Dallas, with seven hundred fifty members of its own. "I prefer White Rock," he told me. "I grew up Southern Baptist. So the Sunday-morning service here is too, uh, Catholic for me." In his reference to White Rock, he reminded me that in Dallas, with its dense culture of churchgoing, even young gays have a long menu of choices. (Attendance at White Rock, though, began to dip below a hundred on Sundays in 2001 when its minister resigned after gaining national notoriety for claiming "amnesia" when it was discovered he'd led a past life as a fundamentalist preacher with a wife and child). Indeed in the greater metropolitan area there are an estimated twenty-five churches that are predominantly gay or lesbian, many of them Baptist in tone. Their ability to jive the doctrine of the inerrancy of Scripture with apparent antihomosexual passages is mainly based on the theory that mistranslation or a misunderstanding of historical context is to blame. They argue that Saint Paul was actually referring to male prostitutes, or that the ban on homosexuality in Leviticus is equivalent to that against eating mussels or working on the Sabbath.

Both Hebrew verses dealing with homosexual behavior are contained within the holiness code of the third book in the Bible—Leviticus 18:22, which states, in the *New American Standard Bible* translation, "You shall not lie with a male as one lies with a female; it is an abomination," and Leviticus 20:13, "If there is a man who lies with a male as those who lie with a woman, both of them have committed a detestable act; they shall surely be put to death." The cautionary tale of the men of Sodom whose town was destroyed after they desired to rape two angels, who had appeared as male visitors, is found in Genesis 19:1–25. In the New Testament the three strictures against "homosexuality" are found in the Pauline letters: Romans 1:26–27, "the men abandoned the natural function of the woman and burned in their desire towards one another"; 1 Corinthians 6:9, "Do not be deceived, neither fornicators, nor idolaters, nor adulterers, nor effeminates, nor homosexuals"; 1 Timothy 1:10, ". . . and immoral men and homosexuals and kidnappers and liars and perjurers, and whatever else is contrary to sound teaching."

Among the few churches in Dallas liberal in their interpretation of these six biblical passages—the only true competition to the Cathedral of Hope—and so most welcoming to gays have been St. Thomas Episcopal and North Haven Methodist. As Reverend Piazza explained North Haven Methodist to me, "People who are not completely 'out' go there because it's comfortable and they don't have to be 'out' yet they can be affirmed without worrying about being discounted." One anomaly is a gay New Age church north of town called the Cathedral of Light—this use of the term "cathedral," whether of light or of hope, to mean a church of size rather than in its traditional usage as the seat of a bishop, is emphatically (though not exclusively) Texan.

Texas is, of course, full of gigantism, and its churches are no exception. The Cathedral of Hope is as quintessentially Texan in its glorying in size and numbers as it is gay in the majority of its membership. (Piazza estimates that approximately 15 to 20 percent of his congregation is heterosexual.) During the weekend I was visiting, for instance, the local news shows were heavily rotating a story about the new Prestonwood Baptist Church, in Plano, Texas, which opened on May 2, 1999. It measures 406,000 square feet, boasts 7,000 members, 2 miles of pews, 450 choir seats, and an additional planned 54,000-square-foot sports and fitness center. There are more of these Brobdingnagian sanctuaries in town:

Highland Park Methodist, one of the largest Methodist churches in the world; Highland Park Presbyterian, until a few years ago the largest Presbyterian church in the world; and First Baptist Church, Dallas, once led by the fabled archconservative W. A. Criswell, still thriving with 26,000 members and remaining the nation's largest church.

This sort of muscle-flexing Christianity—with an emphasis on keeping a high profile using numbers and size—can sometimes look peculiar to an outsider. Malcolm Boyd, an Episcopalian priest who has preached at the Cathedral of Hope and is the author of the sixties classic *Are You Running With Me, Jesus?* as well as a more recent memoir, *Gay Priest: An Inner Journey,* expressed reservations about the cathedral's building fund to me. "It's the 'edifice complex,' " he said. "The construction of churches that cost money. MCC is now following the Roman Catholic, Episcopal and other churches. That means money-raising and ego and careers and prestige. But if we do that maybe we lose our cutting-edge and prophetic quality." It's an assessment with which Michael Piazza, of course, couldn't agree less. "He's exactly right about Episcopalian churches," he said, when I relayed Boyd's remark. "Episcopal churches don't need more room, more symbols, more legitimacy. If I were a Methodist minister again, for example, I would never put pews in a church. But our congregation needs this to feel like church. This is a homeless community, a disenfranchised community, a spiritually disempowered community . . . I don't fault Malcolm Boyd if he doesn't get it. Because he's lived his life in that world. I've chosen to live mine with the exiles. And exiles need a different thing. This church has done a lot of good just because of its size," Piazza went on.

> People haven't been able to discount us, or disregard us, or even criticize us, in some ways, because these conservative churches really have evangelism and growth as their value, and here we are doing it. And they're usually not doing it at the rate that we're doing it. We'll give away a half-million dollars in services and money to the poor and

needy in this city this year. To celebrate the millennium
we're going to give away a million dollars and have challenged every other church in town to do the same. . . . The
result is, we get lots of hate mail but it never has a Dallas
postmark. Fred Phelps has come to picket us. The Ku
Klux Klan. And Operation Rescue. But they're all from
other places. We've never had any harassment from inside
Dallas. I used to think that in Dallas, church was such a
strong value that they disapproved of homosexuality but
they thought if we're going to be homosexual, we ought
to go to church. And they were glad we weren't going to
their church.

Along with size in Texas has always come freedom and individualism. The "Lone Star" mentality remains strong. As Philip
Johnson put it, "Texas is my favorite part of the country. They're
much more open to new ideas. Not necessarily morals. But they're
much more open to new ideas of architecture. They're the land of
the West. It's the last place where you can almost ride horseback
off into the sunset. Yippee! That's in their culture. They all feel
the frontier spirit." And in turn he has certainly been welcomed
professionally in the state, having been the architect of the Crescent and Thanksgiving Square, and the Henry C. Beck Jr. House,
in Dallas; the Water Garden and Amon Carter Museum, in Forth
Worth; and, in Houston, the de Menil House, the Rothko Chapel,
the Transco Tower, NCNB Center, Post Oak Central, the Pennzoil
Plaza, and both the law school and the college of architecture at
the University of Houston. Indeed, the familiarity of Johnson's
name and work in these major Texan cities has been one of the
strongest pulls in Piazza's fundraising.

The individualism that inspires 4x4 truck drivers when faced
with a traffic jam in Dallas to simply drive up and away over the
nearest embankment is considered typically Texan. Gays, however, are not. What the cathedral is proposing to do, with their
highly visible new building, is to link Dallas and homosexuality
in a kind of paradox, with political implications. For while gays

have always operated quite well in the city, they've adopted a more mainstream and camouflaged image than their more radical counterparts in many other American cities. More characteristic of gay politics in Dallas, for instance, has been the Federal Club, an insiders' group established in 1987 by wealthy gays who pay up to $100,000 in annual dues and meet for four lunches a year at the exclusive Tower Club, on the forty-eighth floor of Thanksgiving Tower, to further their political agenda. At the outset, these conservative business types developed a business strategy, drafted a mission statement, and set goals matched to timelines. It's a plan for gay politics that they call the "Dallas approach."

Exposing the operations of this circumspect group, *D* magazine, in a November 1998 article titled "The Pink Mafia: How Gays Gained Power and Status in the Nation's Most Conservative City," also laid out what they determined was the merely tangential access of the Cathedral of Hope to gay financial and political clout. "Indeed, the Cathedral of Hope MCC lacks a strong presence of A-Gays within its congregation," reported the magazine, which classified the church as "déclassé." "Believing the church is 'too gay,' as one successful gay man put it, A-Gays typically worship at Dallas power churches like Highland Park Presbyterian and First United Methodist. As a result, Piazza is forced to look outside the church and outside the city for the bulk of its funds." Curiously enough, when I visited a certain amount of Piazza's fundraising was being directed at straight Dallas philanthropists sympathetic with the building but unwilling to have their name on any of its dedicatory plaques.

I talked with one socially active young woman from Dallas who has shuttled between its gay and straight scenes. She explained the distinction to me, while insisting on remaining anonymous. "Remember, Dallas is a city that dresses. You don't see a lot of that at the Cathedral of Hope. The men in Armani suits are going more to Highland Park Unity Church. The Unity Church is the closest to an open religion for gay people. There's a big congregation in North Dallas and one in Highland Park. North Dallas is nouveau riche. Highland Park is old money. If you go to either of these areas and mention MCC, they're going to look at you like, 'What are you talking about?' The gay community is extremely segregated in Dallas. You have your Cedar Springs area, which is very vocal and very active. It's very downtown. Khakis or jeans with a pressed shirt, that's downtown style in Dallas. Most of the guys who go to MCC are very into country-western. The Round-Up is like MCC at night."

The bar that she was referring to is a country-and-western dance bar, the Round-Up Saloon, on Cedar Springs Road at the corner of Throckmorton, dead center in Dallas's gay neighborhood. (On his visit to Dallas, Johnson was taken on a tour that included this part of town. "They said, 'Now we're getting to our district,'" he recalled. "There were sidewalk cafes all along there. And behind that they have their dwellings. It's a real ghettoization.") I did immediately see an assistant of Piazza's when I walked into the bar, and soon other church members emerged from the crowd. I'd heard that the pastor's "spouse" was an avid two-stepper. A dance with a multiple of two beats per measure, and lots of sliding steps, "two-step" is a tradition in cowboy culture. There was a clash of the iconography of the Texas flags and neon beer signs of traditional country-and-western dance halls with the disco balls, bootshine stand, and pool table of gay dance bars. These men and women in same-sex couples danced on a crowded corral-like dance floor to Garth Brooks's "The Dance" or Travis Tritt's "Here's a Quarter, Call Someone Who Cares," in their painstaking impersonations of the stylized mating rituals of the most stereotypical Texan cowboys, now almost a vanished breed. It mimicked, in a sense, their nostalgic reclaiming of the ceremonies and rites of the mainline Protestant churches that had excluded them the first time around as adolescents.

Finally, though, the churches and social institutions against which the Cathedral of Hope measures itself would still be those of its own denomination, the Metropolitan Community Church, a denomination begun in Los Angeles in the late 1960s with branches that reach far beyond the borders of Texas, to Asia and Africa. Yet it's on this very seminal issue of being a denomination with its own property and its own governing bodies that Piazza feels most distant from Troy Perry. "I don't think there's a future for a gay and lesbian denomination," Piazza confided to me, though he happens to be a minister in the only one. "Troy founded a denomination, a status quo institution, at the end of the sixties. If I were he, I probably would have done the same thing. This is not about intelligence. But it is about really bad timing. It was the end of the age of denominationalism. In retrospect, what should have happened, in my opinion, is that rather than create a nineteenth-first-century denomination, we really needed to begin to create some twentieth-first-century institutions. Rather than be a denomination, we should have been a fellowship of open, affirming, inclusive churches. As it stands now you have to quit being a Lutheran or a Baptist and become an MCC. That's really limited us." And yet, of course, without Troy Perry and his quixotic denomination there would have been no Cathedral of Hope.

Insider ecclesiastical disputes aside, in the history of twentieth-century religious leaders in America, Troy Perry looms ever larger as a fascinating figure as time goes on. What once seemed like a strange vision—a gay church—gains in clarity and importance perhaps even just as it's beginning to outgrow the original mission. Perry's current position is described as founder and moderator of the board of elders of the Universal Fellowship of the Metropolitan Community Church, which is based in a five-story headquarters purchased for $3.8 million on Santa Monica Boulevard in West Hollywood, down the block from the Sports Connection gym. It includes not only the Cathedral of Hope but also a network of churches in forty-five states and eighteen countries—including Canada, Denmark, Great Britain, Indonesia, Mexico, New Zealand, Australia, and Nigeria—that generate an annual income exceeding $15 million. (In 1995, individual members contributed more than $11 million as compared to total individual contributions that year to the Human Rights Campaign of approximately $4 million, and to the National Gay and Lesbian Task Force of about $2 million.)

With his imposing six-foot-two-inch frame, cropped salt-and-pepper beard, and extemporaneous and often rousing speaking style, Troy Perry is the memorable face and voice of the church, its human logo. And his own colorful life story has probably determined the character of the MCC more than any matters theological or political, especially since his background is decidedly southern, and Pentecostal. Born in Tallahassee, Florida, on July 27, 1940, the son of a gas station owner and bootlegger, Perry by the age of thirteen was already a boy preacher at his local First Pentecostal Holiness Church. By the time he was sixteen, he was a paid evangelist, traveling through Alabama preaching, and by the time he was eighteen, he'd married Pearl, the daughter of a local Church of God pastor in Alabama. With Pearl, Perry had two sons, Troy Jr. and Michael. As the authors of the gay history *Out for Good: The Struggle to Build a Gay Rights Movement in America* have described his early years: "Perry had been raised a southern charismatic, among snake handlers, faith healers, shouting, perspiring preachers and people who believed that it was possible to hear the voice and know the mind of God."

In this world where speaking in tongues was considered perfectly normal, homosexuality was not. Twice Perry was forced to bow out of a preaching position, pack up his belongings, and move on because of discoveries of his trysts with other men. His wife, Pearl, stuck by him in a sort of "don't ask, don't tell" marital agreement until he finally decided to live openly as a gay man in 1963 in Los Angeles. In the intervening five years, she'd stayed by his side as he served as a Church of God pastor in Joliet, Illinois, until his homosexuality was uncovered, and then as a pastor of the Church of God of Prophecy—a sect split from the Church of God in 1923—in Santa Ana, California. After his final expulsion from his Santa Ana church, and the return of his wife and sons to Alabama, Perry found himself drafted, in 1965, and soon was serving as a cryptographer in the U.S. Army in Germany, granted a high-security NATO clearance for decoding top secret messages.

In 1967, at the age of twenty-seven, Perry was a civilian again. This was a year before the Stonewall incident—the clash between gays and police in the Stonewall Bar in New York City, viewed in retrospect as the big bang of gay liberation. Yet in Los Angeles, a similarly radicalizing experience for Troy Perry, now a division manager for Sears Roebuck, occurred even earlier, in the summer of 1968 at a raid on the Patch, a large dance bar in Wilmington, across the river from Long Beach and south of Los Angeles. Perry's friend Tony Valdez was arrested in the raid, and a protest was organized by the bar's manager, Lee Glaze, whose customers marched with him on the jail carrying bouquets of flowers and singing "We Shall Overcome." When Tony bitterly complained the next morning, "We're just a bunch of queers and nobody cares about dirty queers!" Perry found himself answering, "God cares." With that consolation, he emboldened himself to start his own gay church to preach what seemed the simplest of messages: that you can be gay and Christian at the same time.

To jumpstart the church, Perry placed an ad in the October issue of *The Advocate,* the gay monthly published in Los Angeles. As Perry recalled for me in a phone interview:

> I had to come up with a name to put in the ad for the first service. I was sitting in my office at Sears and I said to myself, "Well, it's a church." So I wrote the word "Church" on a piece of paper. I knew it was going to be an outreach to the gay and lesbian community but with its doors open to all, so "Community Church." Well, where am I holding the service? Metropolitan Los Angeles. So "Metropolitan Community Church." I put the ad in *The Advocate.* Then I went home and told my roommate, who promptly had a heart attack. He said, "You did what?" We rented together; he wasn't my lover. He said, "Troy, you're the craziest person I've ever met in my life." But I only knew how to do it the way I'd been taught as a young preacher, and that's that you openly and honestly told people who you were, and you told them how to find you.

On October 6, 1968, twelve people attended the first service of the Metropolitan Community Church. They were a mix of Protestants, Catholics, a Latino, a Jew, and a straight couple. The service was held at 1:30 p.m. in the right half of the little pink house in Huntington Park shared by Perry with his roommate, Willie Smith, a movie projectionist at the Encore Theater, who somewhat grudgingly helped lead the singing from borrowed hymnals. Instead of a suit and tie, Perry departed from Pentecostal fashion and wore a Roman collar and black Congregational robes for the first time in his life, at the suggestion of an older friend, Reverend Revel Quigley, a gay Congregational minister. As Perry recalled, "I wore liturgical garb because my friend told me, 'Troy, you need to do that. You can give preacher-style as long as you give them something to be comfortable with. Those from liturgical backgrounds are going to need robes.' So in every Metropolitan Community Church worldwide we wear the liturgical garb." The title of Perry's sermon that day was "Be True to You," based on Polonius's rhetorical advice to his son Laertes in *Hamlet*.

"The next Sunday we were fourteen instead of thirteen," recalled Perry. "I got up and looked around and said, 'If you love the Lord this morning, would you say 'Amen!' They all shouted 'Amen' back to me. It's been that way, too, since then. I also praised the Lord because we were growing. The next Sunday we had sixteen, and I got up and said, 'Well, look at this. Thank you, Jesus, we're on the move.' But the fourth Sunday we only had nine, and I almost died. But here again, God had prepared me. He gave me a sermon entitled 'Despise Not the Day of Small Things.' I said, 'Well, that's the sermon God gave for me.' The next Sunday we were twenty-two in attendance. We'd jumped back up, and we've never dropped since." Willie expanded his music ministry by playing records of religious music on a borrowed phonograph. For Communion, Reverend Quigley supplied wafers, served on a glass plate, and the wine was passed in a "Jefferson Cup," which Perry still keeps as a memento of those first services.

Fourteen months later, the MCC had grown so much that

services were moved to Willie Smith's job site—the 385-seat Encore Theater in Hollywood, large enough for the 348-member congregation. Perry had his own parsonage, a house the church rented on North Virgil Avenue for meetings and choir practice where he lived with his mother and boyfriend. On March 7, 1971, when the members held their first service at their own place of worship, an old opera house at Twenty-second and Union Streets, Governor Ronald Reagan sent a telegram of congratulations, and a crowd of twelve hundred people attended; this marked the breakthrough of MCC Los Angeles as the first openly gay organization in the United States to purchase property of its own. By then the eclectic MCC style of worship had been established, borrowing ritual and liturgy from the Episcopalians, choral music from the Southern Baptists, including many hymns familiar to Methodists, and with the coming forward to the Communion rail, basically an Anglican custom, and a charismatic laying-on of hands straight out of the Pentecostal Church of God. By basing a church mostly on gender issues, the MCC was able to cut through to a fresh, enviable ecumenism that remained elusive for the more traditional, theologically grounded denominations.

The spread of the denomination proceeded quickly. On February 22, 1970, MCC San Francisco, organized by Reverend Howard Wells, held its first service. On May 10, 1970, MCC Chicago, organized by Reverend Arthur Green, began worshiping in Green's home. On May 19, 1970, MCC San Diego, led by a persistent Howard Williams, gathered its congregation in a leased auditorium. During the same season of rapid growth, successful missions were started in Miami and Dallas, and on July 19, 1970, MCC Phoenix, led by Reverend Ken Jones, held prayer services in the offices of ONE, Inc. By September 1970, the first MCC church beyond the shores of the continental United States had opened, in Hawaii, where Troy Perry had gone for what had been intended as a week's vacation. By 1973 the first of the international churches, MCC London, was chartered.

Along with greater visibility came greater dangers. MCC churches became targets for hate crimes, just as black churches had been burned and attacked by white supremacists in the South during the civil rights struggles of the 1960s. The first casualty was the Los Angeles "mother church," which was burned to the ground in January 1973. Two months later a fire in the MCC meeting place in Nashville destroyed some holy objects on the altar. In New Orleans in June 1973, arson was responsible for a Sunday-evening fire in the UpStairs bar, where MCC New Orleans met for services, leading to twenty-nine deaths; many of the casualties were members of the congregation. Over a quarter century, a total of eighteen MCC churches were set on fire, with thirty-three consequent deaths. The stained-glass window of MCC San Diego was shattered by four gunshots. An MCC minister in Stockton, California, was viciously stabbed thirteen times, his neck sliced, and the blood drained from his body. In Louisville, Kentucky, a bullet from a drive-by shooting pierced the stomach of the lesbian pastor's lover.

"Being a Christian, I've taught our people over the years that no one can scare us," said the deeply political and occasionally confrontational Perry, whose engagements in power politics included a meeting at the White House during the Carter administration in 1977 and an award presented for service, along with ninety other clergy, by President Bill Clinton in 1998. "We Christians believe in eternal life. The worst they can do is kill us. But to be absent from this body is to be present in the Lord, as we say. We've got to continue to move out to do what is right. We've made up our minds that we're not going to be chased out of a city, period. Once we lock in, we lock in."

After years of steady growth, the membership of the UFMCC still seems to be increasing. But the evidence can be uneven and contradictory. The next largest church after the Cathedral of Hope is only a quarter its size, and happens to be MCC Houston, which has about 650 members, and it gives more credence to the notion that Texas is the prime location for a churchgoing sensibility among gays. MCC San Francisco has about 500 members and conducts an active ministry to the Castro Street neighborhood. MCC Toronto also draws about 500 people on Sundays, and owns its own large church building. MCC Washington, D.C., is the most interracial of the MCC congregations, with a white woman pastor, an 80 percent African-American laity, and a large gospel choir. Yet by the late 1980s there were ninety-eight charter churches all of which had achieved a minimal degree of self-sufficiency. That number had decreased to eighty-six by 1999. ("Charter churches have to do with how our local districts do their business," claims Perry. "You can't judge our growth based on charter churches.") The total number of churches has grown, but mainly because of the founding of many smaller congregations in smaller towns—the average size of an MCC church is thirty-five parishioners. Meanwhile, the Cathedral of Hope has been responsible for 50 percent of the growth rate of the entire denomination, having doubled its own size in a single decade. In 2001, The Cathedral took a new step by even founding its own satellite, The Cathedral of Hope in Oklahoma City, after two MCC churches in the city had been closed.

This uneven apportioning of growth has been largely attributed to the opening up of the more liberal mainstream churches to gays, either officially or in Sunday-by-Sunday practice. "MCC isn't really a denomination, it's two hundred churches," Reverend Jim Mitulski, the pastor of MCC San Francisco, told me over dinner in June 1999, emphasizing some of the same issues as Piazza.

It can't sustain a bureaucracy. Nor, maybe, should it. It's trying to. But not successfully. I think it will find its own level. It's a little top-heavy right now. It tries to support two levels of governance—a regional one and an international one. So I think it's going to get smaller, one way or another. The success of our church here in San Francisco has to do with making indigenous the best principles of MCC—congregationalism, feminism, liberal causes, commitment to social justice, willingness to experiment with conventional Christianity. The simple reason of its being a gay church is no longer in and of itself a compelling enough reason to organize a spiritual community, though it is in some places. But I think a fellowship, or a loose organization of churches, makes more sense. We're considering an affiliation here, for instance, with the United Church of Christ in northern California and Nevada. The separatist principle, which guided in many ways the founding years of MCC, is changing. It's a different era.

Malcolm Boyd finds weakness less in this jockeying for position among other denominations—its bid for membership rather than observer's status in the National Council of Churches, for instance, seems dead for the forseeable future—than in a weak theological underpinning. "Growth was forced upon MCC," Boyd explained. "But I think that conceivably it has placed on a back burner what I would call issues of gay spirituality and theology that are deep ones. Some very valuable work has been done in the area of what is called 'feminist theology.' I have not seen very much work that has been done in gay and lesbian theology. Maybe everybody's been too busy, and there was a necessary activism when questions of survival became primary. But I think that could be an Achilles' heel in the future if not dealt with. I feel that in the year 2020 you might find theological questions rather more basic than today. Theology can't be beside the point."

Troy Perry, however, refuses to concede any of these issues, remaining the gay Saint Peter, the boulder on which the entire denomination is built. "When I first started I used to say we were working to work ourselves out of business," Perry explained to me in the excited, rolling Southern cadences he speaks with even in phone conversations. "That was my big thing. I said, 'When the Church of God, my old denomination, lets me come home, I will.' Well, even if they changed on gay issues tomorrow, I still wouldn't go home, because there are too many differences still. The way they treat women, for instance. We hold the same place in the gay and lesbian community that the historical black churches do in theirs. Everybody said that when integration came that would be the end of the black church in America. But they continued to grow. I believe with all my heart that in the future there will be hundreds of thousands of us who will continue to look at MCC as our church."

He also refuses to concede that the Cathedral of Hope has become synonymous with growth in the MCC or that it is, in short, a case of Texan exceptionalism. "In the last four years there has been a lot of growth in that particular local church," he admitted. "But we have growth in other cities too. That church has jumped over what we call the megachurch barrier. But I have about four other churches getting ready to jump over that barrier too: St. Petersburg, Houston, Austin, Washington, D.C. They each have almost eight hundred members. Austin has just purchased ten acres of land. The Cathedral of Hope will be one of *several* psychological cathedrals in the MCC. But as the other churches jump over the thousand-member barrier there will be others out there too."

While Piazza and Perry have become increasingly absorbed in counting the number of worshipers in the pews each Sunday, pumping up building funds, or making new nations safe for gay Christianity, the Reverend Mel White has recently taken the spirit and message of the MCC in his own freelance direction. Installed as the dean of the Cathedral of Hope in 1993 and then as national minister of justice for the entire denomination, a post from which he resigned in July 1999, White has recently managed to evoke a response in the MCC at large. He has also given it a political mission that's captured the gay activist imagination and the attention of the national media more effectively than the faded, though still actively pursued, goal of building a gay denomination. (When I asked him about his odd title of "justice minister" at the UFMCC, he joked, "Every time I try to repeat my title I think of an official in a third world country with an old Cadillac and a couple of guards.")

White's ambitious spin-off of the MCC has been Soulforce, Inc., a nonprofit organization founded in early 1999 with his companion of fifteen years, Gary Nixon. It bills itself as inspired by the nonviolent principles of Jesus, Gandhi, and Martin Luther King, its *Stars Wars*–sounding name a translation into Americanese of Gandhi's term *Satyagraha*. In effect, Soulforce has become a sort of spiritual ACT UP. (ACT UP, an acronym for "AIDS Coalition to Unleash Power," is the confrontational guerilla-style movement, begun in 1987 by the fiery activist and writer Larry Kramer. It drew attention to insufficient support for AIDS research and patient care by having protestors block rush-hour traffic in New York's financial district or disrupt a mass at St. Patrick's Cathedral. Its members often stereotyped as sporting shaved heads and wearing Doc Martens, ACT UP, never particularly popular in Dallas, peaked in popularity in the early 1990s.) White's contribution to the unfolding tactics of gay liberation has been to try to link their cause to religion and spirituality, something rarely attempted in the gay community. Indeed, he often describes himself as "homo-spiritual" rather than "homosexual."

Mel White is certainly suited to serve as the face for such a contradictory-seeming enterprise. His entire life has been a contradiction, and much of his political energy could be interpreted as attempting to heal the split between his closeted past and almost flamboyantly in-your-face present as a spokesman for gay rights. Until Christmas Eve, 1991, when he wrote his own "coming out" letter to Jerry Falwell, White was regarded by leaders of the religious right as one of their most talented and productive supporters. He was a speechwriter for Oliver North. He also worked as a ghostwriter for Jerry Falwell on two of his books (*If I Should Die Before I Wake!* and *Strength for the Journey*), as well as for Billy Graham (*Approaching Hoofbeats*), Pat Robertson (*America's Dates with Destiny*), Jim and Tammy Bakker (their dual autobiography remains unpublished), and for the senior pastor of Dallas's First Baptist Church, the former pastor of Billy Graham, and the patriarch of modern Christian fundamentalism, W. A. Criswell (*Standing on the Promises*). He flew on Pat Robertson's private jet, and took walks on the beaches of Acapulco with Billy Graham. What these men didn't know was that White—a graduate with a doctorate in ministry from Fuller Theological Seminary, a senior pastor at the Evangelical Covenant Church in Pasadena, a producer of religious films including *Tested by Fire* and *Like a Mighty Army,* and a family man with a wife, Lyla, and two children, Erinn and Michael—was gay.

Like many members of the Metropolitan Community Church, White spent twenty-five years being counseled in "ex-gay" meetings, exorcised, electric-shocked, prayed for, and nearly driven to suicide because of his buying into his church's teaching that homosexuality was a sin that he must resist in order to be saved. After his public installation as dean at the Cathedral of Hope—on the denomination's equivalent of a holy day, Pride Sunday, June 27, 1993—White's life as a double agent came to a complete halt. His journalistically irresistible story, with its dyslexic confounding of left and right, was featured in the *Los Angeles Times* and the *Washington Post.* He was interviewed on *Larry King Live,* and, in 1994, he, his partner, and his ex-wife were featured on *60 Minutes* in conjunction with the publication by Simon & Schuster of his autobiography, *Stranger at the Gate: To Be Gay and Christian in America.*

In the years following, White traded on his initial media presence with lots of public events designed to draw attention to issues of gay rights, often involving his former bosses. On February 15, 1995, he was arrested for trespassing at Pat Robertson's CBN Broadcast Center, and then conducted a twenty-two-day fast in the Virginia Beach city jail. Finally, Robertson visited him and begrudgingly went on the air to say that he "abhorred the growing violence against gay and lesbian people." On September 1, 1996, White and Nixon began a two-week Fast for Justice on the steps of the U.S. Senate to protest the Defense of Marriage Act. After DOMA passed, 85–14, they and seven others were arrested for praying on the White House sidewalk.

Such abrasive confrontations, though, weren't really in sync with the tone Michael Piazza was trying to adopt for the burgeoning Cathedral of Hope. The friction between the new dean and the church's pastor on these issues of style contributed to White and

Nixon's eventual decision to sell their farm in Ennis, forty-five minutes south of Dallas, and in 1996 move back to Los Angeles, closer to the UFMCC headquarters. When I'd spoken with White the year before, in the piano bar of the Melrose Hotel in the Oak Lawn section of Dallas, he explained why he was an imperfect fit for the Cathedral of Hope. "They're Baptists in Dallas. Even the Catholics are Baptists. In other words, I'm using the word generically. You go to church, wear a tie. Sexually, at the Cathedral of Hope, members talk a lot about monogamy. Gay couples get engaged, and they don't have sex until they're married. They're astounded at promiscuity and don't understand it. It's a Baptist Texas culture. . . . They're also nice, generous, loving people." (White and his own partner met in 1984 at All Saints Episcopal Church in Pasadena, where Nixon, a corporate property manager, sang baritone in the Coventry Choir. They became full-time activists together in 1993.)

After White took Soulforce on the road, Piazza seemed to regret his loss a bit. When we spoke early in 1999, he said,

> When Mel first came out he probably had a lot of guilt. As a result of that, his passion was to take these guys on. This wasn't our passion at all. We were trying to build something positive to be an antidote to their poison. He wanted to organize a bus caravan that would converge on Lynchburg, Virginia, to do this fast on the steps of Liberty Baptist Church. That would have been an extraordinarily expensive effort. I said, "If we do this to Falwell, we should be willing to have him do it to us. The difference is we do it to him and he makes millions from the video footage. He does it to us and we lose millions in contributions from people who won't come to church." He got really angry at me about that, and we decided this probably wasn't going to work. No sooner had we made that decision than he suddenly has this divine encounter with Gandhi and shifted what he's doing 180 degrees. His use of Gandhi and King is a very appropriate way to teach

people a different way of responding to oppression, and really would have been congruent with who we are and what we were trying to do . . . but wasn't before.

A memorable photograph from the civil rights movement shows Martin Luther King sitting pensively with a photograph of Mahatma Gandhi on the wall behind him. The portrait of King works as a bit of casual propaganda, setting up a political lineage and conferring on King's civil rights movement in America between 1955 and 1968 the authority of Gandhi's earlier justice movements in South Africa (1893–1915) and India (1915–1948). Mel White has also used this photograph to publicize Soulforce, Inc., and the implication is that he is the one to succeed King in using the principles of nonviolence to overcome oppression. White has also used the support of Rodney Powell to connect himself to King. Powell, as a young black student at Meharry Medical College, was involved with King in the sit-ins in the early 1960s in Nashville, Tennessee. This involvement was well documented in David Halberstam's *The Children,* but his gay sexuality was hidden at the time. Others who have been active in Soulforce are: King's daughter, Yolanda; William Sloan Coffin, the former chaplain at Yale who marched with King; Jim Lawson, the president of the Fellowship Reconciliation and the instigator of the Nashville student movement; and the Reverend Bob Graetz, the white Lutheran minister who joined King in the original Montgomery bus boycott, and whose home was bombed twice.

"Jesus is talked about with a lot of admiration and respect in the Christian church," explained White. "But Gandhi said, 'You know, I think he meant it.' Gandhi taught me more about Jesus than my twenty-five years in the evangelical church. Gandhi took the Sermon on the Mount and turned it into marching orders. King then added that wonderful mystique of the South, and translated it from a kind of labored Shakespearean prose to the street. Together they have taught me so much."

From his home in Laguna Beach, White then put together a gay version of their mission. As research, he went to India in 1998 to meet with Gandhi's grandson, Arun, on the fiftieth anniversary of his grandfather's death and to successfully enlist him in Soulforce. While on the subcontinent, he responded to an advertisement in a local newspaper offering all of Gandhi's works for $250. He expected five or six books. White was quite surprised when 263 volumes, all as thick as phone books, arrived at his door in southern California. He spent time at the Martin Luther King Center meeting with Coretta Scott King and her executive assistant, Lynn Cochren, a traveling companion to both King and Maya Angelou. "Lynn's a gay white boy who's really positioned himself with a couple of powerful black women," explained White. After this research phase, he then used the Internet to set up an organization whose numbers are hard to count, though White claims to have trained five thousand people in the principles of nonviolence in a seventeen-step "Soulforce Journey" on their Web page, www.soulforce.org, and to answer at least one thousand e-mails a week.

There were many significant events in Soulforce's first two years. In October 1999, two hundred delegates met with the Reverend Jerry Falwell in Lynchburg, Virginia. One month later there was a protest in Grand Island, Nebraska, leading to the arrest of seventy-four Soulforce protestors on the steps of Trinity Methodist Church. They were blocking access to the denominational trial of the Reverend Jimmy Creech, a heterosexual United Methodist Church minister who'd celebrated a covenant ceremony for two gay women, for which he'd been acquitted, and then a holy union for two gay men for which his ordination was withdrawn after twenty-nine years of service. The group closed down the Los Angeles headquarters of Rupert Murdoch's Fox Family Channel in February 2000, protesting the broadcasting of Pat Robertson's *700 Club*. A workshop in nonviolent action took place in May 2000 on the campus of the Trinity Episcopal Cathedral in Cleveland, Ohio, simultaneously with the general conference of the United Methodist Church at the Cleveland Convention Center after they finally stripped Jimmy Creech of his credentials as a minister. One hundred and ten members were arrested on

November 15, 2000, for blocking the entrance to the National Shrine of the Immaculate Conception, in Washington, D.C., protesting the stance of the Roman Catholic Church on homosexuality, an action coinciding with a meeting of three hundred U.S. Catholic bishops. On January 5, 2001, the eve of Epiphany, in a joint action with Dignity/USA, the gay Roman Catholic organization, Soulforce members taped a list of demands for inclusion in the church on the doors of the Vatican. In June 2001, a jazz funeral was held in the streets of New Orleans during the Southern Baptist Convention.

The event that drew the most press coverage, and presented most successfully the new possibilities in Soulforce for dramatizing identity politics, was the Lynchburg confrontation with Jerry Falwell, which I attended. By nine o'clock on Friday morning, October 22, 1999, White and Falwell had already appeared together on *Good Morning America,* presenting the popular *Crossfire*-style format of polar opposites being friendly for a greater good: coverage. (The Soulforce Web site received twenty-eight thousand hits during the hour of the broadcast.) The story was the lead for most of the weekend, in heavy rotation every fifteen minutes on CNN. The *New York Times* ran a news story, an op-ed piece by Frank Rich, and an editorial, "Mr. Falwell's Progress." *Time* magazine chose for their upbeat recap—"An End to the Hatred"—a staged photograph of Falwell in a moment of extreme self-parody propping a lavender Tinky Winky doll on White's shoulder, with White grinning, his clerical collar wrapped prominently around his neck. (The reference was to an alert that Falwell's ministry had put out earlier in the year warning that the suspiciously colored character on the children's show *Teletubbies* was gay, though Falwell later claimed the information had been lifted from the *Blade,* a local Washington, D.C., gay newspaper.)

Confronting Falwell meant confronting the most recognizable face of Christian fundamentalism, partly because Falwell had been so assiduous at making his pulpit accessible to the media since his own born-again conversion in 1952 as a result of listening to a radio broadcast of Charles Edward Fuller's "Old-Fashioned

Revival Hour." The success of his own takeoff on Fuller, a one-man TV show called *The Old-Time Gospel Hour*, was the secret to the success of his own nonaffiliated Baptist congregation, Thomas Road Baptist Church. He founded the church in Lynchburg in June 1956 with a mere thirty-five adults and their children; it grew to 22,000 members, and the TV show expanded to 386 stations and a daily radio program heard on 304 stations nationwide. (The Thomas Road Bible Institute was added in 1972, and the Lynchburg Baptist Theological Seminary in 1973. Early graduates of the seminary in the 1980s then came together to form the Liberty Baptist Fellowship, an entirely new Baptist denomination built on the rock of Falwell.) Rightly or wrongly, Falwell was given media credit, as an organizer of both the Moral Majority Foundation and Moral Majority, Inc., for having delivered the religious right to Ronald Reagan in 1980, thus winning him the election. From that decade of his greatest fame and influence, which has been waning ever since, he piled up a number of trophies of recognition: he was named "One of 25 Most Influential People in America" by *U.S. News & World Report* in 1983, and "Number One Most Admired Man Not in Congress" by *Conservative Digest* in 1983; and he was inducted into the National Religious Broadcaster' Hall of Fame in 1985.

There was a personal sidebar to this event. When Mel White was ghostwriting for Falwell in 1985 and 1986, he had a close friendship with this increasingly powerful spokesman for the religious right. "It was [Falwell's] standing policy to call one senator and two congressmen or -women every day," White recalled in his autobiography. "Even when we were flying across the country in Jerry's private jet, nothing kept him from making those two influential calls, and never once while I was with him did the people in power refuse or even postpone his calls." When White decided to "come out" on Christmas Eve, 1991, he did so in a letter to Falwell protesting a fundraising circular in which his ex-boss claimed he'd been "rescued" from a dangerous "homosexual mob" by the Los Angeles police, implying an assassination attempt. Now, a decade later, they were to confront each other like two generals on opposite sides of a social civil war. Yet Falwell, throughout the weekend, aggrandized White's position as a gay political leader, perhaps as a way to aggrandize his own. "Mel is the titular leader of millions of people in his constituency," Falwell misleadingly told his congregation on Sunday morning at the Thomas Road Baptist Church.

Driving in my Nissan rental from the local Lynchburg airport to a Days Inn on Candlers Mountain Road, I was aware that I was heading into a very public, very staged drama, almost allegorical in its high contrasts. This region of the Piedmont had been politicized as terrain in the public imagination over the past decades by Falwell's very presence, although politics—or even a strong local identity—wasn't evident during the drive. Lynchburg is located sixty-six miles southwest of Charlottesville, on the banks of the James River, equidistant between Washington, D.C., and Appalachia, with a postcard view of the Blue Ridge Mountains. With a current population of sixty-five thousand, it is a tangled network of neighborhoods, circling highways, shopping malls, and a collection of suburbs spread over fifty miles with no discernible center. While Falwell's church and university give him clout in the city, Lynchburg is hardly a theocratic Salem. Most of the business establishment is Episcopalian-owned, and most citizens I spoke with were indifferent, even sarcastic, about the fundamentalist cadre in their midst. (Which is not to say that Lynchburg is not religious in a palpably American way: on Sunday mornings, even the Burger King in this self-described "City of Churches" is closed.)

By default, Lynchburg is a capital of the religious right—because of Falwell's "Old-Time Gospel Hour," the Thomas Road Baptist Church, and especially Falwell's founding there of the now-defunct Moral Majority. Yet he wasn't the first conservative Protestant Christian to call up an army for political, rather than spiritual, action. Even before World War I, Billy Sunday, who grew up in Iowa, played baseball in the National League, and found Jesus in Chicago by listening to a street preacher outside a saloon, was preaching reverence for the flag, the armed forces, and the family. Carry Nation, a Bible-thumping fundamentalist, came roaring out of Kansas, wielding a hatchet meant for the destruction of saloons and inspiring thousands of women to "smash, ladies, smash" in order to fight "the scourge of drink." Her crusade against alcohol led to the ratification, in 1919, of the prohibition amendment to the United States Constitution. In 1925, William Jennings Bryan, former secretary of state and three-time presidential candidate, as well as a devout believer in the literal interpretation of Scripture, rallied fundamentalists to fight "modernism," in his prosecution of a Tennessee public schoolteacher accused of teaching Darwinism in the famous Scopes' monkey trial.

But in the decades following World War II, quietism had been the mode of evangelical, fundamentalist, and charismatic Christians. Registering voters who shared their political views, picketing abortion clinics, or condemning homosexuals was of no real interest to conservative Christians—even the television evangelists Oral Roberts, Rex Humbard, and Billy Graham, who addressed social issues but stayed out of electoral politics (though Graham was certainly a public friend and unofficial advisor of Richard Nixon). Falwell, a local Lynchburg boy born in 1933, his father a bootlegger and gas station owner, was key in eventually leading the conservative churches toward more unabashed activism. His "Old-Time Gospel Hour" was first broadcast in 1956 from Channel 13 in Lynchburg on a ninety-dollar-a-week budget. Yet by 1978, it was featured in a front-page article of the *Wall Street Journal* as a powerful national radio and television ministry, an "electric church" with approximately 1.4 million viewers. In 1979, at the turning point in his career, Falwell met at the Holiday Inn in Lynchburg with a group of conservative leaders—Paul Weyrich, Howard Phillips, Ed McAteer, and Robert Billings—to draw up a plan to save America; this became the Moral Majority, which was so directly involved in presidential politics in the early 1980s.

Along with abortion, homosexuality was a winning issue for Falwell, a card played repeatedly in his fundraising letters. His record has been unwavering and consistent: speaking at one of Anita Bryant's "Save Our Children" rallies in 1977, he said, "So-called gay folk [would] just as soon kill you as look at you"; he supported the failed 1978 Briggs Amendment to ban gay teachers in California; in 1979, while witnessing a gay March on Washington from the lawn of the White House, where he'd been invited by President Jimmy Carter to meet Pope John Paul II, he'd acidly remarked, "God did not create Adam and Steve"; at a rally of the Moral Majority in Cincinnati in 1983 he'd labeled AIDS "the judgment of God" and called for the shutting down of gay bathhouses and a prohibition against homosexuals' donating blood; and just weeks before the meeting with Soulforce he'd issued a press release in which he said homosexuals were "trapped in bondage," and that they "let sin and the devil take control of their lives," "were guilty of a horrible and enslaving sin," and "cannot and will not go to heaven."

Yet Falwell's righteous star had been dimming rather than brightening in the years leading up to the October meeting, and his press releases were far less carefully read. In the early 1990s the Moral Majority had been replaced by the Christian Coalition; Liberty University was $110 million in debt; his television show temporarily left the air; and the Praise the Lord (PTL) television ministry, entrusted to him by Jim and Tammy Bakker when their scandals broke, folded. By the middle of the decade Falwell evened out again, staging a comeback in 1996 with a fifty-two-week patriotic "God Save America" tour. Yet that same year, William Martin, a professor at Rice University, published *With God on Our Side: The Rise of the Religious Right in America,* in which he argued that while Falwell had been the most visible representative of the religious right in the early 1980s, others such as Paul Weyrich, Ed McAteer, and Howard Phillips were its true champions. "If left to Jerry Falwell, the Religious Right would be dead now," said Martin. "He didn't have the grassroots organization." Ironically, by taking a half step toward his nemesis, the gay liberation movement, Falwell was now spending a weekend in the glare of cameras that must have reminded him of press opportunities past.

"The event with Mel White was a chance for him to be back in the limelight," concurred Susan Friend Harding, the author of *The Book of Jerry Falwell: Fundamentalist Language and Politics.* "He does love it, and he misses it. He's actually become an increasingly respectable, mainstream figure. But for outsiders he still seems as far-out as ever. So when he does something like this it seems tremendous. . . . He's got a quiver, and he's got a lot of arrows. Depending on the subject he'll pull out a different arrow and shoot it. Any good preacher does this. Any good politician does this. And I think preachers are a species of politician. Over time Falwell has emphasized one facade more than the other. Right now he's in a more avuncular, grandfatherly mode."

Of Falwell's tendency to migrate in his positions, Gustav Niebuhr commented more approvingly, "Falwell is an almost daring person. He's not afraid to step out and do something you might not expect him to do. Even in founding the Moral Majority. He had a big church. Everything was going fine in Lynchburg. He did not have to get involved in politics. He knew it was probably going to bring him a lot of grief. He got a lot of criticism from among his own conservative evangelicals. But Falwell's got a thick skin. A lot of ministers wouldn't have met with Mel White. Falwell did say it didn't change his beliefs and opposition to homosexuality. But he was willing to consider that certain language in talking about gays was not appropriate."

In the two years following this meeting with Soulforce, Falwell certainly continued his pattern of facade shifting. Evidence of the more moderate Falwell was his support two years later, in August 2001, for President George W. Bush's decision to allow federal financing for limited stem-cell research—a position harshly criticized by many Roman Catholic and evangelist organizations that maintain there can be no compromise of principles involving the sanctity of life. But then just a month later he was back in the news in a more regressive guise when he attributed the terrorist attack on the World Trade Center and the Pentagon to God's wrath against gays and lesbians, abortionists, and the A.C.L.U. His linking of these and other groups, such as feminists and the People for the American Way, in a sort of negative spiritual conspiracy in a discussion with Pat Robertson on the Christian Broadcasting Network's *700 Club* was dismissed by President Bush as "inappropriate."

The activists coming to confront him from Soulforce tended to be members of evangelical churches as well, especially those from the South with ties to the MCC churches. And so they too were in a similar tradition. Most of the Protestant denominations involved in influencing public policy had been mainline: Lutheran, Presbyterian, Methodist, Episcopalian. There had been some exceptions: in the nineteenth century, the fervent, evangelistic preaching of Charles Finny helped mobilize both the abolitionist and the women's suffrage movements; Martin Luther King, a Baptist preacher, and tens of thousands of other African-American evangelical Christians, both clergy and laity, had been responsible for the successes of the civil rights movement; Jimmy Carter had been elected president as an evangelical Christian in 1976.

The first event of this confrontation between mostly evangelical Christians on opposite sides of the same social issue was a gathering of the two hundred Soulforce delegates from more than thirty states at seven o'clock on Friday evening at the First Christian Church, a Disciples of Christ church located on Rivermont Avenue that had been set up as "Soulforce Central." The hosts included the pastor, Roger Zimmerman, and the director of Christian education, Sandy Knodel, wearing identifying green ribbons. The basement was stocked with bagels and coffee donated by other local churches. This three-hour meeting was billed as "Advanced Soulforce Training. Memorial Service. Candlelight Vigil." Its effect, however, as at the Cathedral of Hope, was a group of, as they put it, "God's lesbian, gay, bisexual, and transgendered children"—their shorthand acronym GBLT—making it up as they went along, patching together liturgical traditions and folk rituals of bygone leftist political movements while indifferently dispensing with debates on theological differences that had so vexed the orthodox sects for centuries.

When I entered the red-brick-trimmed-with-maple-wood sanctuary, with hanging lanterns and deep forest green carpeting, and slipped into a wooden pew near the rear, "The Walls of Jericho" was being played by an ensemble of three women on drums, electric guitar, and organ. Their backdrop was a projected slide on a portable screen of a rainbow flag and the words "Soulforce Central. Journey to Lynchburg. October 22–24, 1999." Half the congregation was women, mostly lesbians. Most of the men looked to me like Promise Keepers—there were many gray-haired or hefty men in flannel shirts wearing baseball caps. There were two or three black people, and one woman who'd grown up in New York City. But basically the crowd was white, middle-aged, and as middle-American as Arby's.

Music took up much of the first half hour. When "You've Got the Whole World in Your Hands" was being played, the man in the pew in front of me, a gay born-again Christian from Maryland who'd sent two of his sons to Falwell's Liberty University, turned and said, "Have you guys heard this song before? It's beautiful." A black woman up front shouted, "Everybody sing. We wanna make it inclusive!" The verse "Won't let Falwell blow it out / I'm gonna let it shine" was added to a favorite evangelical standard, "This Little Light of Mine." The new lyrics were typed out on the screen in lavender print. "It's like a good karaoke bar," whispered David, my neighbor, a father of six and grandfather of five from Washington State who'd been partnered with a man for nine years.

All sat up and grew quiet when "Reverend Mel" finally took his place at the front of the church, mike in hand. Tall and spindly, with a shiny bald head edged by gray-white hair, dressed conservatively in a herringbone jacket, clerical collar, and round copper-tinted eyeglasses, he proved to be a lively and often sharply funny leader. At times his e-mails rousing the troops in the past few weeks had bordered on histrionics, giving me pause with all their warnings of violence or of horrible turnarounds on Falwell's part.

Yet in person White seemed to be keeping a calmer eye on the agenda, while obviously relishing the opportunity to rally and perform—requisites in such a leader, whose operating method is events and demonstrations. He seemed ready for prime time.

Sitting on a folding metal chair, White first led a meditation, visualizing going with Jesus into a cave over the sea, leaving behind the pressing multitudes and talking with Him. "Then you look over and notice He's talking to someone else, looking out to sea," said White. "And you look out to sea. And you talk to someone else, too."

White followed up the meditation with some very nice comments about Falwell, hardly in the spirit of some of his recent correspondence. "You're gonna like this man," he promised the group, which would be meeting Falwell at a planned dinner the following evening. "Remember that he was one of the first Southern Baptists to integrate his church and baptize black people. Now he wants to be the first in reconciling that community with this community. And we're here to see that it happens. It's so miraculous. Jerry Falwell is serious about loving us. This is grace a Web page at a time. This is grace a sermon at a time." (White was perhaps being overly generous. The Thomas Road Baptist Church actually remained segregated until 1968, and the first baptism of an African-American person there appears not to have occurred until 1971.)

White's pep talk was followed by testimonials, staples in the evangelical and twelve-step traditions. Brian Randall, class of 1991 at Liberty University, spoke of his "bittersweet homecoming." The not-yet-defrocked Jimmy Creech, from Raleigh, North Carolina, spoke on "spiritual violence." (The following year Creech accepted Mel White's request to serve as chair of the Soulforce board of directors.) Dr. Rodney Powell, a black man with a white beard as electric as Charlton Heston's as Moses in *The Ten Commandments,* recalled his involvement with Martin Luther King: "I feel like I'm transported back in time. I feel like I'm back in the basement of the First Baptist Church in Montgomery. Then we were all in the closet. We aren't ever going back there again."

Paul Dodd of Austin, Texas, until recently the senior Southern Baptist chaplain to the army, who'd been married to the pianist in his father's Baptist church until he came out as gay, said, full of emotion, "I'm glad I'm able to have lived long enough to experience this tonight."

The greatest response was for the testimony of Mary Lou Wallner, an evangelical Christian from Elgin, Illinois, who'd rejected her daughter because she was a lesbian. Her daughter, Anna, hanged herself in 1997, and her mother had been pleading for understanding from gay Christian parents ever since. "If I can steer one person away from living the pain I live, then maybe Anna's death will have some meaning," she said. "I've had to come to terms with who I am and how I treated my own flesh and blood." White hugged Wellner and her husband, Bob, and asked God to "take away the guilt; let it be gone forever."

Moving from speeches to ritual, on a parallel track with a church service, the evening's candlelight memorial began as poster-sized black-and-white photographs of twenty gay men and transgendered individuals killed by violence or suicide were carried out and placed in empty spots of pews next to delegates, with the implication both that they were present and that "it could be you." As they were recognized, people would whisper their names: "Matthew Shepard," "Billy Jack Gaither." The names of the icons were read in a litany, a martyrology, including the manner of death. Several had been bludgeoned to death, others stabbed, shot, and strangled. One had been beheaded. I was reminded of the list of atrocities in Dostoevsky's *Brothers Karamazov*, gleaned from newspaper accounts of sensational crimes of the time. The last three posters held up were of Jesus Christ, Martin Luther King, and Mahatma Gandhi. The last slide projected was a black-and-white cross.

The evening ended with a few announcements about the following day's itinerary, heard above the muffled weeping of many of those present.

Most of the following morning and afternoon was just prologue to the big event: the ninety-minute meeting, closed to the press, with Falwell and his group of two hundred supporters at Lynchburg Christian Academy, the elementary and high school on the grounds of the Thomas Road Baptist Church. One near deal-breaker occurred when word arrived that there would be no food, only water, at the so-called "dinner" because Gary Bauer's Washington-based Family Research Council in its September newsletter had condemned Falwell for violating 1 Corinthians 5:9: "Anyone who calls himself a brother but is sexually immoral . . . With such a man, do not even eat." While many of the protesters were ready to exit at this affront, White talked them down, reminding them of their goal of meeting face to face with people who had demonized them in their minds. "Jerry's people are so much like us," he said, prophetically enough. "They'll be amazed at how normal and boring you look. And you'll be amazed at how normal and boring *they* are."

The only confrontation with any real bite occurred when we left the First Christian Church in a cavalcade, which passed through the protesters restrained at the front curb by local police. Four groups had been granted permits and were stationed either at First Christian or along Thomas Road: Reverend Edward Nelson and his Citizens Against Moral Deterioration; Reverend W. N. Otwell and his followers from the Heritage Baptist Church, in Mount Enterprise, Texas; Reverend Fred Phelps, from the Westboro Baptist Church, his group spouting verses from Leviticus and Romans; and, funnily enough, a gay group, Bob Kunst with the Oral Majority from Florida, who felt White was appeasing the enemy, just as the rightist groups felt Falwell was betraying their cause. ("Groveling and crawling to Falwell for acceptance is the most blatant example of masochism I've ever seen," Kunst told one reporter.) There were signs visible through the windshields with such messages as: "Judas Falwell," "Fags Can't Repent," "Homo Agenda Underminds [sic] Nation's Moral Fiber." But there was no real violence. Altogether about sixty protesters showed up.

All the press and certified protesters were finally left behind when our cavalcade turned into the vast, shopping-center-sized parking lot of Falwell's spiritual complex on Thomas Road. Falwell founded the Thomas Road Baptist Church in a building that had previously housed the Donald Duck Soft Drink Bottling Company. Nearly forty-five years later, he was shepherding there by far the biggest congregation in Lynchburg, jamming a total of four thousand people into the three services on Sunday. In 1967, Falwell founded Lynchburg Christian Academy in the three-story brick school where we'd be meeting, to provide a kindergarten-through-twelfth-grade education for the children of his parishioners, with the goal, according to his Web site, of "training Champions for Christ." He'd also established a home for alcoholics, a summer camp for children, a Bible institute, a correspondence course, and a seminary. In 1971, Falwell founded a separate campus, Liberty Baptist College, now Liberty University, an accredited college with seven thousand students, from which many of his delegates to this meeting had been drawn. Liberty students had a history of being recruited for special events: in 1983, busloads of them came to Washington to form a human chain between the Supreme Court and the Capitol as a way of pleading for a school-prayer amendment.

The foodless "dinner" (snacks and lemonade had also been scratched) was held in the school gymnasium, a gleaming basketball court with a huge American flag hung along one wall, the electronic scoreboard inactive. Beige curtains, like portable infirmary curtains, seemed an attempt to give an atmosphere of a formal dining room to the collection of round tables covered in yellow linen and decorated with fake autumn leaves. Soulforce placed a small white porcelain angel at each place setting. All of the delegates had been entrusted with leis of tea leaves, contributed by a woman delegate from Hawaii, to be given to a new acquaintance as a gesture of friendship. (Many, I noticed, wound up piled in the center of the tables, like streamers at the end of a New Year's Eve party.) The posters from the night before of those killed violently for their beliefs graced the low platform from which White and Falwell would speak. At each person's place was a small bottle of Poland Spring water.

Although the gray metal chairs around my table never filled up, I was interested to sit next to Kim Graham, the athletic director of the university. Long-legged and conventionally handsome, he looked like a sportscaster and said things like, "I hope the world will see that the folks at Thomas Road Baptist Church are open-minded, even though they don't agree with the stand the other side takes." He was evenly friendly, but declined my offer of a lei, choosing instead to explain Liberty's policy against tenuring their professors—the administrators wanted to be free to terminate anyone who strayed from what was called "the Liberty way." Sitting to his left was Gerry Falwell, Jerry's cousin, who instead of speaking with the three delegates to his left had plugged in the earphones of his transistor radio to listen to the Liberty football game they were missing. "Don't tell Jerry or he'll make me stop," he pleaded with a burst of laughter.

The Liberty students tended to cluster by themselves until the time came to disperse to various tables. They were a much sharper bunch than might be expected. It was 1999, and many of the young men wore their hair spiky, almost punk, rather than in military crew cuts. Surfer necklaces were common, and even an occasional earring. The young women wore short skirts and had *Friends*-style hairstyles, like so many NYU coeds. These students may not have fulfilled the early hopes of the evangelical theologian Francis Schaeffer, who had urged Falwell to turn his university into a fundamentalist Harvard, but they seemed to be on their way at least to satisfying the Liberty official who'd more recently told a reporter, "We want to be to that fundamentalist or evangelical young man or woman what Notre Dame is to young Catholics and Brigham Young is to young Mormons."

After a bit of rustling, Falwell—who would later, along with his wife, shake hands with all the delegates—left behind the bulky plainclothes security guard in a tan suit who was with him all weekend to take the podium. Vaguely resembling Martin van Buren, Falwell, at sixty-six, was strong-jawed and portly, with longish white hair. He wore a dark suit, a white shirt, and a red tie, and spoke like someone completely used to relaxing in a public forum. He managed at the very start of his remarks to seize, and reconfigure, the agenda by underlining recent violence and prejudice against Christians—especially the seven Christian young people murdered at Wedgewood Baptist Church, in Fort Worth, and the young woman shot at Columbine High School after purportedly affirming her belief in Jesus—as the moral equivalent of violence against gays, and as the motivation for his taking part in this conference. (It was advertised in a banner hanging overhead as "Anti-Violence Forum. October 23, 1999." Of his own exaggerated diatribes against gays over the years, he did say, "We apologize for that. We're sorry for that." Everyone applauded at this admission, the necessary headline having been delivered.

"Animosity against people who are different is unfortunately a deeply human tendency," he went on. "Unchecked, this natural aversion can degrade to hatred and violence. It is perhaps the most visible evil of modern times. Can anyone argue otherwise at the end of the twentieth century, the century of mass graves and ethnic cleansing?" He then assured everyone, to the pleasure of the Lynchburg officials and the annoyance of the Soulforce delegates, "We love the sinner far more than we hate the sin." (His version of the speech on his Web site a week later was slightly different in tone: "With two hundred homosexuals staring me in the face last Saturday, I accentuated the biblical position that homosexuality is sin. I also cautioned everyone attending that meeting that my position would never falter. I will never presume to counter God's Law.")

During the rambling portion of his speech, Falwell revealed himself to be more fully understandable as a member of the elite congregation of celebrities than as a mere southern preacher, giving us several glimpses into celebrity culture. He bragged about having dinner often with Senator Edward Kennedy, "I eat at the house of Ted Kennedy and he at mine. We don't agree on anything but motherhood. But we're friends." Even more mindbogglingly, he included in his name-dropping Larry Flynt, the publisher of *Hustler* magazine, whom he'd unsuccessfully sued in 1987 in U.S. Supreme Court for printing a "parody" in which he was portrayed, as the court papers described, "engaged in a drunken incestuous rendezvous with his mother in an outhouse." "I'm a friend of Larry Flynt," he assured the audience. "I'm trying to get him to move to Lynchburg and work for me. The last three times I was in California he asked me to spend the day with him." Their friendship seemed as counterintuitive, perhaps, as that played out on TV talk shows in the previous decade between Timothy Leary and G. Gordon Liddy. Falwell also insisted in his talk that "the term 'religious right' didn't exist until I started the Moral Majority."

Falwell seemed most at ease when he'd concluded his formal speech and could move on to displaying his camaraderie with White; their relationship was full of mutual admiration spiced with frat-boy-style put-down's, jibes, and jabs. "Let me introduce you to this balding statement," he said of White. "I can still outrun you," White interjected, as he handed him a framed cartoon depicting a place setting for "Mr. J. Falwell" at a dinner next to a place setting for "Mr. T. Winky." "You're a better writer than an artist," Falwell shot back. Then he added, in a sincere aside to the Soulforce delegates, "Believe me, your guy represents you well."

"You've changed not your view of homosexuality but of homosexuals," said White, into the mike. "When the gay community tries to demonize Jerry Falwell, I'm not going to let them get away with it."

"A guy named Falwell and a guy named White tried this for the first time," Falwell came back. "And the building didn't fall down. This is the South. This is not New York City. This is not just novel, it's *historic.*"

After this self-congratulation, White let some of the testimonies of his delegates be heard again from the floor, this time more as a direct challenge to Falwell. When Liberty graduate Brian Randall said, "It was my perception I would be kicked out of school if I came out," Falwell replied, "There is no sexual activity at Liberty, but we do not have thought police." To Mary Lou Wallner, the mother of the lesbian suicide, he ministered, "There's nothing a child can do that a parent should write them out of their hearts." When Falwell said, "We oppose alcoholism and drugs, not alcoholics and drug addicts," the Reverend Jimmy Creech complained, "I'm hearing things from Reverend Falwell that I consider close to spiritual violence."

A good portion of the men—many of the older ones on both sides in blue blazers, gray slacks, and penny loafers—wound up during the break at the men's room on the first floor of the school. There were lots of male jokes. "Hey, stop running that water!" someone yelled as the line of students, administrators, and Soulforce delegates grew longer. One delegate, a salesperson from Michigan, informed a student draped in a tea-leaf lei what an honor he'd received by being chosen for this token of friendship. "Awesome!" the student politely replied. The resident director of the school, in front of me in line, explained, apparently oblivious to the double entendre, "It's my job to keep these guys straight!"

The second half of the program involved watching live on closed-circuit television a press conference of Falwell and White. Reverend Jimmy Creech also sat on the panel, along with a special guest slipped in by Falwell unannounced, Michael Johnston, an ex-gay who was HIV-positive and led an active speaking ministry trying to inspire homosexuals to change their orientation, as he claimed to have done, in a seventeen-minute radio presentation and in his videotape for sale the following day at the Thomas Road Baptist Church. His organization's "National Coming Out of Homosexuality Day" had recently featured Falwell. Johnston's presence soon created another stir when it was discovered that he was scheduled to speak at the eleven o'clock Sunday service, to which the Soulforce delegates had been invited. (The thinking on the part of the church was perhaps that this would be the perfect opportunity to help the homosexuals toward salvation.) After much cell-phoning back and forth at an emergency meeting back in the basement of First Christian Church that evening, Johnston's pitch was relegated to an earlier service, and Falwell officiated as planned at eleven o'clock.

I did slip in early to catch Johnston's talk. Dark-featured, thirty-something, wearing a bejeweled ring, Johnston told a somewhat dispiriting story of having been the kept boy of a rich businessman in Seattle. When the man lost his house and most of his fortune in a failed business venture, Johnston claimed to have left him and moved to Washington, D.C., where he engaged in a promiscuous lifestyle, involving hustling, which culminated in his AIDS infection and subsequently his born-again-Christian renunciation of the homosexual lifestyle. He hustled his videotape as well during the testimonial to an extremely attentive congregation. I didn't attempt to buy one, though a fellow delegate did walk up to speak with him at the sales table afterward and claimed Johnston—who had appeared with his mother in print and television ads developed by the Campaign for Reclaiming America—bitterly informed the delegate not to be deluded into thinking that the event with Falwell marked any softening on the part of his evangelical constituency toward the sin of homosexuality.

(In his subsequent posting on his Web site, Falwell wrote of Johnston, "Michael, who joined us in Lynchburg over the weekend, was consumed by the homosexual lifestyle for many years. As a tragic result, he now carries the AIDS virus. . . . I am committed to helping Michael Johnston and thousands of other 'ex-gays' declare their message of godly deliverance because I continue to believe that many homosexuals are hungering for an escape from their lifestyle. Furthermore, I agree with Robert Knight of the Family Research Council who said last week, 'Pretending darkness is light does not turn sin into virtue.' ")

Mostly, the tenor of Sunday at the Thomas Road Baptist Church was pleasant, the rain of the day before having been replaced by sun and warm fall temperatures. The church, only an hour's drive from Monticello, is a large octagonal building fronting the street, with a pillared facade and triangular pediment, which evokes the architectural style of this part of Virginia. An echo of the previous day's activities was a protester holding a sign, "Mel Wants to Sodomize Your Sons." All the doorways to the circular sanctuary were guarded by uniformed police officers, as well as by ushers who handed everyone arriving for the eleven o'clock service a program advertising on its cover, "Reaching peo-

ple for Christ since 1956." The sanctuary is an amphitheater carpeted in pale blue, with a series of descending pews in semicircles,
the pulpit set up as the vanishing point up front, sprays of
chrysanthemums lining the floor, and cameras prominently set up
midway down the front aisle, under the overhanging semicircle of
a balcony.

Music established the mood, and the weekly sight and sound
of the choir in their pale blue robes is an important ingredient of
"The Old-Time Gospel Hour," which is simply an edited videotape of this service, with extra footage occasionally added. The
minister of music, Robbie Hiner, asked the congregation to
squeeze to the centers of the pews because of the crowds, and then
led them in a hand-clapping rendition of "Onward, Christian Soldiers" and "How Great Thou Art." Four young men in a sort of
barbershop quartet sang "God's Glorious Church" and "There Is
a River." Older male officials of the church sat on the dais in
dark three-piece suits identical to Falwell's. Like schoolchildren
politely raising their hands, members of the almost entirely white
congregation—the men in suits or pressed striped shirts, the
women in long skirts, hair tied back—would, every so often, signify feeling the spirit. A mother in shiny eyeglasses in front of me
busily underlined in orange highlighter the Bible lessons of the
day while shushing her little boy.

That morning Falwell reminded me of a genial Ed McMahon,
the foil for Johnny Carson on the old *Tonight Show*. "I want to welcome our Soulforce guests and Mel White," he graciously began
his "Morning Message." "We have people here from thirty states
across the nation. I've never met more courteous, gentlemanly
people than you brought here. Mel White, my hat is off to you.
We had a most fruitful meeting. And I say this with the world
looking in. This is being broadcast live." Some in the congregation shifted uncomfortably; a few parents had kept their children
home from Lynchburg Christian Academy on the Friday and
Monday surrounding the meeting with Soulforce.

Employing a preaching technique in place since the Puritan
preachers of the seventeenth century, Falwell then worked his way

verse by verse through the day's lesson, Proverbs 13. He stopped to tell a personal story about buying Grinders, which are shoes with metal strips bolted on the bottoms, for his grandson, Jerry III. He threw in Ben Franklin–style epigraphs, "I believe that you birds who are sleeping past eight o'clock in the morning are living in sin." He reiterated his confession from yesterday that if his own son were gay he wouldn't send him away but he'd pray to the end of his life for his transformation. "We believe the Bible is the inerrant word of God," he assured. The congregation responded in apparent relief to this affirmation of their original sentiments, and gladly ended the weekend with scattered amens.

Falwell then turned to the balcony, where a group of prospective high school students on a visit to Liberty University were seated together. To them he expounded the positive benefits of what he proudly called "living in the box," which was his characterization of living according to the strong rules of "the Liberty Way," with its ban on drinking, smoking, and sex outside of marriage. While he addressed them, I couldn't help thinking back to the emergency meeting last evening when a gay female graduate of Liberty, one of the Soulforce delegates, had told us of smuggling a book by the feminist Gloria Steinem into the school chapel to read while Falwell, in her words, "talked of homosexuals burning in a place hotter than hell."

As we exited following the singing of "Only Trust Him," one delegate, who had been a Southern Baptist preacher for thirteen years but claimed not to have been at a service in twenty-five years, remarked, "They really still are preaching against drinking, smoking, and gambling. Nobody else in the world is. But they haven't caught up."

The only remaining bit of Soulforce business to complete was White's wish that everyone at the dinner the evening before invite one of their new fundamentalist friends out to lunch. I tagged along to Slurpy's, a restaurant in a nearby shopping mall, with two Liberty University students who'd been invited by David, who came from Washington State, and whose interest in talking with these young men was doubled by his being the father of a son who had recently been born again. There was some serious back-and-forth over Cokes and burgers. But most memorable was a rambling account from Daniel, one of the Liberty students, of driving thirty hours straight to Midlands, Texas, to visit his grandmother with his girlfriend, not being able to stop at a motel because he'd need to rent two separate rooms for him and her and he'd been ticketed for speeding and needed to save the money to pay the fine. "The speedometer was off because of oversize wheels on the back of my truck," he explained.

In such comic gaps between intent and the carrying out of a mission, I was made quite aware of the difference between blueprints and life—missions with a spiritual implication tend to be even more exaggeratedly quixotic. Plans were now in place for a Philip Johnson cathedral to rise in Dallas that would be worthy of the cover of the Dallas phonebook and would perhaps cast a long, gay shadow, putting gay spirituality on the world map. Mel White had positioned himself as a gay Gandhi, his subcontinent electronic, his goal as much the transformation of the self-image of gay people as the political reformation of their enemies. And yet what I'd witnessed was a fascinating social civil war between people who were far more alike than different, but seemed either unwilling or afraid to look at themselves in the mirror, this being most obvious in the confrontations between the ex-gay and a gay, or a gay born-again Christian and a straight one. There were a few important connections, of course. But lots of misfires.

Upon returning to New York I found an e-mail waiting for me in my box. "Hey man this is Daniel. Just in case you are racking your brain trying to remember which one I am. I am one of the guys that you had lunch with after church at Thomas Road. I was just writing you to let you know that I really enjoyed getting to meet all of you. This weekend really gave me an education I did not have before. Thank you very much for allowing us to ask questions about our differences without taking offense to them. I would very much like to know your thoughts on the Bible. Meaning do you believe it is inerrant or do you believe there are flaws?"

I wondered if his letter was a school assignment. It certainly had a canned quality. But I composed a response anyway, explaining that parts of the Bible seemed to me debatable, if solely because of problems of translation from Hebrew, Greek, and Latin, but that if anything was inerrant from a Christian viewpoint, perhaps love and mercy might qualify. I didn't receive a response. Noting that in his America Online profile Daniel had listed his occupation as "redneck," I nevertheless wrote a followup a few months later. I mentioned doing an interview for *Talk* magazine with Robert Perovich, a twenty-three-year-old Calvin Klein model who was a born-again Christian and engaged to be married.

"With the male model thing for Calvin Klein I do not think that I understand," Daniel wrote back, revealing some of the new perplexities in spiritual politics. "Is he engaged to be married to a man or a woman?"

Five

A Busy Mosaic:
Islam in New York City

In the 1998 English film *My Son the Fanatic,* Om Puri plays Parvez, an immigrant Pakistani cab driver in the English Midlands who drinks scotch, listens to jazz, hangs with hookers, and hopes his son, Farid, will marry the daughter of the local police chief. Holier-than-thou Farid, however, is forever locked upstairs in his bedroom listening to instructional tapes on how to perform salat, or daily Muslim prayer, and wants nothing to do with his father's smarmy Western values. In *East Is East,* released a year later, Om Puri plays the alter-image of Parvez, George Khan, a tradition-bound Pakistani, described by film critic Roger Ebert as "the Ralph Kramden of Manchester," who's trying to force his six culturally checkered sons into arranged marriages with homely daughters of his Pakistani friends. In both films, Puri's character, the father of the fanatic or the fanatic himself, winds up alone, his family a casualty of cultural dissonance.

This cinematic double image is a sign of the times for Muslim immigrants, not solely in England but also in France, Germany, and, increasingly and quite dramatically, in the United States. The repeal of the Asian Exclusion Act in 1965 allowed in not only an entire generation of Hindus but also of Muslims, for whom New York City has often been only a first stop on a dispersion that is subtly changing the cultural and spiritual complexion of the entire country. Contributing to this Islamization has been fallout from the Lebanese civil war of 1975 and especially the Iranian revolution of 1978, with the escape to the West of many Iranians with ties to the deposed Muhammad Reza Shah Pahlavi. Most recently, Muslim refugees have poured in from Bosnia, Kosovo, Albania, and Afghanistan. Surveys vary, but the United States has been widely estimated to have six to seven million Muslims—more than either Episcopalians or Presbyterians, and soon perhaps Jews—including an entirely new generation of Muslim youth coming of age having grown up on the same Subaru commercials and episodes of *Beverly Hills 90210* as everyone else. As a result, versions of both *My Son the Fanatic* and *East Is East* are running on parallel tracks in the lives of these young adults. With the exceptional interest in spirituality and seeking in the country, they're turning up the volume on spiritual as well as cultural issues.

Yet given the deep shock of Muslim terrorists destroying the World Trade Center and part of the Pentagon and killing thousands of innocent people on September 11, 2001, their spirituality has a certain association of "off-limits" danger to even many liberal seekers. While most of my visits to Muslim communities in the city took place before the attacks, the followers I'd met managed to resume their former lives afterward. Mosques filled with first-generation immigrants remained more directly involved in Middle Eastern politics: the largely Afghani Hazrat I-Abubakr Sadiq mosque in Flushing, Queens, for instance, was divided along ethnic Tajik and Pashtun lines by a denouncement of the Taliban by its Imam. But for second-generation American

Muslims, as well as converts, the times brought anxiety about personal safety but also surprising support and increased curiosity from acquaintances who'd never paid much attention before. "A friend said to me, 'It really is a beautiful religion, I never knew much about it,' " I was told by an Irish-American woman in her late twenties who'd just become a Muslim six months earlier.

To try to get a sense of the lives of Muslims in New York City is to be led through a maze of ideas, people, and locations, never finding resolution, only greater nuance, and never hard-edge clarification, but more and more articulation. Adding to the mystery is the absence of a pope or a chief rabbi who can claim to speak for all Muslims; the religion is organized either mosque by mosque or by organizational affiliations with large foreign nation-states such as Saudi Arabia or Pakistan. As I talked with first-, second-, or third-generation Muslims in the greater New York City area, I found myself taking out subway maps I hadn't looked at in a decade. I visited neighborhoods I'd never visited before: Bay Ridge, Brooklyn; Jamaica, Queens; East Harlem. I drove with new Muslim friends to a Turkish mosque on Fridays. I chanted with Sufi groups. Through introductions, I met many practicing Muslims who might otherwise never have registered on my radar screen, especially those younger believers who—like Farid with his instructional prayer tapes—blend in while being singularly focused, in their inner lives, on a spiritual geography that has Mecca as its epicenter.

Adnan is one such American Muslim, who was introduced to me by a mutual friend, an Iranian novelist. He has chosen, fervently, the *My Son the Fanatic* approach. In his early thirties, he is an intelligent and intense writer of hypertext fiction, with long dark wavy hair, a goatee, and luminous brown eyes that always seem to be looking just beyond you. Adnan graduated from high school in Fort Lauderdale after having spent his junior year abroad in an American school in Karachi. Pakistan had been the home of his parents, though Adnan was born outside London. It was as an undergrad at Bennington College, in Vermont, that he underwent a road-to-Damascus experience, Islamic-style, as he explained when we met for coffee one Sunday afternoon at DeRobertis Pasticceria on First Avenue in the East Village in Manhattan, down the block, probably not coincidentally, from a Bangladeshi mosque, the Madina Masjid. "There's this path between north Bennington and the campus, a straight path that goes through the woods," he recalled. "I'd had this traumatic experience. I walked through there with my eyes closed just relying on an internal navigational system, which was basically a communication from God."

Adnan could be elliptical at times. When I asked if he'd been on the *hajj*—the pilgrimage to Mecca, the birthplace of Muhammad, prescribed for every Muslim at least once in a lifetime—he answered, "Yes, I've been to Mecca," with a faraway look, as though he were thinking of a mystical place rather than a city in western Saudi Arabia. Yet Adnan was quite expressive about his passion for Islam. "Islam is all-encompassing in its emphasis," he said. "It's a vehicle provided by God for anybody as an act of divine generosity. So I can only be grateful for it." He recommended a translation of the Quran by Muhammad Asad. He outlined his following of Muslim practices: prostrating five times daily; attending mosque for jummah, or Friday-noon prayer; and fasting "with my brothers" for a month during Ramadan. Later that evening I received a telephone call, in which he insisted that if I included his birth date in any publication, I should not write 1970, but rather the date according to the Arabic lunar calendar, 1390—counting from Muhammad's desert flight from Mecca to Medina in the summer of A.D. 622. "It's more precise," he insisted.

Adnan is not alone. Samina, a floral designer turned off by memories of the treatment of women in her native Pakistan, where women are supposed to pray at home rather than at the mosque, was brought back to Islam in part by the enthusiasm of her son, Timor. A tall young man in his twenties who's experimented with calligraphic graffiti art, he's been trying to compose a Muslim version of rap. "My son's a born-again Muslim," Samina told me. "He complained to me, 'You didn't teach me my religion. It was your duty.' I said, 'Maybe if I had, you would have gone away from it.' " Timor recounted to me a visit to a mosque in Pakistan that led to his current devotion. He'd been followed out by several older Pakistani men who questioned the brevity of his prayers until they learned that he was American. "One old man said to me, 'Look how straight I'm standing. And without a cane. Who in America as old as me can stand this straight? It's from praying my whole life.' " (Samina, who briefly became a devotee of Gurumayi in 1990, left Siddha Yoga after thinking to herself, "This is so against my religion to bow to a photograph!")

I also spoke with Pedram, who was born in Tehran in 1972 and lives with his family on Long Island. Pedram, his Iranian-born mother, his younger brother, Payman, and I rode home together on a subway one evening after a Sufi gathering at an apartment on the upper West Side of Manhattan. I asked Pedram's mother whether she had enjoyed the evening; she rolled her eyes toward her sons, one of whom was carrying a paperback copy of *The Shapes of Light,* written by a mystic philosopher named Suhrawardi, that he'd just purchased and said, "Oh, sure. It was very nice. But I'm certainly not into it the way those two are." Pedram claimed, "My parents were very modern. They weren't praying five times a day. My grandmother, though, did practice Islam, did the daily prayer, didn't drink alcohol. She was pious." His wake-up call came at the State University of New York at Stony Brook, where he took an "Introduction to Islam" course with Professor William Chittick. "Here I was, this nineteen-year-old kid who thinks I'm Muslim," recalled Pedram, "and this guy who was born in Connecticut can speak Arabic and Farsi ten times better than I can, and he knows more about the religion than I could ever possibly know at that point."

For every Adnan, Timor, or Pedram, though, there's a Hisham Moulay "Sammy" Bouadi, the Moroccan-born clerk at my local Korean deli in SoHo. Born into the Arabic language of the Quran, Sammy, in his late twenties, emigrated with his parents to Paris from the capital city of Rabat when he was eleven. He lacks some of the reverence of his born-again brothers. "I call myself a Muslim, but I know I'm a *moderne* Muslim," said Sammy. His arms were tattooed, and he was dressed all in denim, with an Eddie Bauer baseball cap. "It's hard for me to be like my dad. It's really hard for me to follow Islam in this country. There are a lot of Muslims in New York, but they became religious back home. From here, you gotta change yourself, you gotta stop drinking, you gotta stop dating, smoking the things that make you high, you gotta start praying and reading Quran. Yeah, it's probably easy. At least that's what they think. But that's not the way it is."

Though Sammy lives in Bay Ridge, Brooklyn, now a heavily accented Arabic neighborhood where street signs are often in Arabic script, he's only been to its main mosque, Masjid Musab bin Umayr, or the Islamic Society of Bay Ridge, once. Yet he lives with his father, who prays five times daily. His wife, a Virginia-born daughter of a Muslim father and a Christian mother, has lately been transforming herself into a sort of *My Daughter the Fanatic*. "She started praying for, I think, five months," Sammy told me at Café Dante in the West Village, while drinking a bottle of Heineken and smoking a Marlboro Light. "She gets up at 5:30 in the morning, praying. She covers herself. It doesn't make a difference to me. She started after she married me. My dad, he loved the idea. She's like, 'I don't care if they fire me. I am a Muslim woman, and I have to cover myself.' "

Accelerating this heightened Muslim spirituality in America— as distinct from England—are the converts, who are responsible for moving the dialogue beyond the quaint paradoxes of Old World and New. Films such as *My Son the Fanatic* and *East Is East,* or novels such as *White Teeth,* by Zadie Smith, published in 2000, about two North London families—one headed by working-class Archie, and the other by his best friend, a devoutly Muslim Bengali named Samad Iqbal—play on the confounding, and often comic, cultural crossword puzzle presented by new immigration patterns. But another book, *The Autobiography of Malcolm X* (adapted as *Malcolm X* by director Spike Lee in 1989), contributes the bracing sensation of rediscovery that American converts to Islam have brought. The great surprise of the last quarter century is the number of African Americans—who now constitute perhaps 40 percent of the American Muslim community—who've espoused traditional Sunni Islam under the leadership of Wallace D. Muhammad, the son of Elijah Muhammad. (Elijah Muhammad's Nation of Islam remains intact as a much-diminished organization with as few as ten thousand members, led by Louis Farrakhan.)

"Today the whole world is watching American Muslims to see how we practice this religion in a non-Islamic society," said Yusuf Hasan. He served, in the early 1970s, as a uniformed soldier of the Fruit of Islam, the military wing of the Nation of Islam, and is now the Muslim staff chaplain at the Memorial Sloan-Kettering Cancer Center and assistant Imam at Masjid Malcolm Shabazz, in Harlem: "We've gotten off the track in a lot of Islamic countries. A lot of Muslims have gone to sleep. God is reviving it for us in America to bring the people back to the true religion. Many Muslims have mixed in their culture and now think that's the religion. It doesn't make me a Muslim because I dress a certain way. The Holy Quran came down on the heart of a human being. What makes me a Muslim are my good actions and good conduct and what is in my heart."

Among Caucasian Americans, compared with African American and Latino converts, the trend has been for women to be drawn to the religion more than men, in spite of the popular notion of women as veiled second-class citizens in Muslim societies. Gray Henry, the director of Fons Vitae, which includes the Islamic Texts Society, in Louisville, Kentucky, embraced Islam along with her husband, a Venezuelan filmmaker, in Manhattan in the 1960s. She studied at the venerable Al-Azhar, the Islamic university built in A.D. 970 in Cairo, the oldest continuously functioning university in the Western Hemisphere. Then she accepted spiritual direction from Martin Lings, an English Muslim convert who served as keeper of the Oriental manuscripts at the British Museum, wrote a biography of Muhammad based on the earliest sources as well as three works on Islamic mysticism, and was a member of the Shadhiliyah Sufi order, dating back to thirteenth-century Egypt. "When we met Martin Lings, we realized that it would be possible to achieve a sanctified state and be a Westerner," she said. "Because, frankly, you never see saints in our part of the world." (Many of the British and American converts, especially artists and intellectuals, have come through such Sufi orders, which emphasize the mystical, or interior, aspects of Islam.)

Living in Kentucky since 1990, Gray Henry has pursued ecumenical activities locally, including sponsoring a conference in 1999 called "Merton and Sufism," with the monks from the nearby Abbey of Gethsemani. Her experience has made her sensitive to the plight of converts to Islam in contemporary America. "It would be difficult to be outwardly Islamic in America today," she told me. "Because the prejudice is so bad and so deep. To tell someone you're involved in Sufism would be like telling them a lie, because you know they're defining it as something else. Sufism became part of the American hippie trip. There are even those who say you can be Sufi and not be a Muslim. That's the stupidest thing I've ever heard. It's like saying you can be a monk or a nun and not be Christian."

The bottom line for many younger American Muslims, and converts, is the conviction that, as Imam Yusuf Hasan put it: "Islam is a religion of inclusion." That is certainly the wish of Shaffiq Essaje, who was born in Kenya of Indian background, educated at Oxford and Cambridge, and works as a pediatrician specializing in infectious diseases, at the NYU Medical Center. Essaje is also a member of Al Fatiha, a gay Muslim organization with an unofficial membership estimated at two hundred fifty to three hundred regulars, attendees at its events numbering between thirty and one hundred. "Two doors down from the Bangladeshi mosque on First Avenue there's a little East Village bar," said Essaje. "Out front there's a Black Muslim selling incense sticks . . . but his customers are usually all East Village hippies. I walk past that mosque every day. I never get a sense that the people going to mosque are shocked or horrified as they pass people who they would never come across back in their home countries, who come from another planet almost. At the same time I've never gotten a sense that their presence is a thorn in the side of the neighborhood. I think people do become changed by being in New York City and experiencing this degree of pluralism. I can only hope this will create a greater degree of tolerance for the gay community."

Many of the great worldly cities have staged important moments in the history of Islam: Mecca and Medina, where Muhammad set up his theocracy; Damascus, the oldest continuously inhabited city in the world, and the capital of the early Umayyad Dynasty, between A.D. 661 and 749; Baghdad, in the ninth and tenth centuries the world's center of learning under the Abbasid Dynasty; Cordova, the Muslim outpost in Spain in the twelfth century; and Istanbul, the capital for the Ottoman Turks. Some envision New York City as the current "it" city in Muslim history. As Feisal Abdul Rauf, imam of the Masjiid Al-Farah in Tribeca and founder of the American Sufi Muslim Association, put it: "The new immigrants have maintained relationships with their families back home, especially because of the Internet and cell phones. People can go home for a long weekend. This is now a two-way street. As Islam in America evolves, it's going to have an effect on how the religion is practiced in other parts of the world."

Islam in New York City is a busy mosaic. There are currently about 110 mosques in the city, about a hundred of which were set up only in the last twenty-five years. Their exact number remains uncountable, for a mosque, or *masjid,* is simply any place where prayer occurs or, more literally, a "place of prostration" or *sujud,* the posture of kneeling with forehead on floor captured endlessly as the universal pictograph signifying "Muslim." Mosques don't have the same official institutional status as churches, synagogues, or temples. The first *masjid* was the courtyard of Muhammad's house in Medina, with a palm stump serving as his pulpit. There was a *hadith,* or "saying," attributed to Muhammad that the whole face of the earth is really a mosque. Often without funds to build traditional Oriental mosques with tall minarets and green domes, immigrants to the city have been particularly inventive, transforming factories, storefronts, even cinemas into makeshift prayer halls.

"You often find mosques in apartments or in the basement of nondescript buildings with a majority of residents from the same country," said Louis Abdellatif Cristillo, the field director of an ongoing "Muslim Communities in New York City" mapping project at the Columbia University School of International and Public Affairs. "A number of students of mine were from the Pakistan region, and they told me they lived in a seven-story apartment building where one of the apartments had been converted into a mosque for prayers. There are untold numbers of such functional mosques in the city that don't fall into the public category. The space itself doesn't have to be specifically constructed for that purpose." (Cristillo, an Italian American from California, fits the not uncommon profile of having embraced Islam in 1981 while serving as a Peace Corps volunteer in southern Morocco.)

The city's six hundred thousand Muslims are generally thought to reside in one of a few neighborhoods spread out around dominating mosques: the Al Farouq Masjid, on Atlantic Avenue in Brooklyn (which gained notoriety when some of the 1993 World Trade Center bombers were traced to the Alkifah Refugee Center, which had started out around 1986 as a desk at the mosque before moving a few doors down the street); the Masjid Musab bin Umayr, in Bay Ridge; and the Masjid Malcolm Shabazz, in Harlem. Such landmarks are known worldwide. "I've heard stories of people who've gotten off the plane at JFK, not knowing anybody, meeting somebody by accident from Brooklyn who gave them the address to the Musab *masjid*," added Cristillo. "It serves as a halfway house for new arrivals. The mosque will take them in for a few days until they can get set up with some other brothers in an apartment. It's done very informally, through social networks. They also help people locate jobs."

But many other neighborhoods are demographically shaded "Muslim" as well. In the Fordham area of the north Bronx, there's a growing Muslim population from the Balkans, Montenegro, and Kosovo as well as West Africans, Pakistanis, and South Americans. The Alianza Islamica in the north Bronx is a Latino mosque, founded by a Puerto Rican convert in the early 1970s, which now includes about three hundred families with a strong outreach program to street gangs, its growth reflecting a trend among the nation's estimated twenty-five thousand Hispanic Muslims. (They recently sent a member to Mecca to study religious law and sciences, his mission being to eventually return to teach the rest of the community.) In the Bedford-Stuyvesant neighborhood of Brooklyn, there's a long-standing presence of African-American Muslims, with some recent influx of West Africans. The Arab community in Bay Ridge is being replenished with Palestinians, Egyptians, and Yemeni. A sort of "Little Pakistan" has grown up in Coney Island, where Urdu can be heard spoken on the streets. (Robina Niaz, a social worker from Pakistan, told me of being turned away from Friday *jummah* at the local Coney Island Pakistani mosque, which was still under construction in the summer of 2000. When she complained, they found a place for her in the basement, where she prayed while plaster fell on her from the ceiling each time the men on the main floor performed their thundering prostrations.) On Friday afternoons following the *jummah* at the Turkish Masjid Fatih, on the border of Borough Park and Bay Ridge, Turkish women in white scarves can be seen busily shopping at the corner Birlik Market for *halal,* or ritually pure produce. (Pork products and alcohol are prohibited to Muslims; in earlier decades, they shopped at Jewish kosher delis to ensure their meat was properly slaughtered.)

Visiting any of these "ethnic" mosques can be a sort of subway tourism—the Middle East, West Africa, or even the Caribbean on two MetroCard swipes a day. Among Muslims, they're often known as "homesick mosques." One of the most elaborate of these folk centers is the Imam Al-Khoei Benevolent Foundation, at 88–89 Van Wyck Expressway, in Jamaica, Queens. A seventy-five-thousand-square-foot yellow brick school building, its incongruous minaret rising over a well-traveled underpass like a tower of pale ice cream encircled by blue bands of calligraphy, the center, which opened in 1989, is truly an outpost of Iraqi Shiite culture. Its founding spirit was one of three living Grand Ayatollahs, Seyyid Abulqasim Musawi Al-Khoei, who was born in Iran in 1899 and died in Iraq in 1992 while detained under house arrest by Saddam Hussein following the violent crushing of a popular uprising after the Gulf War. (According to the center's Web site, Al-Khoei had been taken to Baghdad, where, "under duress," he appeared on television with Saddam.) The author of thirty-seven books, Al-Khoei was responsible for founding similar compounds of prayer, education, and social welfare in Bangkok, Islamabad, Beirut, and London. Like those of George Washington or Abraham Lincoln in traditional American public schools, portraits of him—turbaned, ascetic, with a white beard and profile reminiscent of the far more famous Ayatollah Khomeini—hang throughout the mosque.

To walk the gray linoleum halls of the Al-Khoei Foundation makes one feel that one has been dropped without subtitles into a foreign film, particularly one of the classroom scenes of the contemporary Iranian filmmaker Abbas Kiarostami. English is rarely spoken. In the main entrance hall, men pass beneath a huge, glittering chandelier in white knitted prayer caps, women in black-and-white scarves and colorful wraps. Warning signs at each stall in the men's room read: "Please do not urinate whilst standing as the floor becomes *najas* (unclean) & it is *makrooh* in Islam." *Makrooh* is a technical term in Islamic law meaning disliked, but not forbidden. An example would be smoking tobacco. There are no urinals, just pools and faucets for *wudu,* or ablution—the ritual washing of hands, face, and feet required before prayer. The dark wood shelves of the library are filled with tall green and red volumes dealing mostly with Quranic sciences, ethics, and tradition. The prayer hall is vast, and covered with tan wall-to-wall carpeting. On the Friday I visited, dozens of boys from the Al-Imam Junior High School lined up in their blue sweaters with white stripes on the sleeves, as well as about two hundred men— including one sumo-sized bodybuilder in a Nike shirt, reminis-

cent of the infatuation with martial arts and wrestling in the
"houses of strength" *(zur kaneh)* of traditional Iranian Shiite culture. The women and girls had disappeared behind gray screens,
to listen to the Imam Fadhel Al-Sahlani, the U.S. representative of
the Grand Ayatollah Al-Seestani, with his clipped beard, white
turban, and green linen robe, declaim against men giving up their
prayer regimen in the workplace, and women choosing to work
rather than be supported by husbands and fathers. His point: too
much cultural assimilation.

"Some of the Muslims here have been affected by a habit and
by a way of life of a non-Muslim," he underlined his message for
me later in his office. "Some of the ladies have problems with their
husbands. They refer to American law rather than Islamic law.
When she feels she will not get what she wants from Islamic law
she goes to the American system. That is not right. We have problems with the children. Some of them have bad habits. They
smoke, and do drugs, and maybe drink. But as far as the government is concerned, we don't have any problems. In Arab countries
we don't have this kind of freedom in the practice of our religion. . . . During the Gulf War the police came, and they just
wanted to make sure that everything is well and there is nobody
attacking us."

To help me get my bearings, Sayyed Nadeem Kazmi—
"Sayyed" is the honorific title of any descendent of Mohammad's—
the senior consultant in humanitarian affairs to the international
Al-Khoei Foundation, interrupted in his British accent to explain
to me that "Sheikh Sahlani here is one of the appointed representatives of the Grand Ayatollah Al-Seestani. It's the equivalent of
talking with a bishop. And when you're speaking of Najaf, the
university in Iraq where the Ayatollah Al-Khoei taught, and
which is over a thousand years old and one of the oldest universities in the world, you're talking about something akin to the Vatican or Westminster Abbey." (*Ayatollah,* meaning "Sign of God," is
the title of a high-ranking Shiite religious leader. Shiites are a
minority party of Muslims, prominent in Iran, Iraq, and Lebanon,
who believe leadership should have been passed down through

Muhammad's descendants, beginning with his first cousin and son-in-law, Ali, rather than as it was, through the Companions of the Prophet—Abu Bakr, Umar, then Uthman—which is the position of the Sunni Party. The Sunnis make up about 90 percent of the worldwide Muslim population of 1.2 billion followers.)

The feel of Muslim life is just as strong on sidewalks and in cafes and specialty stores selling fragrances, flowers, or head scarves as in the multiplying mosques. "In Bay Ridge, they're all Muslims," said Sammy, the deli clerk. "We're talking about 75 percent Arabs—Palestinians, Egyptians, Moroccans, Algerians. They have all these cafes where they sit outside together. The only language you hear on the streets is Arabic. All the letters on the stores are in Arabic. It's fun. But to me personally, I don't want to sit there. They're just talking about people. I never learn anything. I just hear, Oh, this guy he just got married with this woman. This guy, he was selling hashish. That guy was fooling with bank accounts, they locked him up. That's all the things you hear. Some religious people talk about Islam. I like those people. At least they're talking about something."

In the south Bronx, where there are virtually no Muslims, the Muslim Yemenis are still easy to spot, in their delis with bullet-proof shields at the cash counters, giving the impression of being besieged. Along Broadway up to Washington Heights are Lebanese entrepreneurs selling sporting goods, sneakers, and dress shoes. Of the approximately forty-two thousand cab drivers in New York City, the vast majority are from the Indian subcontinent, and the vast majority of those are Muslim, as can be detected from the surnames on their posted driver permits that can be traced back to seventh-century Arabia, or from the lettering on the scent bottles on their dashboards. An increasingly common character is the "taxi convert," someone who's been driven by a zealous cabbie to a mosque and winds up embracing the religion. "A friend of mine was first brought to a mosque by a cab driver," corroborated Husayn Fruhstorfer, a Swiss-born businessman who later became Muslim as well. "He was half-black, half-white, smart, but had gone into the army instead of finishing college. It only took him two meetings to convert."

If some of the more recent Muslim immigrants who've taken to driving cabs might not know every street, bridge, and tunnel in the molten grid-work of the five boroughs, they almost always know their way to a singular landmark, the New York mosque of the Islamic Cultural Center, at the corner of Ninety-sixth Street and Third Avenue, in Manhattan. It officially opened in 1991, designed by Skidmore, Owings and Merrill, and built at a cost of $17 million raised over twenty-five years mostly by Muslim ambassadors to the United Nations who sat on its board of trustees. The eighty-eight-thousand-square-foot property was purchased in 1966 with the help of gifts from the governments of Kuwait, Saudi Arabia, Libya, and Malaysia. It was the first mosque in New York City with a traditional dome and minaret— the first one in the United States had been officially opened on Massachusetts Avenue, in Washington, D.C., in 1957, with President Eisenhower in attendance. Like the Episcopal cathedral of St. John the Divine in upper Manhattan, the Ninety-sixth Street mosque is less a parish than a weekly gathering place or public sifter for a particular flavor of spirituality. Its entire demographic is represented weekly: sub-Saharan Africans, Middle Easterners, Caribbean islanders, Balkanites, Indo-Pakistanis, African Americans, and Europeans.

Islam is actually a simple formula of a religion with a very complex manifestation. It can be reduced to five basic rules, the famous Five Pillars: witness *shahadah*—to become Muslim you must recite three times a short creed claiming that there is one God (Allah) and Muhammad is His messenger; perform *salat* five times a day, facing Mecca; give *zakat,* or alms, of 2½ percent of yearly income; fast while the sun is up during the entire month of *Ramadan,* though eating, drinking, smoking, and sex are permitted at night; and make the *hajj* to Mecca, if physically and financially able. The five daily prayers consist of two, three, or four cycles, or *rak'at,* of bowing, kneeling, and prostrating (the prayers can also be recited sitting unobtrusively, if needed). Muslims often carry tiny pocket compasses to be able to identify the direction of Mecca while traveling. Communal prayers on Friday noon are required for men, optional for women, hence the need for the panregional Islamic Cultural Center—a "center" simply being an expanded mosque that offers social services and, in this case, a bookstore, an Islamic school on weekends, and a bulletin, the *Resallah*.

The religion is more correctly known as al-Islaam, meaning "submission" to the will of Allah, as well as evoking peace, from the root word *"salaam."* Its last fundamental is the Quran, more properly al-Qur'an, or in its Western transliteration, Koran, meaning "recitation." It's the Holy Bible of Islam, a work of poetic prose in 114 *suras*, or chapters, generally arranged in order from longest to shortest. In his fortieth year, Muhammad, who'd married a rich, older widow, Khadija, and prospered as a trader between Damascus, Busra, Mecca, and Yemen, secluded himself in a cave in Mount Hira, two miles north of Mecca, for meditation. Muslims believe that during Ramadan, in July of A.D. 610, Allah began to reveal His words to the avowedly illiterate merchant through the angel Gabriel on the "Night of Power." The first words revealed to him—now recorded in Sura 96 of the Quran:

> In the name of God, the Compassionate, the Merciful,
> Recite: in the name of thy Lord who created,
> Created man of a blood-clot
> Recite: And thy lord is the Most Generous,
> Who taught by the Pen,
> taught man that he knew not.

Unlike Jesus, who died violently at a young age, Muhammad's mission consumed his middle and old age, and involved setting up a theocracy under his rule in Medina, where he'd escaped after a decade of persecution in Mecca. As the Quran continued to be revealed over twenty-three years, until his death, in 632, many of the later *suras,* which tend to be longer and more practical, precede the shorter, more ecstatic passages from the early years of ineffable illumination and stammering prophecy. All these divine messages were reputedly memorized or written down by Muhammad's followers on animal skins and bones, flat stones, tablets, tree branches, and trunks. The entire production was then standardized in a canonic edition under the third caliph, Uthman ibn Affan (644–656), and has remained unchanged for fourteen centuries.

On the Friday in spring when I attended the *jummah* for prayer and reading from the Quran at the New York mosque of the Islamic Cultural Center, the warm sunlight was reflecting off the vertical lines of the minaret, and shimmering on the overlapped layers of the celadon green glass forming the arch of the entrance. The inside of the mosque had the feel of an aquarium with a vast dome of distant sky hovering overhead. Green tones, associated in Islam with paradise and oases, were used in the glass, the walls, and the green marble of the floor. A *mihrab,* or niche of aquamarine layers of glass set in the front wall, pointed in the direction of Mecca. White light blazed mutely through windows decorated with ceramic fret. The only interruption in this saucer of open space with no pews, altar, or choir were a large gold-framed clock set on a stand near the *mihrab* and a chair set in a vertical latticed box at the top of a flight of red-carpeted stairs. The effect was of a streamlined yet extremely peaceful flotation chamber.

As the men arrived for prayer that Friday, two weeks after the end of Ramadan, they first slipped their shoes into racks at the rear or along the ledges of the windows. (The shock of leaving anything in such a free-for-all lump in New York City was perhaps the most startling gesture of the entire service.) The crowd, numbering nearly one thousand by the time the service concluded, at 1:30, seemed energetic and vital. Young men turned their baseball caps backward when they entered, to conform with the embroidered prayer caps and pillbox hats of other worshipers. Well-dressed businessmen arrived in black, blue, or tan suits. A few more wore white, blue, or gold African robes. A mound of shoes began to surround those of us sitting cross-legged on the floor in the rear: Nike sneakers, Italian leather loafers, sandals. Many brought prayer beads of light wood or colored beads of glass or held small editions of the Quran in green and red embroidered with gold calligraphic lettering. As women hurried up a flight of stairs to the rear mezzanine, the crowd on the ground floor began to exude a fervent brotherhood, or male bonding, of the sort associated with all-male sports teams, fraternities, or monasteries. Singly, as they arrived, the men would begin their choreographed cycles of prayer. Facing the front, they stood with hands cupped behind their earlobes while saying, *"Allahu Akbar,"* "God is great," bending with hands on knees, saying, *"Subhana-llah,"* "Glory be to God," kneeling, standing again, prostrating their entire bodies with foreheads touching the floor, and then standing again.

The service became focused when Muhammad Salem Agwa, the Imam, the leader of group prayer at the Islamic Center, climbed the narrow steps enclosed by the handrails of the pulpit. The pulpit, where he would deliver his *khutba,* or Friday sermon, was covered by a canopy, leaving the top step empty in recognition of Prophet Muhammad's preeminence. In white robes trimmed in gold and a white prayer cap, he spoke first in Arabic, punctuating his themes by pointing with a finger toward the sky, slicing his arms up and down, and extending his open palms outward. He then translated, explaining that all people are called to a special relationship with Allah that goes beyond what we know as love and friendship; that reading the Quran and praying are two ways to establish such a relationship; that there is no point in grieving for loss since all is ordained; and that the meaning of life is not in serving one's own needs but in working for the larger nation of Islam.

The hour concluded as the Imam approached the *mihrab* to lead the congregation in prayer. "Shoulder to shoulder, shoulder to shoulder," shouted the usher in his turban. "Fill the gaps, fill the gaps." He created a wind of activity as he incited everyone to fall into ranks. At the moment of prostration every forehead was touching the floor, without any deviation or undisciplined looking around. Like the moment of consecration in the Catholic mass, the communal prostration was the satisfaction of all that had gone before, the expression of complete submission and humility to Allah and of the equality of all people before Him. After the final prostration, many greeted each other in Arabic or English before retrieving their shoes. "Hello, brother," said a mustached, gray-haired man in a red padded jacket, wool pants, and light blue socks who had been sitting next to me.

During the past hour—or perhaps during the past five minutes—the front courtyard and nearby sidewalks had been transformed into a haphazard simulation of a Middle Eastern bazaar. Many women stood with brown paper bags outstretched asking for money from those exiting the prayer hall. One held a clipping about Sarajevo, implying that she or her family had been victims of the war. A man handed me a leaflet from Best Deal Travel, Inc., offering round-trip airfare to Saudi Arabia, including lodging in Mecca and Medina, for $2,200. The package also offered "Free stopover in Cairo, free gifts and more!"

Walking around the block to the rear entrance of the mosque, I met a young man in a tattered brown topcoat who held out his palm in the brisk breeze to ask for money. When I gave him two quarters, he rewarded me by pointing to a pigeon perched on a stone truss running partway up an angle of wall, the exterior marker of the *mihrab* within. "The bird is praying to Mecca, too," he informed me as gleefully as a godly man out of Attar's thirteenth-century collection of mystical tales, *The Conference of the Birds.*

There's always a certain amount of exoticism, or orientalism, at play for visitors in these urban mosques, even with the cosmopolitan mix in such a modern and sleekly abstract domed prayer hall as the Islamic Cultural Center of New York. The fresh news in American Islam, though, is its suburbanization, its translation into a second or third generation. Like the Jews who passed from the ghettos of the lower East Side to settle in the "Five Towns" of

Long Island and beyond, so the Muslim population has now dispersed from city to suburbs in the past two decades as well, becoming equally enamored with higher education, professionalism, and assimilation. And so the very defining scent and flavor of the religion itself has moved on and is being duly updated.

"I never bought into Islam as a culture," I was told by Pedram Samghabadi. "I don't want the culture of the Prophet and his Companions. I want their character. Anyone can grow a beard. But not everyone can go through the stuff the prophets did and come out the other side. Growing a beard doesn't make you a better Muslim. . . . For my friends, it's almost a nonissue that I'm Muslim. It's like, okay. But then New York City is such a heterogeneous place. Here people don't care if you're walking down the street on your hands. My experience might be different if I lived in Nebraska or the Bible Belt. I was having this interesting Internet chat with this kid from the Bible Belt, and he thought that since I was Muslim I was writing to him from a tent in Egypt. I was like, 'Dude, you better get out more. I live in New York, man. What are you talking about?' "

Pedram became increasingly taken with Islam after his graduation from college: "One night running in the backwoods of the north shore of Long Island, something inside me just cried out to God, it was like being in love with God." His instinct was to learn Arabic, which is actually only spoken by 18 percent of the world's Muslims. Having lived in Iran until he was eight years old, he'd been introduced to Farsi, the Persian language, which has the same alphabet but is a different spoken language. So he went to classes on *tajweed,* the proper recitation of the Arabic of the Quran, offered at the Islamic Center of Long Island (ICLI) in Westbury, Long Island. And he began attending Friday prayer: "It's basically a Sunni mosque. I prayed as a Shiite. But it didn't matter to them or me. They pray with their hands crossed. I pray with my hands down. Shiites have this tiny piece of earth they put down so their forehead only touches something natural. That's about the only difference."

For Pedram, as for so many other young people and their families, this first traditional mosque on the island was an eye-opener. Its blue-green ivory-stone dome rises austerely on Brush Hollow Road. The mosque had been built in 1991 by a Jewish architect, David Hirsch, at a cost of $2 million. Its manicured lawn has earned several awards for best lawn from the Westbury Civic Association, and within a decade, the mosque has become only one of fourteen mosques serving the estimated seventy thousand Muslims living in Nassau and Suffolk Counties. (The first Long Island mosque, in Selden, which opened in 1978, is housed in a former Baptist church.) Along with its classes in chanting of the Quran, and the Friday prayers, the center provides Sunday school, spiritual support for prison inmates, a domestic harmony committee for families seeking crisis intervention, funeral services, and a media committee to answer questions when crises arise (such as the crash of EgyptAir flight 990 or the bombing of the World Trade Center).

One of the low-key patriarchs of the Islamic Center of Long Island has been Dr. Faroque Khan, born in Kashmir in 1943, a chest specialist who arrived in New York City in 1967 with his wife, Dr. Arfa Khan, a radiologist. He is now a professor of medicine at SUNY Stony Brook, and a regent of the American College of Physicians' American Society of Internal Medicine. In the early 1960s, New York City still had only two mosques: the Islamic Center of New York, which was then located at One Riverside Drive, and another on State Street in Brooklyn. Living as recent immigrants in Queens, Khan and his wife discovered that the only place available to them to celebrate *Eid ul-Fitr,* the festival similar to Thanksgiving marking the end of Ramadan, was in a hall rented in Roosevelt Hospital in Manhattan. "We got stuck in traffic and missed the whole thing," recalled Khan.

A kindly, intelligent man with white-gray hair and eyebrows who tends to dress in a suit, or at least a white shirt and trousers, wears a classic Rolex, and drives a middle-of-the-line Lexus, Khan began casting around for a supportive community because of such practical disappointments. He was acutely aware of the awkward position in which suburban American life was putting his two children—his son, Arif, who went on to graduate from Yale Medical School, and his daughter, Shireen, who's planning to pursue a career in child psychology. "When our children started growing up they started asking questions," recalled Khan. " 'Dad, where's my Christmas tree? Dad, where are the Hanukkah lights?' That was a wake-up call." But the Khans soon discovered that they were not alone, and they eventually joined with eight or ten other families who were similarly trying to reestablish some connection to their Muslim heritage after the shuffle of trying to get ahead in America. Many of these first founding families also had a doctor in the house, as Khan told a reporter from the *New York Times* in 1988: "Our Islamic Center is a Who's Who of physicians."

An early gathering spot was a storefront on College Point Boulevard in Whitestone, Queens, which was owned by a family of Muslim Tartars from southern Russia. From there, the group moved to a private kindergarten in Garden City, Long Island, next to a huge parking ramp where their children played tag. They then moved to the basement of a Baptist church in Westbury. Among these early pioneers were Dr. Jamil Khan, chairman of pediatrics at Brooklyn Jewish and St. John's Hospital, who eventually served for two years as president of the Islamic Center of Long Island; his wife, Dr. Farida Khan, who works on its domestic harmony program, which recently purchased a house adjoining the mosque property; and Ghazi Y. al-Haaj Khankan, born in Syria in 1934, who was then the host of his own radio program on 105.9 FM, "The Voice of al-Islaam," which he'd begun in 1967. In 1984, after a decade of wandering, these families—with Faroque Khan bringing along the Kashmiris, and Jamil Khan the Indo-Pakistanis—finally raised enough money to purchase an acre of land along with a shuttered two-story red brick house that still serves as offices behind the mosque, its basement having been used during the seven intervening years for prayer. "I remember the first Friday prayer, three people showed up," confessed Faroque Khan.

The ersatz Sunday-schooling of the earliest years was recalled with something less than enthusiasm by Dr. Faiz Khan, Jamil

Khan's son, who emigrated from Alighar, India, with his parents in 1970 when he was a one-year-old baby, and so grew up entirely in America. "We used to dread going to those classes when I was a kid," said Faiz Khan, now an attending physician in emergency and internal medicine at Long Island Jewish Hospital. "You'd rather be outside playing football. There was no organized curriculum. The teachers couldn't really speak English. They were of my parents' generation and they didn't understand the culture, and so we kids couldn't really relate to them. It was more of an attempt of my dad's generation to reestablish their roots. Everyone came here in search of economic opportunity. But in the process they underestimated the cultural diffusion. They didn't realize what they were up against."

Faroque Khan's niece Daisy, who came from Kashmir in 1973 as a teenager to pursue her education in architectural design, lived with her uncle and his family. She remembers the Iranian revolution as jumpstarting the community's more serious phase. "Pre-Khomeini, the Muslims I met in America seemed more relaxed about their religion," she said. "But during the revolution, they began to feel defensive because their religion was being portrayed in the media in a way that was fanatical and aggressive. It was a brand of Islam we didn't identify with or understand. In Kashmir I grew up with an Islam that was loving, giving, and tolerant towards other religious groups. So some of us started turning inward to learn about our religion. There was a new birthing of people wanting to learn about their faith to be able to defend it."

The result of the investments of these few Muslim families on Long Island in the 1980s is now a seven-thousand-square-foot tan brick sanctuary supported by about seven hundred families and accommodating seven hundred or eight hundred people for weekly prayer. About forty different nationalities are represented, though the majority are South Asians from Pakistan, India, Kashmir, and Bangladesh, with a good percentage from the Middle East and a sprinkling from the United States. On any given Friday, the parking lot is filled with a standard mix of current makes: Toyotas, Subarus, Tauruses, Mercedeses, BMWs. Men in prayer caps and women hastily fastening their head scarves make their way under a green awning, often stopping to sign one of the weekly petitions left on a picnic table outside addressing Muslim concerns, such as the Arab-Israeli peace talks or a United Nations referendum. A second picnic table is covered with ingredients for a lunch catered for a small price by a local family: pita bread, falafel, cans of Sprite.

"Our community is a cross section of the classes of American society," said Faroque Khan. "When you come to Friday prayer, you find the guy who pumps your gas, the guy leading the corporation, and the fellow running the deli down the street all standing shoulder to shoulder. I think that one of the appeals to African Americans is that if you are the first to arrive at the mosque, you go to the first row. If you're last, you go to the last row. There's equality based on your practice. You can't really walk over people to come to the front. That kind of equality was a very important message for them. If you're coming from the South and all your life you've been in the back of the bus, suddenly you find a religion where you can be the driver of the bus, if you're qualified."

A surprising ally emerging from the stresses and strains of the construction years—from 1989 through the official grand opening, in 1993—was Michelle Depew, a building inspector then in her early twenties who was working for the village of Westbury. Many residents were quite upset by the prospect of having a mosque in their midst, both because of worries over traffic congestion and because of fears of terrorism and dark plots being hatched just over the garden hedge. Indeed, about ninety Westbury residents signed a petition to ban construction when the land was first bought. An Oriental oddity was deemed to have no place in the land of muffler shops, pancake houses, and churches. Ms. Depew was, by default, siding with the irate neighbors, as she was committed to enforcing the building codes, including one that didn't allow the congregation to use their mosque without a temporary certificate of occupancy. A showdown occurred when she chained the entrance closed on a holy day. ("Some of the opposition was understandable," allowed Faiz Khan. "Some worshipers exhibited obnoxious manners characteristically found in their homelands. On Fridays, I'm sure some residents of Westbury perceived what appeared to be a storming of the town between the hours of 12:30 and 2:30. The assailants were abrupt, unfriendly, ethnocentric immigrant types, who on occasion blocked their driveways or littered, did their thing, and left.")

The upshot of Depew's skirmishes at the mosque was that she wound up embracing Islam. "I spent lots of time there because I was always getting complaints on the place and had to respond," Depew explained.

> The neighbors were quite angry about the entire situation. But even when we were battling over the temporary certificate of occupancy there was respect and communication. You don't see a lot of respect out in the world at large. But if you have people who believe, anywhere, you're going to have people who respect each other. So I felt very comfortable. I guess that was why I decided to sit down and study the situation, and to attend their Sunday discussions.
>
> I found that I liked the simplicity of Islam. It has the same basic ground rules as Christianity, you have your apostles and prophets. But there was a lot of warmth there that I could feel. It seemed like a natural way to live. I'd grown up Episcopalian in a little town in upstate New York, very white, very narrow-minded, with a lot of hypocrisy and racism tied in with the religion. I went to church all those years, but there was always a distance. Going to the mosque was just very simple. It brought me back on the trail again.

Yet she still hasn't told her family of her "apostasy": "My family doesn't know anything about it. It's nobody's concern except for mine and God's."

The problems of the construction years are now smoothed over, and the mosque is a well-running center of both prayer and civic activism. Its degree of homogenization can be witnessed every Friday, as the usual ethnic inflections of city mosques are lost in its whitewashed hall. The front half is for the men, the rear half for the women, with no calligraphy evident anywhere. Lots of light pours in through a green octagonal dome lined with windows, and through side windows, the sills lined with volumes of the Quran, looking out on leafy trees and neat, white two-story homes with shingled roofs. As clean as an architectural model, efficiently cooled by central air-conditioning, the mosque holds the usual mix of men with red-and-white checked turbans, or caps of gray lamb's fur, and women in yellow, blue, green, and black scarves and Pakistani chemises. But there are also women in blue suits and tiger-print scarves. And there are plenty of teenage boys sporting an Abercrombie & Fitch aesthetic in their cargo pants and rugby shirts.

The two-part sermon on the day I visited was given by an Egyptian gentleman who is one of the rotating Imams—the mosque has divided the leadership roles among a core group. Speaking from a dark wood podium with the initials of the center, ICLI, in gold lettering on the front and flanking star-and-crescent medallions, he gave a traditional sermon on a *sura* dealing with the Day of Judgment, a concept shared with Christianity, which could just as easily have been given at the Ninety-sixth Street mosque. "You will not take anything with you into the next life except your good deeds," warned the Imam. He spoke with an Egyptian accent and wore a white cotton tunic and pants, and a white prayer cap. "You will work in this life and be accountable in the hereafter. Allah won't need to ask about your good deeds and sins. It will show very clearly from the light on your face." Some more contemporary activity went on among the listeners sitting cross-legged on the green carpet during the talk: one boy rolled a plastic motorbike over his brother's crew-cut head; a young man in a reversed Yankees cap put together a cell phone from a kit; someone's beeper went off accidentally.

Another member of the leadership team—the man behind

many of the petitions on the picnic table at the entrance, as well as the face the press puts to the public life of the center—is Ghazi Y. al-Haaj Khankan, the director of interfaith affairs and communication, a dashing gentleman in his late fifties with a flourish of a silver-gray mustache and a resonant voice with which he parlays his passion for Islam to the world. Having studied at the American University in Beirut, his American career began in the late 1950s when he taught Arabic at a U.S. Army language school in Monterey, California, followed by his appointment in 1960 as director of the Muslim Students Association of the U.S.A. and Canada, based in New York City. Khankan helped found the National Council on Islamic Affairs, which eventually merged with the American Muslim Alliance, the first group dedicated to organizing Muslims into a major voting bloc at the national level (a recent gathering of theirs featured the theme "How to Get 2,000 Muslim Americans Elected to Public Offices in 2000"). "Ghazi's a very high-profile guy," a mosque member told me. "He'll talk to congressmen, try to court their favor. It's through him that the Islamic Center of Long Island has become very much involved in the activist scene—petitioning, lobbying, political sloganeering."

Khankan's sense of the political consequences of stereotyping has made him a particularly strong apologist for the equality of men and women that he claims is built into the Muslim religion. "From day one, Muslim ladies had the right from God Almighty to run their own businesses and to keep their inheritance separate from their husband," said Khankan. "Prophet Muhammad's boss was his wife. So obviously, women have the right to an independent income, to be their own bosses, to keep their maiden name. Many tribes used to bury their newborn daughters alive. Islam prohibited that. . . . In Saudi Arabia, you cannot drive if you are a woman. These are cultural things. It has nothing to do with Quranic teaching. Because in the day of the Prophet, women rode camels, horses, and donkeys. So why can't they drive a car nowadays?" He explained their relegation to the rear of the mosque, and inability to serve as Imams, as a gender "difference" rather than inequality.

Khankan's liberalism concerning women does not extend to gays. The position he explained to me as mainline Islam was more in line with that of the pope or Jerry Falwell: "The Quran and the Bible both say that homosexuality is an abomination. And you know the story of Prophet Lot and what happened to his people. God destroyed people who did this lewd behavior. Now under Islamic law not just homosexuality, but promiscuity, in the sense of a man and woman performing the act of sex outside of marriage, or adultery, are all sinning. And there are punishments for such acts. Muslim leaders are there to help those who feel they want to leave the homosexual way of life. When they do that and repent, God will forgive them. We do not go out and pursue homosexuals for the purpose of harassing them. If they want our help, we will help them." (The story of Lot in the seventh *sura* of the Quran generally follows the drift of the version in Genesis.)

"I've heard, though, that there is a group of homosexuals who claim to be Muslim who use the name of 'Al-Fatihah,' the opening chapter of the holy book of al-Qur'an," he went on. "I feel very hurt by their choice of name. Since the Holy Book does not approve of homosexual behavior, they should not really infringe upon the name. If that's their choice in life, that's their choice. But part of the belief system in Islam is that everyone is personally responsible on the Day of Judgment for his or her actions, and there will be hellfire or paradise. I advise them to look towards the hereafter. They still have a chance to return to the natural way of life that God has prescribed in his Holy Book."

While Khankan's is a voice of authority, the place to hear the true medley of voices that make up the center is at one of their Sunday discussions, such as the one I attended on a hot July afternoon on the topic "The Four Most Frequently Asked Questions by Non-Muslims about Muslims and How to Address Them," led by Farouk Khan. The day's list of questions—concerning Jesus; women ("Why do you treat your women so shabbily?"); the relation to the Nation of Islam; and living as Muslims in a secular nation—were soon blurred in a roving hour-long discussion taking place between noon and one among fourteen men and eight women, who automatically divided themselves by male and female on either side of Khan in a circle of folding chairs in the rear room of the prayer hall, which is consigned to women during Friday prayers.

A Middle Eastern gentleman told of having a debate with a Christian chaplain who came to minister to his wife while she was in the hospital, since no Muslim chaplains were on staff. While Jesus is treated as a prophet, like Muhammad, and Sura 19 of the Quran is devoted to his mother, Mary, including an account of the virgin birth, Muslims do not believe in the Trinity, or the divinity of Christ. The man felt frustrated, apparently, by this misunderstanding by the chaplain.

"There is a great deal of theological debate right now in Christianity about Jesus as the Son of God," interjected a second Middle Eastern man. "We Muslims should be smart and reach out to these people. They are trapped in their own thinking and don't know about Islam."

"But our position is right. We should put some *attack* into it," said the first gentleman.

"Vinegar never attracts a bee," counseled Khan.

"But one book is right from the beginning to the end. Only one book. The Quran."

A Caribbean man in a black turban, one of two black men and three black women, interrupted. "I read in the Quran that even if a people is saying that a cow is god, you do not make fun of their god."

The addition of his voice opened up the discussion to conversion from Christianity to Islam, as all of them had been brought up within some Christian denomination.

"I couldn't deal with the Trinity since I was a kid," he continued. "I'm from Haiti. If Islam went there, every Haitian would believe Islam. Christianity was forcefully introduced into Haiti."

"What facilitated *your* attraction?" asked Brother Yousuf—a young man with parents from the Middle East—of one of the women.

"I grew up Christian," replied Sister Linda. "I'd go to Bible study but I was always confused by what they were trying to tell me."

With the hour nearly used up, and the time approaching for a cycle of group prayer, a young African-American brother, who would join in the prayers on the rug but not follow through on all the motions, voiced a response that could probably fill in for hundreds of thousands of African Americans not present in the room. "I'm not converted to Islam yet," he said. "But I have an open mind. . . . I was brought to it by the brother known as Malcolm X."

The mosque that today doubles as a memorial to the young man's inspiration, Malcolm X, is the Masjid Malcolm Shabazz, formerly Temple Number Seven of the Nation of Islam. Its green aluminum pumpkin-shaped dome rises above the busy intersection of 116th Street and Malcolm X Boulevard, formerly Lenox Avenue, at the center of the African-American cultural capital of Harlem. The mosque's own name change reflects the Islamic name change of Malcolm X to El-Hajj Malik El-Shabazz, following his *hajj* to Mecca in 1964, and his personal transition from a Black Muslim to an orthodox Sunni Muslim. (The first, Christian name of this boy, who was born in 1925 in Omaha, Nebraska, and went on to become such a highly visible Black Muslim leader, civil and human rights advocate, pan-Africanist, and pan-Islamist, was the much more diminutive Malcolm Little.)

Malcolm X kept coming up as a figure of fascination in my talks with the younger generation of Muslims, certainly for African Americans but also among the immigrant group; he was often felt to be the closest to an American Muslim saint. One Algerian in his twenties told me of the power of reading *The Autobiography of Malcolm X;* the book sounded in his description like a sort of St. Augustine's *Confessions.* For Timor, the nascent Muslim rapper, Spike Lee's movie version ranked second in his personal film library only to *The Message,* a 1976 epic starring Anthony Quinn, filmed in both an Arabic and an English version, based on the life of the Prophet.

The Malcolm X championed by black America has generally been the intense revolutionary with short-cropped hair and simple black-framed eyeglasses, caught in midconversation or midinterview (this was the image on the thirty-three-cent commemorative stamp issued for Black Heritage month in 1999). His media fame through most of his adult life came from his role as the fiercely articulate national representative of the Nation of Islam. He had been converted in 1948, while serving a six-year prison term for larceny in the maximum-security Norfolk Prison in Massachusetts, where his brother Reginald revealed to him during a visit, "The white man is the devil." Dropping his surname and taking on an X, standard practice in the movement, was an outward symbol of inner changes: ex-Christian, ex-Negro, ex-slave. During the early 1960s, he intractably played bad cop to Martin Luther King's good cop, puncturing King's nonviolent message with audacious statements, such as his take on John F. Kennedy's assassination, in 1963, as "chickens coming home to roost."

The Nation of Islam may have used the symbols and trappings of orthodox Islam, but its teaching had definitely strayed from the universal message of Islam, and its insistence on Muhammad as the last prophet. Often identified with its founder, Wallace Fard Muhammad, a silk peddler in Detroit in the 1930s, the Nation of Islam has suggested that God is a black man who would liberate African Americans and destroy Satan—their white oppressors— and that Elijah Muhammad was God's messenger, The main attraction of the separatist philosophy of the Nation of Islam was its political empowerment of blacks, and its insistence as a social movement—in the tradition of Marcus Garvey's "Back to Africa" movement—of "Do for Self," including the peddling of bean pies and whiting fish to improve nutrition and physical health. "You are what you eat," wrote Elijah Muhammad in *How to Eat to Live,* published in 1972. His linking of religion and nutrition put him in a line going back to Seventh-Day Adventist Ellen Smith, as well as to Dr. John Harvey Kellogg of the Sanitarium.

"Elijah Muhammad wasn't teaching us Islam, he was a social reformer," Yusuf Hasan told me. "He was trying to socially reform African Americans. He said, 'Do for yourself, pull yourself up by your own bootstraps, take care of your wife and children, stop the drinking, especially you men take control of your community and your lives.' We saw Dr. King as having been a leader in the Christian religion, and in Islam today we love Christians because a lot of our people are Christians. But the Dr. King thing was passive. If someone slapped you on one cheek, you turned the other cheek. The Nation of Islam was totally the opposite. If you hit me, I'm going to hit you back. If you fight me, I'm going to fight you. If you respect me, I'll respect you."

The involvement of Malcolm X with orthodox Islam wasn't fully expressed until his break with Elijah Muhammad. The break followed his temporary suspension in December 1963 for his comments on the Kennedy assassination, and his withdrawal from the Nation of Islam in March 1964 as he publicly separated from Elijah Muhammad on issues of immorality when the leader was accused of having fathered illegitimate children. (His vindictive exposure of the issue, about which he'd first heard in the 1950s, was read by some as politics rather than morality.) After he transformed himself into "Malik" during his *hajj,* he returned to lead the short-lived Muslim Mosque, Inc., and the Organization of Afro-American Unity (OAAU), which were founded in March and June 1964, respectively. Most American Sunni Muslims, however, were unconvinced of his sincerity at the time of his assassination. On February 21, 1965, he was killed by members of the Nation of Islam, with the apparent complicity of government authorities, while giving a speech to the newly formed OAAU at the Audubon Ballroom in Harlem. He was given a Muslim burial by an obscure African-American Sunni organization.

It is "Malik," rather than Malcolm X, who has attracted the attention of the younger American Muslims—hence the young man's careful emphasis at the Westbury mosque on "the brother *known* as Malcolm X." Exhibit A in this shift has been the famous "Letter from Mecca," which stands in African-American literature with Martin Luther King's "Letter from a Birmingham Jail," but which can become a veritable Pauline epistle in the eyes of believers. "During the past eleven days here in the Muslim world, I have eaten from the same plate, drunk from the same glass, and slept in the same bed (or on the same rug)—while praying to the *same God*—with fellow Muslims, whose eyes were the bluest of blue, whose hair was the blondest of blond, and whose skin was the whitest of white," he wrote home to his assistants at the newly formed Muslim Mosque, Inc. "And in the *words* and in the *deeds* of the 'white' Muslims, I felt the same sincerity that I felt among the black African Muslims in Nigeria, Sudan and Ghana." Whether he abandoned the notion of a special relationship between European and American whites and Satan, as opposed to the phenotypic whites he saw in Mecca, however, remains an open question.

Upon his return, Malik's transformation appeared to speed up daily. In a basically accurate scene in Spike Lee's 1992 film, the returning pilgrim, (played by Denzel Washington), in a neat suit and bearded for the first time, his wife, Betty Shabazz (Angela Bassett), beside him, stands before a bank of microphones in a roomful of reporters and popping flashbulbs at the overseas-arrival building at New York's Kennedy International Airport on May 21, 1964. In the film, Malcolm X gives a rendition of the prepared speech delivered that day: "In the Muslim world, I saw, I felt, and I wrote home how my thinking was broadened! Just as I wrote, I shared true, brotherly love with many white-complexioned Muslims who never gave a single thought to the race, or to the complexion, of another Muslim. . . . The true Islam has shown me that a blanket indictment of all white people is as wrong as when whites make blanket indictments against blacks."

By then Malik had ceded his Harlem Temple Seven, though under his lieutenancy the Nation of Islam had achieved a membership estimated at 500,000. His position as head minister and national representative was filled by Louis Farrakhan, a twenty-two-year-old calypso singer from Boston recruited to the Nation of Islam in 1955 by Malik. When Elijah Muhammad died in 1975, however, his son and successor, Warith Deen Muhammad, an ally and friend of Malcolm X's as well as a scholar of Arabic and Islam, began to dismantle the Nation of Islam and move it in the direction of orthodox Sunni Muslim, basically implementing the vision of Malcolm X. (Farrakhan balked at the changes and resurrected the old Nation of Islam in 1978.) The temple—in an earlier incarnation the Lenox Casino—has remained identified ever since with Malcolm X. The only radical changes in its appearance since his death were caused by the five-alarm fire set on the night his body lay in a casket at the nearby Unity Funeral Home; the fire gutted the main hall, the Gethsemane Church of God in Christ on the floor beneath, and seven street-level stores, including the Black Muslim restaurant that Malcolm X had used as the canteen of his operation.

As I exited the 116th Street IRT station on a sweltering Friday in August 2000 to attend *jummah* at the renovated Masjid Malcolm Shabazz, a taped *adhan,* the call to prayer in Arabic, was already being broadcast by loudspeaker over the rooftops of the surrounding commercial district. Though the area was busy, there was a fallowness to the streets and businesses; not all the storefronts were occupied. Across the street the *masjid* was definitely the landmark, occupying half the block between Malcolm X Boulevard and Adam Clayton Powell Boulevard. The brown brick of the four-story domed building was interrupted by crescent windows faced in yellow metal, and, around the length of its entire first level, a dark green painted stripe. The building contained various mosque-related businesses, including a barbershop, offering "Perms, Curl, Fade Out, Afro," a real estate office, the entrance to the Clara Mohammed School, and the cramped check-in lobby for the *masjid,* where an attendant took calls on a wall pay phone, the counter piled high with copies of the newspaper *Muslim Journal.* (In 1961, Malcolm X founded the Nation of Islam's first newspaper, *Muhammad Speaks,* in the basement of his house in Elmhurst, Queens, and initiated an early practice of requiring every male Muslim to sell an assigned quota of newspapers on the street as a recruiting and fundraising device.)

The prayer hall on the third floor was long and low, its open half-moon windows letting in the noise of outdoor construction as well as views of rooftops crowded with industrial heating units. With simple light green carpeting and white walls, the broad room gained lushness from its thin yellow-and-red tile pillars and the whir of tropical propeller fans overhead. A few feet out from the corner *quibla* was a green podium with a floor mike, into which a young black man dressed simply in a pressed white shirt and blue jeans, with a trim beard, was singing the *adhan* in a beautiful tenor voice. For most Muslims worldwide, he would have brought to mind Bilal, the African slave reportedly chosen by the Prophet as the first *muezzin,* or caller to prayer. Bilal climbed a roof near the mosque that the prophet helped build in Medina to recite the words still in use to this day, translated as:

> God is greater
> God is greater
> I witness that there is no god but God.
> I witness that Muhammad is the messenger of God.
> Rise to prayer.
> Rise to felicity.
> God is greater.
> God is greater.
> There is no god but God.

Indeed, when Warith Deen Muhammad disbanded the Nation of Islam, he renamed his followers the Community of al-Islaam in the West, and their newspaper, the *Bilalian News.* (The group's name was then changed to the American Muslim Mission, with the *American Muslim Journal,* and then to the Muslim American Society, with the *Muslim Journal,* which is now edited by a Muslim woman.)

The congregation that day was entirely black; the men were in shorts, or tan suits, or cargo pants. One construction worker prayed by a freight elevator to the side with his hammer hanging off his tool belt. Some wore African garb—gold tunics with dark red fez. A few dreadlocks were in evidence; otherwise there were white and brown prayer caps, knit green stocking caps, and reversed baseball caps. The women in the rear were in cotton wraps and scarves of green, purple, dark blue, and gold, with their little boys and girls tumbling about them. Some black plastic chairs were set to the side and back for both sexes; the men numbered about two hundred, the women seventy-five. The prime difference from the Ninety-sixth Street mosque and all other mosques I've visited is that everyone was handed a plastic bag for their shoes on the way in, which they then carried with them, though there was an optional and sparsely used traditional shoe rack at the entrance.

The sermon, given by the current imam, Izak-el M. Pasha, lasted nearly an hour. Pasha is a short gentleman in his fifties with a round face, brown eyes, and full lips; he was wearing a white prayer cap, tan shirt, white pants, and sandals with tan socks. He began slowly on his topic, "The responsibilities that we have as Muslim believers." He enumerated these as common sense, faith, and a self-accusing spirit. As the sermon on what he called "Islam 101" progressed through its two parts—with the passing of plastic buckets for charitable offerings in between—he began to strike at deeper issues. "Any drugs you take not from a prescription, you have taken willingly," he reprimanded. "Anyone engaging in sexual activity proscribed by Allah, you're doing willingly." By his conclusion, he'd built in intensity to animated old-time preaching, to which his congregation responded with shouts of *"Allahu Akbar,"* in the manner of the punctuating of sermons in gospel churches with "Amen." "Islam is real," he wound up. "It's reality. It's the ultimate reality."

Immediately following the service, I waited in the corridor outside while the Imam spoke with Saikou Diallo, the father of Amadou Diallo, the twenty-two-year-old West African street vendor who was shot by four plainclothes police officers as he stood unarmed in the entrance to his Bronx apartment building in February 1999. (His funeral at the Ninety-sixth Street mosque had turned into a sometimes unruly political rally with shouts of *"Allahu Akbar"* as his coffin was carried teeteringly through the surging crowd). Diallo's father nodded quietly on his way out, and I was shown into the office by an assistant. "This office is where Malcolm was at," the Imam told me, obviously used to satisfying visitors on this point. "This is actually the office, and there's another upstairs which he worked out of, doing the daily work, as I do. So Malcolm was here. There was a fire after his passing, though this part of the building is basically the same except for the renovation." He said that the assistant who'd shown me in, and who then sat in on our interview, had known Malcolm X, as "he's been here since he was a young boy." "But myself personally, no," he went on. "I saw him when I was a young man with my brother. I just came to meetings. I hadn't joined. Malcolm was a great man, a great worker, with a love for humanity, really a love for all people. He wanted to be right. He wanted to be just. That was Malcolm."

The historical office where I found myself was large, solid, and obviously heavily trafficked, with black-and-white photographs of Malcolm X and other movement leaders propped on bookcases full of hefty volumes, bound reports, and piles of loose papers. A long conference table ran down the center of the room, where I sat to one side, forming a T with the wide wooden desk where Pasha sat in a red padded leather swivel chair, wooden prayer beads piled on a phone book next to him, a scarlet Bible stuck in a line of volumes of the Quran propped up by a bronze bust of Abraham Lincoln. Across the front of the desk were displayed official plaques identifying the Imam as Commissioner of New York City's Commission on Human Rights and as the Muslim chaplain of the Police Department. These ties to the city were evident a year later when he spoke as the sole Muslim religious leader at the on-site memorial service for victims of the World Trade Center attacks. On the wall behind him was a poster-sized facsimile of a page of the Quran as well as two "Register to Vote Here" signs with arrows pointing down. A wheezing fan worked overtime on a windowsill.

Pasha had been a plumber by trade. He was appointed in 1993 by a group of elders in the community when Imam Ali Rashid, who'd held for the post for seventeen years, passed away. Having been raised Baptist in Brooklyn, Pasha attended meetings as a teenager with his brother of what was then officially called "the Lost and Found Nation of Islam in the West." Married in 1972, he soon joined Temple Number 7C in Brooklyn. As a member of the Fruit of Islam (FOI) in which he was part of the force responsible for importing and distributing whiting fish, he would always attend the central meetings at this mosque, then under the leadership of Farrakhan. "I became a Muslim feeling that was the best way for me to express my manhood, and to be with other men who were not afraid to stand up for what was right," he told me. "It was the philosophy we today would see as a kind of black nationalist movement, but based on strong religious overtones."

Those overtones became the dominant chord when Warith Deen Muhammad was named supreme minister after his father's death in Chicago, on February 25, 1975. Within two months, he had declared that whites were no longer viewed as devils and could join the movement. He dispersed the elite corps, the Fruit of Islam and the Muslim Girls Training, and he lifted the dress code so the men would no longer have to wear suits and bow ties, and the women did not have to wear long gowns and cover their heads. The traditional Muslim creed, the *shahadah,* was introduced, and the Quran and the Sunni tradition were followed. "When he came here in 1975, he told us to take down the Quran from the shelves where we'd kept it in a high, safe, respectable place," said the Imam. "We knew that one day we would be learning more about it. But up until then most of our lessons came from the Bible."

One of the so-called "Pioneers," who's been in the mosque since the beginning, Gladys Muhammad, recalls those first steps regularly in her column in *The Thinker,* a newspaper of the Harlem *masjid.* "The first big change that I remember was when he had the beautiful plush chairs taken out of the temple and rugs laid in order for believers to pray in the correct way," she wrote. "This big change automatically changed the temple into a *masjid.*" Assistant Imam Yusuf Hasan recalled for me, with relief, the slacking of the uniform: "I was glad we wouldn't be in a straitjacket anymore. Because in the Nation of Islam we were like soldiers. We had to march around and do everything the captains and lieutenants told us to do. Get up at four or five in the morning. Guard people's homes. We were like robots. Sometimes at meetings they would shut the door of the temple and not let us out until we raised a certain amount of money, until people went into their pockets and came up with it. Some people lost their homes, their wives, their families. So when Imam Muhammad took over he said, 'The men are free. Go out and take care of your families now.' " Partly as a result of these changes, African-American Sunni Muslims number more than two million, making up about 90 percent of the converts to Islam in the United States.

Pasha particularly stressed the social activism of Islam—predictably enough, given his Nation of Islam upbringing. His priority was obvious on the streets when I made my way back toward the subway, through a neighborhood that now includes the Malcolm Shabazz Harlem Market; the Malcolm Shabazz Gardens, a development of new three-family homes; a Renaissance Project to open new stores up and down the block, such as the House of Jewelry, with "Islamic Outfits for Men and Woman"; the Malcolm Shabazz Cultural Center, where the Muslim Coalition for Political Improvement was presenting "Jazz Night" that Friday night; and the Malcolm Shabazz Mosque Development Corporation. "Before we ever engaged with them, the government came to us and said, 'We know these blocks and stores used to be empty,' " Pasha told me. "They said, 'We know all the revenue sources. We know you're not getting the money from us. We know you don't sell drugs. So we'd like to find out how you're making these successes.' "

The mosques of the immigrants lose some of their local coloring as they begin to be camouflaged in suburban settings. So, too, the mosques in New Jersey and Long Island of those followers who've evolved from the Nation of Islam seem less filled with the angst of urban politics. At the Masjid Malcolm Shabazz, with its intense history and its blurring of identities, one is unsure where the Nation of Islam stops and orthodox al-Islaam begins. In Pasha's office, you feel as if Minister Malcolm might walk through the secured door at any moment. Yet as Pasha put it: "The stereotypical quote unquote Black Muslim is out the door."

This transformation is most obvious in a mosque such as the WARIS Cultural Research and Development Center, a primarily African-American mosque in Irvington, New Jersey, a somewhat economically distressed suburb of Newark. As the Islamic Center of Long Island is more suburban in contrast to the Ninety-sixth Street mosque or the Al-Khoei Foundation, so the WARIS Center is to the Masjid Malcolm Shabazz.

Formerly a dental laboratory and tooth factory, this one-story center is barely noticeable at the edge of a parking lot that was baking in the noon heat when I visited that same August. Jiggling the lock of the front glass door, the Imam, and director of religious affairs, Wahy Deen Shareef, laughed as I told him of my visits to Long Island. "The Islamic Center of Long Island has all those wealthy families," he said. "If there are some people with money, you'll draw lots of people. We haven't found that group in New Jersey yet." The leaders of the WARIS Center, though, reveal similar professional know-how. An engineer for Nabisco in his late forties, with short thick brown hair, brown eyes, and goatee, Shareef was dressed slickly in a green checked sports coat, black slacks, a green shirt, and sunglasses. He seemed almost pleased at the focused energy called for by the challenge of trying to make the project work against all odds, and he was suavely engaging as he showed me around a complex that was so obviously a work in progress.

Shareef led me up and down beige hallways lit by fluorescent lights over lots of linoleum floors, ticking off the various social services set up in empty rec rooms or tucked in cubby holes: the drop-in center for job placement; the child care center; the karate school; the computer lab; the Boys and Girls Club of Northern New Jersey; drivers-ed school; and a culinary-arts cooking school in the works in a deconstructed kitchen. The main conference room, with a long table for meetings, and a tall fridge as well, was basically an all-purpose living room. Black-and-white photographs were displayed on its tan walls (of Muhammad Ali, Miles Davis, Billie Holiday), as well as illustrated prints (of Rosa Parks, Frederick Douglass, Malcolm X, Elijah Muhammad, Nelson Mandela). One strip of wall, with an American flag hanging, was a memorial to black soldiers who fought in the Civil War.

The Friday *jummah* took place in the main prayer hall, with venetian blinds on the windows, prayer rugs laid across its linoleum floors, insulated ceiling board above, and a floor fan churning. At the front of the room was a purple Quran set on a music stand, which served as a podium; on the wall behind it hung a framed calligraphic verse from the Quran on a light green background. The bright room, feeling like a student activities room in a high school, filled by 1:15 with about sixty men and twenty-five women, all black, mostly African-American, most of whom performed the suggested four cycles of prayer before the beginning of the service. The *khutba* that day was given by Abdul Alim Mubarak, also in his late forties, who was a news editor at CNN. Dressed in a white cotton tunic, white socks, and black sandals he was balding, with a clipped beard and brown chesnut eyes. The theme of his talk was, in his words, "honoring the womb that bore you," inspired especially by a recent vacation to his birthplace, Richmond, Virginia, and his visits with relatives and friends at the Baptist church where he'd been active as a choirboy and usher. He addressed the heated early days of the Nation of Islam, when harsh breaks were often made with family members unsympathetic to the cause. In its place, he was recommending the Quranic injunction to honor your father and your mother.

Between the lines of his talk was the ever-present issue of the many shifts in allegiance and identity in just a few decades in all of these black mosques. "Lots of our people have had as many name changes as Malcolm X," Shareef had briefed me earlier. "I've had four names. My Christian name, my Nation of Islam name, an African name when I was involved in a pan-African organization affiliated with what Amiri Baraka was doing in Newark at the time, and my Muslim name." As Abdul Alim Mubarek, born Ronald Carl Rowe, told me afterward in the conference room: "In 1975, there was uncertainty for us, resistance from some; some didn't know what to make of the changes. There was fear of the unknown. Though for me it was easy. Because orthodox Islam was intellectually stimulating and spiritually productive." Shareef, who was standing nearby, added: "Some people were affected by it traumatically. A lot of families broke up because of that change. My own was one, in terms of my first wife and I. Changing your belief system can cause you to stop and question some of the other things you're doing with your life."

But neither man owned up to having ever entirely bought the creed of the Nation of Islam. "It kinda made sense, but it kinda didn't make sense," said Mubarek of such Nation of Islam mythology as the black mad scientist, Yacub, who rebelled against Allah by creating the white race. "So I was just going to have faith and run with it. Maybe some myths were concocted, but they were rooted in the reality of circumstances. We were asking how we got in this position in America. You had all this religious imagery where God is lily white and Caucasian. But then you had this white slave master who was raping you. It was easy for us to say, Okay, yes, this is the devil." To which Shareef, who joined the temple in Newark at age eighteen after reading *The Autobiography of Malcolm X*, added, "The whole concept of Fard being God, I never put too much emphasis on that. I think it was more of a vehicle for social change. And to develop relationships with people who were struggling for the same things I was struggling for."

At the close of the service that afternoon, Shareef stood to introduce a tall gentleman in a gray suit and a purple, lightly bejeweled prayer cap, who was in charge of procuring a section of a local New Jersey cemetery as a gravesite for Muslims. "I'm writing over a check today for nine hundred dollars for my wife and I," testified Shareef. "The odds you'll be needing one of these plots is one to one." The gentleman then stood up with an artist's rendition of a lovely, Moorish-style gateway that would mark the entrance to the gravesite. He warned, "Many of us come from Christian families who'll give us last rites if we don't have a plan. Think of your Muslim family members and your Muslim children." (Emphasis on family values is quite pronounced in Islam, with membership numbers in a mosque usually given in terms of how many families, rather than individuals, belong; Muhammad taught that marriage is half the religion.)

Afterward I spoke with the Imam in his office. He was less politically charged than Imam Pasha, but a degree more concerned with the theological message of Islam. Most prominent in this masculine den, decorated by his wife, with a big wooden desk, padded office chair, and thick tan carpet, was a framed calligraphic rendering of one of the most notable verses of the Quran—*ayat al-kursi,* or verse 255 in the second *sura,* "The Verse of the Throne":

God
there is no god but He, the
Living, the Everlasting,
Slumber seizes Him not, neither sleep; to Him belongs
All that is in the heavens and the earth. . . .
His throne comprises the heaven and earth.

Sipping from his bottle of Poland Spring water, Shareef told me of his own evolution; his allegiance to Warith Deen Muhammad, as distinct from Elijah Muhammad, was obvious. "Imam Muhammad came here when we first bought this building," he said, proudly. "He said that he considers me his friend. And I consider him to be my friend, and my leader of course."

A life-changing moment for him was a visit of W. Deen Muhammad to the Newark temple in 1974. As Shareef was serving on the secretarial department of the Nation of Islam, his assigned job was to record the lecture. "The striking thing about the event was that when he started his lecture . . . to show you where we were at the time . . . he looked on the podium and asked where the Quran was," Shareef recalled. "Nobody who was sitting in the front-row seats knew where the Quran was. Except me. I found the Quran on a podium downstairs, covered with papers. I went and got it and handed it to him. And then he taught from the Quran. That was the first time I ever witnessed anyone teaching from the book we claimed to believe in. Up until that point rarely did we even quote from the Quran. . . . That was actually still a year before the passing of Elijah Muhammad."

The name of the WARIS Center, a puzzle to some on first hearing, is an homage to W. Deen Muhammad as well. The word comes from *warith*, an attribute in the Quran of Allah, meaning "inheritor." But it was used by Imam Muhammad in an address in East Orange, New Jersey, soon after he was unanimously elected supreme minister of the Nation of Islam, in which he was talking about the need for African Americans to establish their identity. "He said if you want respect, than call yourself *'Warith'* and the white man will respect you. In other words, name yourself. Give yourself an identity." A friend of Shareef's, a construction worker, Isa Muhammad, who now owns a construction referral business, heard the speech and thought about bringing together a group of people who would call themselves the "Waris." So in 1976 he and four others met at Isa Muhammad's home to form the association, with Shareef's house as its first official address, eventually moving to an office building in Hillside, then to Nesbitt Terrace in Irvington, until moving in and beginning renovation at this location in 1995.

"We have about thirty families now," estimated Shareef. "When we started we were fairly young, but now we have grandchildren together. I have a granddaughter. The composition of our congregation is pretty much working people like myself. You met a council person from Irvington. The president of the Irvington city council is also a member but wasn't here today. Many of our members wear their work uniforms, whether suits or otherwise, and then go back to the worksite from here. Because of our location we have a predominantly African-American community, but we have some people from Asia, India, Pakistan, who periodically come here. We have a couple of European Muslims. . . . I'm on the board of the West Orange Public Library. And the man who recommended me was a Jewish attorney in the town." Shareef had also been invited to a breakfast in September, along with Imam Muhammad, at the state mansion of Governor Christie Todd Whitman.

Women, according to Shareef, were prime movers in their center. "African-American women have always been active in churches, always active spiritually," he said. "And they come from a different culture than these Middle Eastern women. They're not gonna be pushed into the background." So he'd arranged for me to talk with Linda Salaam, who had been raised as a teenager in the Nation of Islam and had attended a Muslim high school in Newark. "What I enjoy about the covering is the respect I receive from Muslims and non-Muslims alike," said the poised forty-five-year-old woman, her head covered with a black-and-gold scarf, her straw bag set on the conference table beside her. "If anything, at my job, I'm envied by the other women. I've been able to hold that stature of being a Muslim woman throughout. . . . The Muslim woman, as I see her, is a helping mate. She helps the men." Salaam worked for the United States Postal Service.

After she left, the wife of the chairman of the burial project added a few helpful thoughts, in more of a "Now, you listen to me" tone. Like Salaam, her head was covered with a scarf that wrapped around her neck, but the rest of her was simply blue jeans and a blouse. "Sometimes in the Nation of Islam you'd hear that the place of the woman was to be behind and to serve the man," she said, getting a rhythm going. "And some of the women from the Middle East were raised to believe that women are subservient. We as American Muslims have a different perspective. I guess through the sexual revolution those ideas about women at home and in the workplace have changed. That has permeated the Muslim community, too. Women are no longer going to sit back and be ruled and you do this and you do that. No woman of the *millennium* is going to stand for that nonsense! We respect our men, but in turn they respect us too."

Driving me back to the South Orange Amtrak station, Shareef talked of the place of the African-American Muslims within the wider *ummah,* the community of all faithful Muslims. Basically, they remain *in* but not entirely *of* the *ummah.* On the upcoming Labor Day weekend, for instance, the annual convention of the largest representative organization of American Islam, the Islamic Society of North America (ISNA) was to be held in Chicago at the same time and in the same city as the yearly gathering of the Muslim American Society, yet their leaders somehow could not devise an event where they might come together. Even though Warith Deen Muhammad serves on the ISNA Shura Council, relations are still uneasy. As Jane I. Smith wrote in her *Islam in America:* "In some cases, blacks even feel that they are unwelcome and unappreciated by those involved in ISNA, although the clear movement of most African Americans to identify with Sunni Islam will, many believe, serve to ameliorate that problem."

Shareef also talked about the different nuances of emphasis of the WARIS Center or the Masjid Malcolm Shabazz as well as another Muslim expression popular in America, Sufism. A month earlier Feisal Abdul Rauf, the Sufi Imam, had spoken as a fellow traveler on a Friday at the WARIS Center. "He talked about listening." Shareef smiled. "A real Sufi message . . . learning to listen. I love that." He told me that what he was really stressing with his own people was knowledge and social responsibility. "At the end of the day, though, I don't see too many differences," he said. "I think our emphasis is very similar. The establishment of peace with oneself, then peace with God, the creator of this self, then peace with others and the environment."

Set on a tree-lined block of West Broadway in Tribeca is one of the most subtle of Manhattan's mosques. An anonymous white storefront with a tracery of a green metal fire escape, its two front windows covered in plain white venetian blinds, it contains a small jewel box of interior design known as the Masjid Al-Farah. Adding to its mystique is its reputation as a Sufi mosque where members of different Sufi orders often pray on Fridays, and as home to a Sufi circle of the Nur Ashki Jerrahi Order, whose spiritual leader is an American woman, Shaykha Fariha al-Jerrahi, born Philippa de Menil.

Sufism, the mystical dimension of Islam, can be quite controversial. One night I was riding in a jalopy of a yellow cab driven by an obviously American-born young man from Brooklyn whose shaved head was only my first tip-off to his fervent espousal of Islam. "I'm ready for the *hajj,*" he bragged. Rock music blared noisily from his radio as he shouted back at me his strident case against Sufism: "Sufism is not really Islam. Islam is simple. Islam is clear. You pray. You believe in certain things—the Day of Judgment, the angels, the Prophet Muhammad, God. Sufism is trying to complicate Islam. That's how you know it's wrong. . . . Sufis take drugs. They do weird stuff." Sammy, the Moroccan deli clerk, had actually never even heard of Sufism, though he grew up in a country hosting some of its most fervent orders.

Speaking up movingly for the other side was Faiz Khan, whose adolescence was spent organizing Muslim summer day camps at the Islamic Center of Long Island but who joined a Sufi order three years ago. "The Center of Long Island is a very nice administrative organization," he explained. "It's run by people who know what they're doing, have wealth, and professional attitudes. It's steered in the right direction. But for a lot of young people, Islam goes beyond that. There's this spiritual yearning you start to feel. And if you can't find it there, you look for it elsewhere. Some have considered Buddhism or Hinduism, though the only person I know who almost became Buddhist ended up remaining a Muslim once she discovered authentic Islam."

There is a maxim often heard in Sufi circles repeated by scholars of Islam such as Professor William Chittick, whose latest work is *Sufism: A Short Introduction.* This is in fact a complaint first made by a tenth-century Sufi teacher, Bushanji: "Today Sufism is a name without a reality, but it used to be a reality without a name." The "reality without a name" refers to the mystical experiences Muslims believe Muhammad underwent: being instructed in a visitation by the angel Gabriel to begin to recite the Quran; riding the flying horse, Boraq, during the *Al Isra,* or "Night Journey," to the ruins of the temple in Jerusalem and then being lifted from the *al-Haram a-Shareef,* or "Dome of the Rock," to the seven heavens. The "name without a reality" has most recently become attached to an uneasy sense that Sufism was kidnapped during the 1960s by whirling hippies, high on marijuana and mellifluous flute melodies, looking for a quick fix of trance spirituality but not bothering with the tougher love so evident in the frequently harsh Quran. As Faiz Khan put it, "Initially, I was very anti-Sufi. The term in my mind conjured up images of earthy-crunchy-type throwbacks to the sixties who purposely neglected any formalism, or Sharia, when it came to spiritual growth. I preferred the hardline activist scene."

The term "Sufi," either with or without a reality, is probably derived from the Arabic *Suf,* meaning "wool," since Sufis as early as the eighth century were dressing in coarse woolen garments to advertise their rejection of luxury. They traced their simplicity to a saying of Muhammad's: "Do not wear silk or silk brocade, and do not drink in vessels of gold or silver, and do not eat in bowls made for them; for they are for them in this life and for us in the next." Through silence, solitude, hunger, and wakefulness, the Sufis sought to attain direct knowledge of God. They also meditated on the Prophet as the "Divine Light of Illumination." Such was the teaching of the Andalusian Sufi Ibn 'Arabi (1165–1240), known as the "Great Master," who met Rumi, the great poet of Sufism, in Damascus. Rumi, who spent forty years composing his epic poem, *Methnawi,* in which he fuses divine and human love, opens with the *nay,* the flute, which symbolizes the soul after its separation from God. And so the followers of the *tariqah,* the Sufi path, of Rumi use music and dance in their search. These are the whirling dervishes—*dervish,* or disciple, being Persian for "poor."

The whirling dervishes—with their white robes and tall, conical caps, pivoting on a single foot as they twirl with one palm turned up toward heaven and the other turned down toward earth—have become synonymous for many with Sufism; their guest appearances at City Center or the Cathedral of St. John the Divine can have the atmosphere of a New Age Woodstock. (The Threshold Society, the American Mevlevi Order of Whirling Dervishes in northern California, which does much of this "performing," is led by Kabir Helminski, a translator of Rumi's poetry and the author of a collection of essays, *The Knowing Heart,* published in 1999 by Shambhala Press. This American-born sheik was appointed to the position in 1990 by Dr. Celaleddin Celebi of Istanbul, Turkey, a twenty-first-generation descendent of Rumi.) But there are many Sufi *tariqah* that don't involve music and dance. The heart of the enterprise has always been, rather, the chanting of the *dhikr,* the methodical repetition of certain names of God or Quranic formulas, as a way to experience the same sort of beatific vision and direct contact with the divine as Muhammad. In the sixteenth century, the Mevlevis constructed early clocks to regulate the time of prayer; they also used prayer beads, similar to a rosary, in their meditation. From Mecca to Samarkand, the Sufis have since used a string of ninety-nine beads to recite the ninety-nine names, or attributes, of God such as "Mercy" or "Compassion" mentioned in the Quran.

Sufism has often been the spice tempting new converts to Islam. Sufi orders such as the Qadiriyah helped expand Islam in Africa. The Shattariyah order was a force in the Islamic life of people in Java and Sumatra. Sufi thought influenced nineteenth-century Western intellectuals such as Ralph Waldo Emerson. In the late twentieth century, the writings of Idries Shah could be found easily in popular New Age bookstores. Martin Lings, a Western convert, has written inspiringly of the Tunisian Sufi Shaykh Ahmad al-Alawi in *A Sufi Saint of the Twentieth Century.* Thomas Merton's account of his meeting at the Abbey of Gethsemani in the fall of 1966 with an Algerian Sufi, Sidi Abdeslam, and his remark in his taped lectures to his Cistercian novices that "in Sufism they are after what we're after . . . the dissolution of one's present status to be reintegrated on a new level" has been circulated widely. Indeed, Rumi, who was born in what is now Afghanistan and who died in Konya, Turkey, in 1273, may currently be the best-selling poet in America. (Salon.com reported in October 2001 that he was also the one most played on Afghan radio stations.)

By 1990, the Nimatullahi order already had centers in nine major cities in the United States, and was publishing *Sufi* magazine. Other Sufi orders currently popular in America are the Naqshabandis, led by Sheik Muhammad Nazim al-Haqqani, which have been quite well financed and seek to spread an appreciation of Sufi devotion among non-Muslims as well; the Tijanis, who are strong in the African-American community; and the International Association of Sufism, which publishes the journal *Sufism, An Inquiry,* and includes a Sufi Women's organization to push for women's rights within the Muslim community. Particularly appealing to Europeans and Americans has been the Sufi Order International, founded in 1910 by Hazrat Inayat Khan and now led by his son and successor, Pir Vilayat Inayat Khan, with nearly one hundred centers in the United States and Dances of Universal Peace sponsored in dozens of cities. Especially venerable is the Bawa Mihyaiyadeen Fellowship, whose founder arrived from Sri Lanka in the midtwentieth century to live in a Philadelphia row house and teach a Hinduized version of Islam.

Certainly among artists, intellectuals, and academics in America, Sufism has provided a poetic portal into Islam, which otherwise might seem unapproachable and forbidden. Salar Abdoh, an Iranian-born first novelist whose *The Poet Game,* about a Hezbollah-style group of terrorists operating in New York City, was a literary thriller in the elegant style of Graham Greene or John le Carre, has met many such converts since arriving in 1979 in the United States to earn a master's degree in English literature at the City College of New York. "I've seen lots of Americans convert to Islam," he told me. "And then they become very devout usually. It really puzzled me. Often they find something interesting in Sufism and then they decide that to be a real Sufi they need to be a Muslim. In Muslim countries the way I live would be very typical. I'd go to the mosque to pray and then come home and open a bottle of wine. But in America when people convert they become, in Farsi we say, 'a bowl that is hotter than the soup.' "

I learned to detect the telltale signs of Sufism from Abdoh. One Friday we attended a *jummah* of New York University students in a cramped basement room of a student center. The Imam, a young, bearded man dressed in a white tunic, who spoke to the gathering of about two dozen students, sat hunched rather humbly on a low box, speaking in quiet tones about the message he had gleaned that day from the Quran. His attitude was quite unlike that of the Imams of the Ninety-sixth Street mosque or the Al-Khoei Foundation, who were more strident in their warnings about behavior, about moral crime and its punishment. On the way out Abdoh muttered to me, "He seemed to have something of the *Suf* about him . . . very sweet." Sweetness more than any other trait marks a Sufi, as they have no actual differences of belief or practice from other Muslims.

Yet this sweetness, when mixed with a mystical and somewhat looser temper, has riled Muslims in various times and places. The more forceful and best known of its antagonists were the Wahhabis, an eighteenth-century revivalist movement in Arabia founded by Muhammad ibn Abd al-Wahhab, which was vigorously opposed to the Sufi orders and became the formative influence in Saudi Arabia today. "In my opinion, they threw out the baby with the bathwater, doing away with much of Islam's spiritual core, leaving only a shell of puritanical do's and don'ts," said Faiz Khan. "That was pretty much the brand of Islam taught to me in America . . . growing up, I went to those big Islamic conferences seeing a very incomplete, politicized, and even distorted version of Islam."

So the living debate between hard and soft, behavior and spirit, belief and faith goes on within America just as it has been played out for centuries in Arabia, north Africa, and the Indian subcontinent. A singular figure who has been trying to make Sufism a live option in America, and indeed using some rather bold strokes in the creation of a style suited to the culture, has been Shaykha Fariha. Her spiritual chain of command is traceable back to her predecessor, Lex Hixon Nur al-Jerrahi, an American convert to Islam with an unusual layering of religious studies in his background, and their own link to the tradition, Sheik Muzaffer Ozak, author of *The Unveiling of Love,* who was the sheik of the Halveti-Jerrahi order in Turkey, and taught a brand of Sufism with more emphasis on love than on intellectual discernment. (During a crackdown on Sufi orders by Mustafa Kemal Ataturk in his attempt to Westernize the new republic of Turkey during the 1920s and 1930s, the Halveti-Jerrahi order was the only group defying the ban, and so was tolerated as a "folkloric center.")

I sat on the floor in a robing room of the Masjid al-Farah one evening, having tea with Shaykha Fariha, to try to sort out some of these strains, and to hear her own story. A rose scarf draped over her white cotton Sufi cap, the shaykha was barefoot and sat cross-legged in a white tunic, tan wooden prayer beads hung around her neck like a long necklace. Striking, though not unprecedented as a woman in a place of spiritual authority in Islam, she also defied type because of her obviously European pale skin, high forehead, and fair brown hair. Next to her during much of our talk sat Ali, her current husband, an Iranian-born painter with hair tied back and a long black-gray beard who has lived in the city since the 1970s. White robes hung in a glass cabinet, on which was piled a giant prayer-bead necklace, a gift from Turkey. Among the many black-and-white photographs framed on the wall was one from the early part of the twentieth century of Muhammad's tomb in Medina. A stained calligraphic window representing the Arabic word *Hu,* a pronoun meaning "He," referring to God, in mirror image had been crafted by two of her women dervishes in Mexico City.

As Philippa de Menil, Shaykha Fariha was born in 1947 in Houston to one of the wealthier families in America and Europe—Schlumberger, Ltd., the international oil-service firm founded by her French maternal grandfather. Her father, banker and Catholic activist John de Menil, and her mother, Dominique, had moved to Texas in the 1940s, where they became leading patrons of the arts. By the time she died in December 1997, Dominique de Menil had been one of the greatest patrons of the arts ever. In Houston she was responsible for the octagonal Rothko Chapel designed by Philip Johnson and Howard Barnstone, which opened in 1971, with fourteen of Rothko's soaring abstract paintings in black, deep maroon, and raw umber with tinges of blue; the Cy Twombly Gallery; *Broken Obelisk,* Barnett Newman's monumental sculpture; the Byzantine Chapel, which houses two thirteenth-century frescoes ransomed by the Menil Foundation from art thieves; and the Menil Collection, which includes fifteen thousand works of art, from paleolithic to pop, as well as a survey of surrealism, housed in a simple gray clapboard museum designed by the Italian architect Renzo Piano that opened in 1987. The home Philippa grew up in was Philip Johnson's first commission—a modernist one-story brick rectangle with a glass roof, in Houston's River Oaks.

Like her parents, de Menil as a young woman had been involved in commissioning artists as well. She finished Brearley School, in New York, in 1965, and attended Barnard, the University of California in Los Angeles, and Harvard. She married her first husband, an Italian anthropologist, Francesco Pellizzi, in 1969. But her friendship with Heiner Friedrich, a German art dealer she met in 1973 who shared her interest in Buddhism and Sufism, led her back into the family "business," as it were. She and Friedrich, together with a close associate of the de Menil family, Helen Winkler, set up the Dia Foundation in 1975 to help contemporary artists such as Donald Judd, Dan Flavin, and Walter De Maria realize large-scale projects; *Dia* is Greek for "through" or "the godlike one." "You have to understand, there were the Medicis, and then there were Heiner and Philippa," La Monte Young, a minimalist composer who was one of the original Dia artists, later told *Vanity Fair.* Her commitment was intense enough that by 1984 she had reportedly poured more than $35 million of her inheritance into the foundation.

But all along in the de Menil family there was a spiritual story running parallel to that of art and finance. Dominique de Menil had been moving toward Catholicism before she actually converted prior to her marriage in 1931. Together she and her husband shared a lifelong interest in spirituality, and indeed much of the art they collected had a spiritual, if not always an overtly religious, dimension. At the dedication of the Rothko Chapel, the celebrants were Catholic, Protestant, Jewish, Muslim, and Greek Orthodox. As Fariha later described a moment at her mother's deathbed, "On Christmas Eve, we were sitting around her bed, and Mother asked for wineglasses, one for everybody. She looked at me and said, 'The Dalai Lama says that what you are offered you should accept,' and it dawned on me that she wanted me to share in the sherry drinking, although, as a Muslim, I don't drink. I thought, *Okay, why not?* It was a kind of playfulness on her part, but also like Holy Communion." Speaking at a memorial service at the Rothko Chapel, Fariha recalled a moment before her mother left the hospital: "She seemed to be suffering, and I bent down to ask whether she was in pain. 'Pain means nothing to me now,' Mother whispered. 'I am being shown such extraordinary things.' " Because of her own idealism and intense interest in spiritual matters, Fariha has often been singled out from her four older brothers and sisters as most similar to her deceased mother.

Sitting on the Persian carpet drinking chamomile tea, she detailed for me how her parents' interest had been seminal in creating a greater interest in Sufism in America. "I actually met Sheik Muzzafer because my mother had made a kind of deathbed promise to my father that she was going to bring the whirling dervishes back to this country," she said, recalling her father's death, of cancer, in 1973. "They had seen them together in the sixties and had both fallen passionately in love, especially him. She was determined to go to Istanbul to get them and invite them here. In the process we met a representative of Sheik Muzaffer's who talked about his sheik, and it was like a fragrance. I could smell the fragrance of this being named Sheik Muzaffer. At the time the sheik was with ten of his very close dervishes in Rennes, France, at a springtime festival. We said, 'Well, why don't we try to get them stand-by tickets?' We did. And they came. And that was the beginning."

In April 1979, in a Sufi ceremony, Philippa and Heiner "took hands" with Sheik Muzaffer Ozak, joined his Halveti-Jerrahi order of dervishes, embraced Islam, and married, all in the same brief ceremony. (The initiation rite is modeled on the handclasp known as *bay-at al-ridwan,* which Muhammad exacted as fealty from his companions at Hudaybiyah.) Sheik Muzzafer gave the bride her new name, Fariha, which means "Ease and peace of paradise." Heiner Friedrich became Haydar, "Lion of God." They also had a civil ceremony at the city hall, and subsequently two children, Duha, a girl whose name means "the Glorious One in Light," and Aziz, a boy, "the One Powerful in Love." The Dia Foundation expanded its mission by creating a mosque, replete with light works by Dan Flavin and living quarters for the sheik's visits, in an old firehouse at 155 Mercer Street. "I did love art, but in a way what I was looking for in art I found here," she told me.

Sheik Muzaffer Ozak cut a figure spiritually in Manhattan in the late 1970s not dissimilar to that of Baba Muktananda's for the proto-Hindus a few years earlier. His was a sparking charisma clothed in the colorful garb of a foreign culture. "I happened to be walking by the building on Mercer Street one day and the door was opened," an American convert to Islam told me at the Turkish mosque in Brooklyn one Friday. "I saw this man who was like a live wire, you could just see his energy from the street. I thought to myself, 'Who's *that?*'" Sheik Muzaffer, affectionately known as "Effendi," was a large man—not tall, but wide of girth. He had a resonating baritone voice, was prone to smoking clove-scented cigarettes, and was distinguished by his strong Turkish bone structure and hawkish nose. He was nineteenth in the line of successors to Nureddin Jerrahi, who lived three hundred years earlier in Istanbul, Muzaffer's own line branching from the Khalwatis, who had been established in Anatolia and settled in Egypt in the thirteenth century. Having served as a *muezzin* and Imam in many of the mosques of Istanbul, Sheik Muzaffer was by then retired from the office of Imam and simply preached a sermon on Fridays at a mosque near the Istanbul book market, where he owned a shop specializing in antique and religious books. An ecstatic poet in the style of such Sufi classics as Rumi and Kabir, Hafiz and Farid al-Din, some of his translated lyrics under his pen name of "Ashki" were collected in a volume titled *Ashki's Divan.*

"Taking hands with a teacher is like returning to being a child," Fariha explained to me. "When a child is born and they're gazing at their mother and father, what are they learning? It's just gazing at life and seeing how life is, how it communicates with people, how it drinks tea, how it invites people, the graciousness of it, the love of it. . . . Sheik Muzaffer wasn't just in some fixed, inalterable state of divine bliss. He fluctuated. To see him in *dhikr* was magnificent. He would disappear in divine light. But at other times you could just sit with him and laugh and be together in a very ordinary way." One of the places where Sheik Muzaffer could often be found in more relaxed circumstances, surrounded by his rough-looking Turkish male dervishes, was at the five-story Friedrich de Menil townhouse on East Eighty-second Street. It was stripped of detail in 1977 by the architect Richard Gluckman, and has bare wooden floors, white-painted walls, curved stairs, and wooden handrails; the first floor is a nearly empty minimal setting with a fluorescent piece by Dan Flavin and a steel-and-marble sculpture by Walter de Maria in the foyer. The sheik would sit with his guests at Donald Judd–designed wooden tables full of platters of lamb heaped over mounds of pilaf and vegetables, bowls of yogurt flavored with garlic and cucumber, baskets of fresh bread, and finally—all the courses punctuated by prayers—hot cups of black tea, fresh fruits, and Turkish delights.

Soon after his arrival, Sheik Muzaffer met Lex Hixon, who would later become his dervish and eventual successor. Hixon interviewed him for his radio program, *In the Spirit,* broadcast on WBAI-FM radio in New York from 1971 to 1984. The program introduced spiritual teachers from around the world, including Mother Teresa and the Dalai Lama. Hixon was the son of a wealthy old Pasadena Episcopalian family with roots in Wisconsin, where the original family fortune was made in lumber. As a preppy college student, he studied philosophy at his father's alma mater, Yale, and went on to receive his Ph.D. in world religions from Columbia University in 1976, did extensive research in Greek, European, and Indian philosophies, and eventually delved into a syncretic mix of Buddhism, Hinduism, Christianity, and Islam. As his introduction to Islam, he'd been a disciple of Bawa Muhaiyadeen. Hixon's lively presence on the alternative spiritual scene of the 1970s was attested to later by the poet Allen Ginsberg, who called him "a pioneer in the spiritual renaissance in America."

"The moment they met it was like Rumi and Shams," said Fariha, comparing Muzaffer's first meeting with Hixon to that between the poet and the traveling Sufi who inspired the outpouring of more than seventy thousand verses. "There was an amazing spark ignited there which opened a new door for lovers of God. When Sheik Muzaffer met Lex I think he realized that the entire lineage could flower in this country, but in an American form. He said that Islam is like pure water and it takes the form and the colors of the bottles it's put into. He meant that we didn't have to impose any cultural form on America. It will simply blossom from within. And that's what we're seeing happening." By 1980 Hixon, renamed "Nur," meaning "Divine Light," by Muzaffer, had already become licensed as his formal successor along with Philippa de Menil. As Hixon described the double ceremony in his *Atom from the Sun of Knowledge:* "I knelt before him, side by side with my spiritual sister Fariha al-Jerrahi, at the Mosque of Divine Ease, the Masjid al-Farah, in New York City. After placing his green and gold turban upon my head, the Grand Shaykh opened his palms and offered this supplication. 'May whatever has come into me from Allah and from the Prophet of Allah now enter into him.' After his brief prayer, Shaykh Muzaffer removed his turban from my head and placed it on the western woman beside me. I would have enjoyed wearing it longer, but spiritual transmission, like turning on an electric light, is instantaneous." That same year the three of them traveled on *hajj* together to Mecca.

The transmission came true, at least organizationally, in 1985, when Muzaffer Ozak died after twenty years as head of the order and Lex Hixon, still in his early forties, suddenly found himself Sheik Nur al-Jerrahi. Those were traumatic times for the downtown circle. "The passing of a very strong teacher is always dramatic, and shakes up all the disciples tremendously," said Fariha. In her case, the shake-up doubly included her own Dia Foundation, which was in enough financial trouble that her mother retired both Heiner Friedrich and Helen Winkler and appointed as new chairman of the board the vice president and counsel to the board of the Metropolitan Museum, Ashton Hawkins. "I remember our first board meeting, which Philippa attended, was on the same day that the head of their Sufi sect had died in Istanbul," Hawkins recalled. "She said she thought it was a sign from heaven that as we took over the board their spiritual leader died." One of the casualties was the mosque on Mercer Street, which was subsequently set up independently of the Dia Foundation in the smaller space on lower West Broadway. "Sheik Nur used to say he was actually happy to have a smaller container," said Fariha. "He called it the 'jewel box' that housed the jewels of the Hazreti Pir, the founding saint of our order. The other place was a little grander, but suited the kind of royal style of Sheik Muzzafer, who at that time had reached the apex of his life."

Sheik Nur inspired much love and devotion among Sufi followers during the ensuing decade, especially Americans, who appreciated his more informal interpretation of Islam. "Sheik Nur was so full of love, he was pure love," a female dervish of his confided in me. "He took on a lot of people's burdens. At the same time his life was sad. As much love as he gave to people and as much perfection as he tried to bring into people's lives, his own life was sort of torn." Part of the "torn" quality was perhaps his very universalism. His wife was a practicing Buddhist at the time, and one of his daughters was a Christian. As the dervish told me, "He was teaching universal religion, which was very appealing to people who believed in the oneness of God. And New York was the perfect place to impart this knowledge. And yet when I asked him for advice about marrying someone who was not prepared to accept Islam, he surprisingly said, 'If I were you, I wouldn't do it. You and your children need to have one foundation.' . . . To reinforce this point, he told me a story about the time when he went to church with his daughter and grandson. During the service, his grandson turned to him with concern and said, 'Grandpa, when are we doing our ablution?' Over the four years I knew him it was clear he was getting more and more grounded in Islam. He started growing a beard and talked about the importance of *shariah,* which he never had before, and when he died his universalism followed him to the grave. He was given a Christian burial." Hixon had one daughter, Alexandra, from his brief first marriage and three children by his second wife and widow, their names being Dylan Huckleberry, India Thoreau, and Shanti Sunlight Hixon.

Hixon's search, comparable to Thomas Merton's in its painful inclusion of sophisticated doubt and its cosmopolitan longing for universality, was cut short by his death from colon cancer, which spread to his liver, on November 1, 1995, at the age of fifty-three. "Naturally he only used a Tibetan doctor and wouldn't let many people in New York visit him for fear of exhaustion, though Bob Thurman did visit him a lot," recalled Gray Henry. "I went two or three times. Each time he got thinner and thinner. I have the most beautiful picture of him and his wife, Sheila, standing there. You know, for one of us, he made it. I could see the difference. In Islam, illness is there to purify you. He was very concerned that he forgive everyone and be forgiven. His first wife, from whom he was divorced, came and forgave him. He said to me, 'You know if it were only for that, this will have been worth it.' I discovered that all my early prejudices about his being into too many spiritual bags at once were unfounded. He was a great soul."

Hixon's extreme ecumenism, which he credited to an early reading of *The Gospel of Sri Ramakrishna,* the great work of the Divine Mother tradition of Bengal, was definitely reflected in his memorial service in December 1995 at the Episcopal Cathedral of St. John the Divine in New York City. The service opened with a welcome by its dean, James Morton. Dervishes of Hixon's *masjid* danced, of course, led by Shaykha Feriha. But other traditions were equally represented. Roshi Glasssman, a Zen teacher in the lineage of the White Plum Sangha, posthumously performed a Dharma Transmission, which Hixon had been scheduled to receive on December 8 to proclaim him a Zen teacher empowered to give the Bodhissatva Precepts to all creation. Juliana Schmemann, the wife of the deceased dean of St. Vladimir's Seminary, also spoke. Hixon and his wife had spent three years studying theology at the seminary after having been Chrismated into the Orthodox Church of America in 1983. A close friend, Rabbi Don Singer, recited the last verse of the Kaddish. Robert Thurman's eulogy was titled, "Praises of Lex." Philip Glass performed his own composition, "Satyagraha."

"The memorial service was like no other," recalled Wheelock Whitney, Hixon's first cousin. "My most enduring memory is of the somewhat bemused, if always very dignified, expressions on the handsome faces of Lex's parents, Alec and Adelaide, as they sat in the front row and received the effusive homage of hundreds of Lex's friends and followers, which ranged from bear hugs to complete prostration at their feet. I was also very moved that the service ended with a gospel song, since his spiritual journey presumably began in Christianity." Indeed during the year of his illness Hixon had found inspiration in listening to tapes of Gospel music, and so a medley of these African-American hymns was sung by two associate ministers from Mt. Nebo Baptist Church. Hixon was buried in the cemetery of the little town of Sayner in northern Wisconsin near the woods of Plum Lake, where he and his wife had kept a log cabin with no running water.

Spiritual leadership passed to Shaykha Fariha, who, since 1995, has been caring for a community with satellite groups now running in Mexico City, Boulder, Crestone, Atlanta, Honolulu, Chicago, Lansing, Kansas City, Albuquerque, Nashville, Washington, D.C., and Yonkers. "Our circles in Mexico City, Honolulu, Boulder, Albuquerque, and Kansas City are led by women, and Washington, D.C., is shared by a man and a woman," she told me, evidently pleased. "That was one of Sheik Nur's gift. He unveiled women as spiritual guides in our time. The Sufi Order of the West also has women sheiks as do other American Sufi orders. They've existed in the Middle East too, though they are not usually recorded in the history books, except for some exceptional Sufi women. . . . There were certainly male dervishes in this order who couldn't accept having a woman teacher and left after Sheik Nur's death. There was a certain sifting out.

"I've battled with people in my group who want to tell a woman she must put a scarf on," she went on. "I said, 'No, you can't tell anyone anything. They're a guest.' Even with the dervishes, I never make mention of things like that. It just seems to me nonessential. We're concerned with essence, with reaching God, with disappearing into God, not with wearing a scarf or not wearing a scarf. That's not important. How is your heart? How are you behaving with other people? Are you being loving and kind and truthful? That's what's important." The Islamic connection of the Dia Foundation exacerbated mistrust in the New York art world, yet Fariha's personal philosophy can do the same within her chosen religion. But, as she told me, "One of our dervishes dreamt that I was being attacked for being a woman and for calling people onto the path of love, beyond the rigid limits of formality. In the dream Sheik Nur came to me and said not to be concerned about what people thought. The only thing that matters is to uphold 'La ilaha ilallah,' the absolute, all-pervading, blissful oneness of existence. But I'm well protected. I'm not around constant confrontation at all. Generally, it's fairly peaceful, with occasional exceptions." (*La ilaha ilallah* is the basic Muslim statement of belief, "There is no god but God.") As Fariha recalled, "When I was fifteen years old, I first heard the words '*La ilaha ilallah*' spoken by a Pakistani high school classmate. I was so struck by their beauty and healing power that for one whole year I would repeat them to bring peace to my heart."

On the first evening I attended a Thursday-evening gathering of her circle at the Masjid al-Farah, I witnessed one of the rare rough moments. It certainly did not come from the dervishes, about forty of whom were seated quietly on the densely woven ruby, crimson, and green Persian carpets in the prayer hall. Located on the first floor of this converted office building, this hundred-foot-long rectangular space is a simple construction of white brick walls, white tin ceilings, a glass chandelier, and ceiling fans, as minimal as the former de Menil townhouse. On its walls hang six medallions in dark forest green with gold calligraphy of the names of "Allah," "Muhammad," his early companions, "Abu Bakr," "Umar," and "Uthman," his son-in-law and cousin, "Ali," and his grandsons, "Hassan and Hussein," as well as a framed piece of black cloth, which once covered the *kabah,* or cube-shaped shrine, in the center of the Grand Mosque in Mecca. (The cloth is cut yearly and mailed to mosques around the world.) A tall, dark wooden *qublah* in the corner is flanked with Tiffany-style floor lamps; the *mihrab,* in the shape of a rolling shelf ladder in a library, is draped with green curtain threaded with gold. "Sheik Muzaffer commissioned those two wooden structures from two great carpenters in Istanbul, and they were then constructed here in SoHo in some garage," Fariha said. "These carpenters were like remnants from the Ottoman Empire working in SoHo making these beautiful things. They were originally for the other mosque. When we came here, *alhamdulillah,* they fit. That set the tone." (*Alhamdulillah,* which recurs often in conversation with practicing Muslims, is Arabic for "Thank God.")

For the *dhikr* that evening Shaykha Fariha used a white booklet following a litany dating back three centuries to Pir Nureddin Jerrahi that was full of chants, prayer, and readings from the Quran. However, the usual bliss in the circling of words and prayers was disrupted by the presence of a young man from West Africa with a full, almost cherubic face, wrapped in a black turban, sitting in the back of the hall with a wooden staff at his side. With him were two American companions. When Fariha instructed her followers to line up for their prayers, with one of her male followers assigned as Imam, and the women in lines behind the men, the figure squatting in the rear came to sudden life and strode forward. He threateningly approached the shaykha, shouting, "This is *bidah.*" (Often translated as "innovation," and definitely a negative term in Islam, a more accurate translation is "deformation," as in taking a bite out of something, which is its literal meaning.)

The shaykha refused to engage him in dialogue after a few hopeless attempts, and instead urged everyone, "Keep praying, keep praying . . . don't look at him, don't talk to him. Remember why you're here. This is a test." Ali tried to calm the menacing interloper, explaining that they were trying to pray, and that he was in a different culture now. "You're playing with Allah," the man shouted back, occasionally pounding his stick on the carpet. "If you play with Allah, Allah will destroy you. I feel the love of Allah. And I feel the anger of Allah. Right now I am feeling the anger of Allah." Eventually he and his two accomplices were drawn upstairs for further debate, and the evening returned to script, with a dancing circle as its denouement, accompanied by the beating of drums, followed by sweets and tea, and the shaykha sitting on the floor, a rose-colored candle flickering nearby, inter- preting dreams of full moons and sapphire temples for her dervishes. But hovering over the proceedings was the reminder that even in this mellowest of settings, the tensions of Islam are those of a relatively young world religion undergoing an identity crisis in a new and unfamiliar land. For Shaykha Fariha, with her vision intact, the sum of the lesson of the disruption was, "There's a spiritual awakening everywhere in America. It's happening at such a rate that we can see it. It's like corn growing in Kansas. You can hear human hearts opening."

While Sheik Muzaffer Ozak was setting the future in motion with his double-crowning of Lex Hixon and Philippa de Menil with the *taj,* the green turban, of the order, he also surprisingly put Feisal Abdul Rauf in place in 1983 as Imam, to give the ser- mons on Fridays in the downtown mosque. Rauf was a young man in his early thirties with a more traditional Muslim pedigree, and was outside the circle and not even one of Muzaffer's dervishes. Born into a family of *seyyed,* descendents of Muhammad, Rauf's father was Dr. Muhammad Abdul Rauf, born in 1917 in Egypt, a graduate of al-Azhar University with an M.A. from Cambridge and a Ph.D. in philosophy from the University of London. He was in charge of the Islamic Center of New York City (1965–1970) while negotiations were under way for the purchase of the land for the Ninety-sixth Street mosque, and between 1970 and 1980 he served as director of the Islamic Center in Washington, D.C. Among several more specialized books, he wrote *Islam: Creed and Worship,* a basic Islamic catechism in English. As he was helping devise the early circuitry for disseminating Islam in America, his son, Feisal, who'd been born in Kuwait in 1948 and grew up in England, Malaysia, and the United States, earned an undergraduate degree at Columbia University and attended Stevens Institute in New Jersey, where he studied physics in the doctoral program. He's since written two books of his own: *Islam: A Search for Meaning* and *Islam: A Sacred Law,* the latter subtitled, "What Every Muslim Should Know About Shariah."

"I was invited several times by a close friend to go to the mosque on Mercer Street," Feisal Rauf recalled of his unexpected deputizing.

> I finally went one day, and my friend said, "Feisal, I sense there's a role for you to play in this mosque," I said, "Funny, I feel the same thing." I returned on a Friday. Sha'ban, who was *muezzin* and Imam while Sheik Muzaffer was away, invited me, "Please call the *adhan.*" He implored me later, "You must come and call the prayer on Fridays. I'm all alone here." I wasn't keen on it. But that Sunday I went to my *hadith* collection and the book just opened to the merits of calling the *adhan.* I felt a hand tapping me and my heart realized—*Uh oh. It's something I've got to do.* This was an example of one of those times where you know you're getting a very clear message. On Sheik Muzaffer's return I was invited to meet him at his house in Yonkers. He said, "I want you to be Imam in the mosque." I answered that I'd be happy to serve if it didn't exacerbate the rivalry among his representatives at the

Masjid al-Farah. But he said, "Don't worry about it. When I mandate something, it's law."

Soon after Rauf took hands with Sheik Muzaffer.

For almost twenty years since, Feisal Rauf has been giving the Friday sermons at the Masjid al-Farah. In those weekly talks his poise and, of course, sweetness are blatantly Sufi, yet there is no hint of a bohemian soft sell. On Friday, June 9, 2000, for instance, he read most of his *khutba* from a sheaf of white typed pages where he'd carefully prepared the bulk of his remarks, as might be expected from someone whose expertise was Islamic jurisprudence. He looked very gentlemanly, with white hair and a clipped white beard, his brown eyes clear and calm, speaking English with a British inflection, and dressed in a white cotton tunic. He addressed the usual gathering of about 150 men and women on his topic. "Degrees of Divine Sound," the women separated at the rear by an ankle-high string run across the long, narrow prayer hall. Given an unofficial two-party system in Sufism between the so-called "sober" Sufis, who observe rules and etiquette in their relations with God, and their "drunken" cousins, who prefer open, swooning union, Rauf definitely seemed on the "sober" side.

Yet there was nothing dry or authoritarian in his style. You would never imagine for a moment you were listening to a fire-and-brimstone orthodox Muslim exhortation. "We begin, my dear brothers and sisters, by entering into a state of submission before the presence and the throne of Almighty Allah," he said, holding on to the cherry wood rail of the *mihrab* and putting space around his words so that he seemed like someone who'd suddenly dropped down an atmosphere underwater. "We do this by emptying our hearts of all the distractions, from all the emotional issues which grip us. Empty your minds of all thoughts after a week of work, of issues and debates with other people. Leave that behind you with your shoes. And enter into a space that is sacred."

He delivered a talk similar to that he gave a few weeks later at the WARIS Center, on listening—that is, on the power of sounds in the Quran to transform, most obviously in the chanting of the rough melody of the Arabic that is part of many Sufi gatherings. But he included a few detours as he worked his way through his pages. He spoke of the importance of heart, another favorite Sufi theme: "Your role in being messengers of the Messenger of Allah has to do with how you touch other people. We all know that there are a lot of people out there who have lots of knowledge and want to hold you by the neck and say, 'Listen to me while I tell you about Islam,' and all you want to do is run away from them. But there are people who will touch your heart in such a way that they will make you want to love Allah even more. . . . That's the quality the Prophet had, peace and blessings be upon him."

Following his talk, we walked across West Broadway to the Franklin Station Cafe, a clean, white triangular restaurant billing itself as a "French and Malaysian Bistro," which he frequents as a reminder of his years spent in Malaysia, where his father taught before moving to America. Having removed his white tunic, he was now dressed in civilian clothes—a button-down Brooks Brothers–style striped shirt and tan pants. He did carry with him a Moroccan cane several centuries old tipped with beaten copper that had been given him recently by a Moroccan sheik. He filled me in on some of the details of his adult life: taught remedial math in the New York City public school system following graduation; manages real estate as a "bread-and-butter" business; lives in North Bergen, New Jersey, with his wife, Daisy Khan, the Kashmiri niece of Faroque Khan who designs office space for a publishing company; and is president of the American Sufi Muslim Association (ASMA), a member of the board of trustees of the Islamic Center of New York, and of the Interfaith Center of New York, and lectures at the New York Seminary, an institute for training interfaith ministers.

We talked about the reputed magic of the Quran, the magic of sound he hinted at in his sermon, yet that is often missed in flat translation. "Reading a translation of the Quran is like reading a translation of one of Puccini's operas, in English, without the music," he said, over a mango salad and a dish of spicy salmon with cold noodles. "The Arabs used to pride themselves on their complex poetry. It was the only art form a nomadic people could develop and carry with them, so they developed it to the highest possible degree. Yet when the Quran came along it blew the minds of the people of the time. It was as if you had lovely oil paintings and then Monet and Picasso come along and produce something not along these rules but even better. But if you don't have an artistic sensibility, you can't appreciate what they've done. There are pre-Islamic poems that continue to exist. They're very desert, very nomadic. You can smell the air of the desert. But the Quran has an entirely different odor, a different smell." ("I read the Arberry translation when I was young, and it didn't make much sense to me," Fariha confessed to me. "But it's actually said that the chanting of the Quran is God speaking. Just as thunder and lightning is said to be God speaking. It opens the heart tremendously.")

Relying on lots of qualifications and hypothetical examples and quotations from *hadith,* Rauf also talked of contemporary social issues. As Sufis often do, he seemed flexible and liberal, especially up against the cliché of Islam as preaching a simple "Boy Scout" moral code. When I mentioned the discussion of homosexuality I'd had with Ghazi Khankan, he said, "If you ask me what the majority of Muslims believe, I would say they believe exactly what Ghazi told you. As in the Old Testament, homosexuality is referred to in the Quran in the story of Lot. But the primary crime that the people of Lot committed was rejection of God and His Prophet Lot. All Muslims assert that God is most merciful, most compassionate. That's the attribute that opens every chapter of the Quran. Some Muslims therefore believe that for God to create you with a desire then punish you for seeking to fulfill it is inconsistent with an all-merciful and all-compassionate Creator. But Islam condemns promiscuity and adultery, and flaunting one's sexuality, apart from the question of sexual orientation. We therefore need to be clear on what the nature of the sin is."

By the time we'd finished our coffees and a light rain was

beginning to fall in Tribeca, he revealed that he was now himself a sheik of a Sufi group, which met on Friday nights for dinner and *dhikr* at an apartment he and his wife keep on the upper West Side. When I asked how this came about, he told of a series of encounters that packed some of the spiritual thrill of G. I. Gurd-jieff's *Meetings with Remarkable Men,* a classic account of meetings with mystics and saints in the Middle East and Central Asia at the turn of the last century: "Eleven years after Sheik Muzaffer's death, I was invited to go to a sacred music festival in Fez, Morocco. Before I left, Heiner, Philippa's husband at the time, who's very perceptive, said, 'Now don't go and take hands with another sheik there.' This was in 1996. After one of the shows, a lady comes up to me and says, 'Are you a Sufi?' Well, no one ever said that to me in my life. It was like someone coming up to you at a Woodstock festival or in Central Park and asking, 'Are you a Sufi?' We became friends."

His friendship with her eventually led to his meeting a Sufi sheik of the Shadhili-Qadiri order in Morocco in spring of 1997. Formerly a three-star general in the Moroccan military, this sheik, who claimed he would have preferred to remain in the military, had been appointed years before to be successor to the mandate by his own father, who supposedly told him, "You will hold it in trust for its owner, who will come from abroad to assume it, and you will convey it to him. . . . You will know him when you see him." In December 1999, during the month of Ramadan, he realized, with the help of a dream, that Feisal Rauf was the rightful owner of the mandate. "I am now responsible for introducing the *tariqah* in the West," explained Rauf. "This *tariqah's* spiritual chain of authority goes back to both the Shadhili and Qadiri branches of Sufism, except that now it is to be presented to the West in ways it can understand and comprehend. . . . As for me, I have intensive prayers to help me in fulfilling this task of a spiritual teacher precipitating positive and uplifting transformations in the seeker." (Organized in the twelfth century around the teachings of 'Abd al'Qadir al Jilani from Iraq, the Qadiri order grew rapidly and became the most widespread of the early orders;

the Shadhili likewise were established in Egypt and north Africa by Abu al-Hasan al-Shadhili, who died in 1258.)

Rauf invited me to attend his circle, which I did over four months during the summer of 2000. If the Islamic Center of Long Island and the WARIS Center showcase the possibility of an American Islam, stripped of djallabahs and of some misogynistic attitudes as well, Rauf's Sufi group does the same for Sufism, avoiding both Masonic Lodge–style esotericism and hippie feel-good syncretism. Certainly the location is as normal for New York City as a scene in a Woody Allen film: a tenth-floor apartment in a doorman building a block from Broadway on West Eighty-fifth Street. One evening the Latino doorman remarked to Daisy Khan, "You have very interesting people visiting you every week, very well dressed." The arrivals prompting his observation were a Sufi from Africa with a retinue of four men, all dressed in full African regalia, with tall spherical hats. Usually, however, the thirty or forty gathered blend quite well with the rest of the *New York Times*–carrying, bike-riding tenants crowded in the slow elevator at the end of a busy work week.

The apartment is a large one-bedroom, which is almost exclusively used for the Friday get-togethers. Most of the gathering took place in the main living room, with two couches set along two walls, a few framed examples of Quranic gold-leaf calligraphy on the walls, a desk with displayed books, tapes, and CDs for sale pushed into a far corner. In the eastern corner, a tall floor lamp with an orange shade marked the *qibla.* When Feisal's Casio watch, accessorized with an arrow pointing to the *qibla,* would beep, set for the five prayer times, the rugs would be unrolled and the living room transformed into a mosque—once at sunset, once at the end of the night. In the narrow adjacent kitchen, his Indonesian cook and others helped prepare food for dinner and dessert, squeezing past a line of stove and counter. On the largest windowsill, with a view onto a roofscape of wooden water towers, looking particularly Oriental against a setting summer sun, a large air conditioner blasted. And in the hallway near the entrance, two small shoe racks were set to prevent inconvenience to the uncomplaining neighbors, evidently inured to multiculturalism, on their way into their own one-bedrooms.

The group was a mix of ethnicities. The women—always covered for prayer with scarves they generally put on in the bedroom after arriving—included Pakistanis, Turks, Egyptians, Indians, even a Russian make-up artist. A young artist from the lower East Side converted to Islam to marry his fiancée from Uzbekistan, their marriage performed by Imam Feisal one Friday evening. (Muslim women must marry Muslim men, though the reverse is not true.) A young Hispanic-American woman, Diana Castro, seemed among the more liberal in her interpretation of her presence there, not feeling the need to give up her love of the teachings of Christ from her Roman Catholic upbringing to embrace Islam. "It was just like confirming my faith again to do the *shahadah,*" she said. "You're not talking to Cat Stevens here. I always believed in the unity of God and the truth in all faiths, even when I was Christian. Embracing Islam has actually doubled my love for Christ's teachings, since in teaching the 'Our Father' to his disciples Christ was asking them to connect directly to the one God. . . . I basically come here to meditate. I say my prayers and I feel I'm being purged." (Her reference was to musician Cat Stevens's rebirth, in 1977, as Yusuf Islam, a strictly orthodox Sunni Muslim, after his near drowning in Malibu.)

The men sat on one half of the room during prayers and were warned regularly by Imam Feisal, "Don't look at members of the opposite sex when you're doing your *dhikr.* Stay focused within." Among them were a Turkish owner of a dry cleaning business; a creative director in an advertising firm whose grandfather had once been president of Syria; an African-American radio-show host; a European-American sound engineer; an Iranian day trader; and a diplomat from Senegal. "There is obviously not an attraction here to cultural or ethnic expression as in so many mosques in New York City," said Daisy Khan. "Rather, it's getting to the universal core or essence of what Islam is."

The drill each week was nearly identical. A long yellow-and-red cloth would be spread on the floor, with plastic plates, utensils, cups, and a Middle Eastern potluck supper: roast lamb, pita bread, sesame paste, sliced salmon, tomato and cucumber salad, and goat cheese. As supper ended, a chosen *muezzin* would stand, his hands at his ears, and begin to wail the call to prayer in the direction of the floor lamp for *maghrib,* the sunset prayer, and the men and women each formed their parallel lines. Afterward, the Quran would be distributed as everyone sat on the floor to chant Sura 36, *"Ya Sin."* Increasingly shorter chants would follow, the later *suras,* and the repetition of *"Ya Latif"* ("O subtle Lord, have mercy"), or *"la ilaha illallah,"* or simply *"Ya Allah."* Faisal Rauf would then deliver a meditation for twenty minutes. The night prayer, the *salatu-lisha,* would be called. Finally, the cloth spread would reappear and be covered with sliced oranges and watermelons, cookies, Turkish delights, and even Pakistani ice cream, which is basically frozen cream on a stick, while glasses of black or herbal tea were passed.

The real juice of the evening was the chanting over and over the name of Allah. With eyes shut, and prepared already by an hour of repetitive mantras, the members joined in a singsong reciting of the sacred name in the company of others who believe in its power. Such calling out would result in a rise and fall in crescendo, a growing in volume and excitement, even a kind of a cappella harmony. At times the entire group would sound like cars honking in some celestial traffic jam, at other times, like flocks of geese following the leader, Rauf, whose voice could always be heard somewhere up above, down below, or out ahead. There would be evenings of turbulence, others in which you heard just the bare struggling of unmatched voices weakly trying to keep up, and a few where the sound did seem amplified by Dolby stereo. Those were the evenings in which the angels were apparently singing backup, at least according to the spiritual connoisseurs in the group, who would recap the event. "How was your *dhikr?*" they would ask probingly afterward.

"What an authentic spiritual circle like this does is put you in touch with that reality that didn't have a name at the time of the Prophet, the essence of religion, what people feel," said Pedram

Samghabadi, who prays with the upper West Side group. "That's what really causes change. Seeing is believing. You start doing the *dhikr* and your physical acts of worship take on new life. Ours is a very authentic, sincere group. No one asks for money. We don't worship Feisal. He's like a spiritual coach. He's not gonna run for you, he's not gonna lift the weights for you. He's there to guide you through it. But in Islam there's no intermediary between you and God. Most of the people in the group have no relationship to each other. It's like, 'Why am I hanging out with this Pakistani guy?' But this bond is so strong it'll bring us together every Friday night."

During my months making my way through the maze of Islamic life in New York City, I became less distracted by the charm and busyness of the surface of the mosaic, the sensation of walking into a virtual Damascus or a virtual Cairo, and more taken generally with the regional, suburban dialect of much of the Islam actually being practiced. Muslims in America these days often blend in with the other nine out of ten Americans who profess to believe in God. And wherever I went I kept hearing a familiar God talk being spoken.

One afternoon at the Masjid al-Farah, I sat with Ali, the Jordanian caretaker, who came to this country four years ago, leaving his nine children behind. We had one of those front-stoop theological talks I'd experienced dozens of times in dozens of locations in spiritual America.

"Do you believe in God?" he asked, fingering his mustache.

"Yes," I said.

"Well, if you believe in God, then you are Muslim," he cheerfully informed me. "Any Christians who believe in God, they are Muslim too. They just don't know it. And anyone who does not believe in God, he is not Muslim."

A few weeks later, on a Friday evening at Imam Feisal's Sufi circle, I stood in a narrow hallway waiting for the bathroom. It was time for everyone to do their ablutions before prayer, so there was a line. In front of me was Shazad Rashid, a thirty-two-year-old actor with long, black, wavy hair combed back and deeply inset brown eyes, from Kashmir by way of the Strassberg acting school in L.A., who'd assiduously been avoiding being cast as a taxi driver or a terrorist in indy student films.

"Do you believe in God?" he suddenly asked, as we both leaned against the same wall.

"Yeah," I answered.

"Really?" he went on. "How do you know?"

"Uh, it's like a hunch I have," I answered.

"Oh," he said, thoughtfully.

He then disappeared into the bathroom to perform his ablutions in the sink: washing with clean water three times over the tops of the hands (right hand first), face (including mouth and nostrils), forearms (right arm first), top of the head, back of the head, neck and feet (right foot first) to the ankles. This ritual designed for the remembrance of God and completed faithfully by the inquisitive Shazad—in front of a contemporary medicine-cabinet mirror, next to a rack filled with cotton hand towels, a water tower atop a nearby apartment building visible through a narrow window—was identical to that reportedly first choreographed and repeated daily in the Arabian desert by the Prophet Muhammad nearly fourteen centuries earlier.

NOTES

INTRODUCTION

xvi   "I expect that" Harold Bloom, *Omens of Millennium* (New York: River-head Books, 1996), p. 225

"I didn't feel ready." Kathleen Norris, *The Cloister Walk* (New York: Riverhead Books, 1996), p. xvii.

xx   "Happiness is man's proper good" St. Thomas Aquinas, *Treatise on Happiness,* trans. John A. Oesterle (Englewood Cliffs, N.J.: Prentice-Hall, 1964), p. 67.

xxi   "95 percent" This collection of statistics is taken from Marc Gunther, "God and Business," *Fortune* 144, no. 1 (July 9, 2001), p. 61.

ONE

3   *The Truth about Spiritualism* (Chicago: McClurg, 1923).

The Mind at Mischief: Tricks and Deceptions of the Subconscious and How to Cope with Them (New York: Funk and Wagnalls, 1929).

The Urantia Book (Chicago: URANTIA Foundation, 1955).

4   "He predicted": "Dr. Sadler, 93, Dies," *Chicago Tribune,* 28 April 1969.

"a donation": Ibid.

5   *The Elements of Pep: A Talk on Health and Efficiency* (Chicago: American, 1925).

Theory and Practice of Psychiatry (St. Louis: Mosby, 1936).

5   "this grand flat": Alice Sinkevitch, ed., *AIA Guide to Chicago* (New York: Harcourt Brace, 1993), p. 194.

6   "This man is": Cited in Mark Kulieke, *The Birth of a Revelation: The Story of the Urantia Papers.* (Green Bay, Wisc.: Morning Star Foundation, 1991), p. 383.

7   "Being a sister": Deposition of Helen Carlson, June 29, 1994. Record Excerpt of Appellant Urantia Foundation, Docket 174.
    "I remember": Deposition of Helen Carlson.

14 "milestone": Eric Cosh, ed., *Dr. Meredith J. Sprunger on the Origin of the Urantia Papers: Two Historic Interviews* (Boulder: The Invisible Fellowship of Urantia Book Believers, 1994).
    "ranging from": Program from "Living Faith: The Fellowship's 1996 International Conference," p. 9.

15 "When I vacuum": Interview with Carolyn Kendall, 2/6/97.
    "chloroform in print": Quoted by Walter Kirn, in "Walking a Mile in Their Shoes," *Time,* 4 August 1997, p. 58.

16 "Spiritualism is": Cited in *Encyclopedia of Occultism and Parapsychology* (n.p.: Gale Group, 2000), p. 873.

17 "This is a course": Introduction to Frances Vaughan and Roger Walsh, eds., *Gifts from A Course in Miracles* (New York: G. P. Putnam, 1995). p. 2.
    "In the spring": Neale Donald Walsch, *Conversations with God: An Uncommon Dialogue.* Book I. (New York: G. P. Putnam: 1996), p. 1.

18 "As a science journalist": Martin Gardner, *Urantia: The Great Cult Mystery* (Amherst, New York: Prometheus Books, 1995), p. 181.

19 "'This far-distant": *The Urantia Book,* p. 170.
    " '875,000,000,000 years ago": Ibid., p. 652.
    "The limit of velocity": Ibid., p. 260.
    "Thus is the sense of' ": Ibid., p. 379.

20 "The laws of revelation": Ibid., p. 1109.
    "If the spirits are so wise": Cited in *Urantia: The Great Cult Mystery,* p. 224.

21 "I used to read tons": Interview with Robin Jorgenson, 2/14/97.

22 "*The Urantia Book* is remarkable": Interview with Martin Gardner, 6/17/97.
    "The *UB*'s cosmology": *Urantia: The Great Cult Mystery,* pp. 12, 33.
    "The triodity": *The Urantia Book,* p. 1265.

26 "But many years ago": Cited in *Birth of a Revelation,* appendix A, p. 33.
    "You can have": Quoted in G. Vonne Muessling, "William S. Sadler: Chautauqua's Medic Orator" (Ph.D. diss., Bowling Green State University, 1970), p. 4.

27 "We recognize that": William Sadler, *Americanitis: Blood Pressure and Nerves* (New York: Macmillan, 1925), pp. 36–37.

28 "bizarre behavior": Personal interview with Bud Kagan by David Kantor in "The First Century of the Fifth Epochal Revelation: A Timeline of Events Related to the Spread of the Urantia Book," p. 3.
"Here was a": Quoted in *Urantia: The Great Cult Mystery*, p. 115.
"Eighteen years of study": Cited in *Birth of a Revelation*, appendix A, p. 383.

29 "My father had in his salad days": William Sadler Jr., personal transcription of an audiotape recording made in the home of Berkeley Elliott, 2/18/62.

30 Sadler claimed: William S. Sadler, *History of the Urantia Movement: From the Beginning Until 1960* (Boulder: Jesusonian Foundation, n.d.), p. 5.
"One evening": William Sadler Jr. audiotape, 2/18/62.

31 "We acknowledge": *History of the Urantia Movement*, p. 8.
"This individual": William Sadler Jr. audiotape, 2/18/62.

32 "I'm a psychiatrist": "The First Century of the Fifth Epochal Revelation," p. 7.

33 "The truth is that": Quoted in *Urantia: The Great Cult Mystery*, p. 149.
"Someone other than": *Birth of a Revelation*, p. 8.
"Dr. Sadler appeared": "William S. Sadler: Chautauqua's Medic Orator," p. 12.

34 "I thought Dr. Sadler": Interview with Carolyn Kendall, 2/6/97.
"I think there": Interview with Carolyn Kendall, 2/6/97.
"Doctor wanted": Interview with Nola Smith, 7/21/97.

35 "The transition from": "William S. Sadler: Chautauqua's Medic Orator," p. 18.
"The readers": Interview with Carolyn Kendall, 2/6/97.

36 "The work of such": "Defendant's Statement of Facts in Support of its Motion for Partial Summary Judgement as to Plaintiff's Claim for Copyright Infringement," December 17, 1995, Docket 205, p. 10.
"employees . . . work for hire": Rosey Lieske, "Update on Appeal: The Significance of *The Urantia Book*'s Origins to a Court of Law" (Agondonter Foundation, 1996), p. 2.

38 "Stay where you are": This quotation and subsequent quotations are taken from interview with Mo Siegel, 2/27/97.

41 "Mo would read from": Phone interview with Lucinda Ziesing, 8/22/99.

45 "You can't equate": Interview with Paula Thompson, 2/7/97.
"I think there is": Quoted in "Kristen Maaherra Requests: URANTIA Foundation Arguments: Brotherhood Charter Argument."

46 "I'm just very private": Phone interview with Lynn Lear, 8/6/97.

47   "As far as possible": *The Urantia Book,* p. 1343.

48   "The important thing": Interview with Matthew Block, 2/7/97.
     "a young, devout": *Urantia: The Great Cult Mystery,* p. 321.

49   *"The Urantia Book,* which I found": Interview with Block, 2/7/97.

50   "a welcome island": Matthew Block, "Morontia Mota: A New Perspective," *The Circular* (July-September 2000), p. 28.
     "Not long since": *The Urantia Book,* p. 556.

51   "more than one thousand": Ibid., p. 556.
     "No one at": "Morontia Mota," p. 33.
     "I always felt": Interview with Matthew Block, 5/12/01.

55   "Starting for any one": Cited in Matthew Block, "Some Human Sources of *The Urantia Book,*" *Spiritual Fellowship Journal* (spring 1993), p. 10.

56   "felt he had been put": *The Urantia Book,* p. 1481.
     "It's true that": Interview with Block, 5/12/01.

59   "Do you not comprehend": *The Urantia Book,* p. 1664.

60   "This is unique": e-mail to author from Matthew Block, 6/11/01.

                              TWO

67   "They love an": Interview with Deepak Chopra, 3/13/97.
     "I was sitting": Deepak Chopra, *Return of the Rishi: A Doctor's Story of Spiritual Transformation and Ayurvedic Healing* (Boston: Houghton-Mifflin Company, 1998), p. 184.

70   "monkish": Chip Brown, "Deepak Chopra has sniff a cold," *Esquire* (October 1995), p. 125.

73   "When I was six": Interview with Deepak Chopra, 3/13/97.

74   "My ambition was": *Return of the Rishi,* p. 86.

76   "I look like": Dennis McLellan, "The Guru Turns to Fiction," *Publishers Weekly,* 24 July 1995, p. 44.

84   "the one indispensable text": Introduction to *The Nectar of Chanting* (South Fallsburg, NY: SYDA Foundation, 1983), p. xiii.

86   "beautiful and rare trees": Swami Muktananda, *Ashram Dharma* (South Fallsburg, NY: SYDA Foundation, 1995), pp. 11–12.

87   "wheels for feet": Quoted in William K. Mahony, "The Ashram," *Meditation Revolution: A History and Theology of the Siddha Yoga Lineage* (South Fallsburg, NY: Agama Press, 1997), p. 558.

88   "It's time": Interview with Melynda Windsor, 6/17/98.

91   "There is one mind": Ralph Waldo Emerson, "History," in *The Selected Writings of Ralph Waldo Emerson,* ed. Brooks Atkinson (New York: The Modern Library, 1992), pp. 113–114.

96 "When I was in medical": Interview with Deepak Chopra, 3/13/97.

97 "In the spring": Diana Eck, "The Mosque Next Door," *Harvard Magazine* (September-October 1996), p. 40.

109 "The St. Tropez": "Page Six," *New York Post*, 26 October 1998.

"It occurs to me": Linda Johnsen, *Daughters of the Goddess: The Women Saints of India* (St. Paul, MN: Yes International Publishers, 1994), p. 79.

112 "I think in one": Interview with Swami Durgananda, 7/10/98.

113 "not your typical Joe": Interview with Melynda Windsor, 6/17/98.

"If he ever": Swami Muktananda, *From the Finite to the Infinite* (South Fallsburg, NY: SYDA Foundation, 1994), pp. 227–229.

114 "I stood there": Swami Muktananda, *Play of Consciousness* (South Fallsburg, NY: SYDA Foundation, 1994), p. 72.

115 "In Kashmir": Interview with S. Ramachandran, 6/21/98.

116 "Baba Ram Dass": Interview with Melynda Windsor, 6/17/98.

117 "Erhard and est": Swami Durgananda, "To See the World Full of Saints," *Meditation Revolution* (South Fallsburg, N.Y.: Agama Press, 1997), p. 81.

"When I was on trial": Interview with Ericka Huggins, 7/10/98.

"New York had": Interview with Melynda Windsor, 6/17/98.

118 "He looked": Phone interview with Arnold Weinstein, 9/8/98.

"I went to a Diana": Interview with Joe Lalli, 5/12/97.

119 "I pulled my hair": Interview with Swami Akhandananda, 5/31/98.

122 "not exactly sex": Quoted in Lis Harris, "O Guru, Guru, Guru," *The New Yorker*, 14 November 1994, p. 97.

"I knew from my own": Interview with Janet Dobrovolny, 6/7/98.

"Part of being": Interview with Swami Durgananda, 7/10/98.

"This kind of behavior": "O Guru, Guru, Guru," p. 97.

123 "He was a kid": Interview with Joe Lalli, 5/12/97.

"There's an old": Interview with Swami Akhandananda, 5/31/98.

124 "They were all gossiping": Interview with Joe Lalli, 5/12/97.

"Well, those pictures": Interview with ex-devotee, 8/31/98.

"At this time I was in": "A Message from Gurumayi to All the Devotees of Siddha Yoga: Part II," http://www.c2.net:80/~truth/32386.htm.

"I was part": Phone interview with Dan Shaw, 9/1/98.

125 "There's so much": Interview with ex-devotee, 11/7/98.

"I brought my mother": Interview with Joe Lalli, 5/12/97.

126 "manageable bite-sized": Interview with Swami Durgananda, 7/10/98.

"Sometimes Gurumayi's": Interview with Janet Dobrovolny, 6/7/98.

127 "When I knew": Phone interview with John Gregory Dunne, 7/30/98.

128 "There was a whole group": Interview with Swami Durgananda, 7/10/98.

129 "I used to lie in bed": Sally Kempton, "Cutting Loose: A Private View of the Women's Uprising," *Esquire* (July 1970), p. 56.

"Uncomfortable with adult": Ibid., p. 54.

"I became a feminist": Ibid., p. 53.

"Women's liberation is finally": Ibid., p. 57.

"I'd used up": Interview with Swami Durgananda, 7/10/98.

130 "Let them go": Quoted in Sally Kempton's "Hanging Out with the Guru," *New York,* 12 April 1976, p. 41.

"There were about": Interview with Swami Durgananda, 7/10/98.

131 "laughable . . . ridiculous": Quoted in "O Guru, Guru, Guru," p. 98.

"It's true that": e-mail from Swami Durgananda, 6/4/99.

132 "My experience of": Interview with Swami Durgananda, 7/10/98.

133 "I always thought": "Hanging Out with the Guru," p. 36.

"If you shake up": Interview with Swami Durgananda, 7/10/98.

134 "Deepak is a visionary": Interview with Gayle Rose, 3/13/97.

135 "If you talked": Interview with Deepak Chopra, 9/3/98.

136 "When I finally": Interview with Gayle Rose, 3/13/97.

"There's one medical": Interview with Stephen Bieckel, 3/14/97.

137 "When we invited him": Interview with David Simon, 3/14/97.

141 "At the center": Interview with Stephen Bieckel, 3/14/97.

142 "If you take": Phone interview with John Renner, 12/29/98.

"Deepak Chopra is": Phone interview with James Randi, 12/22/98.

143 "In India, too": Interview with Deepak Chopra, 3/13/97.

"I do not take any income": e-mail to author from Deepak Chopra, 11/02/01.

147 "I can't talk about": Phone interview with editor, 12/22/98.

148 "The classical traditional": Interview with Deepak Chopra, 10/31/98.

149 "He's like": Phone interview with Deepak Chopra, 12/8/98.

151 "Oh yes": Phone interview with Deepak Chopra, 12/8/98.

THREE

156 "The monastery is": Thomas Merton, *The Seven Storey Mountain* (New York: Harcourt, Brace, 1948), p. 372.

"Tell this talking": Robert Giroux, "Thomas Merton's Durable Mountain," *New York Times Book Review,* October 1998, p. 35.

"People are now": Quoted in Anne Savord, "A Nun's Tribute," in *Thomas Merton/Monk,* ed. Patrick Hart (Kalamazoo, MI: Cistercian Publications, 1983), p. 198.

159 "The past year": Interview with Timothy Kelly, 9/20/98.

160   "Please don't mention": Tamala M. Edwards, "Get Thee to a Monastery," *Time,* 3 August 1998.

"Since 1995": Phone interview with Gustav Niebuhr, 1/26/01.

162   "Then suddenly": *The Seven Storey Mountain,* p. 320.

163   "So Brother Matthew": *The Seven Storey Mountain,* p. 372.

"strangely urban": Quoted in Dianne Aprile, *The Abbey of Gethsemani: Place of Peace and Paradox* (Louisville, Kent.: Trout Lily Press, 1998), p. 163.

164   "We are a little": Quoted in Sidney E. Ahlstrom, *A Religious History of the American People* (New Haven and London: Yale University Press, 1972), p. 491.

165   "The United States": *A Religious History of the American People,* p. 491.

166   "the sports page": Interview with Timothy Kelly, 9/20/98.

"Ocean breeze": Paul Quenon, "The New Watertower," in *Terrors of Paradise* (Windsor, Ontario: Black Moss Press, 1997), p. 44.

168   "I think that recent events": e-mail to author from John Pawson, 10/2/01.

169   "Most monks": Interview with Matthew Kelty, 9/17/98.

170   "Listen, carefully": *The Rule of St. Benedict* (New York: Vintage Spiritual Classics, 1998), p. 3.

"When they live": *The Rule of St. Benedict,* pp. 47–48.

"Are you hastening": *The Rule of St. Benedict,* p. 70.

173   "I entered as": Interview with Alan Gilmore, 9/16/98.

175   "I think the changes": Quotes in Frank Bianco, *Voices of Silence* (New York: Anchor, 1991), p. 112.

"Vatican II stripped": Interview with Brother Augustine, 8/26/98.

176   "In Louisville": Lawrence S. Cunningham, ed., *Thomas Merton: Spiritual Master. The Essential Writings* (New York: Paulist Press, 1992), p. 144.

177   "I remember John": Phone interview with Robert Imperato, 1/7/99.

178   "Many people thought": Interview with John Eudes Bamberger, 1/28/99.

180   "His assignment": Michael Downey, ed., *My Song Is of Mercy: Writings of Matthew Kelty, Monk of Gethsemani* (Kansas City: Sheed and Ward, 1994), p. 226.

182   "I believe": Interview with Timothy Kelly, 9/20/98.

183   "We wanted to live": Interview with Paul Quenon, 9/20/98.

"The first thinking": Interview with Brendan Freeman, 2/19/99.

184   Information on the communal movement in America during the 1960s is taken from Gilbert Zicklin, *Countercultural Communes* (Westport, CT: Greenwood Press, 1983).

185   "With Brother Lavrans": Interview with Timothy Kelly, 9/20/98.

"eighty-two going": Interview with Alan Gilmore, 9/16/98.

186 "Not just from": *My Song Is of Mercy,* p. 256.
"Gays make": Interview with Matthew Kelty, 9/17/98.

187 "One brother was fond": Fenton Johnson, "Beyond Belief: A Skeptic Searches for an American Faith," *Harper's* (September 1998), p. 40.
"I did blow the whistle": Phone interview with Robert Imperato, 1/7/99.

188 "[Being gay]is taken": Letter to author from Matthew Kelty, 2/14/99.
"I had always": Interview with Francis Kline, 10/24/98.

190 "I noticed": Interview with Geshe Thubten Tandhar, 9/16/98.

192 "Twenty-five years ago": Interview with Timothy Kelly, 9/20/98.

193 "Thomas Merton's greatest": "Beyond Belief," p. 51.
"There was a kind": Interview with Paul Quenon, 9/20/98.
"On the last day": *The Seven Storey Mountain,* p. 3.

196 "Jesus' Father": Quoted in Andrew Harvey, *Son of Man: The Mystical Path to Christ* (New York: Putnam, 1958), p. 141.

197 "There was a purging": Interview with Brendan Freeman, 2/19/99.

200 "a convent ready": *Our Lady of the Mississippi Abbey: 1964–1989* (Dubuque, IA: Union-Horemann Press, 1989), p. 17.

203 "Although some would balk": Lucy Kaylin, *For the Love of God: The Faith and Future of the American Nun* (New York: William Morrow, 2000), p. 12.

205 "The Midwest moved": Interview with Gail Fitzpatrick, 2/17/99.

207 "My friend Rita": Interview with Columba Guare, 2/17/99.

208 "With this system": *Our Lady of the Mississippi Abbey,* p. 16.

209 "Mother Columba would": *Our Lady of the Mississippi Abbey,* p. 26.
"With Father William": Interview with Columba Guare, 2/17/99.

210 "kind of like the nuns' ": Interview with B. J. Weber, 4/27/99.

211 "We try": Interview with Columba Guare, 2/17/99.

212 "After Solemn Profession": Mark Salzman, *Lying Awake* (New York: Alfred A. Knopf, 2000), pp. 97–98.

213 "I'm not sure": Interview with Gail Fitzpatrick, 2/17/99.

214 "largely forgotten": *Son of Man,* p. 162.
"Look now": *Dante's Paradiso,* trans. John D. Sinclair (London: Oxford University Press, 1939), p. 467.

215 "Woman has": John Paul II, *Mulieris Dignitatem: On Women, 1,* quoted in M. Rosario Spreafico, "The Place of Women in the Cistercian Family," *Regional Mailbag* (January-February 1999), p. 13.
"For so many years": Interview with Gail Fitzpatrick, 2/17/99.

218 "I felt like": Interview with Sister Rebecca, 2/17/99.

219 "as a kind of support": Interview with James Kerndt, 2/18/99.

220 "I had a ponytail": Interview with B. J. Weber, 4/27/99.

221 For a discussion of lesbianism among women religious, see Jeannine Gramick, ed., *Homosexuality in the Priesthood and Religious Life* (New York: Crossroad Publishing, 1989).

"I just feel": Interview with Kate Mehlmann, 2/18/99.

FOUR

225 "What is": Interview with Philip Johnson, 7/30/99.

227 "thirty-two of the": Phone interview with Michael Piazza, 8/5/99.

"In truth": Rena Pederson, "In Search of Beauty," *Dallas Morning News,* 21 March 1999.

228 "This will be the most": Interview with Michael Piazza, 4/30/99.

"Please welcome": Quoted in Brad Gooch, "Divine Design," *Out* (May 1996), p. 68.

"I'd never heard": Interview with Philip Johnson, 1/17/96.

"I'm not a gay": "Divine Design," p. 68.

"That was really": Interview with Philip Johnson, 7/30/99.

229 "We saw Warsaw": Quoted in "Divine Design," p. 66. Originally in a letter to Frau Bodenschatz, probably in December 1939.

"It's spiritual": Interview with Philip Johnson, 7/30/99.

230 "Schuller brought in": Interview with Michael Piazza, 12/15/95.

231 "twenty-two acre": Quoted in Calvin Tompkins, "Forms Under Light," *The New Yorker,* 5 May 1977, p. 44.

"When we walked": Interview with Michael Piazza, 12/15/95.

232 "Why are you restricting": Quoted in "Forms Under Light," p. 44.

"My whole feeling": Interview with Philip Johnson, 7/30/99.

233 "I have an idea": Interview with Philip Johnson, 1/17/96.

"It didn't accomplish": Interview with Michael Piazza, 4/30/99.

235 "Bilbao influenced": Interview with Philip Johnson, 7/30/99.

236 "I was just amazed": Interview with Philip Johnson, 1/17/96.

238 "None of the church bond": Interview with Michael Piazza, 12/15/95.

239 "Here I found": George Exoo, "God's Country," *D* (September 1997), p. 120.

240 "Dallas MCC": Interview with Michael Piazza, 12/15/95.

245 "We've been very conscious": Interview with Michael Piazza, 4/30/99.

247 "The main Cathedral": Interview with Mary Warejka, 4/30/99.

249 "People who are not": Interview with Michael Piazza, 4/30/99.

250 "It's the edifice": Phone interview with Malcolm Boyd, 5/3/96.

"He's exactly right": Interview with Michael Piazza, 4/30/99.

251 "Texas is my favorite": Interview with Philip Johnson, 7/30/99.

252 "Indeed, the Cathedral": Kimberley Goad, "The Pink Mafia," *D* (November 1996), p. 67.

"Remember, Dallas": Anonymous phone interview, 1/11/96.

253 "They said, 'Now'": Interview with Philip Johnson, 1/17/96.

254 "I don't think": Interview with Michael Piazza, 4/30/99.

255 "Perry had been raised": Dudley, Clendinem, and Adam Nagourney, *Out for Good: The Struggle to Build a Gay Rights Movement in America* (New York: Simon and Schuster, 1999), p. 180.

256 "We're just a bunch": Rev. Troy D. Perry with Thomas L. P. Suicegood. *Don't Be Afraid Anymore: The Story of Reverend Troy Perry and the Metropolitan Community Church* (New York: St. Martin's Press, 1990), pp. 34–35.

"I had to": Phone interview with Troy Perry, 1/17/96.

260 "Charter churches": Phone interview with Troy Perry, 8/21/99.

"MCC isn't": Interview with Jim Mitulski, 6/16/99.

261 "Growth was forced": Phone interview with Malcolm Boyd, 5/3/96.

"When I first": Phone interview with Troy Perry, 1/17/96.

262 "In the last": Interview with Troy Perry, 8/21/99.

"Every time": Interview with Mel White, 12/10/95.

263 "homo-spiritual": Richard Goldstein, "Believers Who Brunch," *Village Voice,* 2 November 1999, p. 53.

265 "They're Baptists": Interview with Mel White, 12/18/95.

"When Mel": Interview with Michael Piazza, 4/30/99.

266 "Jesus is talked": Phone interview with Mel White, 7/21/99.

269 "It was [Falwell's]": Mel White, *Stranger at the Gate: To Be Gay and Christian in America* (New York: Simon and Schuster, 1994), p. 146.

"rescued": *Stranger at the Gate,* p. 248.

272 "So-called gay folk": *Out for Good,* p. 306.

"God did not create": *Out for Good,* p. 409.

"the judgment of God": *Out for Good,* p. 488.

"trapped in bondage": "What We Believe: JFM's Definitive Stance on Homosexuality." (Jerry Falwell Ministries, www.falwell.com, October 14, 1999).

"If left to": John W. Kennedy, "Jerry Falwell's Uncertain Legacy," *Christianity Today,* 9 December 1996.

273 "The event with Mel White": Phone interview with Susan Friend Harding, 1/28/01.

"Falwell is an almost daring": Phone interview with Gustav Niebuhr, 1/26/01.

274   Falwell's comments: on the *700 Club: New York Times,* 9/15/01.

278   "Groveling and crawling": "Believers Who Brunch," p. 53.

280   "We want to be": William Martin, *With God on Our Side: The Rise of the Religious Right in America* (New York: Broadway Books, 1996), p. 197.

281   "With two hundred homosexuals": Jerry Falwell, "Why Did I Do It?" reprinted from WorldNetDay, *www.falwell.com/pressstatements/prsarchives/prswhy.htm.*

282   "engaged in a drunken": *Hustler Magazine Inc. et. d. v. Jerry Falwell,* 485 U.S. 46 (1988).

FIVE

289   "The Ralph Kramden": Roger Ebert, "East Is East," *Chicago Sun-Times,* 4 April 2000.

292   "There's this path": Interview with Adnan Ashraf, 4/2/00.
       "My son's": Interview with Samina Imam, 5/25/00.

293   "My parents": Interview with Pedram Samghabadi, 5/18/00.
       "I call myself": Interview with Hisham Moulay Bouadi, 5/12/00.

295   "Today the whole world": Interview with Yusuf Hasan, 5/22/00.

296   "When we met": Phone interview with Gray Henry, 5/18/00.
       "Islam is": Interview with Yusuf Hasan, 5/22/00.
       "Two doors down": Interview with Shaffiq Essaje, 5/24/00.

297   "The new immigrants": Interview with Faisal Abdul Rauf, 4/28/00.

298   "You often find": Interview with Louis Abdellatif Cristillo, 7/10/00.

301   "Some of the": Interview with Fadhel Al-Sahlani, 6/22/00.
       "Sheikh Sahlani here": Interview with Nadeem Kazmi, 6/22/00.

302   "In Bay Ridge": Interview with Hisham Moulay Bouadi, 5/12/00.
       "A friend of mine": Interview with Husayn E. Fruhstorfer, 5/9/00.

304   "In the name of God": *The Koran Interpreted,* trans. A. J. Arberry (New York: Simon & Schuster, 1956), Sura 96, 11.1–5, p. 344.

308   "I never bought": Interview with Pedram Samghabadi, 5/18/00.

309   "We got stuck": Interview with Farouk Khan, 6/29/00.

311   "We used to dread": Interview with Faiz Khan, 8/10/00.
       "Pre-Khomeini": Interview with Daisy Khan, 8/14/00.

312   "Our community is a cross section": Interview with Farouk Khan, 8/10/00.

"Some of the opposition": Interview with Faiz Khan, 8/10/00.

313   "I spent lots": Interview with Michelle Depew, 8/8/00.

315   "From day one, Muslim ladies": Interview with Ghazi Y. al-Haaj Khankan, 8/12/00.

320   "Elijah Muhammad wasn't teaching": Interview with Yusuf Hasan, 5/2/00.

321   "During the past eleven days": Alex Haley, *The Autobiography of Malcolm X* (New York: Ballantine Books, 1999), p. 347.

"In the Muslim world": Ibid., p. 369.

325   "This office is where": Interview with Izak-El Pasha, 8/2/00.

327   "The first big change": Gladys Muhammad, "Through the Eyes of a Pioneer," *The Thinker,* 23 September 1998, p. 6.

"I was glad": Interview with Yusef Hasan, 5/22/00.

"Before we ever engaged": Interview with Izak-el Pasha, 8/2/00.

330   "In 1975, there was": Interview with Abdul Alim Mubarek, 8/25/00.

"Some people were affected": Interview with Wahy Deen Shareef, 8/25/00.

"It kinda made sense": Interview with Abdul Alim Mubarek, 8/25/00.

"The whole concept of Fard": Interview with Wahy Deen Shareef, 8/25/00.

333   "What I enjoy": Interview with Linda Salaam, 8/25/00.

334   "In some cases, blacks": Jane I. Smith, *Islam in America* (New York: Columbia University Press, 1999), p. 17.

335   "The Center of Long Island": Interview with Faiz Khan, 8/10/00.

"Today Sufism is a name": Quoted in William C. Chittick, "Sufism: Name and Reality," in *Merton and Sufism: The Untold Story* (Louisville: Fons Vitae, 1999), p. 15.

"Initially, I was": Interview with Faiz Khan, 8/10/00.

337   "in Sufism": Quoted in *Merton and Sufism,* p. 148.

338   "I've seen lots": Interview with Salar Abdoh, 4/9/00.

339   "In my opinion": Interview with Faiz Khan, 8/10/00.

342   "On Christmas Eve": Quoted in Calvin Tompkins, "The Benefactor," *The New Yorker,* 8 June 1998, p. 67.

"She seemed to me": Ibid., p. 67.

"I actually met": Interview with Fariha al-Jerrahi, 7/13/00.

345   "a pioneer in the spiritual": Quoted in "Farewell to Lex Hixon, A WBAI Programmer," *www.wbai/free.org/folso/hixon.html.*

"I knelt before him": Lex Hixon Nur al-Jerrahi, *Atom from the Sun of Knowledge* (Westport, CT: Pir Publications, 1993), pp. v–vi.

346   "The passing": Interview with Fariha al-Jerrahi, 7/13/00.

"I remember our first": Quoted in Bob Colacello, "Remains of the DIA," *Vanity Fair* (September 1996), p. 199.

"Sheik Nur": Interview with Fariha al-Jerrahi, 7/13/00.

347   "Naturally he used": Phone interview with Gray Henry, 8/23/00.

348   "Our circles in Mexico City": Interview with Fariha al-Jerrahi, 7/13/00.

352   "I was invited": Interview with Feisal Rauf, 8/14/00.

355   "I read the Arberry": Interview with Fariha al-Jerrahi, 7/13/00.

"If you ask me": Interview with Feisal Rauf, 8/14/00.

358   "It was just like": Interview with Diana Castro, 5/26/00.

"There is obviously": Interview with Daisy Khan, 8/14/00.

359   "What an authentic": Interview with Pedram Samghabadi, 5/18/00.

INDEX

ABOUT THE AUTHOR

Brad Gooch is the author of City Poet: The Life and Times of Frank O'Hara, Finding the Boyfriend Within, *and the novels* Scary Kisses *and* Zombie00. *He lives in New York City.*

A NOTE ON THE TYPE

The text of this book was set in Garamond No. 3. It is not a true copy of any of the designs of Claude Garamond (ca. 1480–1561), but an adaptation of his types, which set the European standard for two centuries. It probably owes as much to the designs of Jean Jannon, a Protestant printer working in Sedan in the early seventeenth century, who had worked with Garamond's romans earlier, in Paris, but who was denied their use because of Catholic censorship. Jannon's matrices came into the possession of the Imprimerie nationale, where they were thought to be by Garamond himself, and were so described when the Imprimerie revived the type in 1900. This particular version is based on an adaptation by Morris Fuller Benton.

Composed by Creative Graphics,
Allentown, Pennsylvania

Printed and bound by Berryville Graphics,
Berryville, Virginia

Designed by Iris Weinstein